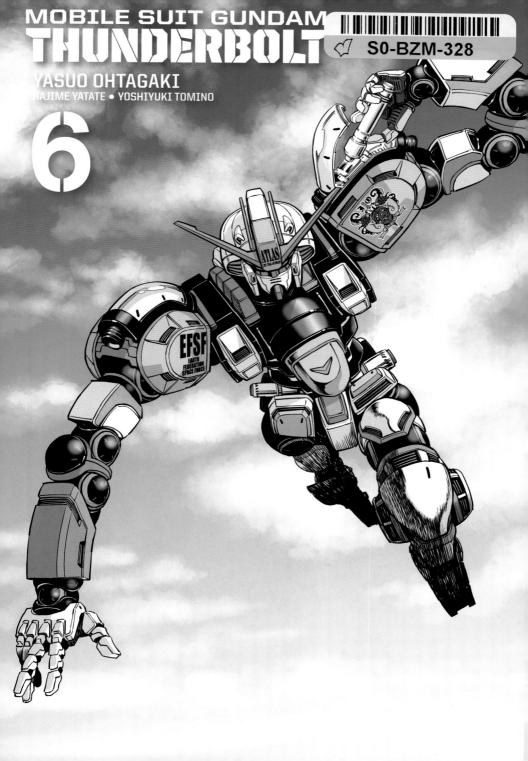

MOBILE SUIT GUNDAM
THUNDERBOLT

YASUO OHTAGAKI
HAJIME YATATE • YOSHIYUKI TOMINO

6

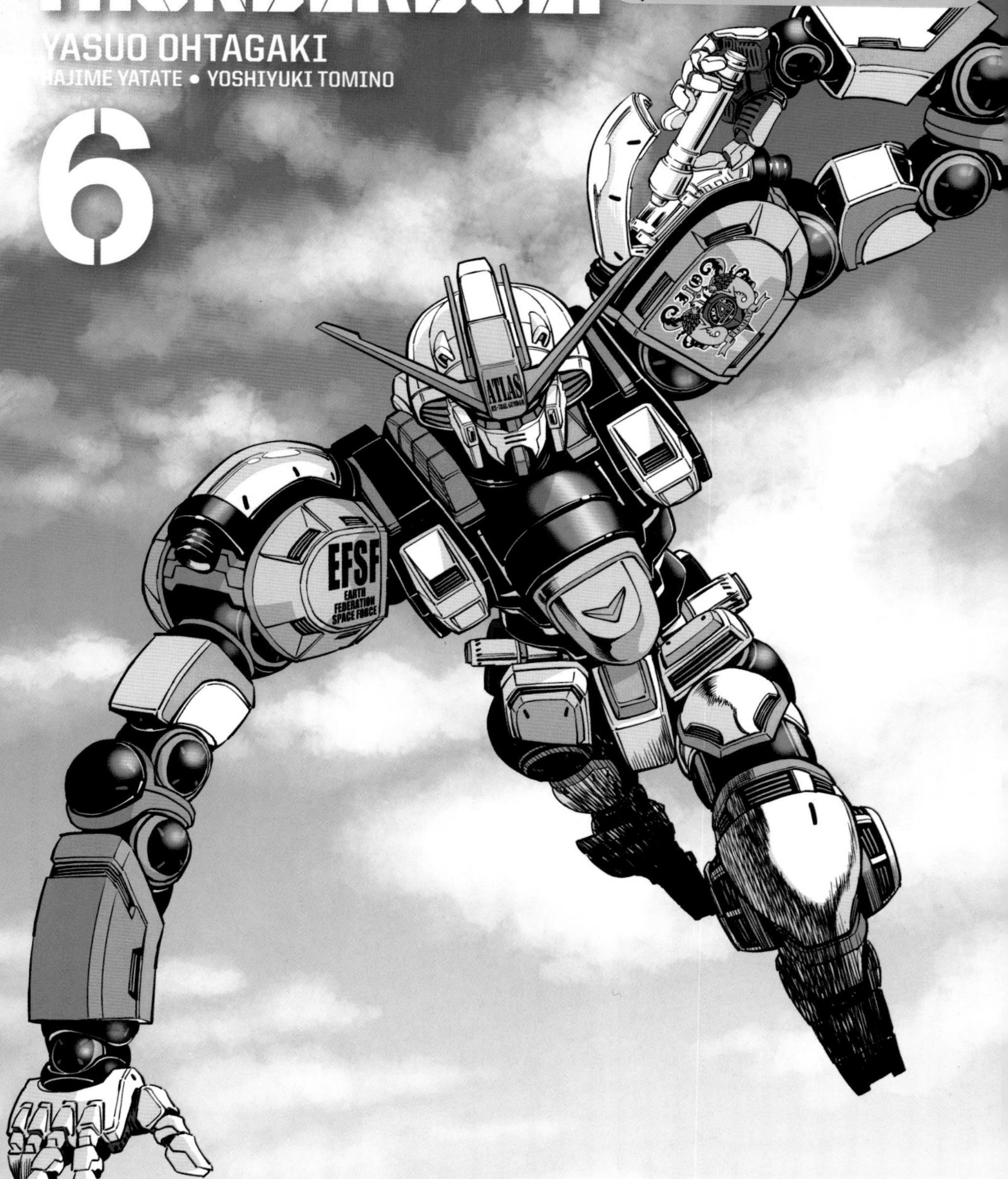
ATLAS
EFSF
EARTH
FEDERATION
SPACE FORCE

EARTH FEDERATION

RX-78AL ATLAS GUNDAM

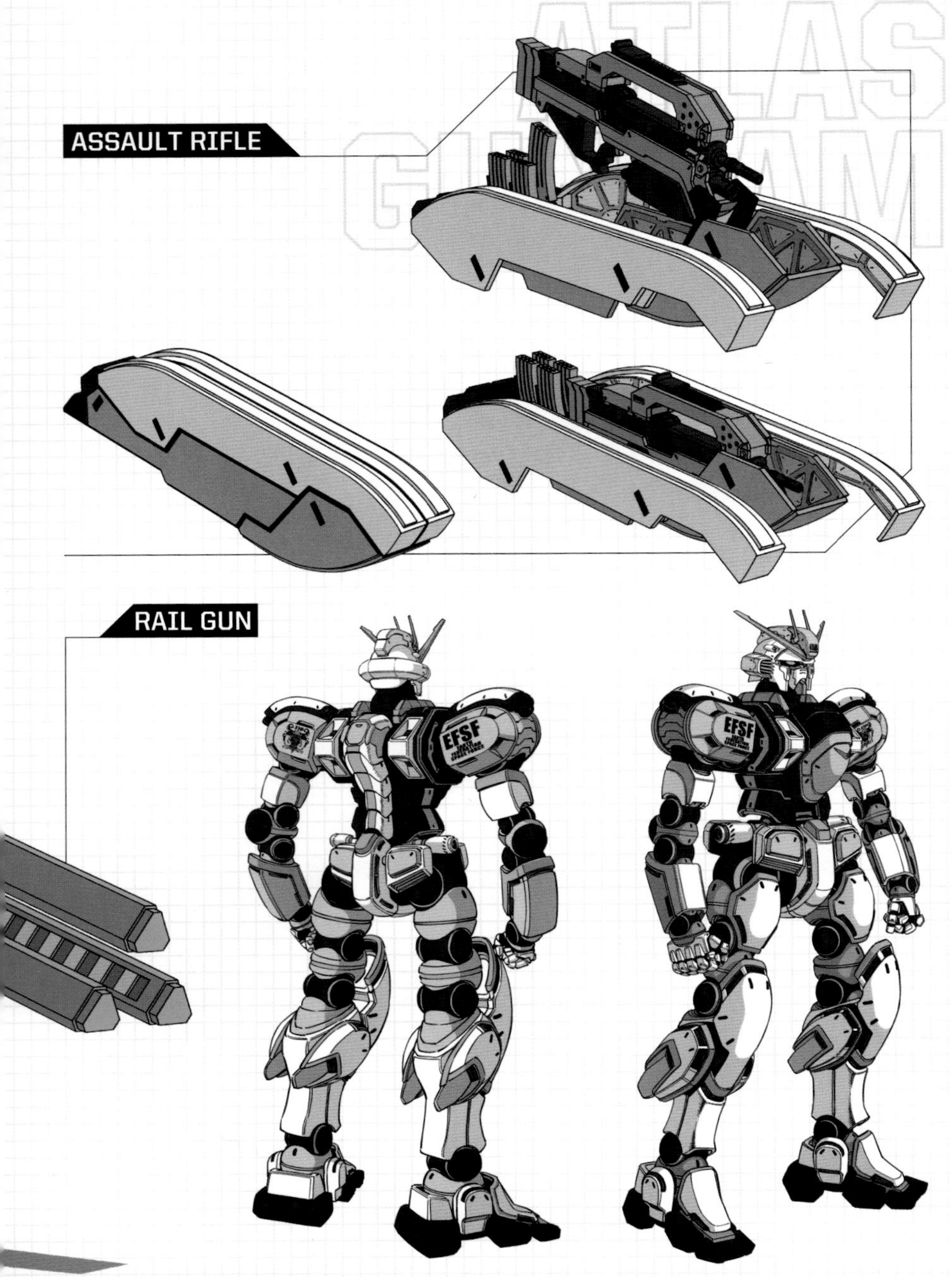
ATLAS GUNDAM
ASSAULT RIFLE
RAIL GUN
EFSF
EFSF

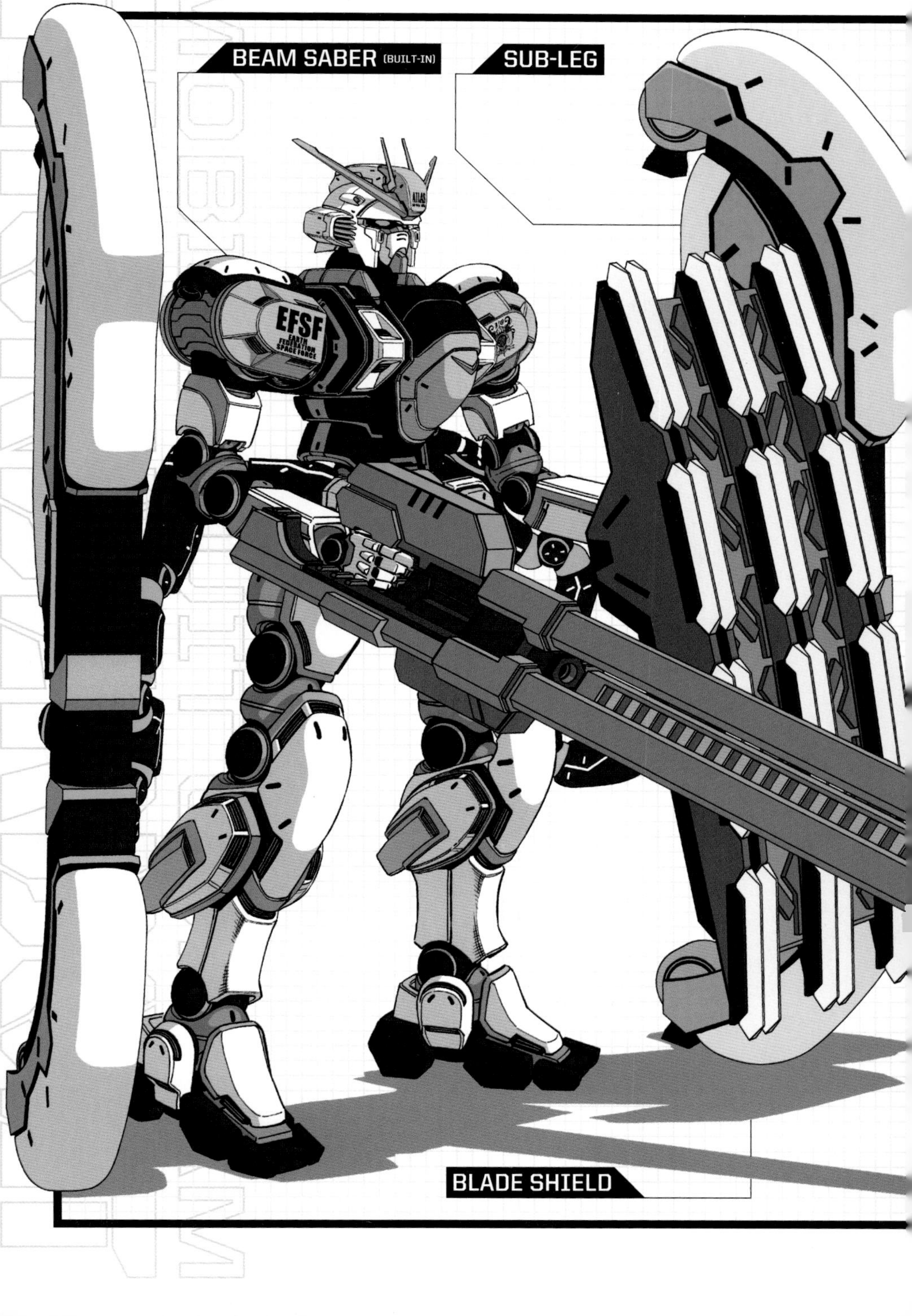
BEAM SABER (BUILT-IN)
SUB-LEG
EFSF
EARTH FEDERATION SPACE FORCE
ATLAS
BLADE SHIELD

MOBILE SUIT GUNDAM
THUNDERBOLT

6

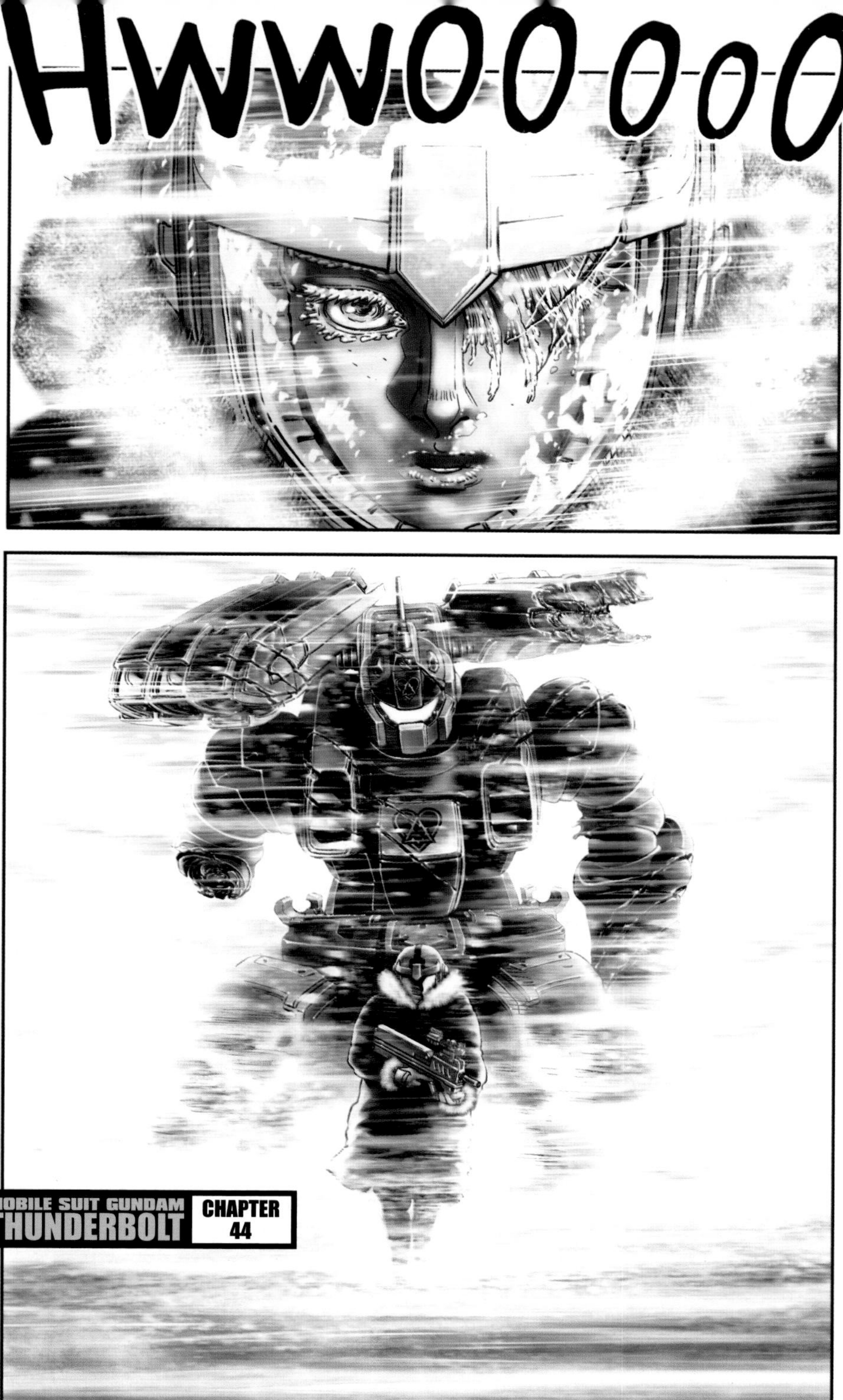
HWWOOOOO
MOBILE SUIT GUNDAM
THUNDERBOLT
CHAPTER
44

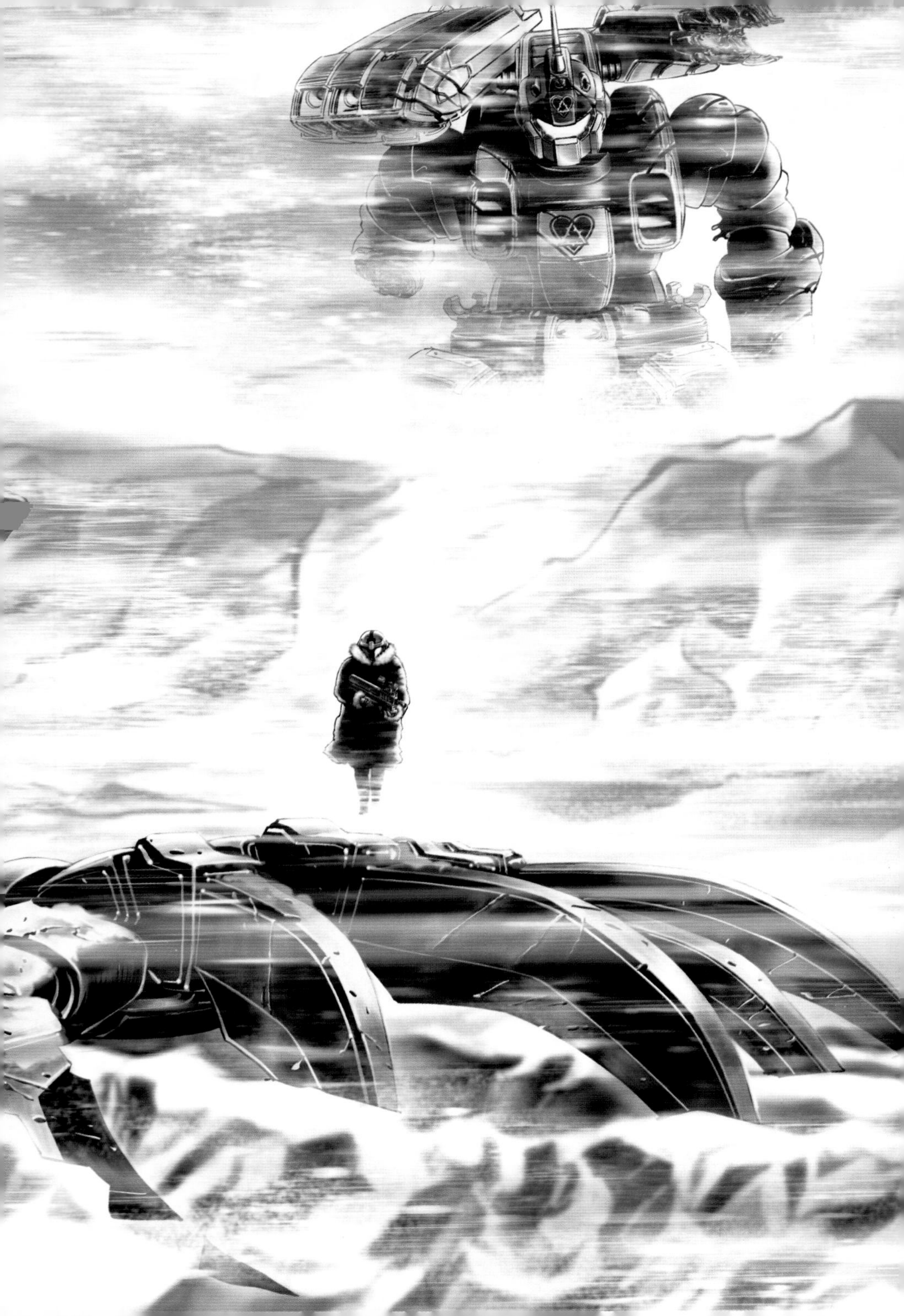

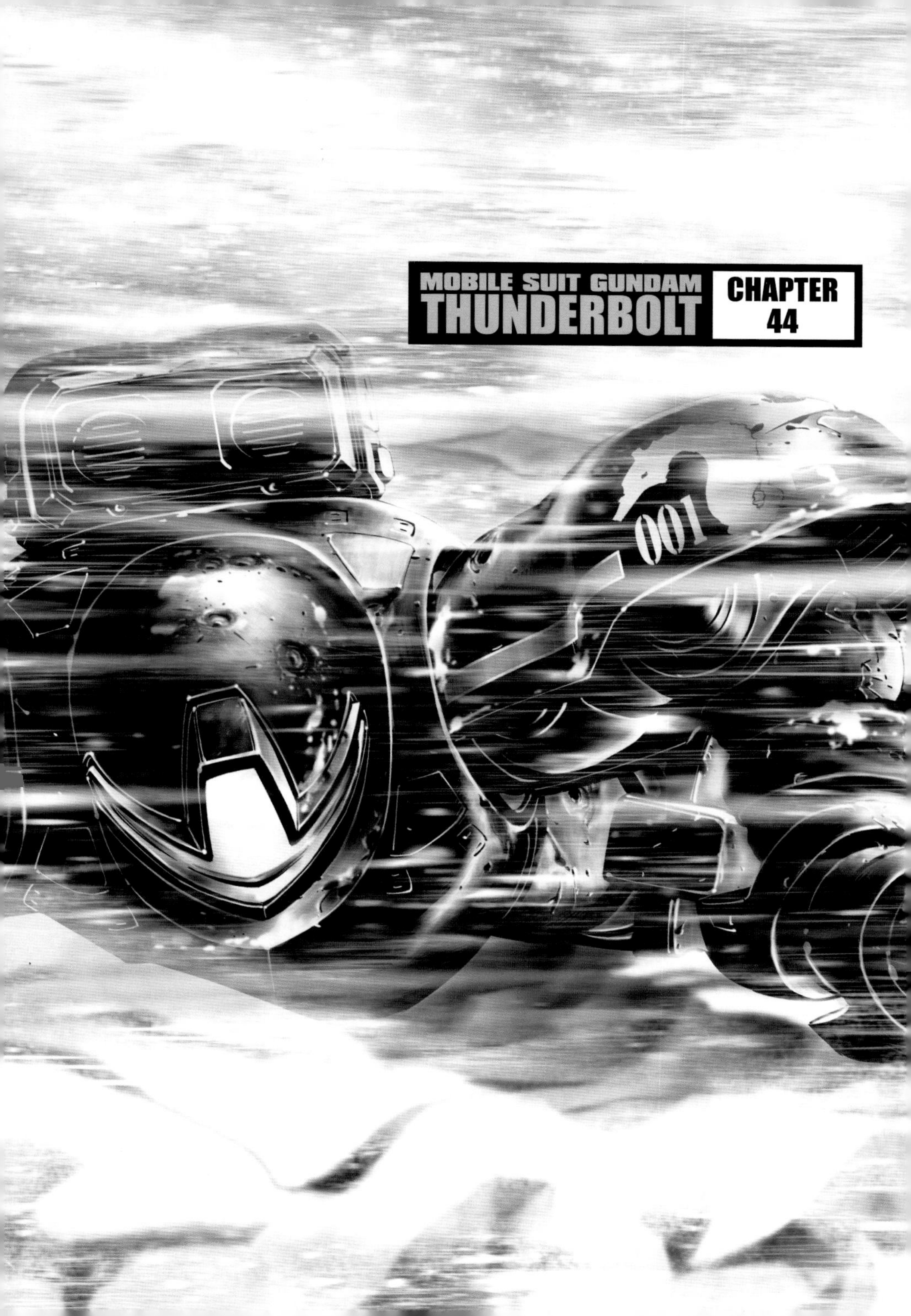
MOBILE SUIT GUNDAM
THUNDERBOLT
CHAPTER
44
001

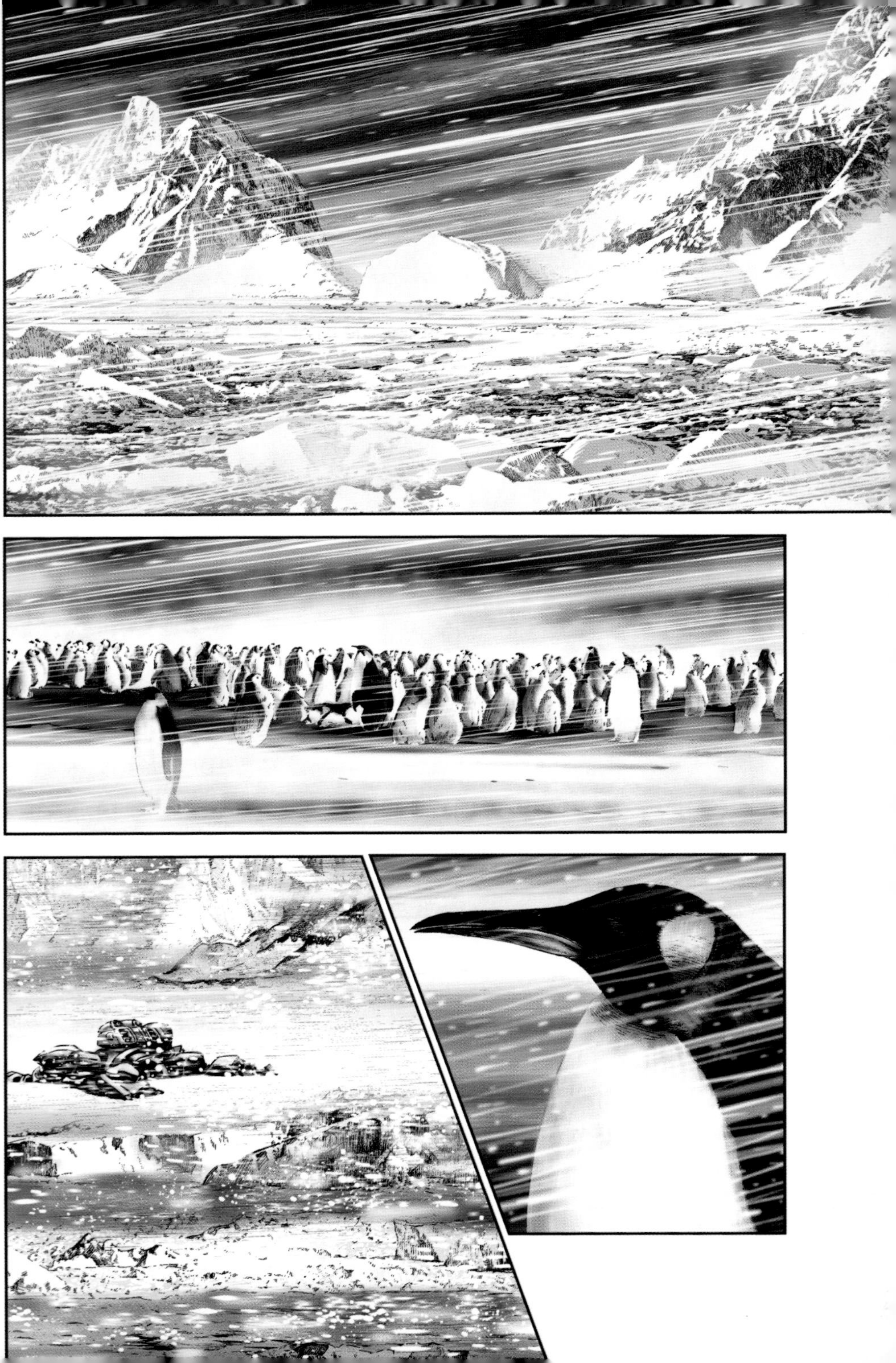

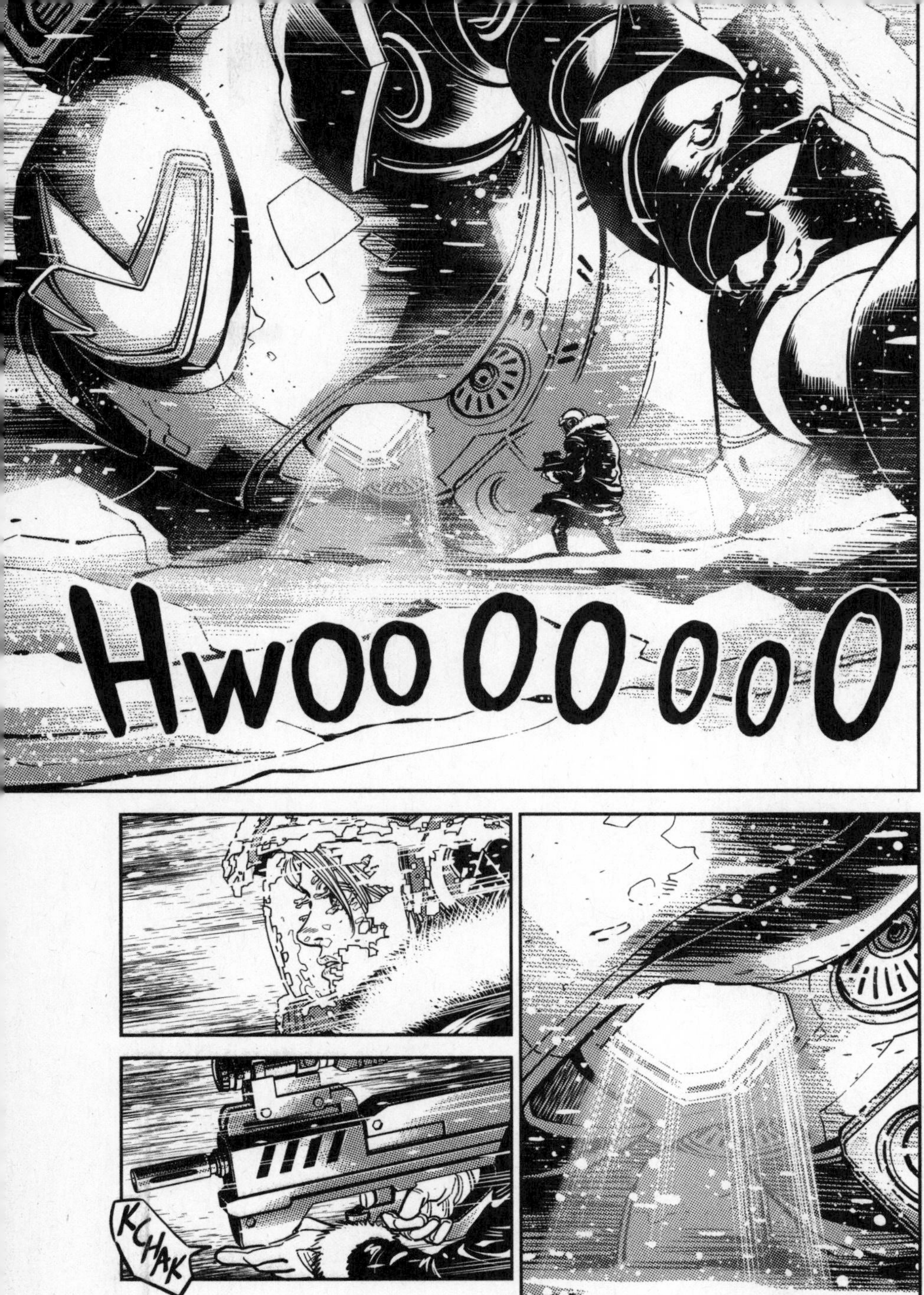
HWOOOOOOO
KCHAK

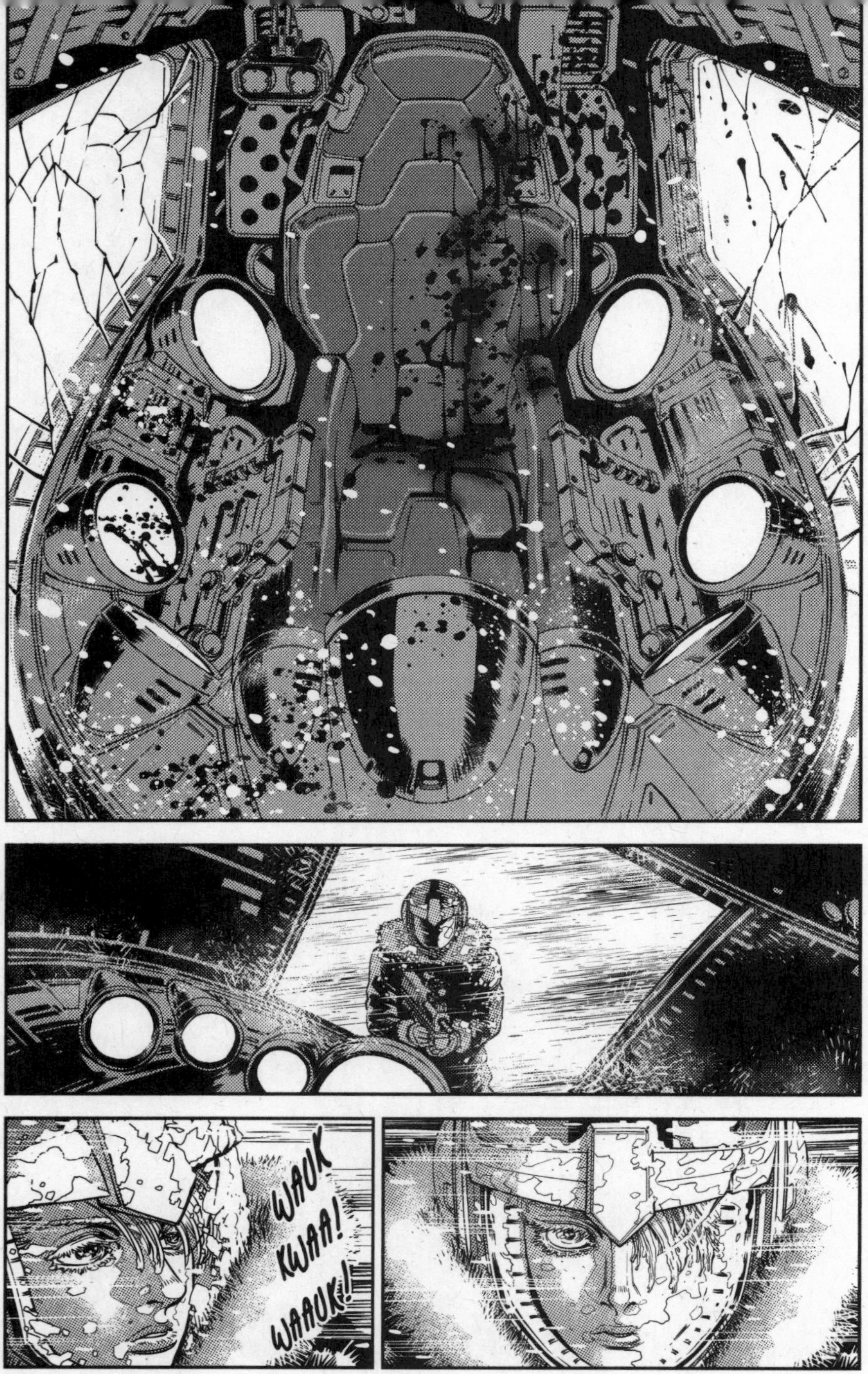
WAUK KWAA! WAAUK!

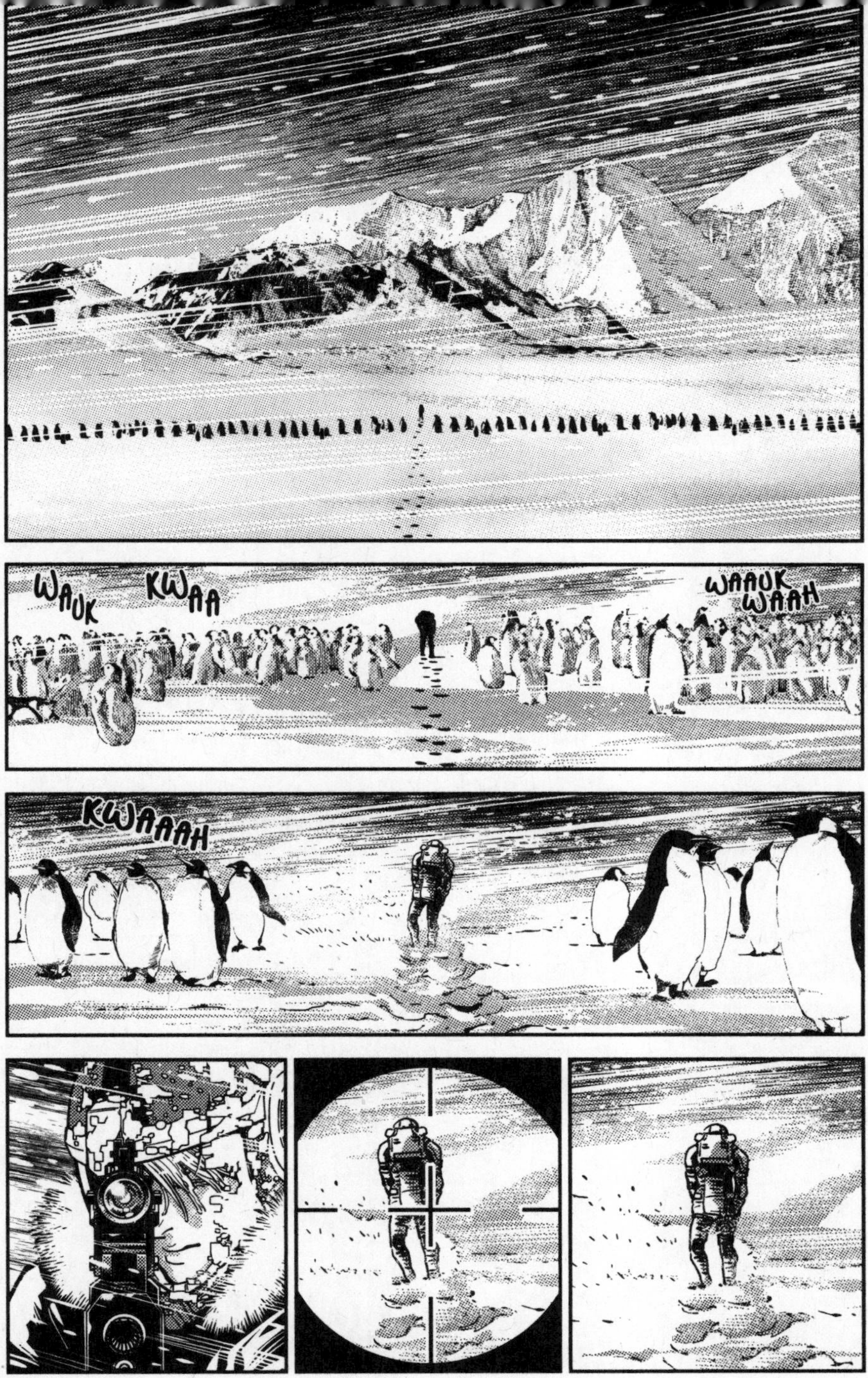
WAAUK WAAH
KWAA
WAUK
KWAAAH

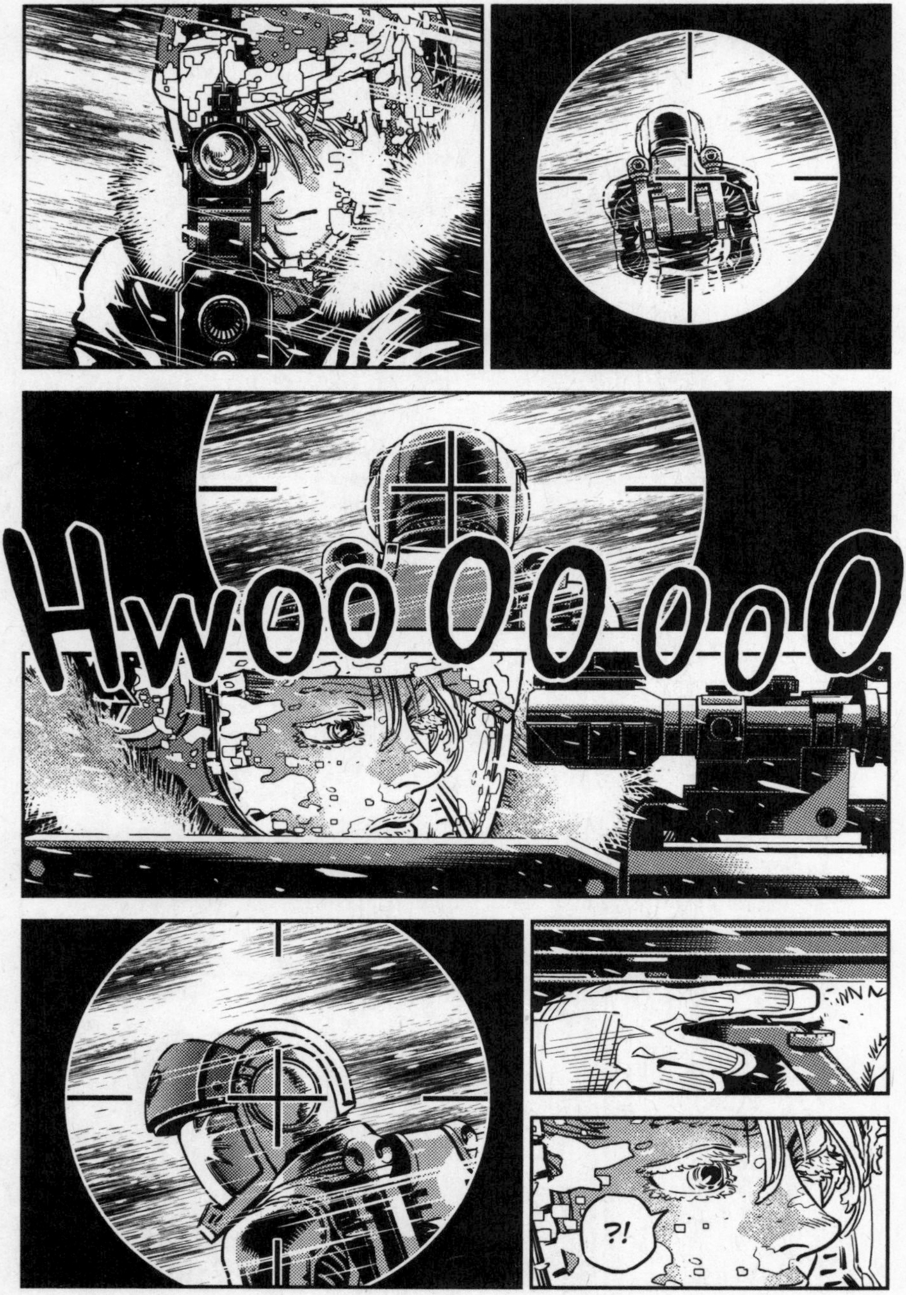

Hwooooooo
?!

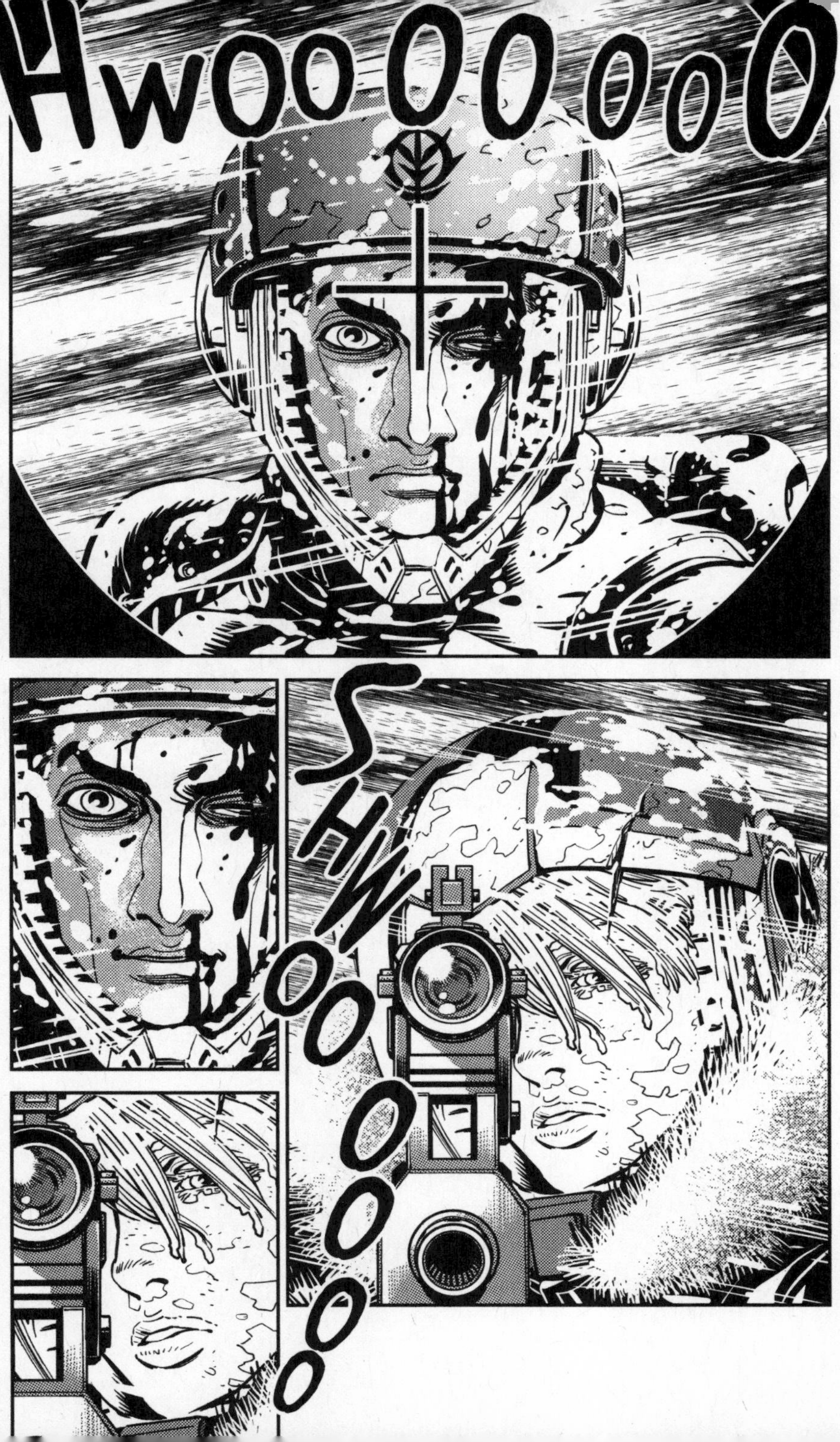
HWOOOOOOO
SHWOOOOOOOOOO

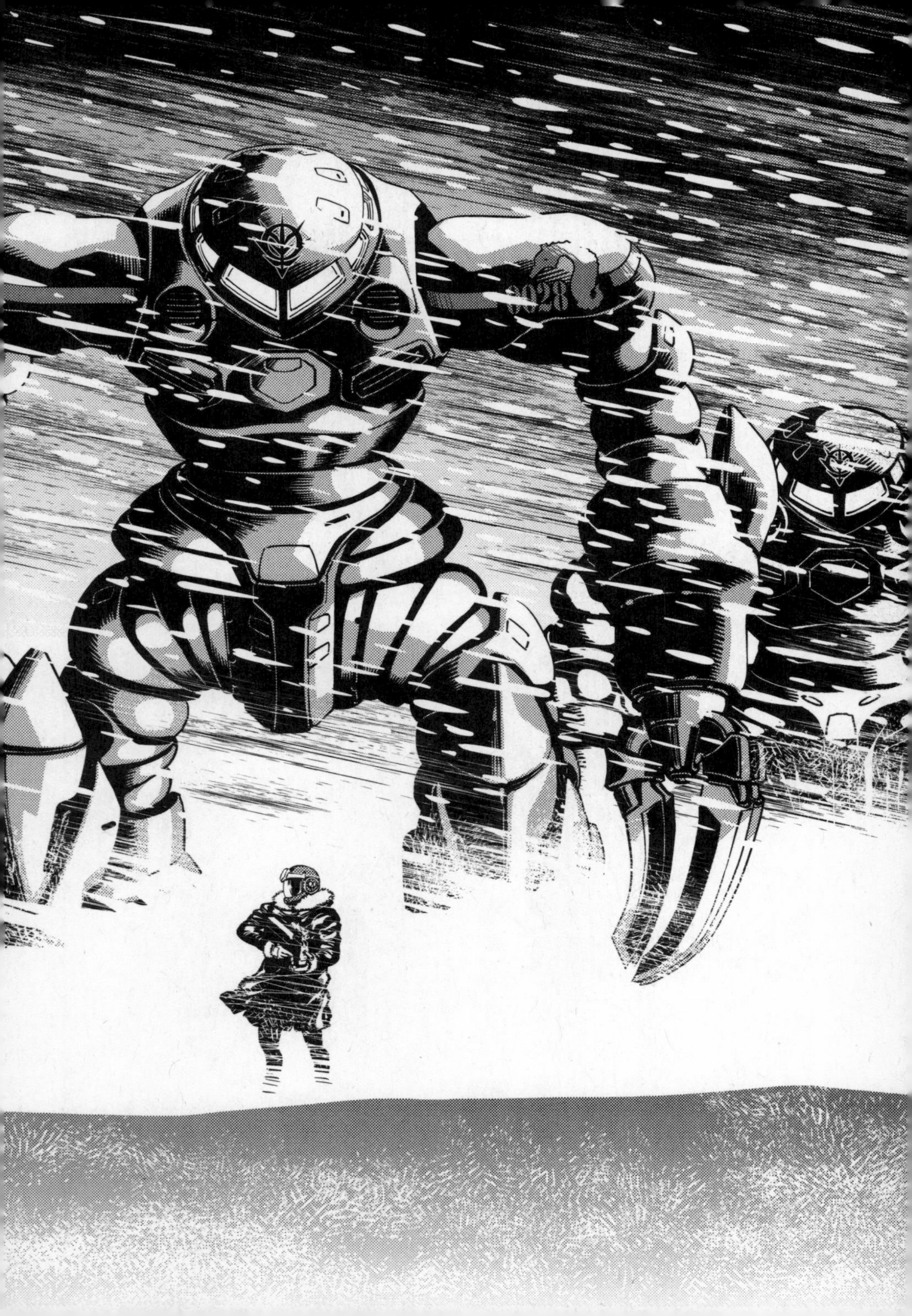

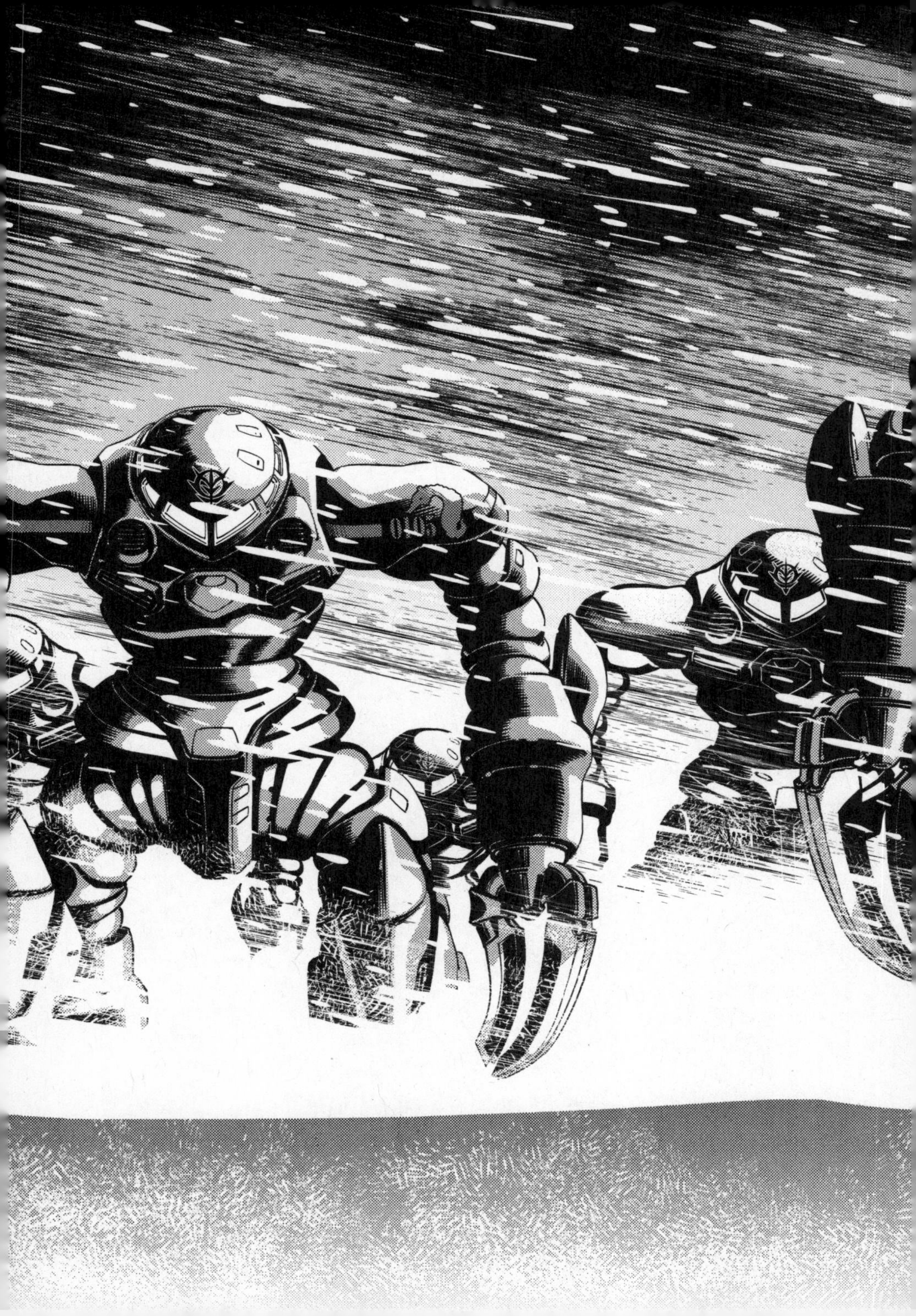

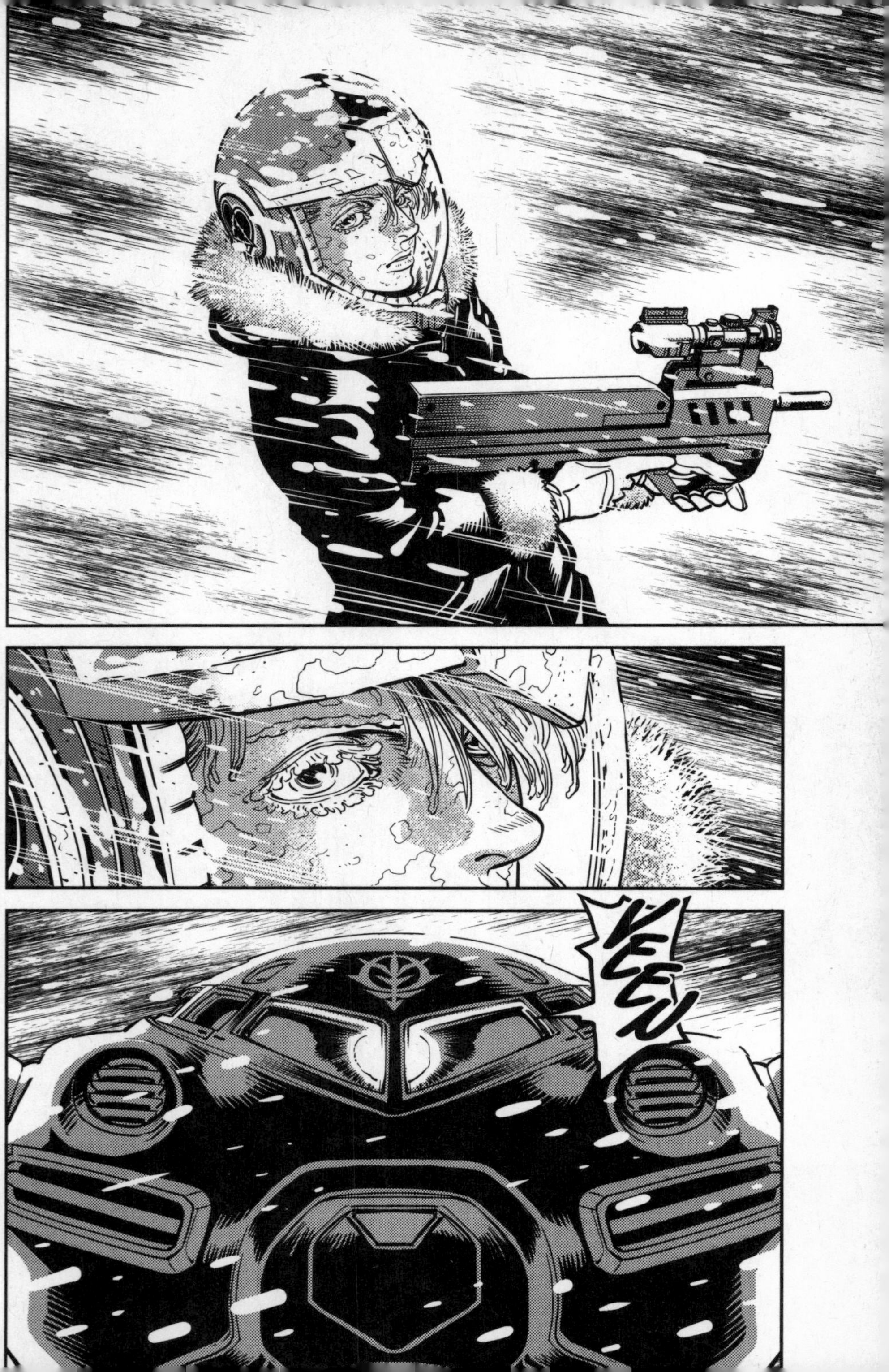
VEEN

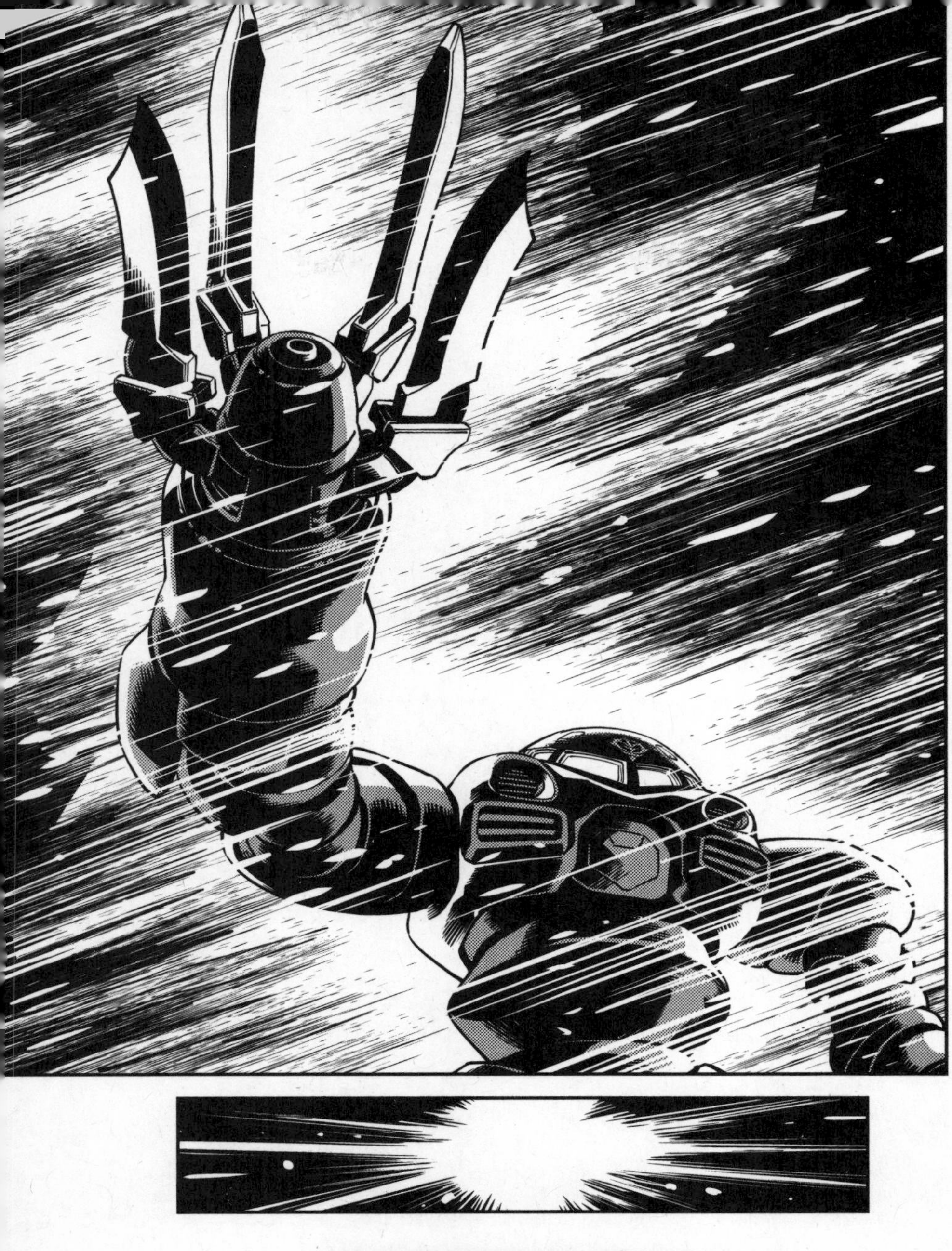

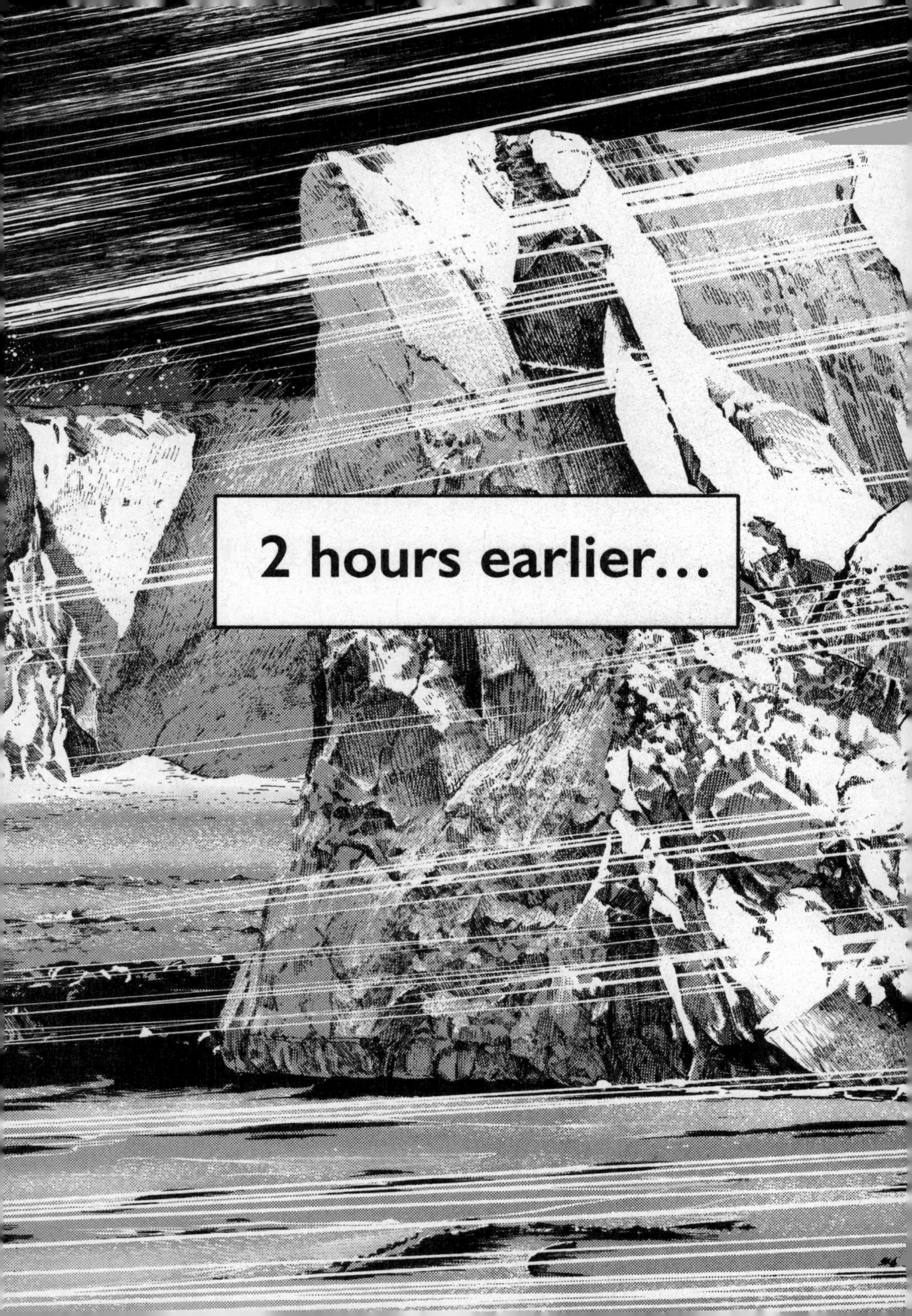
2 hours earlier...

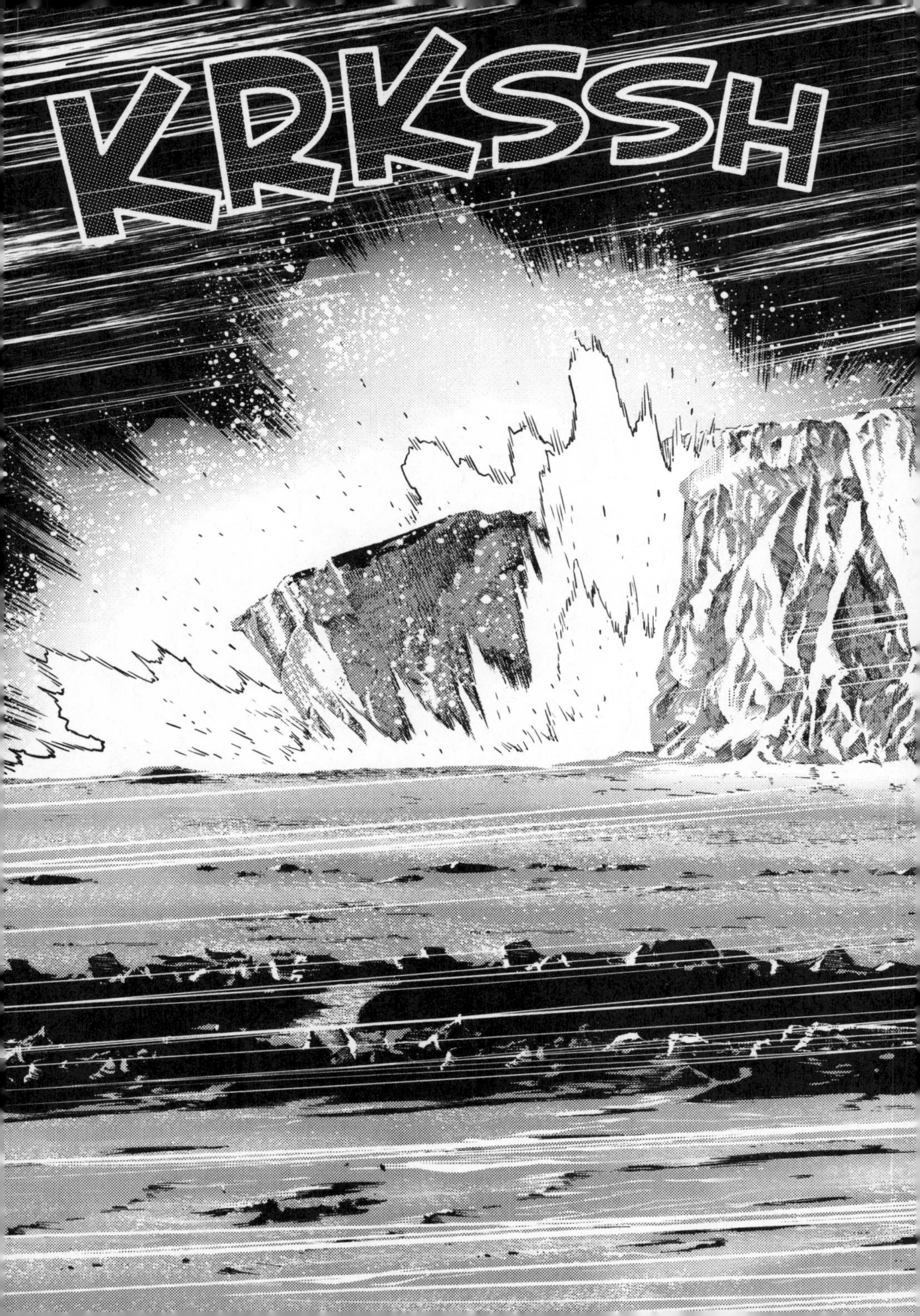
KRKSSH

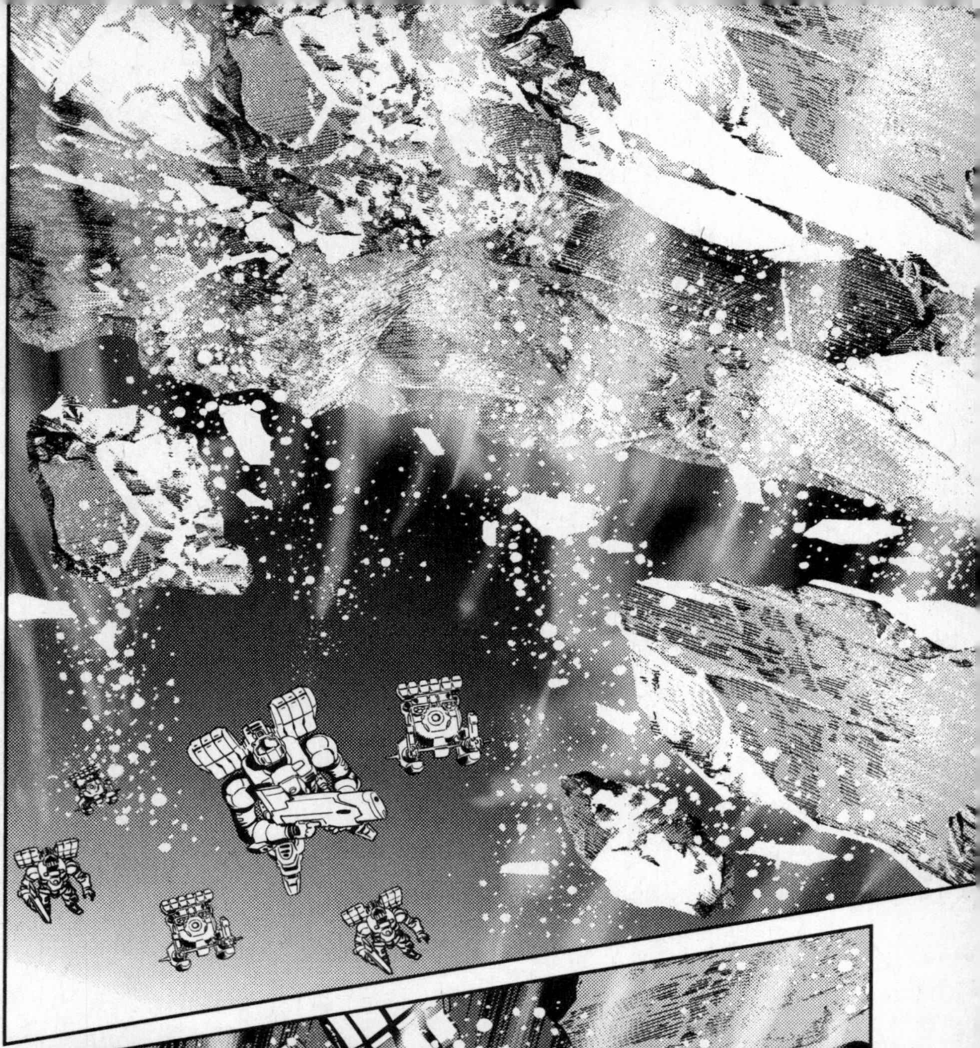
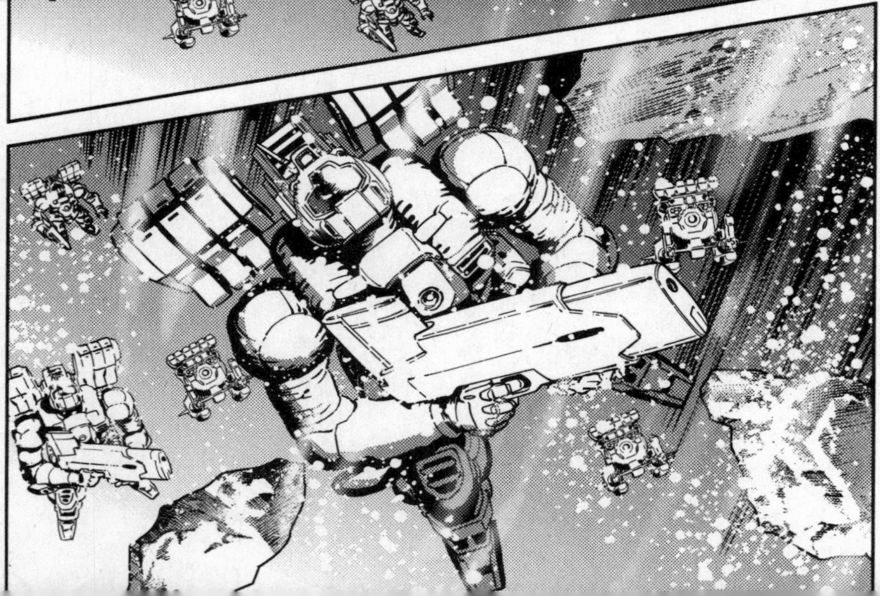

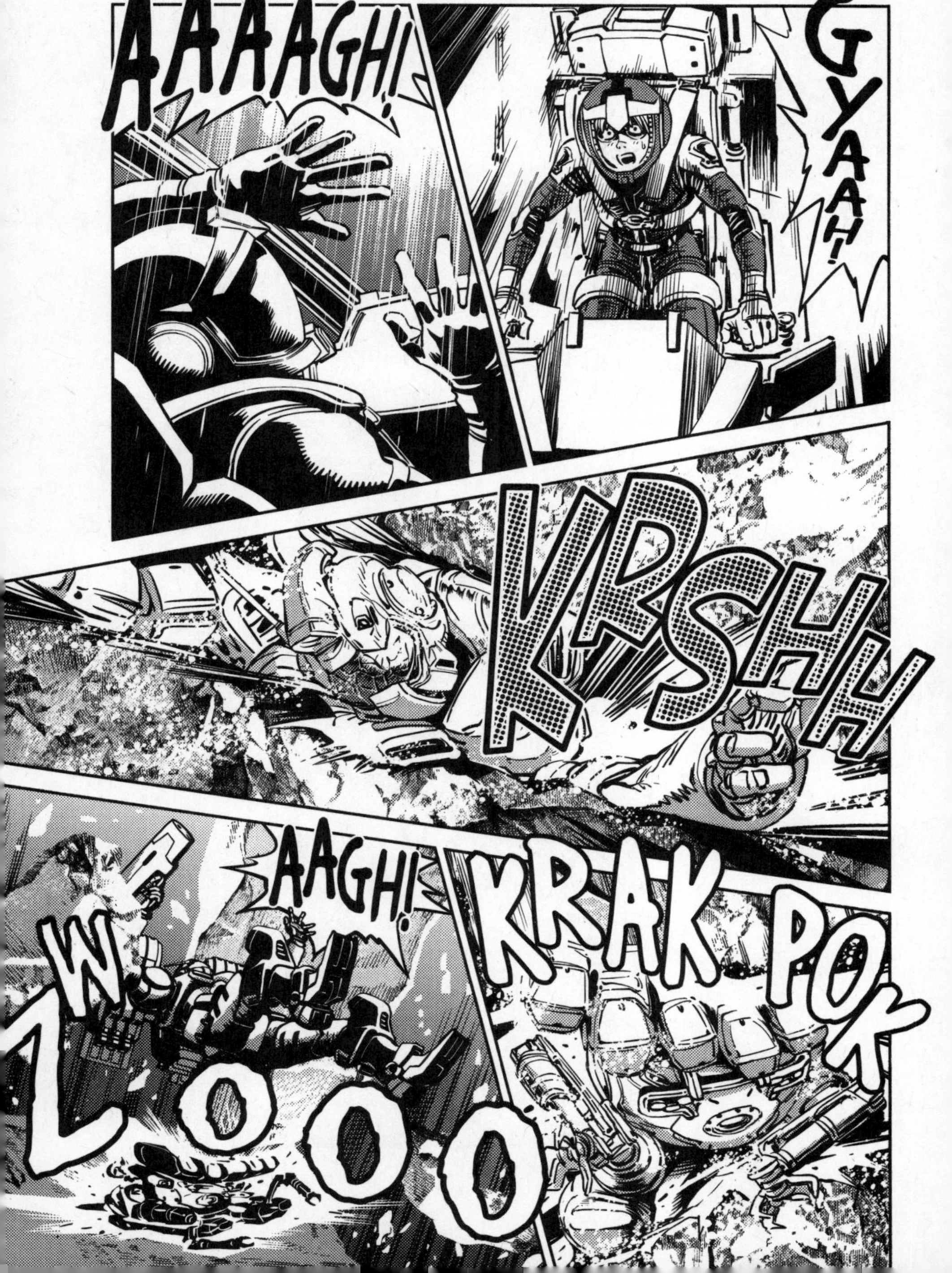
GYAAH!
AAAAGH!
KRSHHH
KRAK POK
AAGH!
WZOOOO

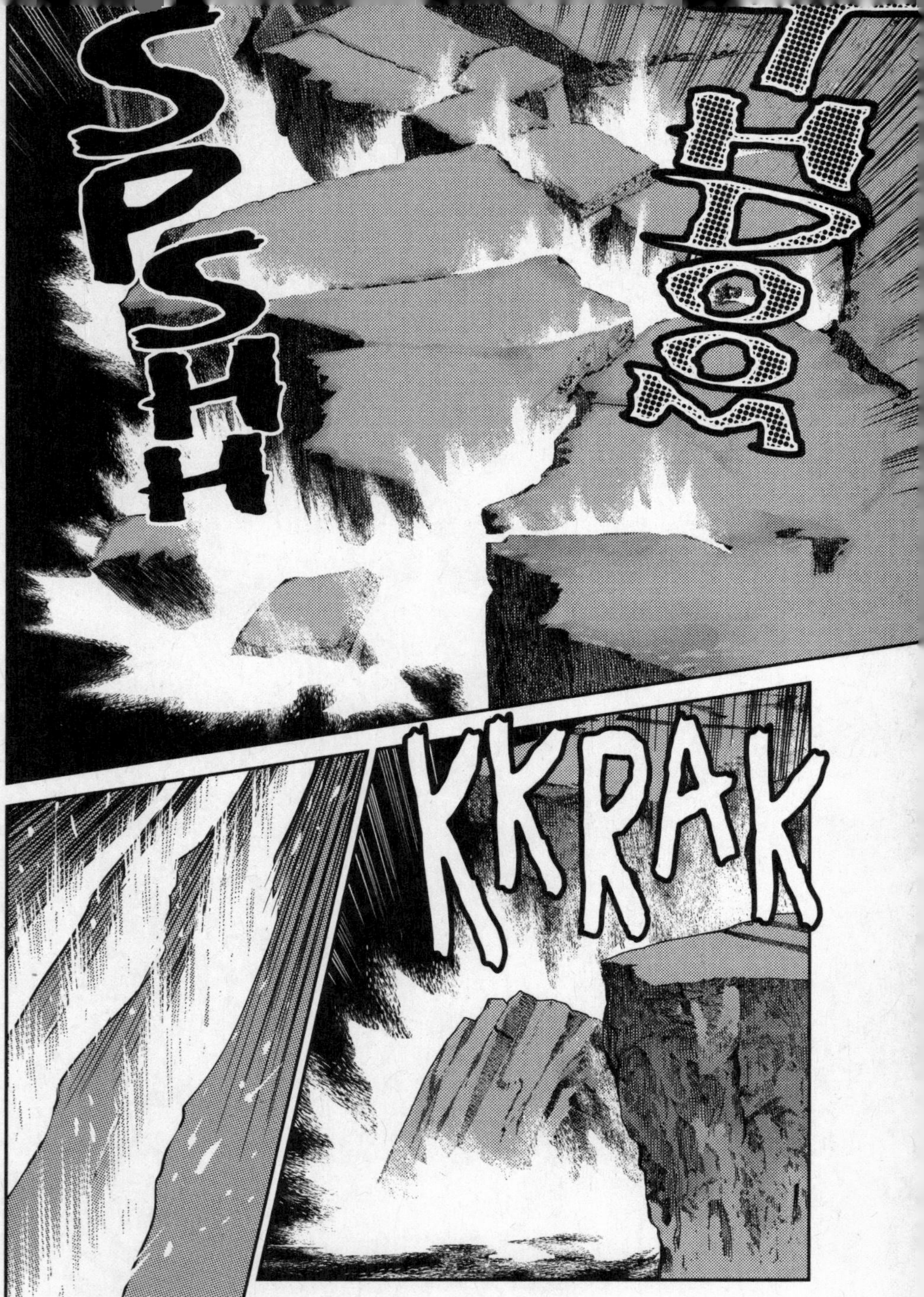
THOOOM
SPSHH
KKRAK

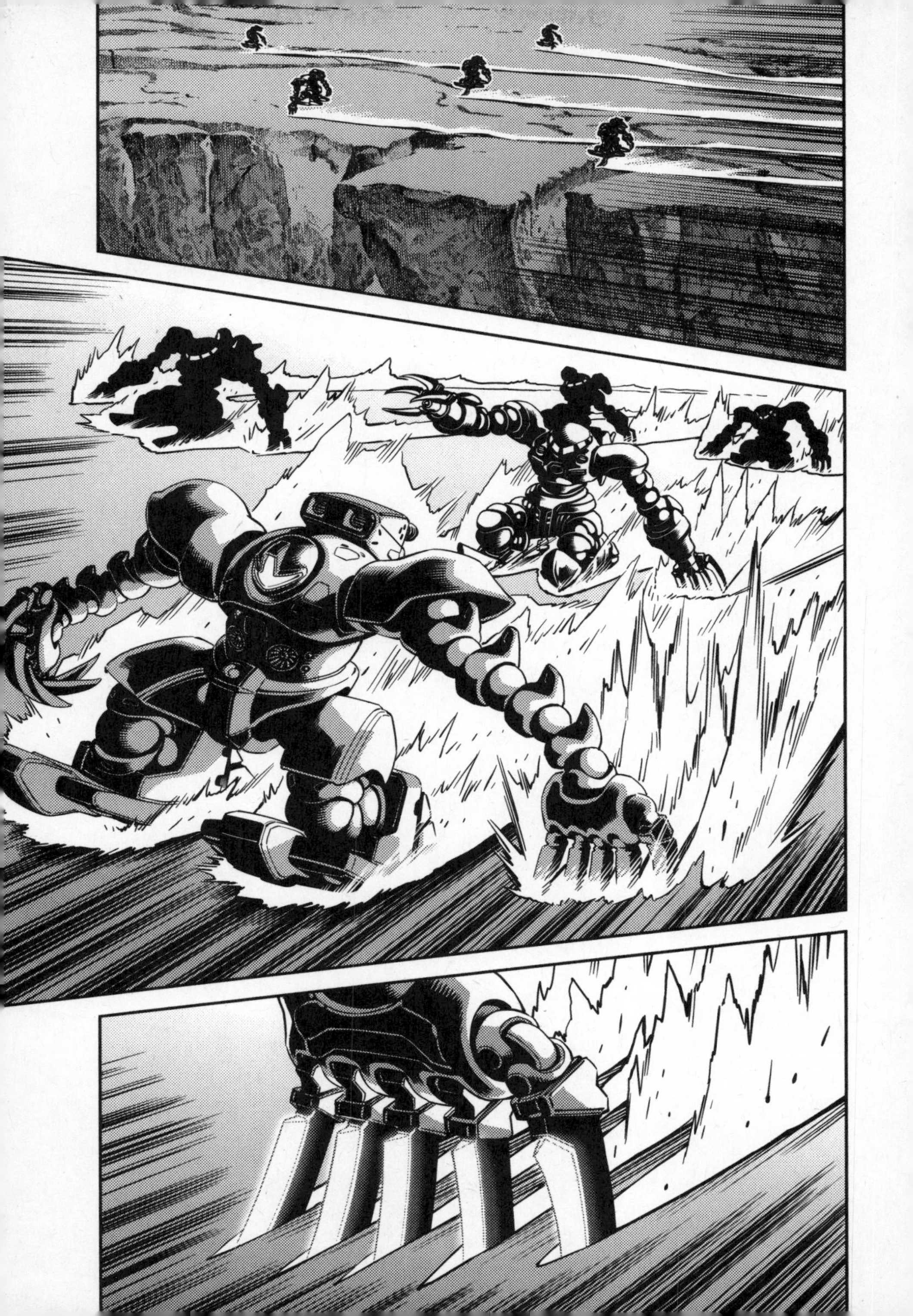

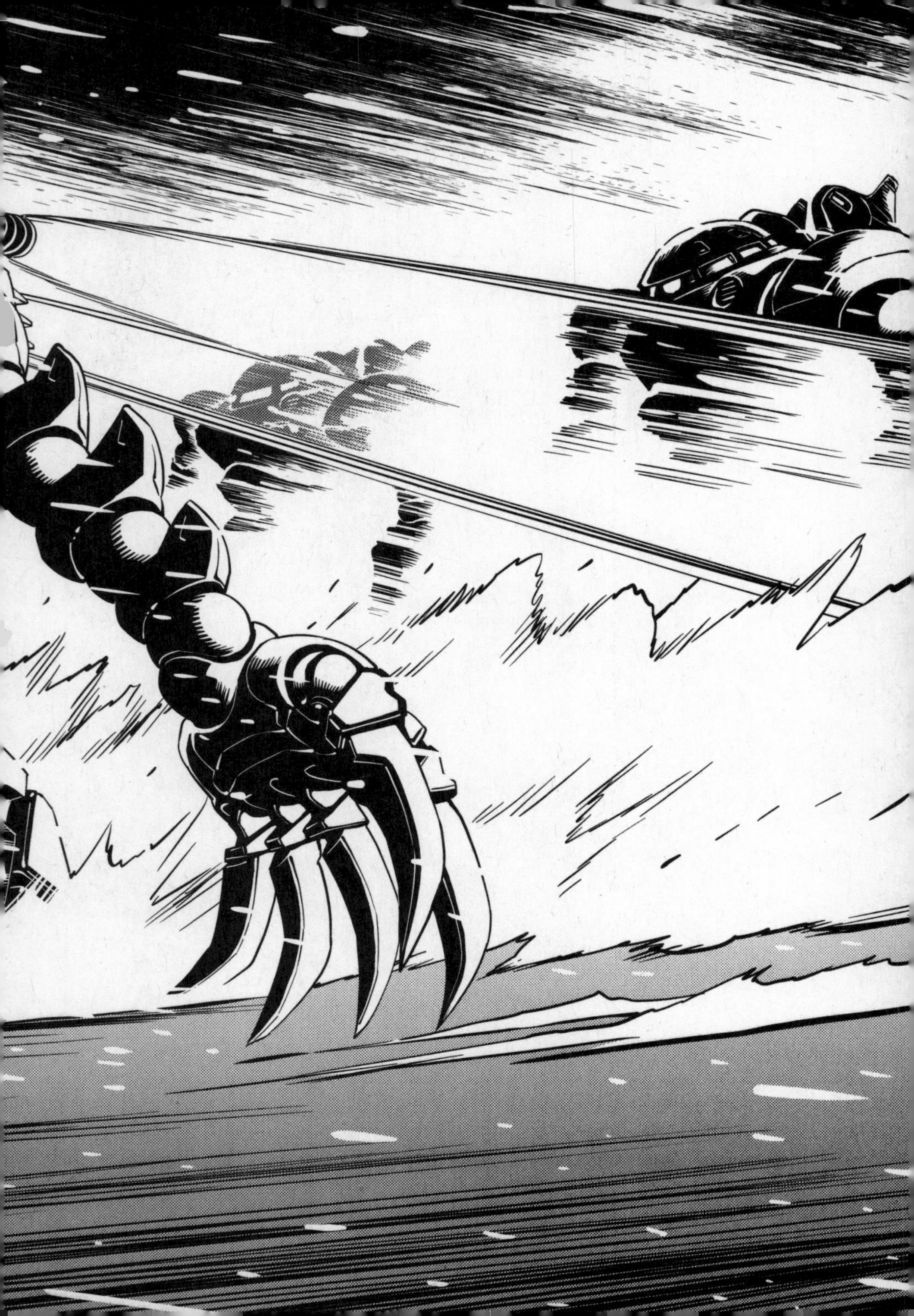

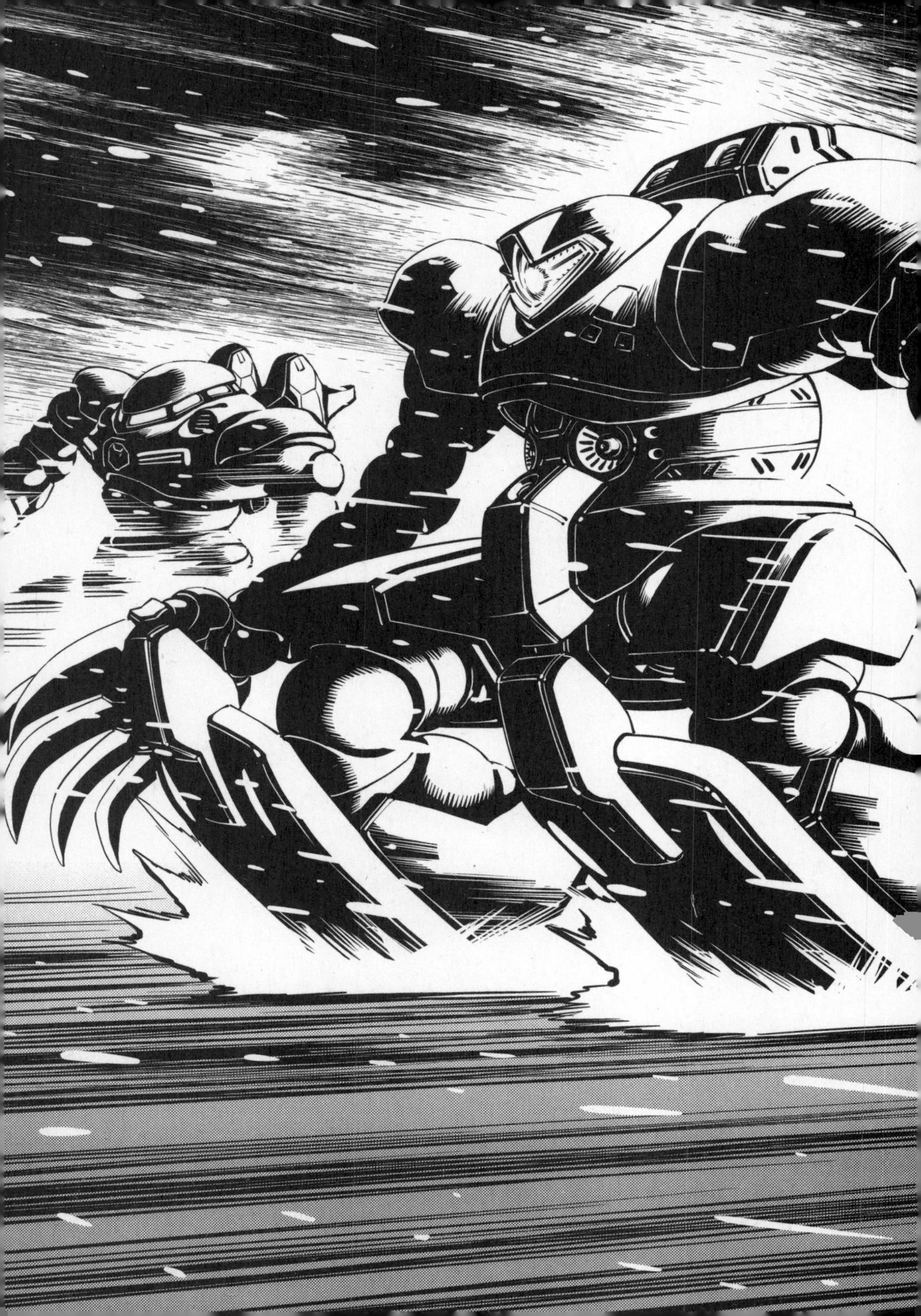

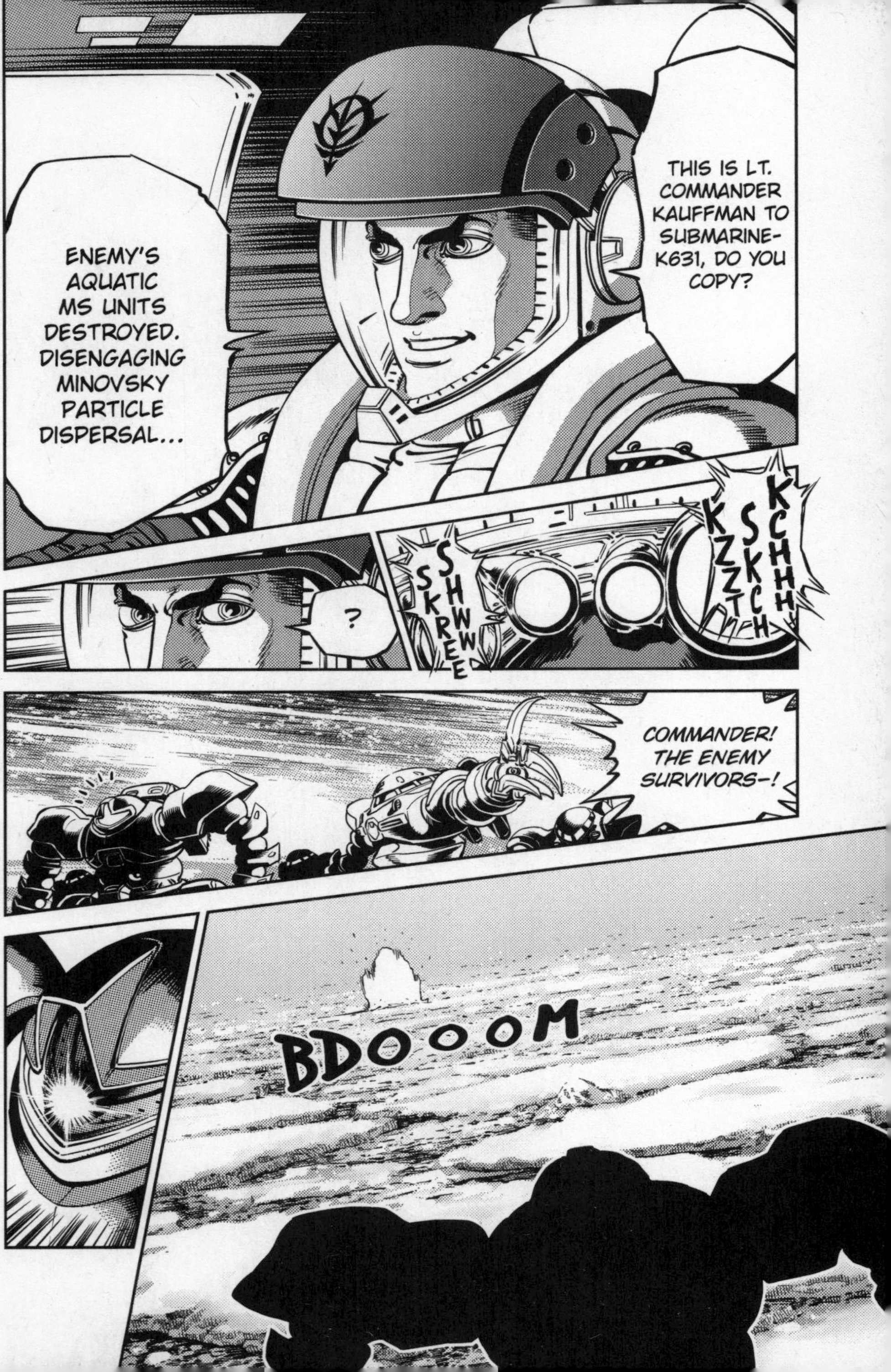
THIS IS LT. COMMANDER KAUFFMAN TO SUBMARINE-K631, DO YOU COPY?
ENEMY'S AQUATIC MS UNITS DESTROYED. DISENGAGING MINOVSKY PARTICLE DISPERSAL...
KZZT
SKCH
KCHHH
SKREE
SHWWWE
?
COMMANDER! THE ENEMY SURVIVORS–!
BDOOOM

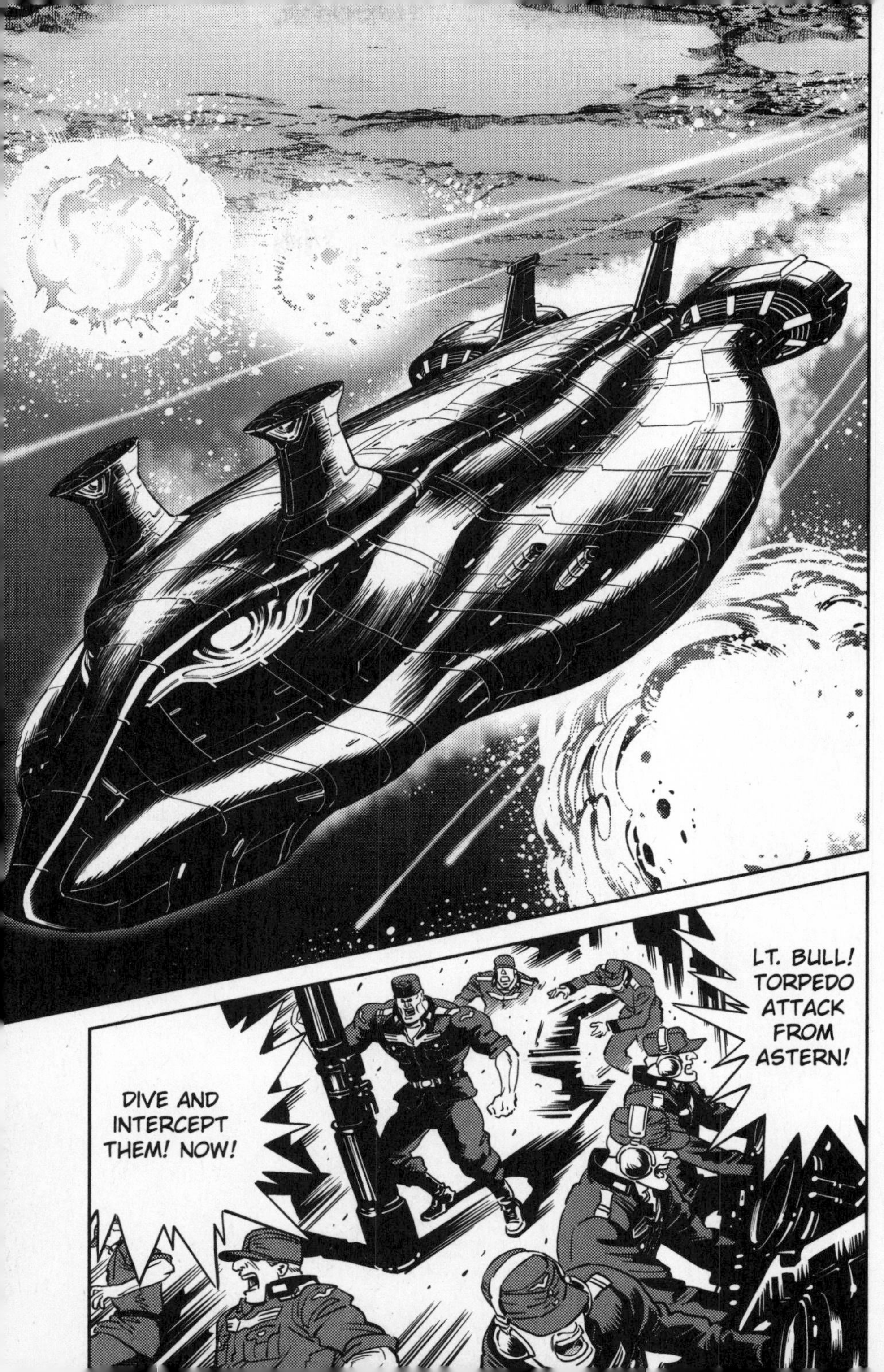
LT. BULL! TORPEDO ATTACK FROM ASTERN!
DIVE AND INTERCEPT THEM! NOW!

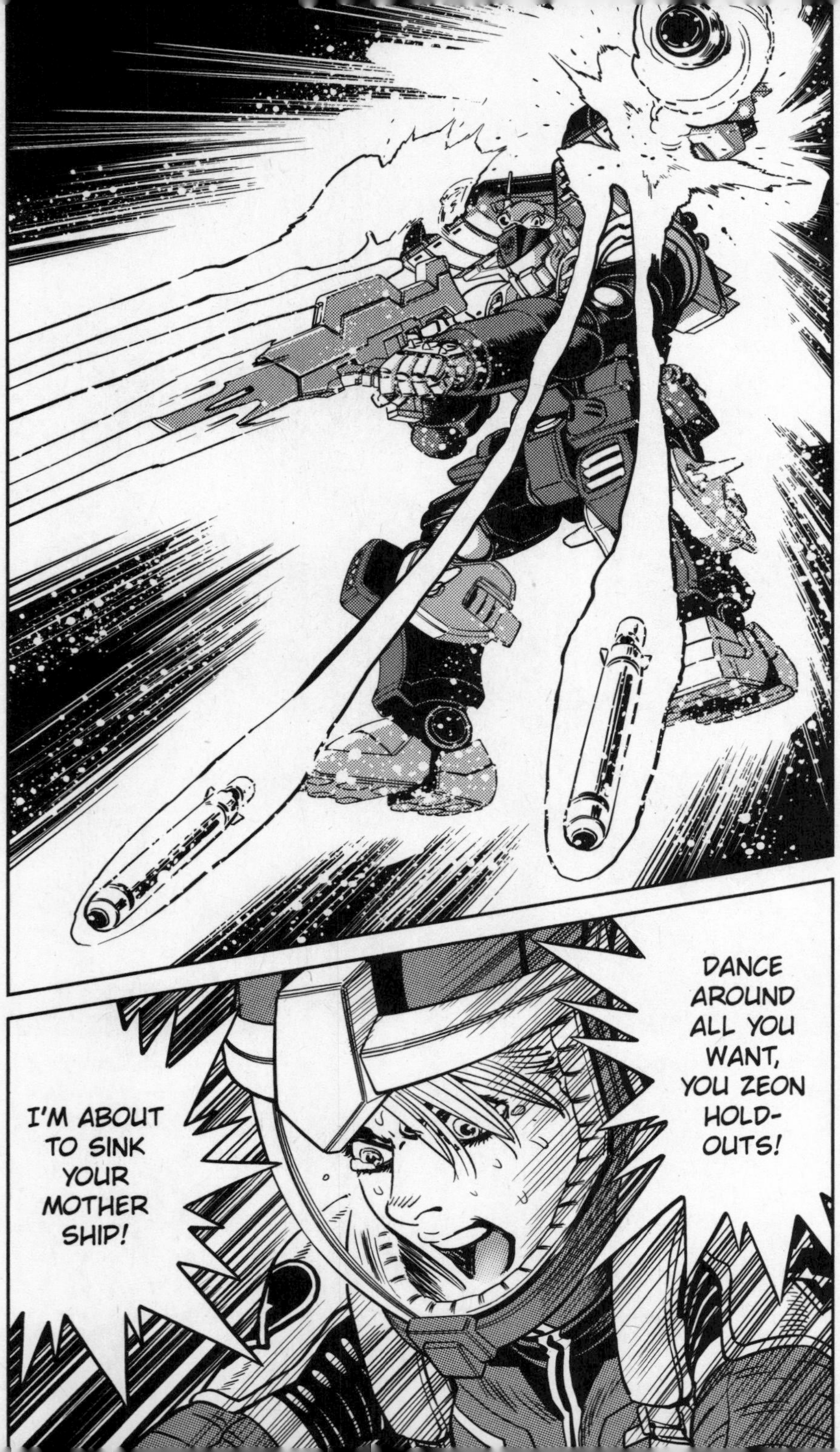
DANCE AROUND ALL YOU WANT, YOU ZEON HOLD-OUTS!
I'M ABOUT TO SINK YOUR MOTHER SHIP!

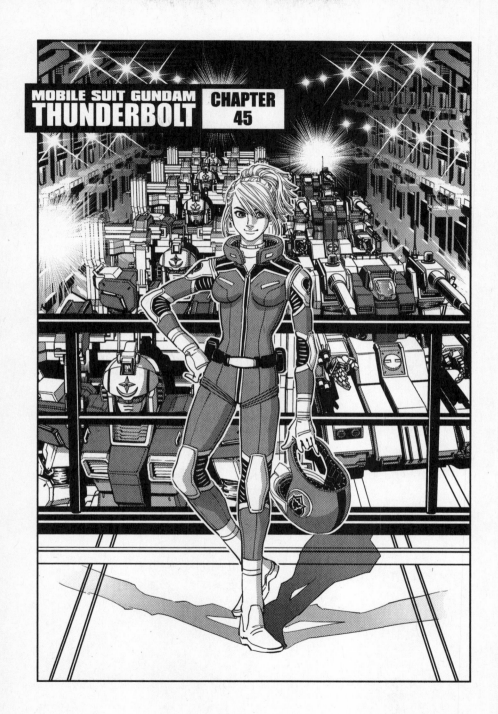

MOBILE SUIT GUNDAM
THUNDERBOLT

CHAPTER
45

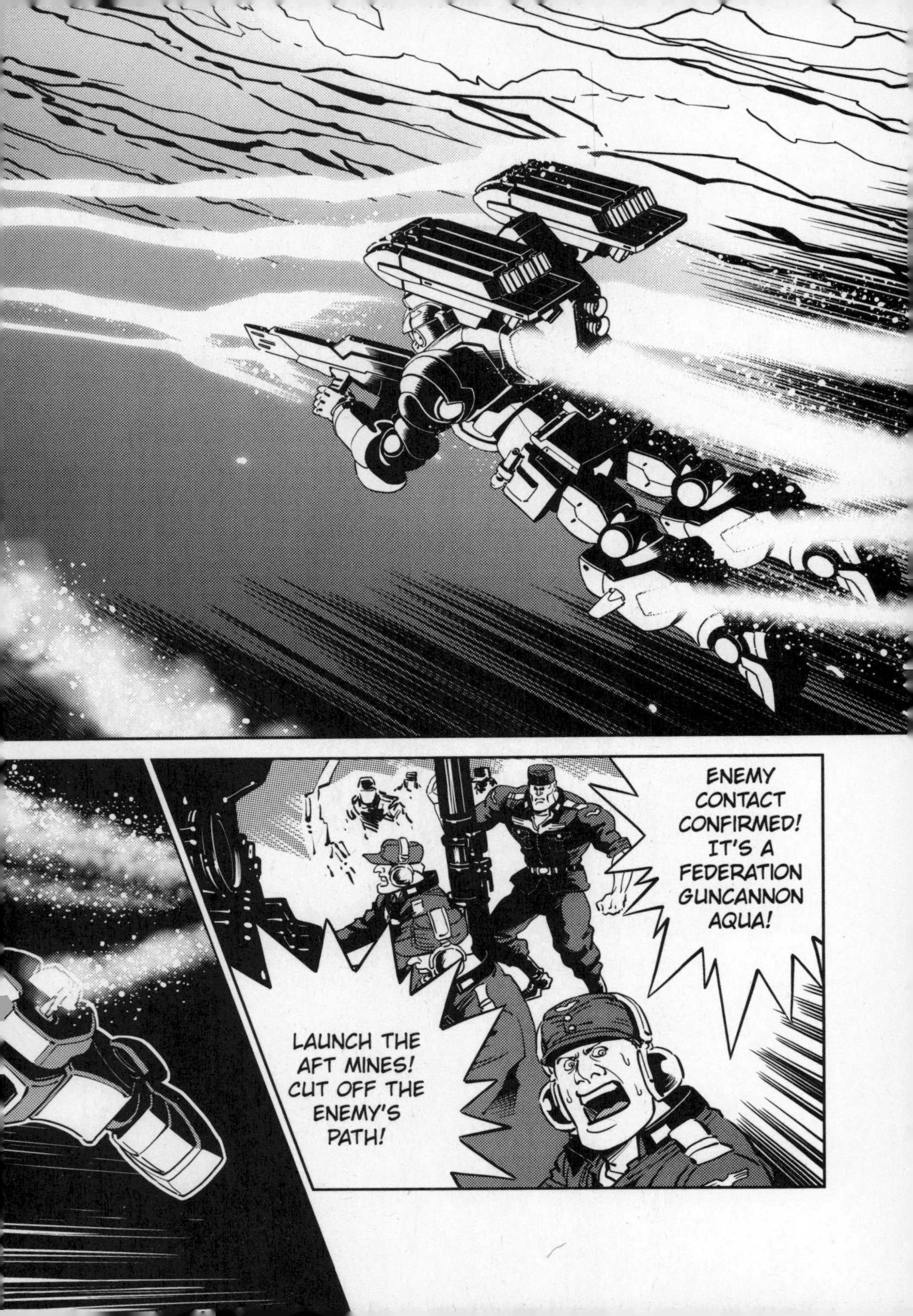
ENEMY CONTACT CONFIRMED! IT'S A FEDERATION GUNCANNON AQUA!
LAUNCH THE AFT MINES! CUT OFF THE ENEMY'S PATH!

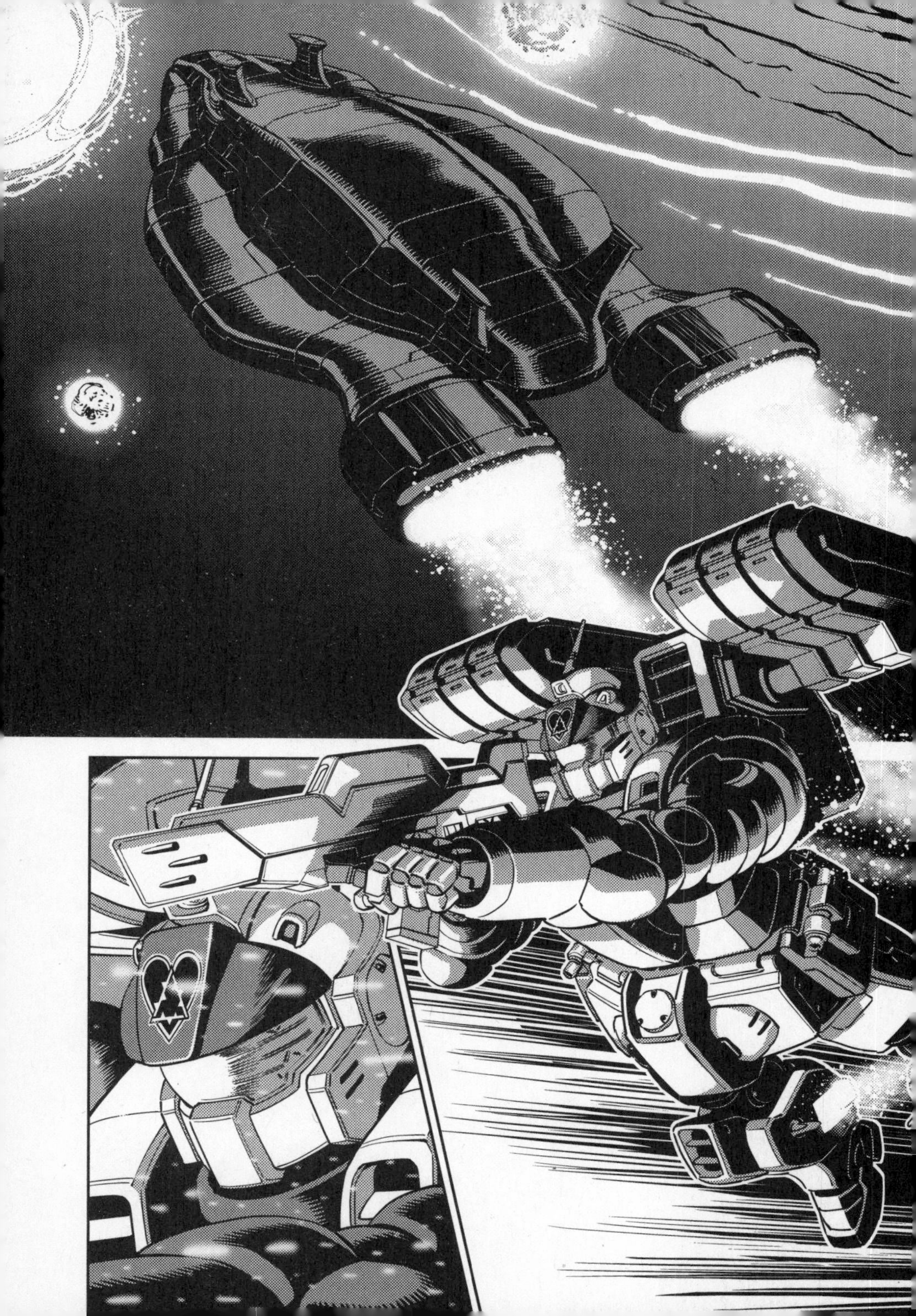

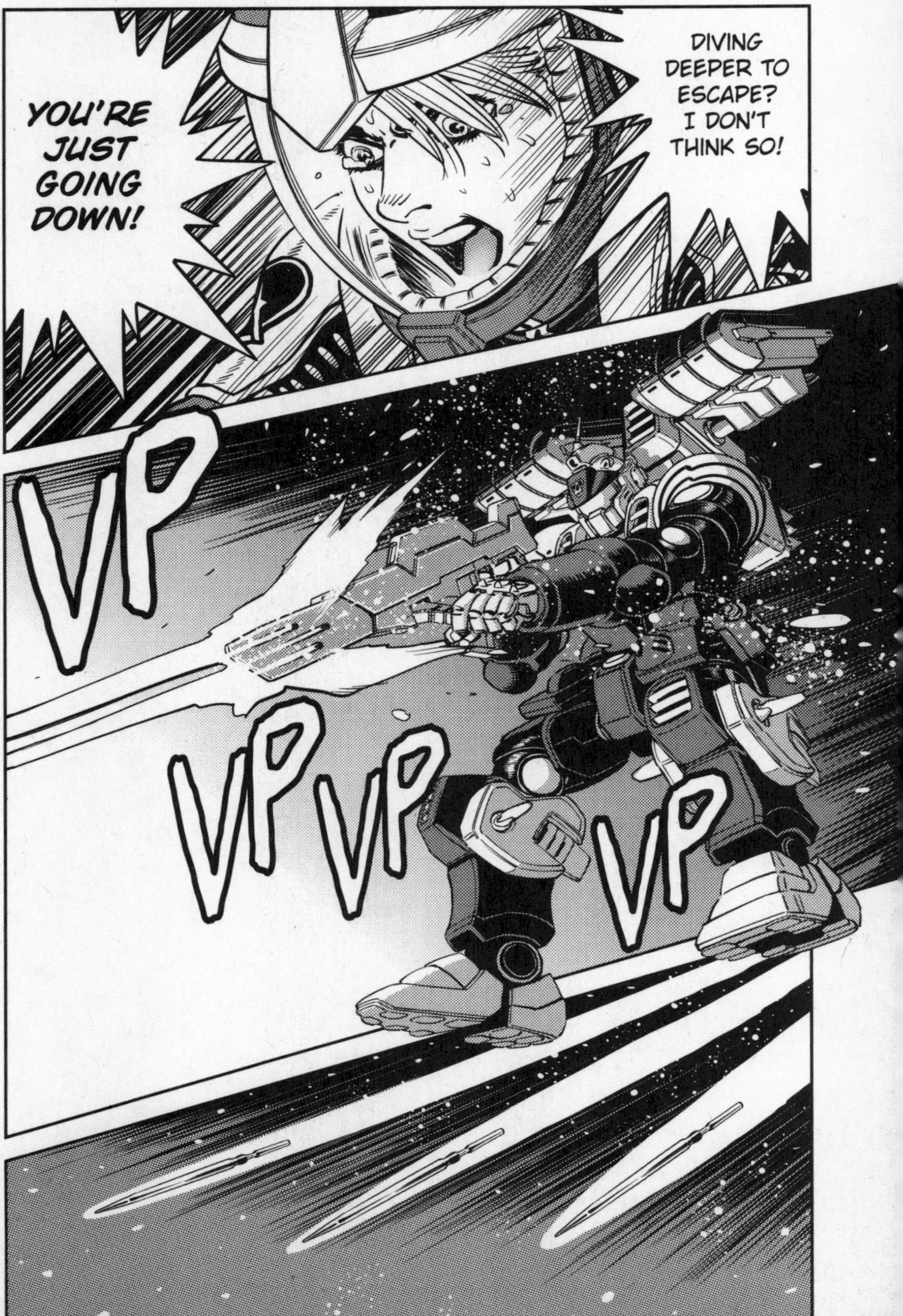
DIVING DEEPER TO ESCAPE? I DON'T THINK SO!
YOU'RE JUST GOING DOWN!
VP
VP VP VP

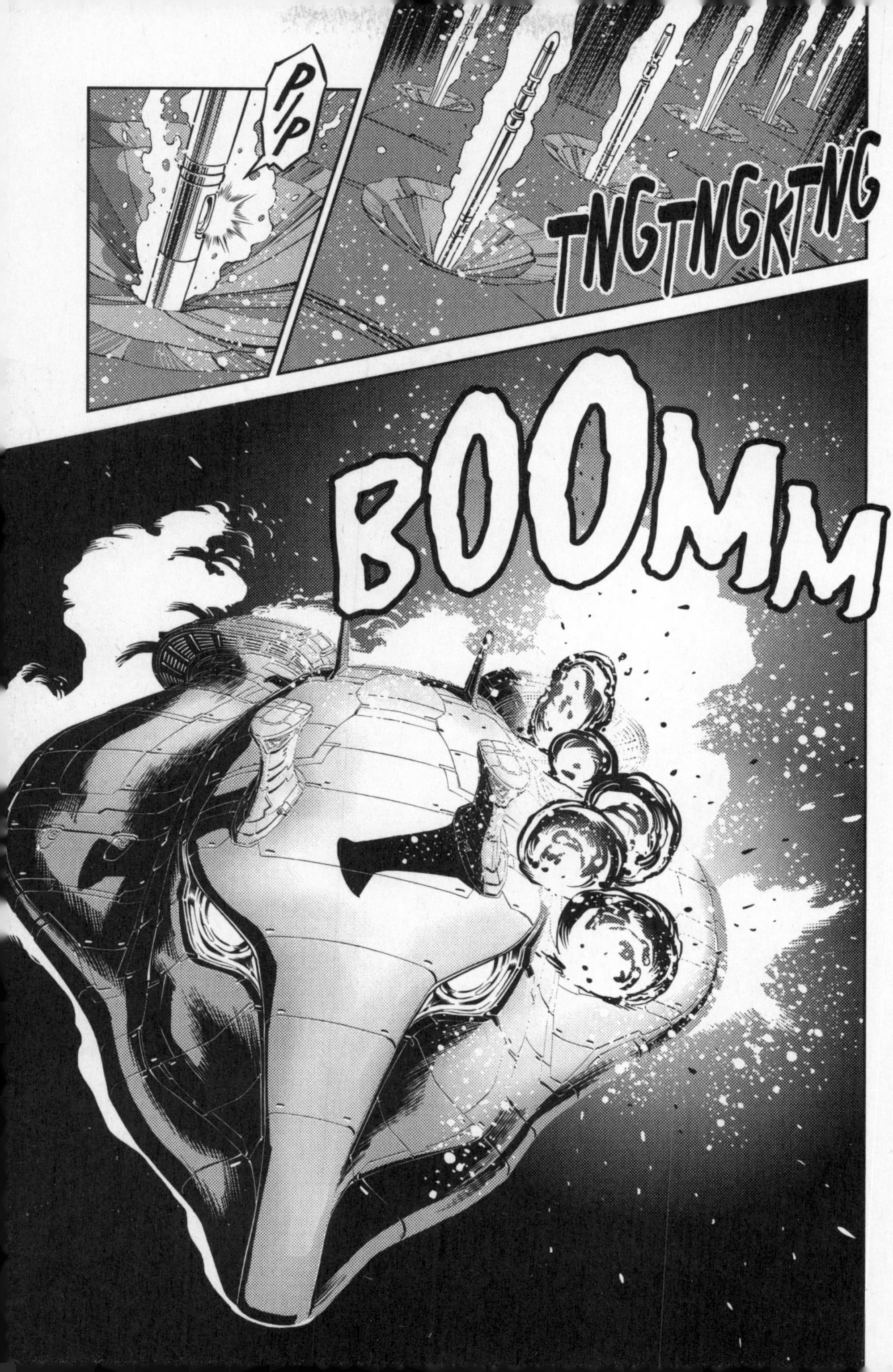
TNGTNGKTNG
PIP
BOOMM

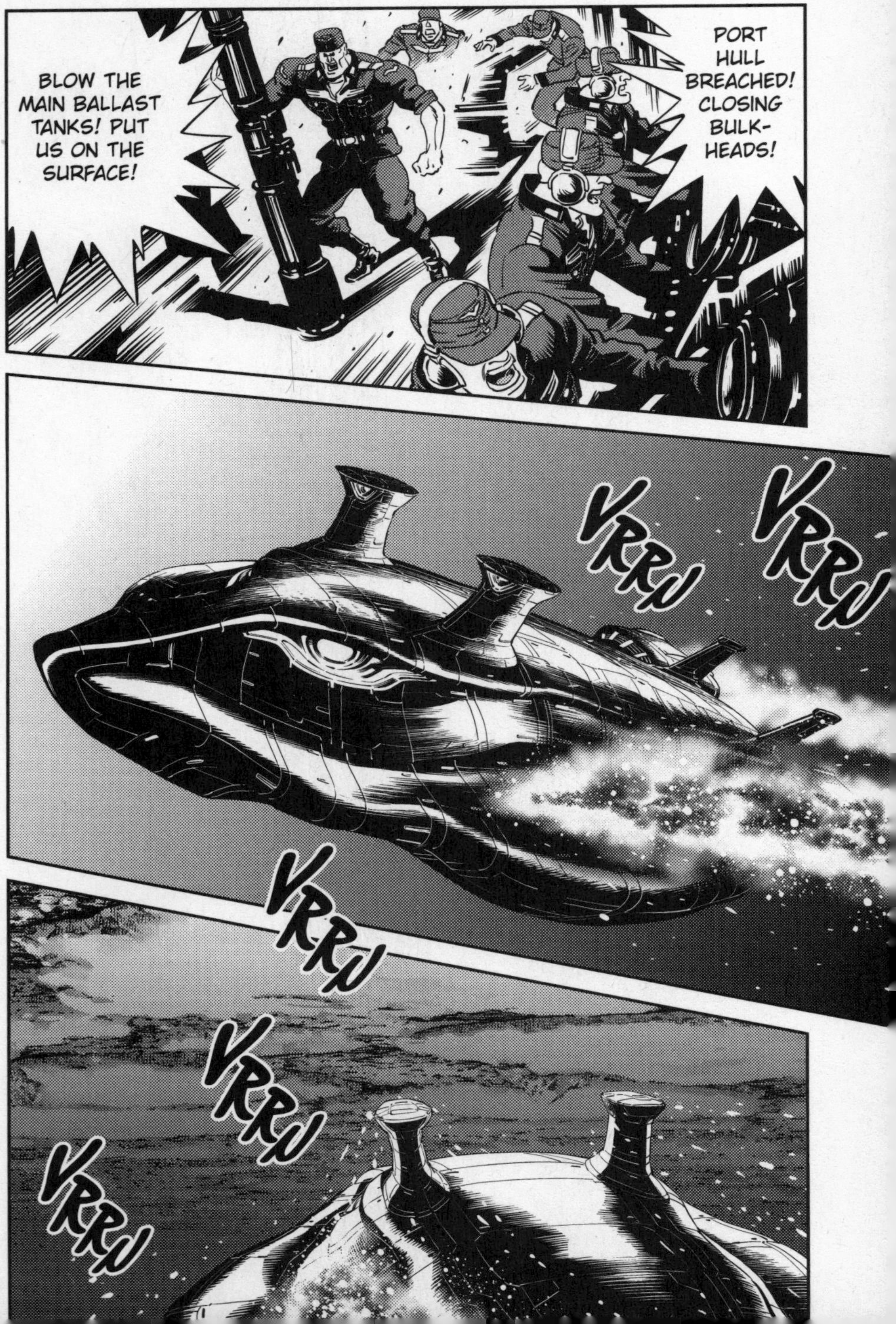
PORT HULL BREACHED! CLOSING BULK-HEADS!
BLOW THE MAIN BALLAST TANKS! PUT US ON THE SURFACE!
VRRN
VRRN
VRRN
VRRN
VRRN

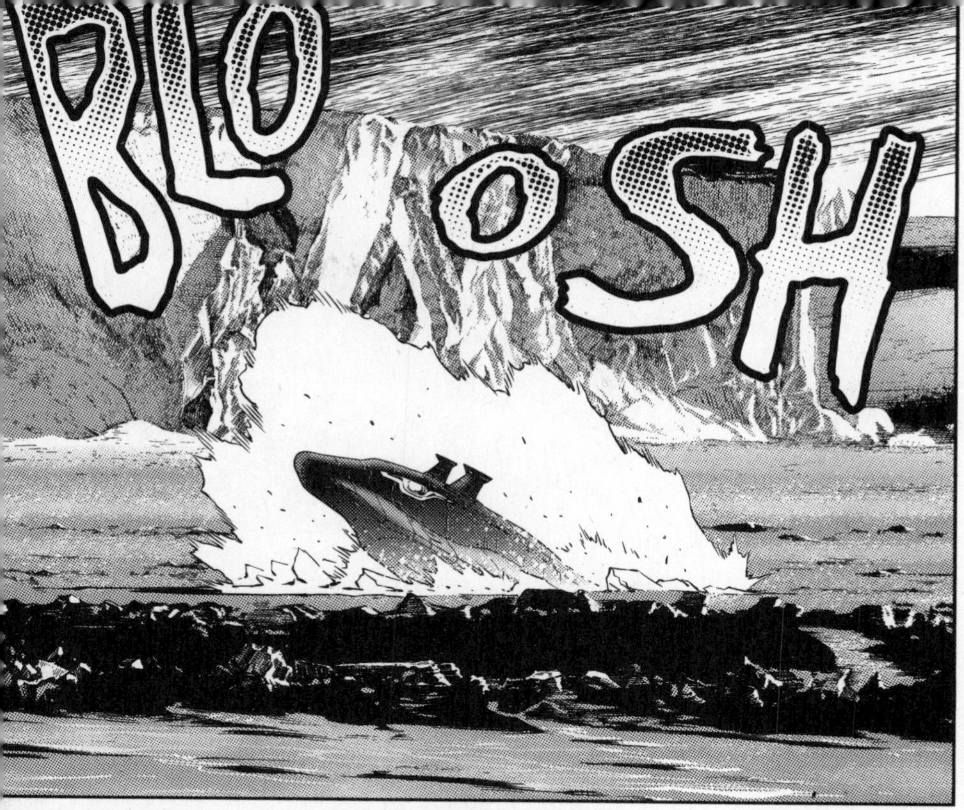
BLOOSH

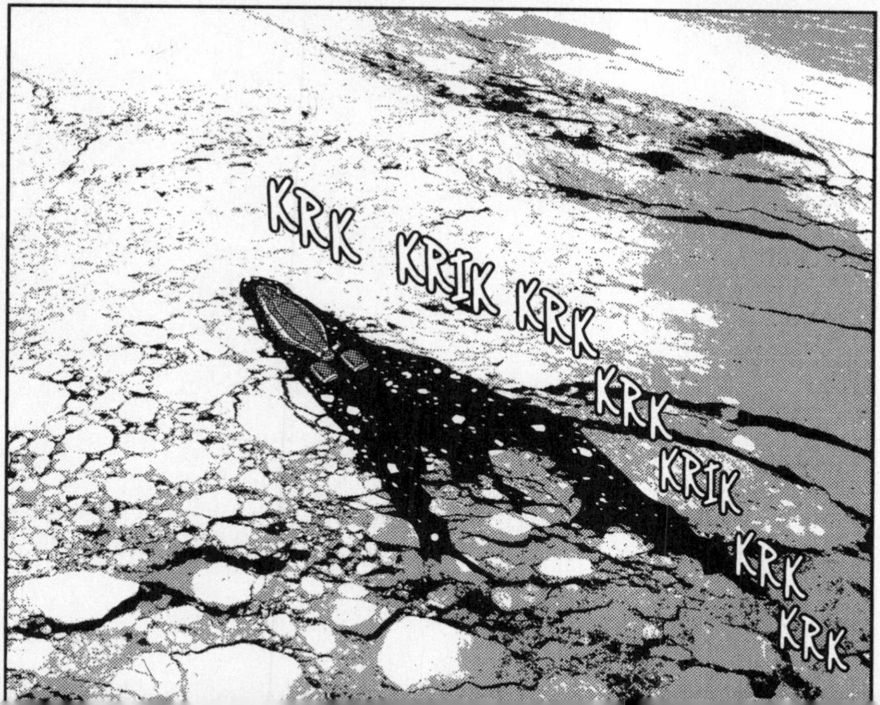
KRK
KRIK
KRK
KRK
KRIK
KRK
KRK

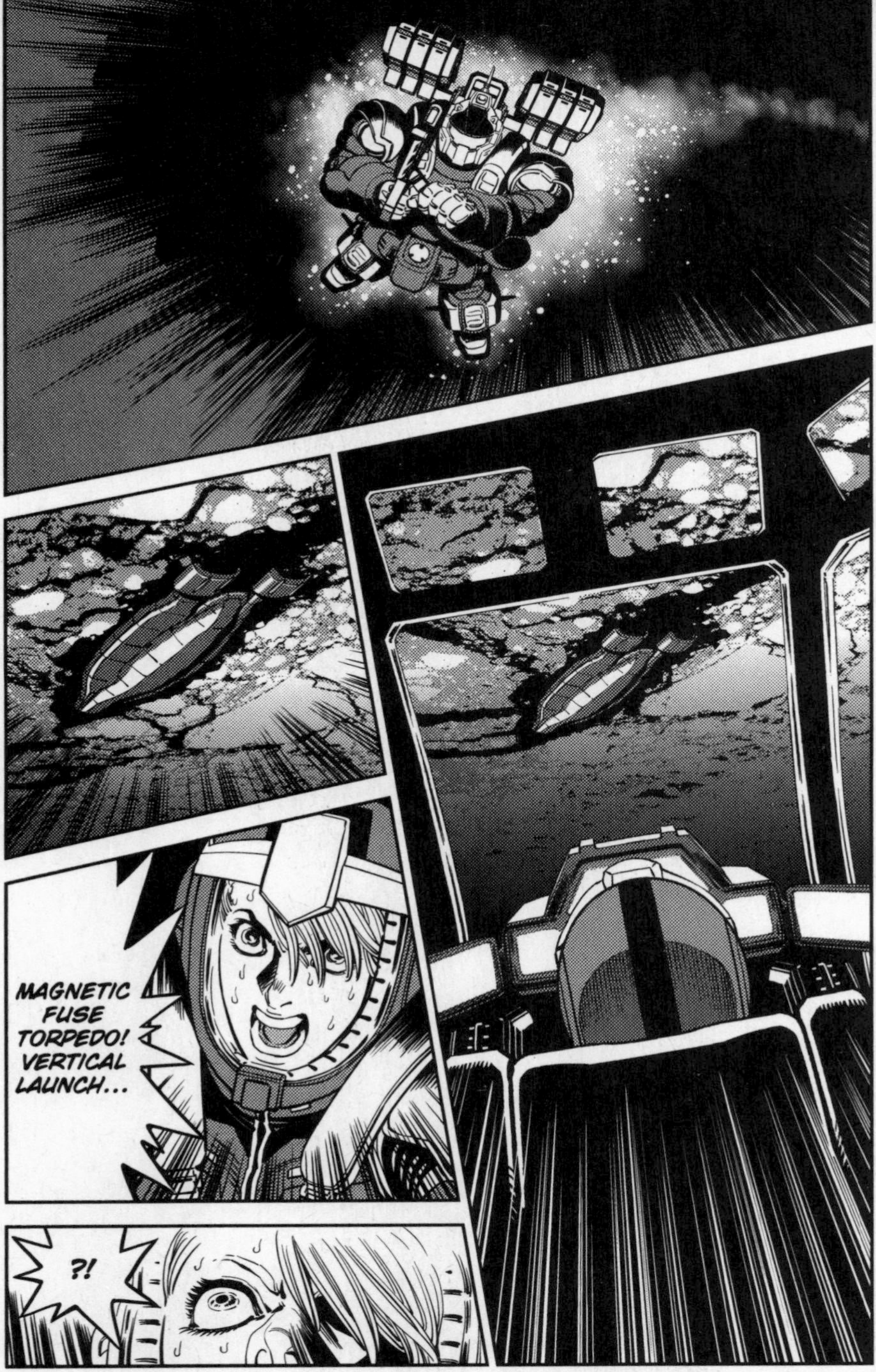
MAGNETIC FUSE TORPEDO! VERTICAL LAUNCH...
?!

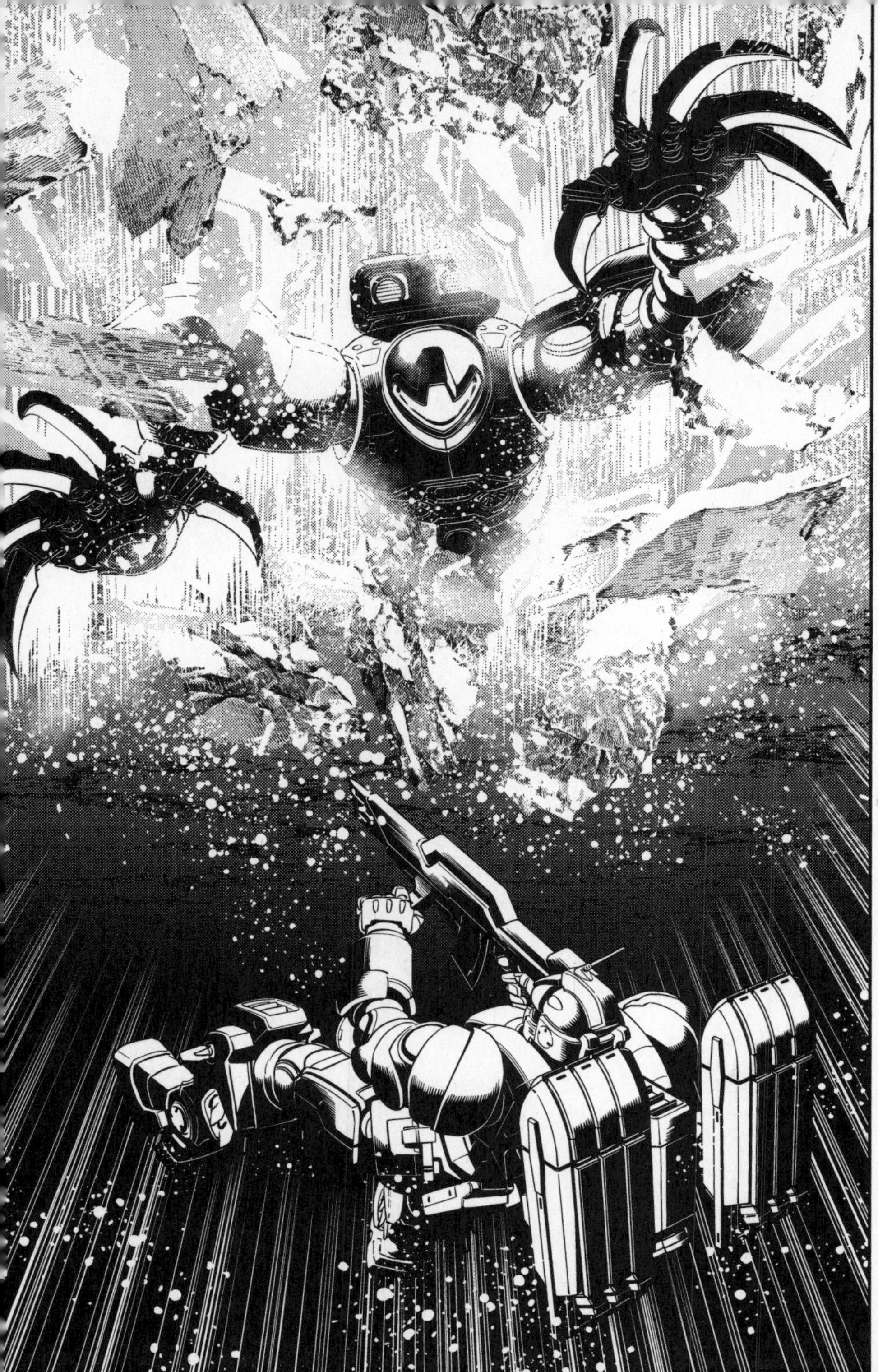

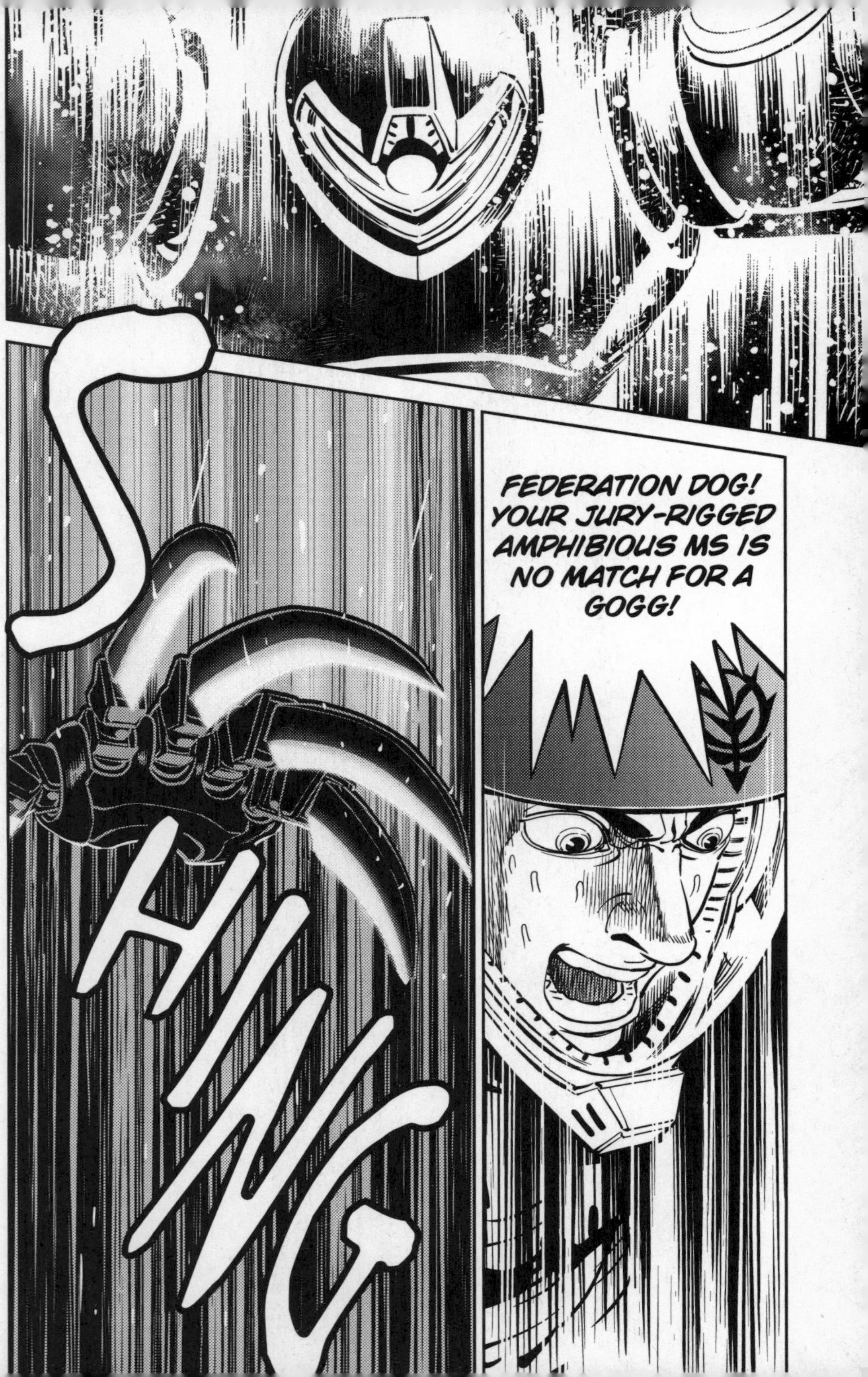
FEDERATION DOG! YOUR JURY-RIGGED AMPHIBIOUS MS IS NO MATCH FOR A GOGG!
SHING

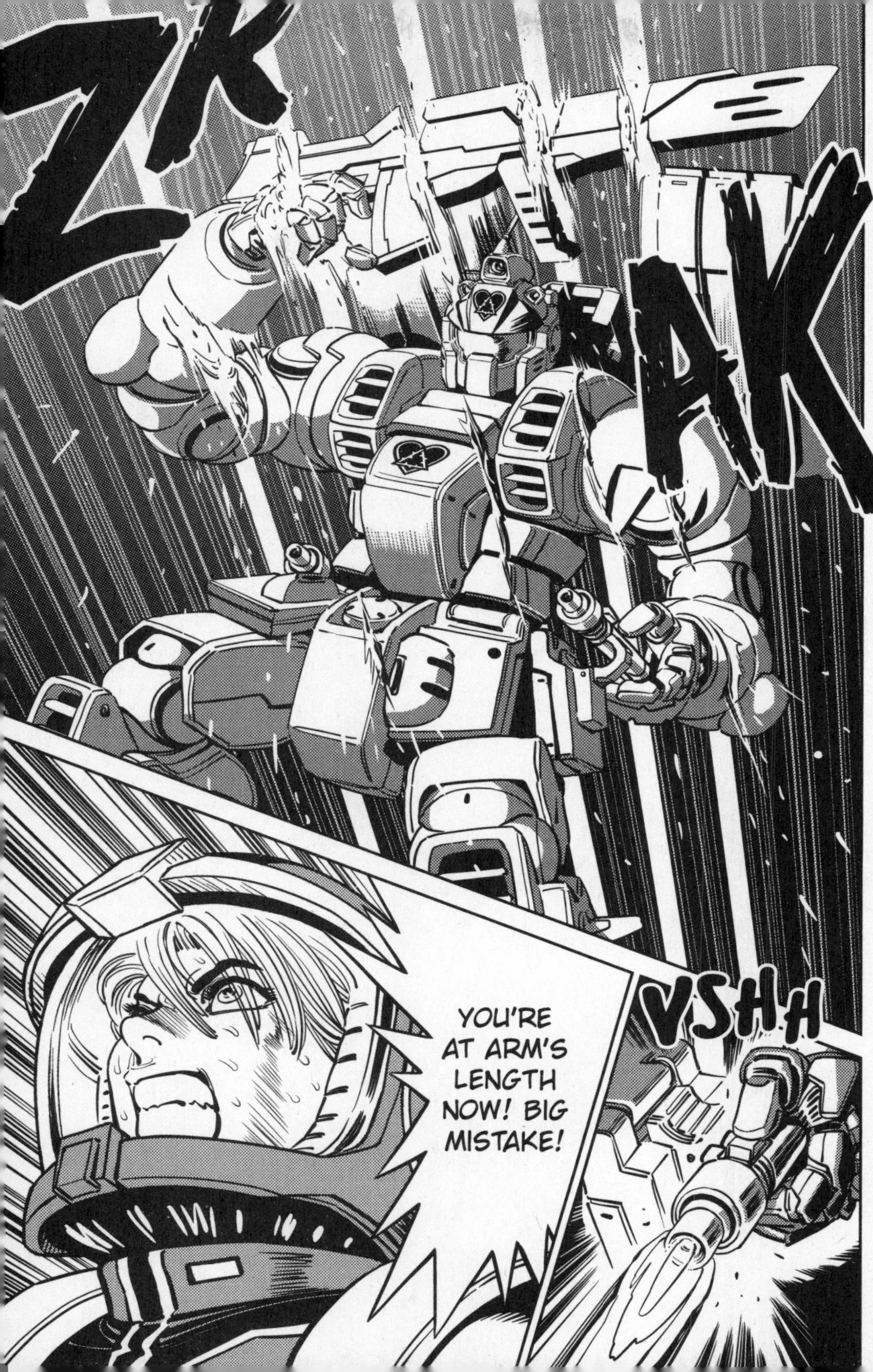
ZK
RAK
VSHH
YOU'RE AT ARM'S LENGTH NOW! BIG MISTAKE!
AAA

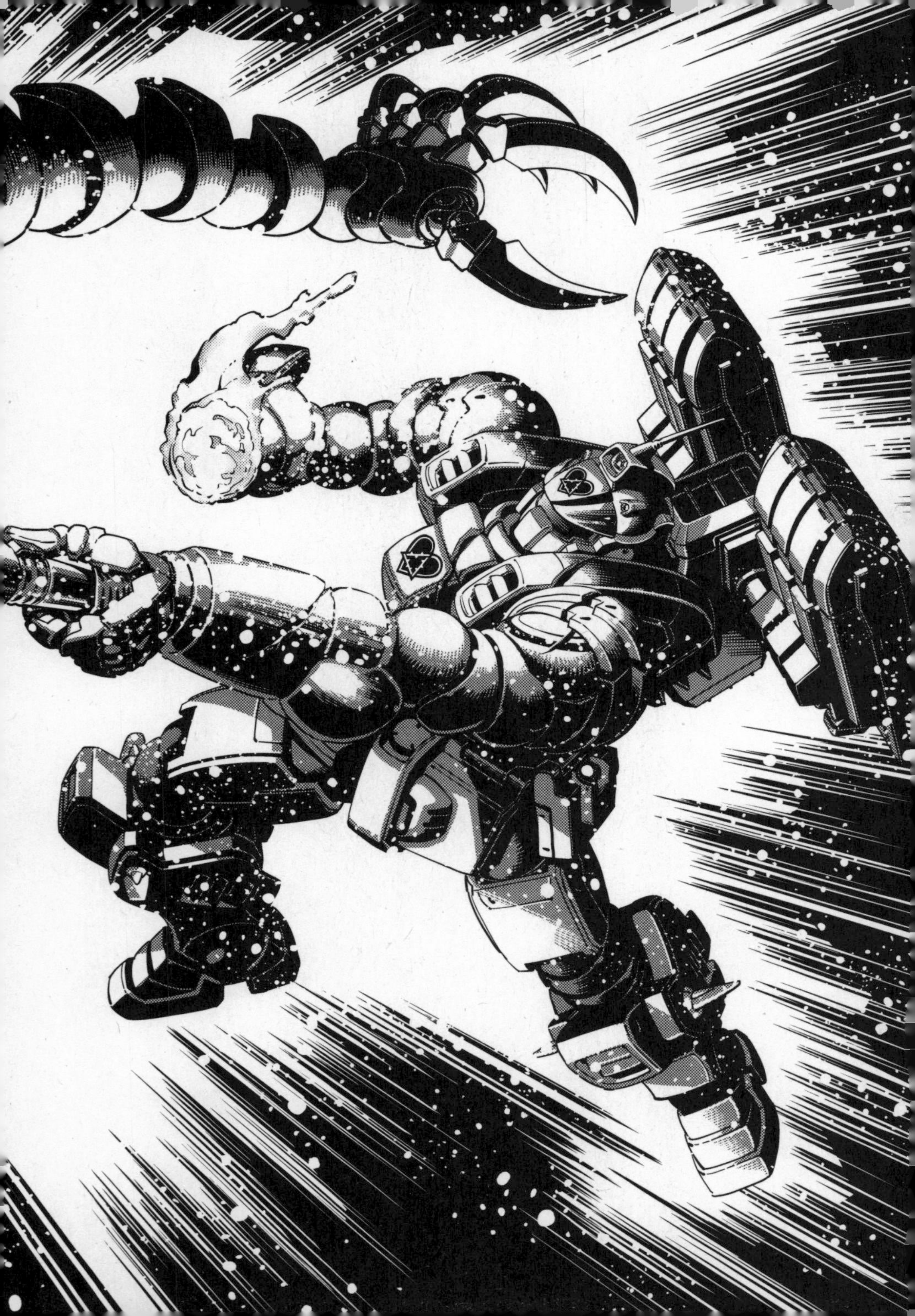

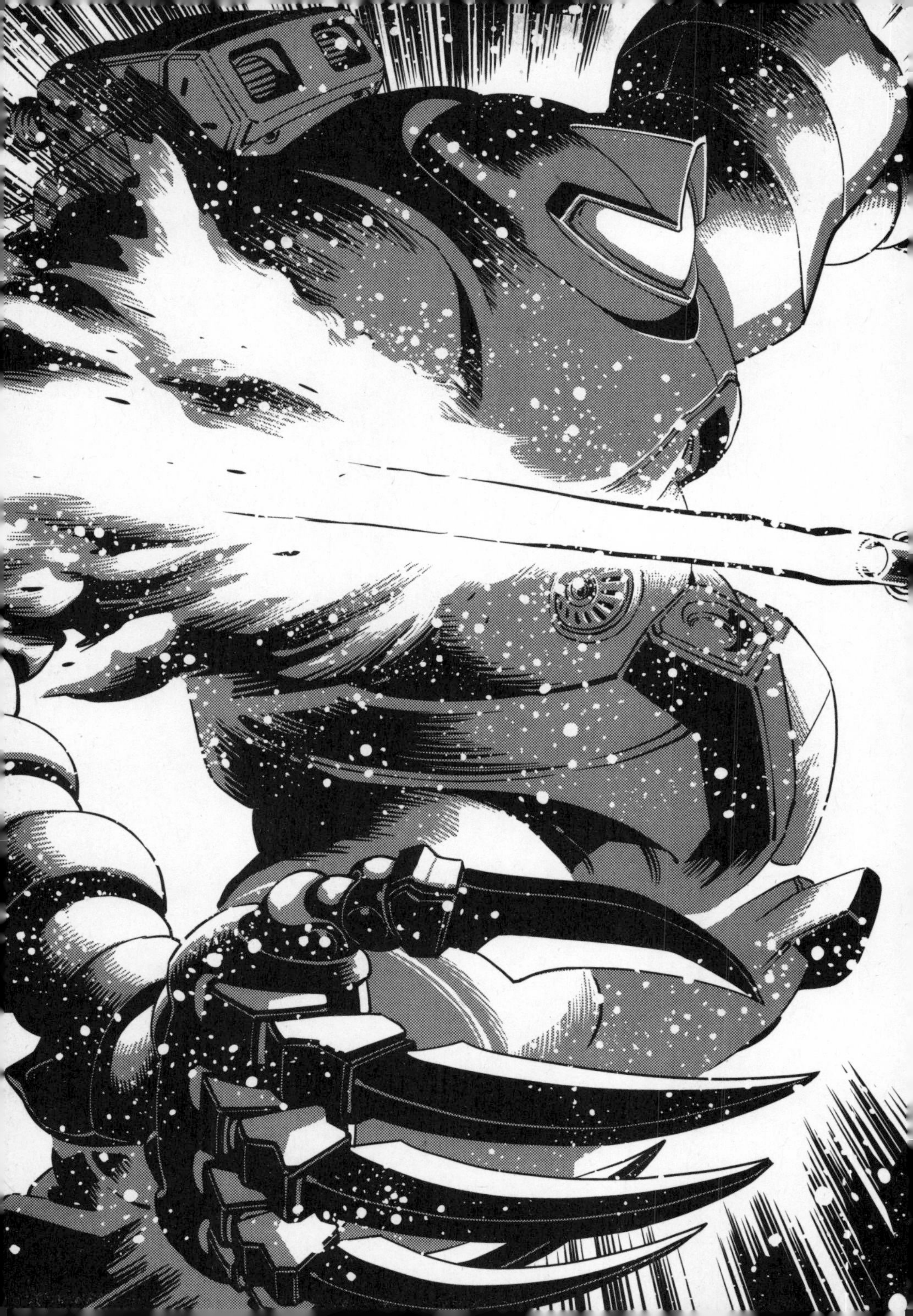

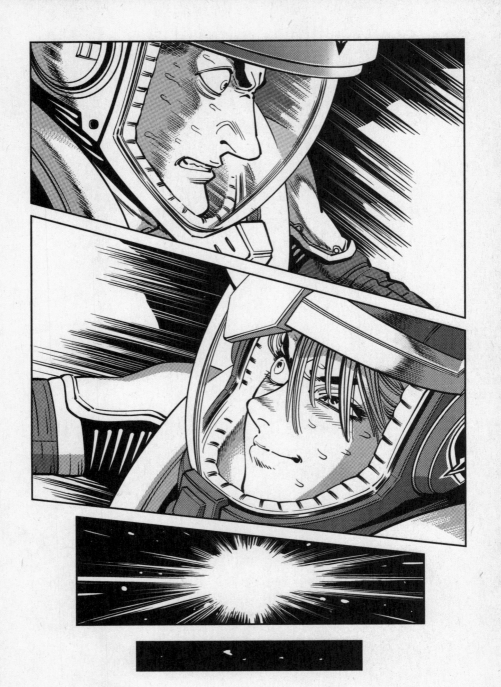

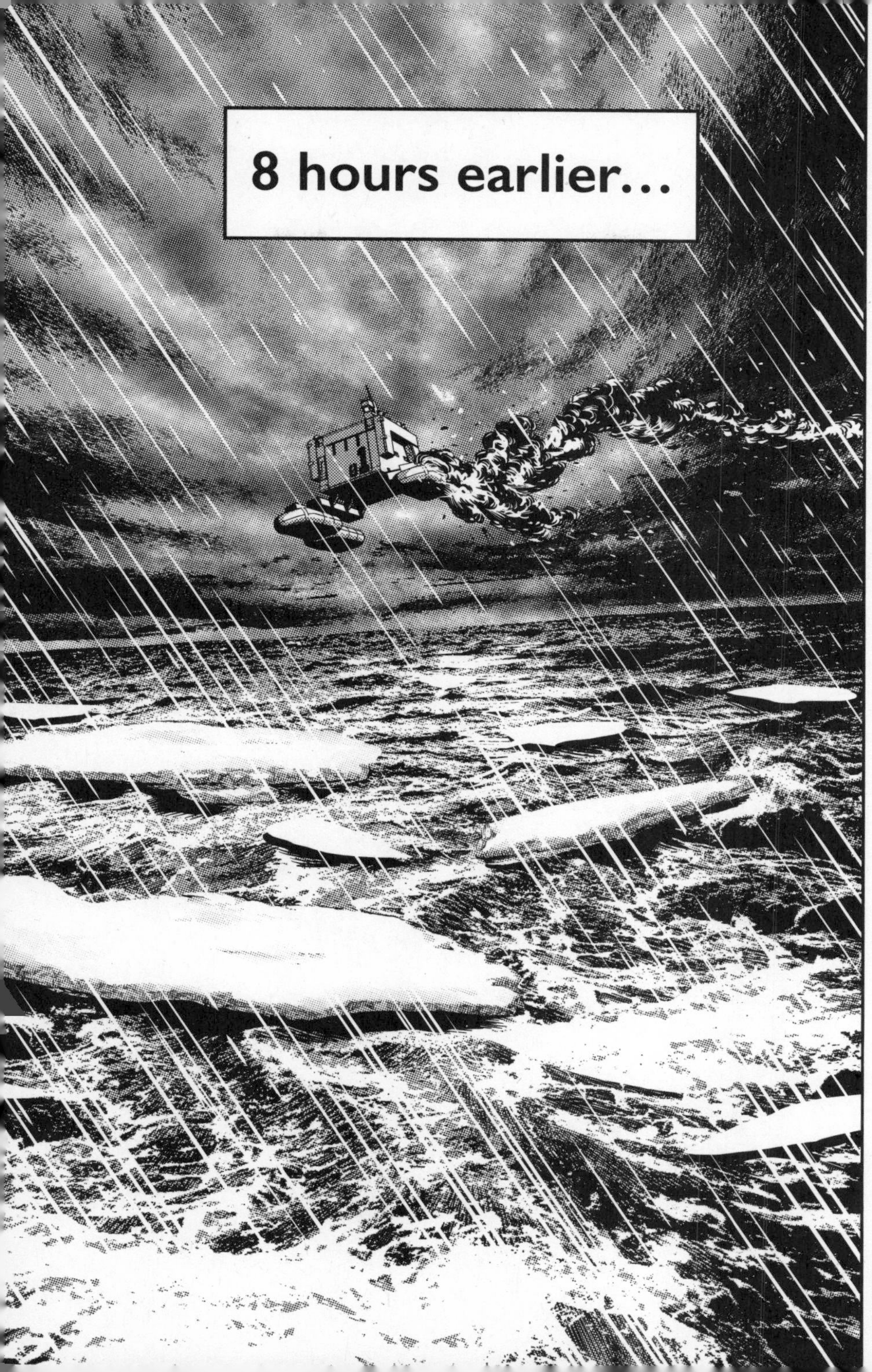
8 hours earlier...

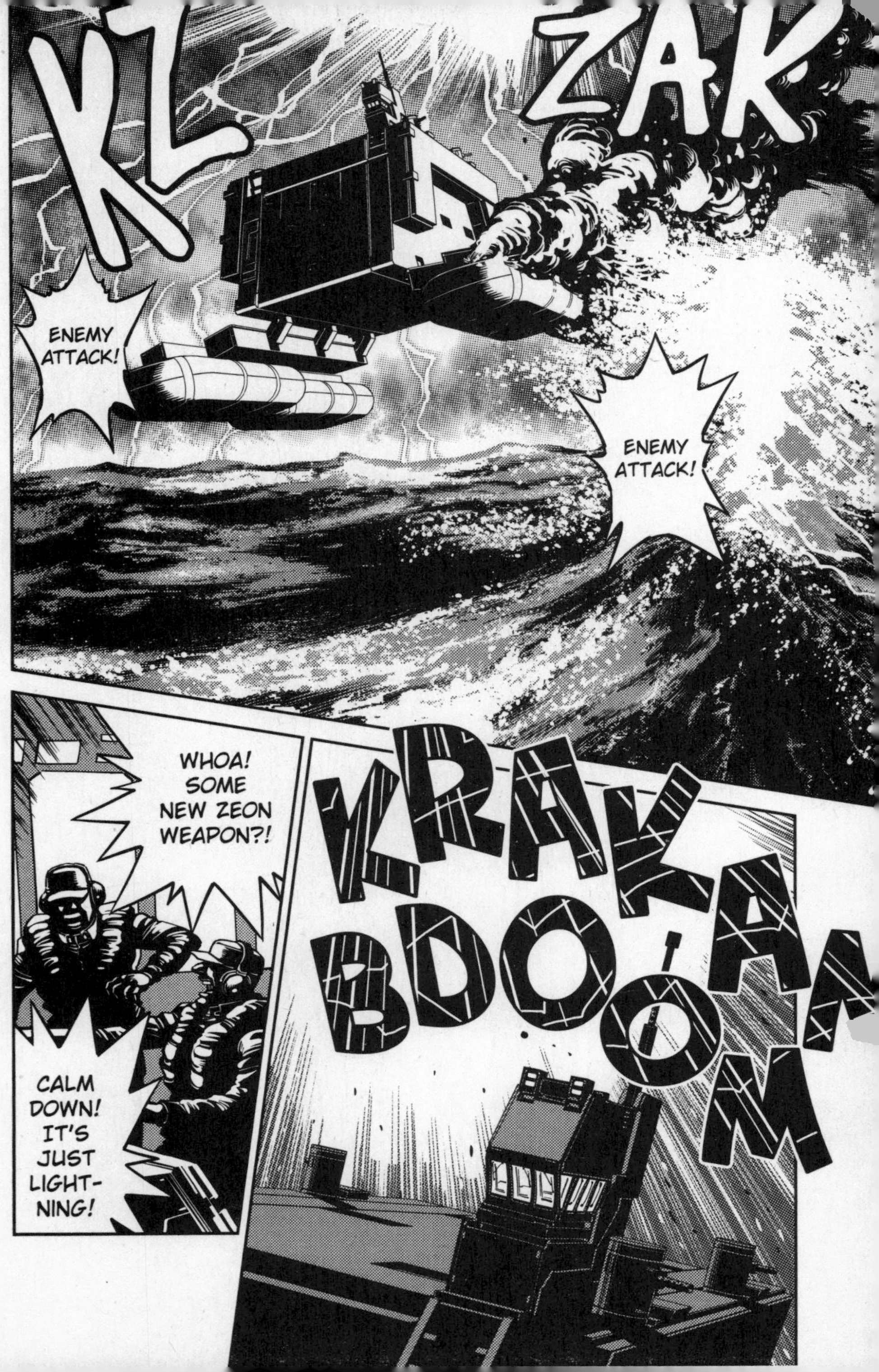
KZZAK
ENEMY ATTACK!
ENEMY ATTACK!
KRAKA
BDOOOM
WHOA! SOME NEW ZEON WEAPON?!
CALM DOWN! IT'S JUST LIGHT-NING!

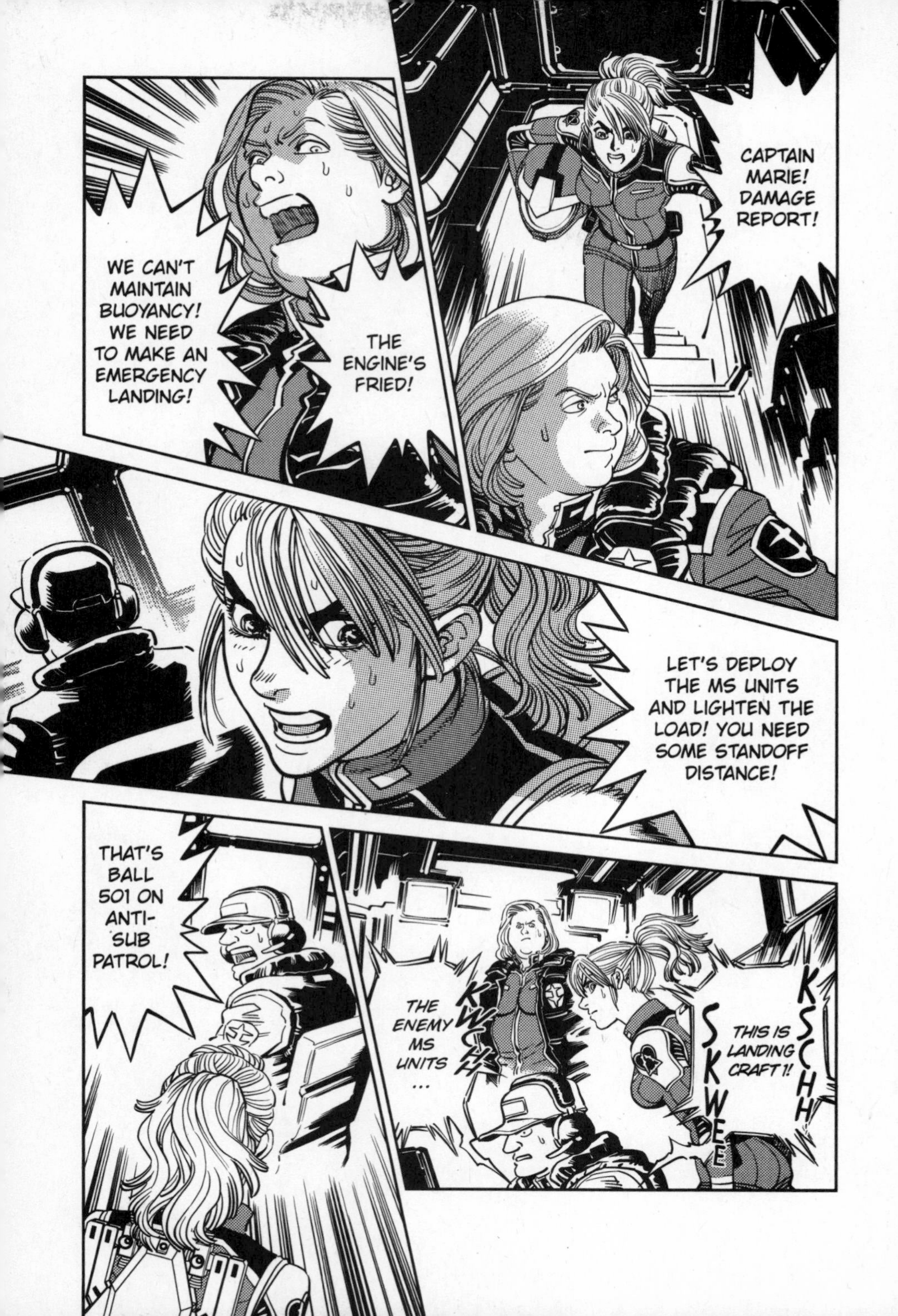
CAPTAIN MARIE! DAMAGE REPORT!
THE ENGINE'S FRIED!
WE CAN'T MAINTAIN BUOYANCY! WE NEED TO MAKE AN EMERGENCY LANDING!
LET'S DEPLOY THE MS UNITS AND LIGHTEN THE LOAD! YOU NEED SOME STANDOFF DISTANCE!
KSCHH!
THIS IS LANDING CRAFT 1!
SKWEE
KWSHH
THE ENEMY MS UNITS ...
THAT'S BALL 501 ON ANTI-SUB PATROL!

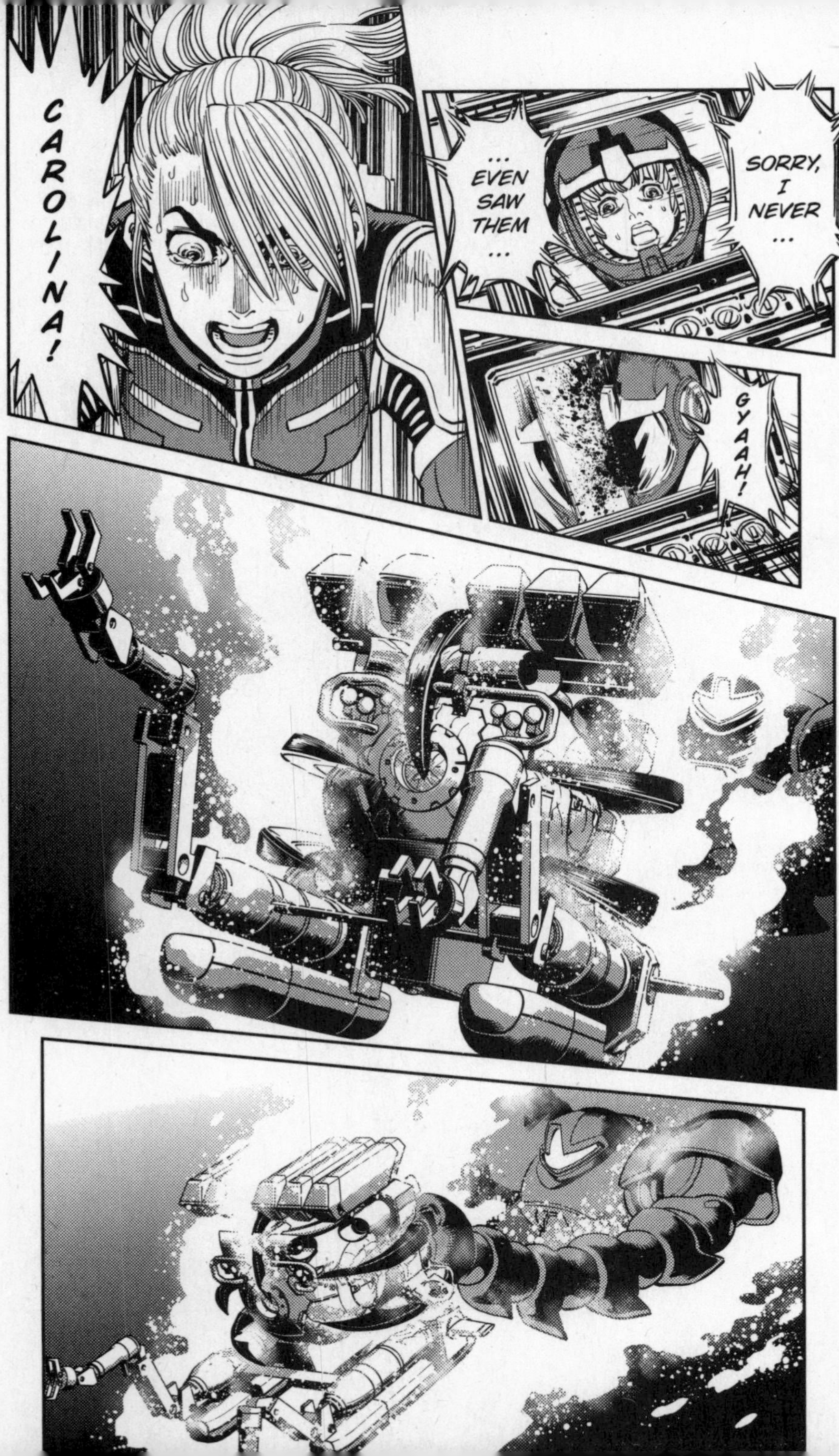
SORRY, I NEVER ...
... EVEN SAW THEM ...
GYAAH!
CAROLINA!

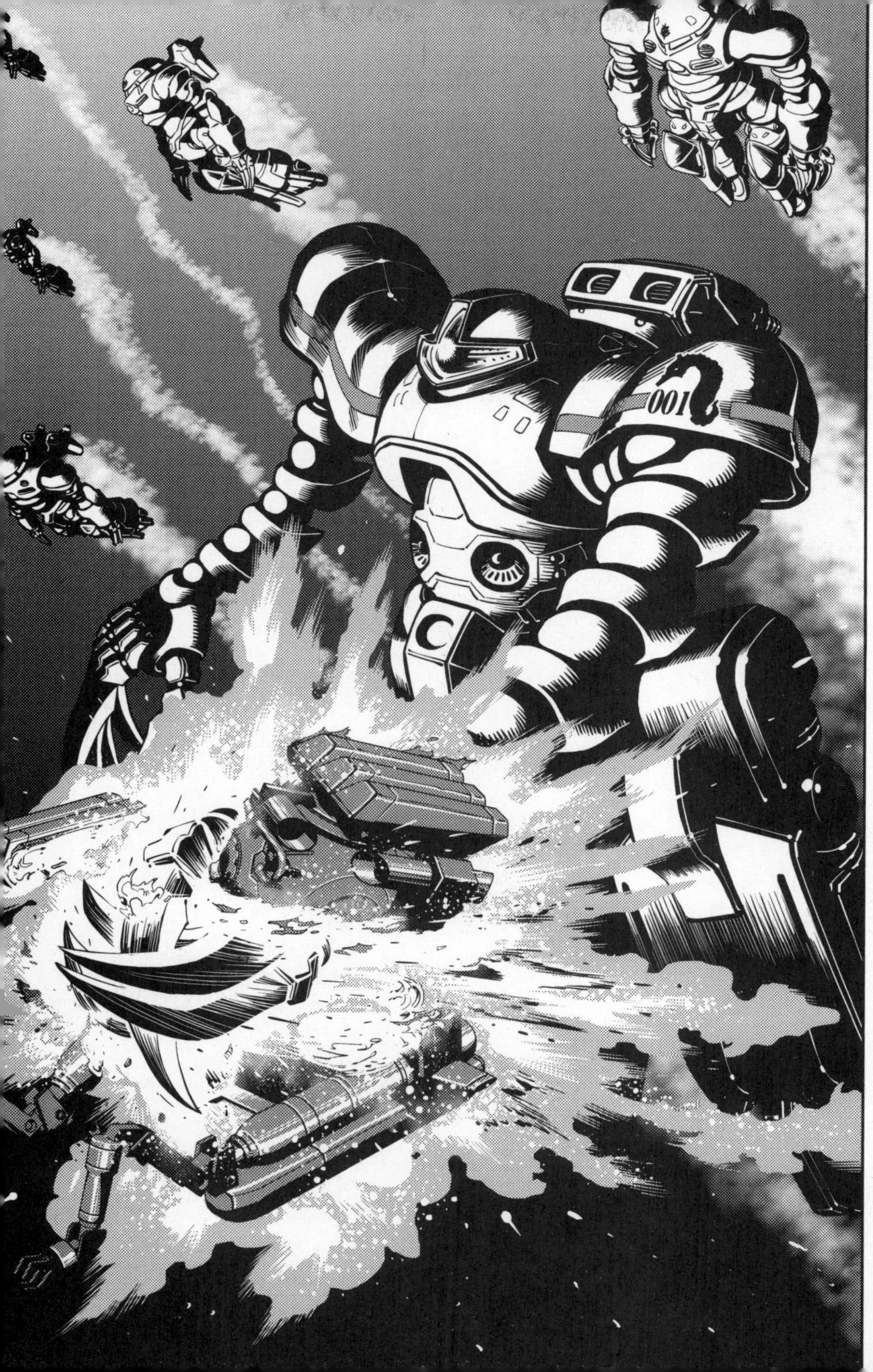
001

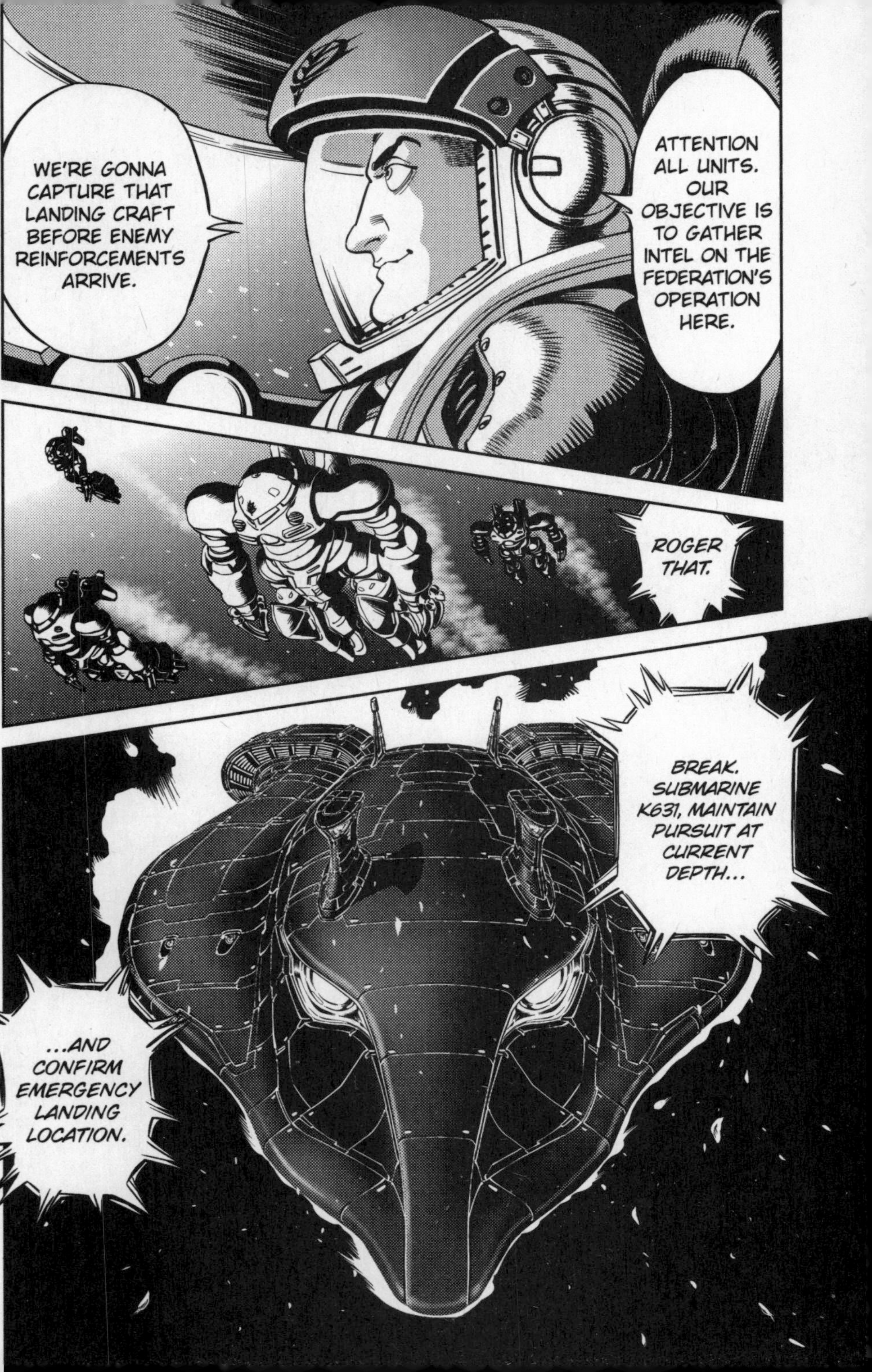
ATTENTION ALL UNITS. OUR OBJECTIVE IS TO GATHER INTEL ON THE FEDERATION'S OPERATION HERE.
WE'RE GONNA CAPTURE THAT LANDING CRAFT BEFORE ENEMY REINFORCEMENTS ARRIVE.
ROGER THAT.
BREAK. SUBMARINE K631, MAINTAIN PURSUIT AT CURRENT DEPTH...
...AND CONFIRM EMERGENCY LANDING LOCATION.

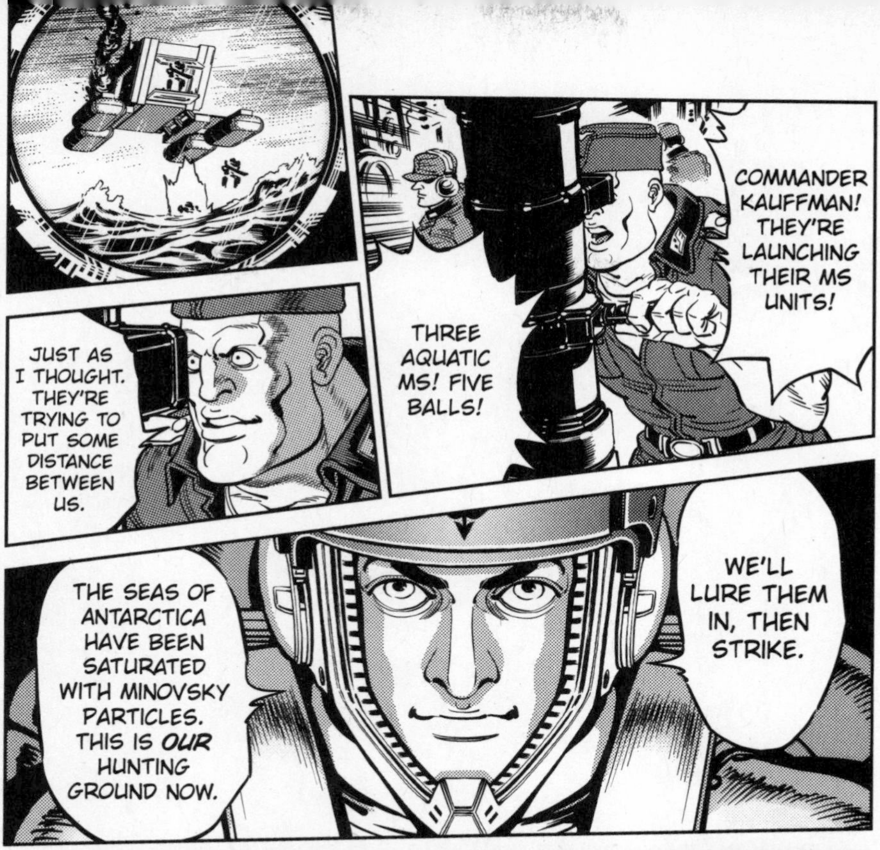
COMMANDER KAUFFMAN! THEY'RE LAUNCHING THEIR MS UNITS!
THREE AQUATIC MS! FIVE BALLS!
JUST AS I THOUGHT. THEY'RE TRYING TO PUT SOME DISTANCE BETWEEN US.
WE'LL LURE THEM IN, THEN STRIKE.
THE SEAS OF ANTARCTICA HAVE BEEN SATURATED WITH MINOVSKY PARTICLES. THIS IS *OUR* HUNTING GROUND NOW.

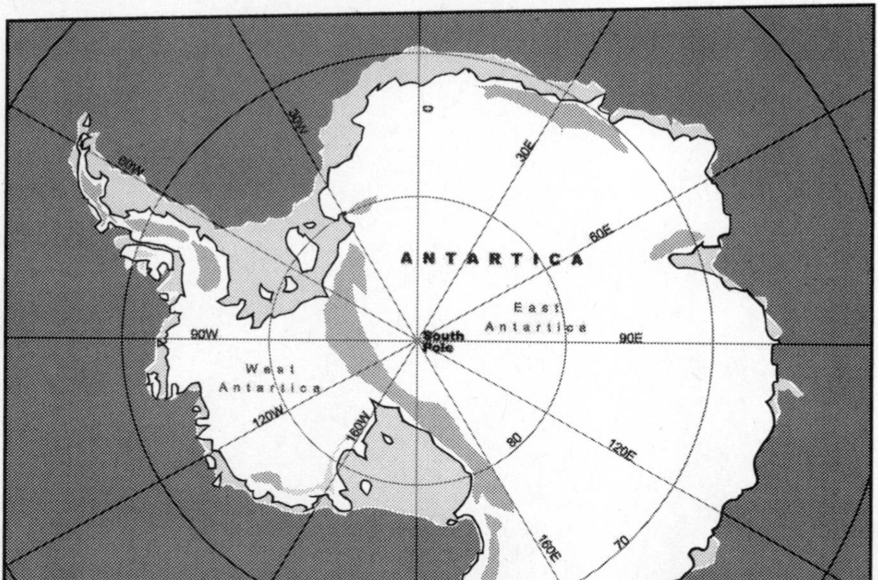
30W
60W
30E
60E
ANTARTICA
East Antartica
South Pole
90W
90E
West Antartica
120W
150W
80
120E
150E
70

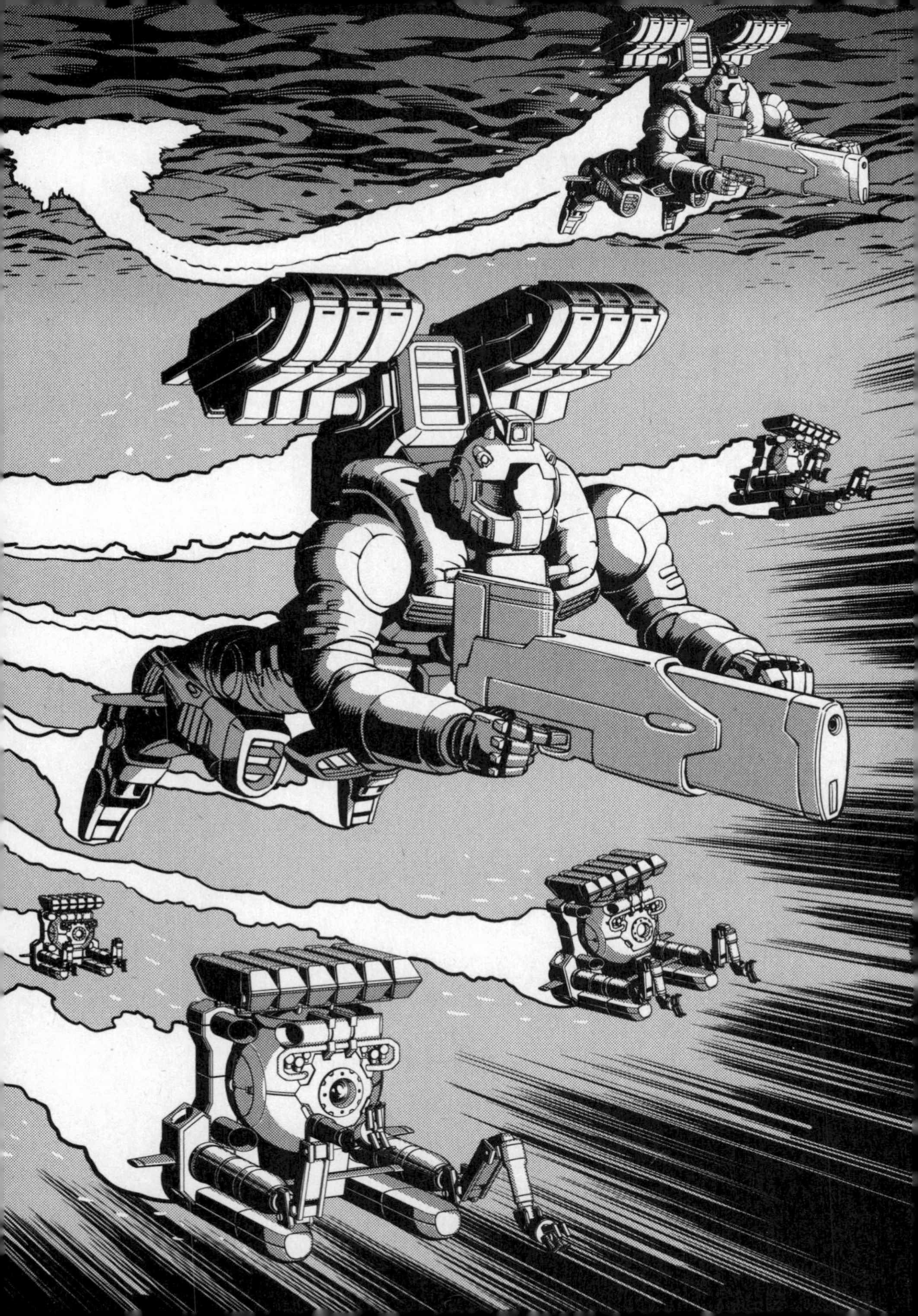

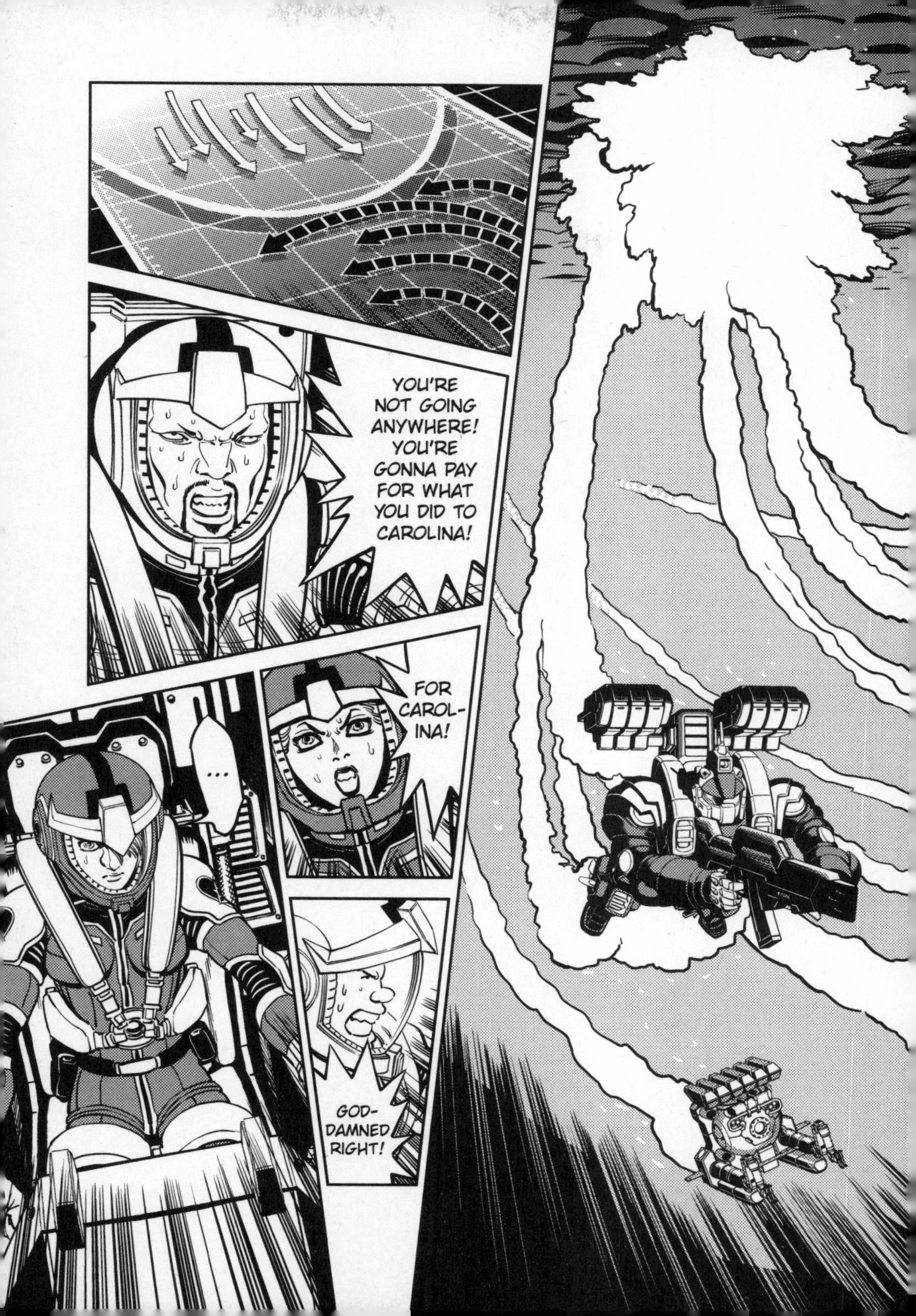
YOU'RE NOT GOING ANYWHERE! YOU'RE GONNA PAY FOR WHAT YOU DID TO CAROLINA!
FOR CAROL-INA!
GOD-DAMNED RIGHT!
...

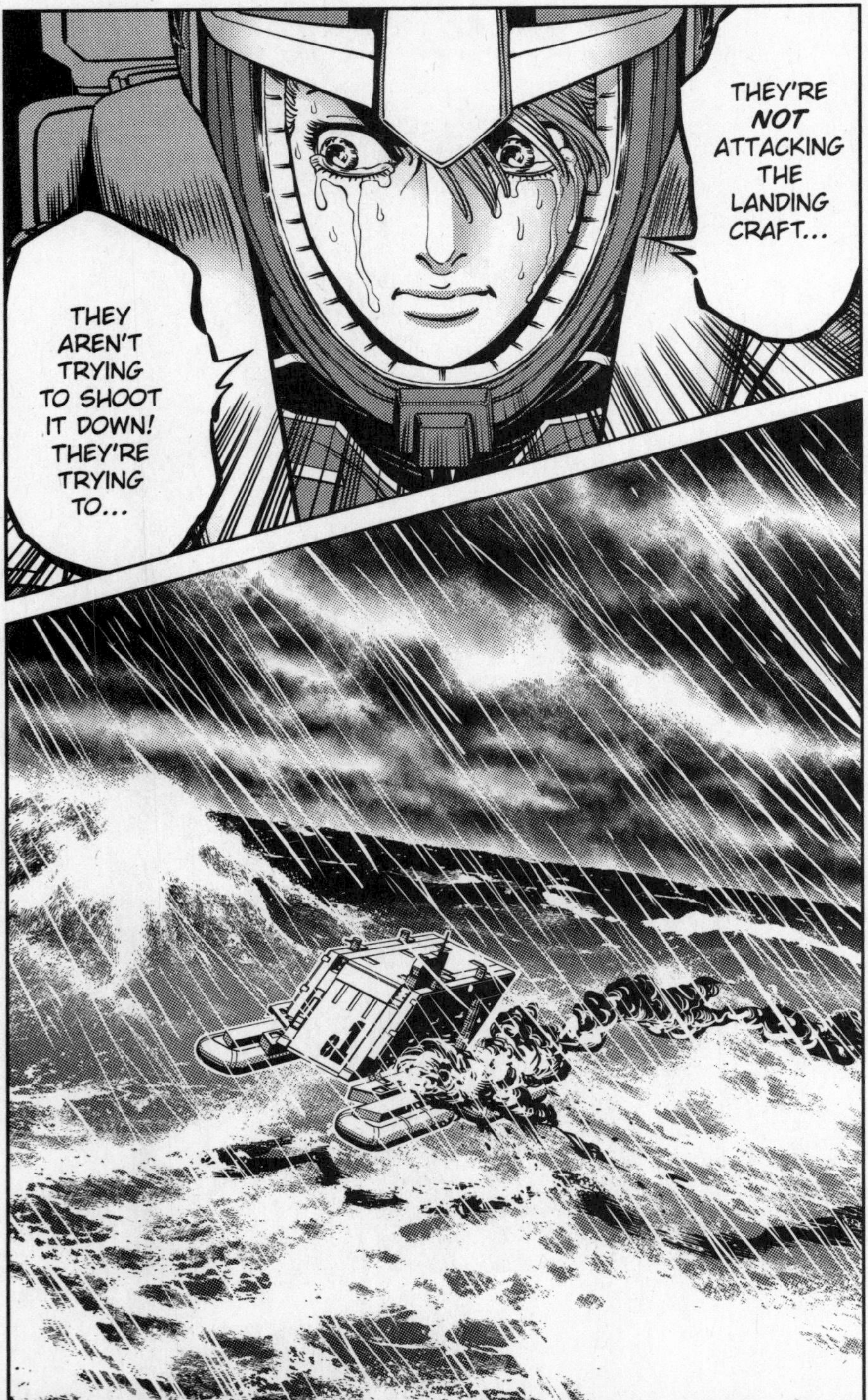
THEY'RE *NOT* ATTACKING THE LANDING CRAFT...
THEY AREN'T TRYING TO SHOOT IT DOWN! THEY'RE TRYING TO...

MOBILE SUIT GUNDAM THUNDERBOLT

CHAPTER 46

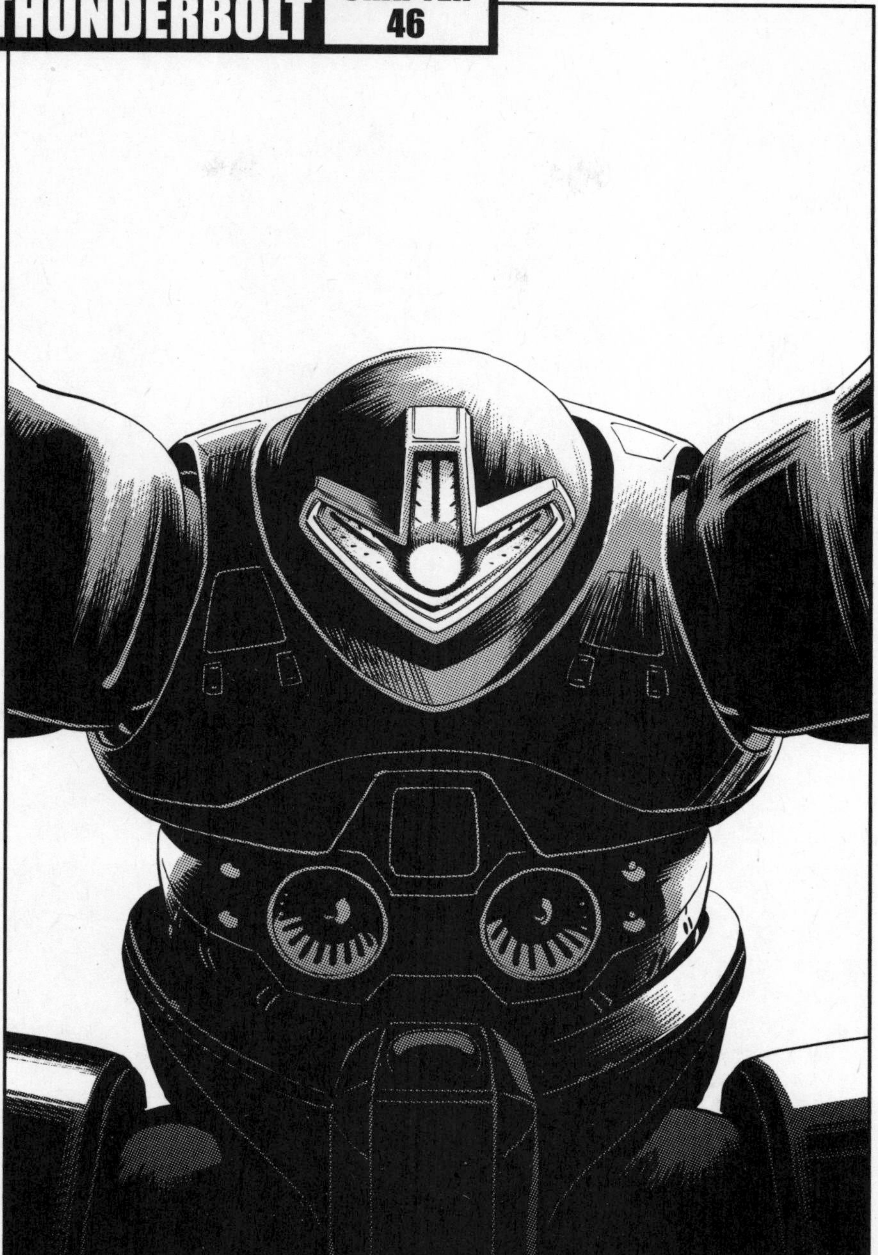

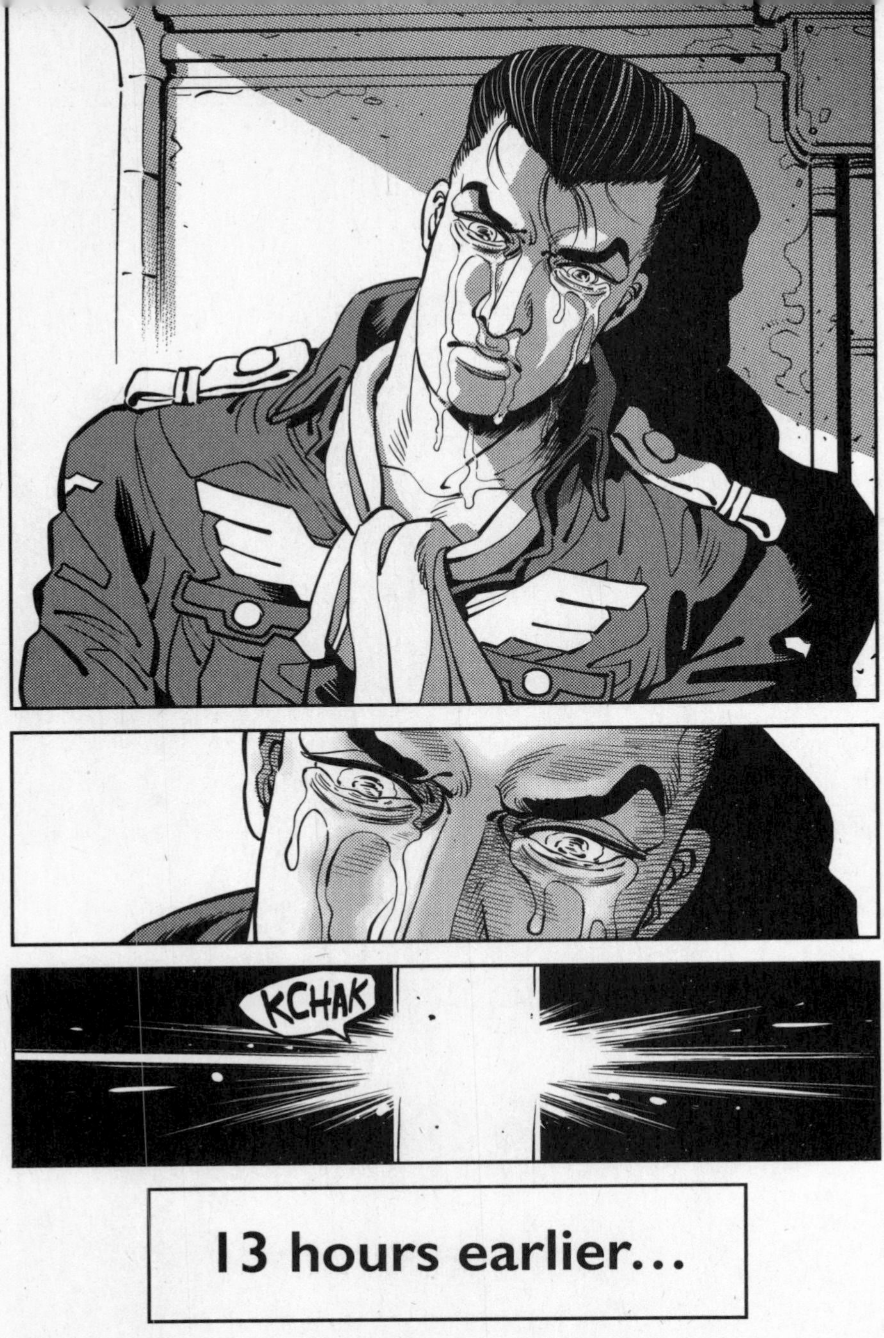
KCHAK

13 hours earlier...

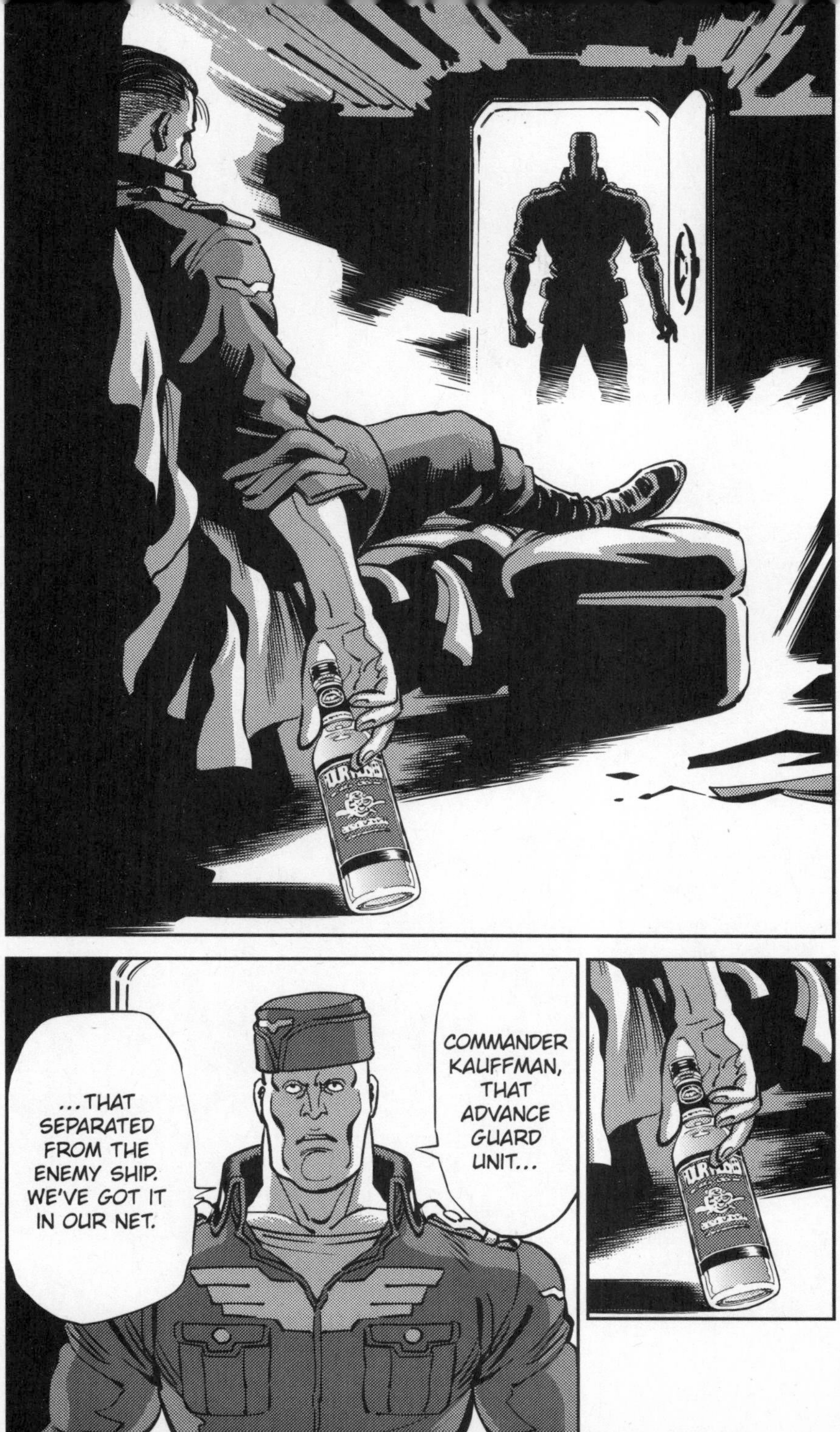
COMMANDER KAUFFMAN, THAT ADVANCE GUARD UNIT...
...THAT SEPARATED FROM THE ENEMY SHIP. WE'VE GOT IT IN OUR NET.

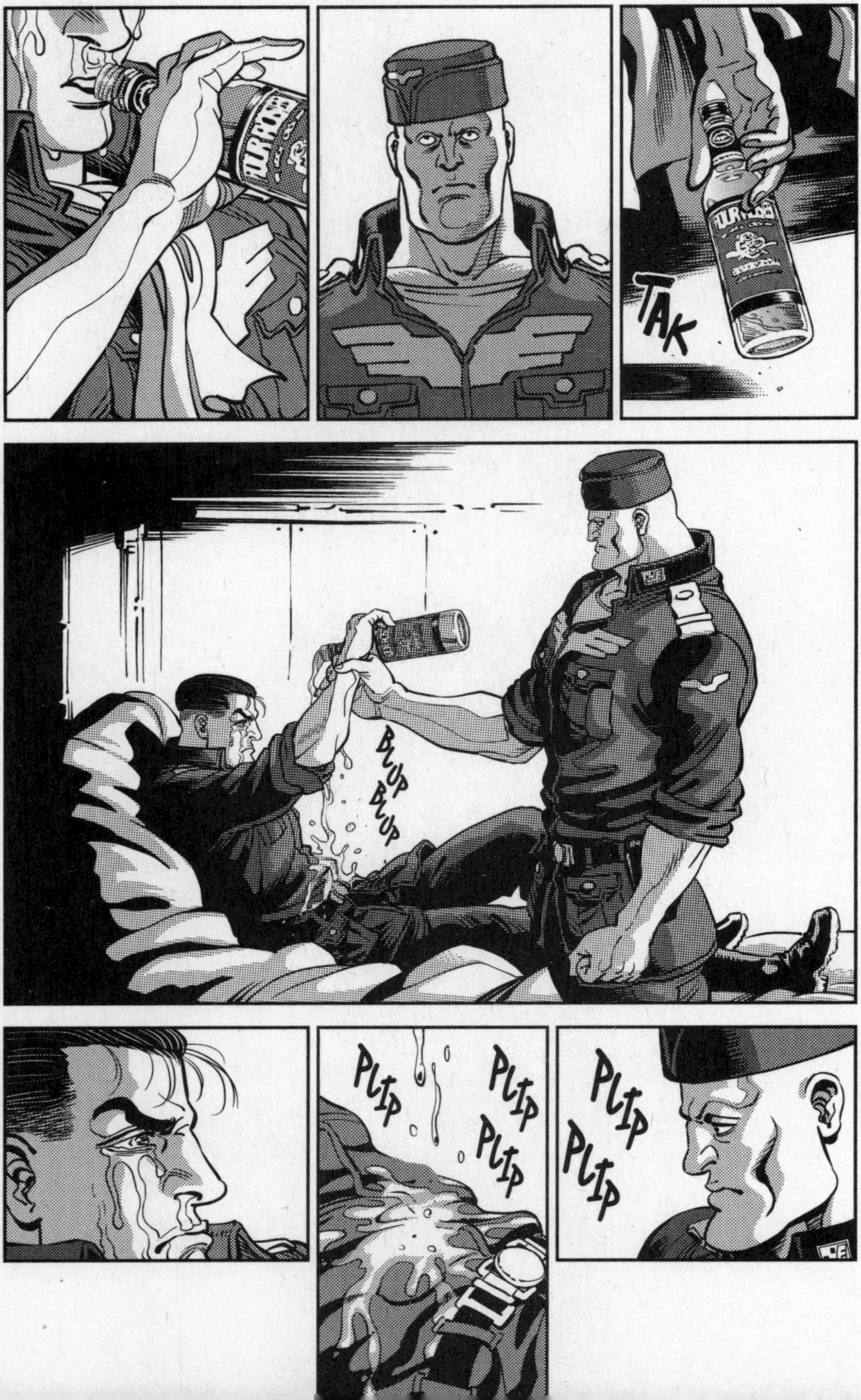
TAK
BLUP
BLUP
PLIP
PLIP
PLIP
PLIP
PLIP

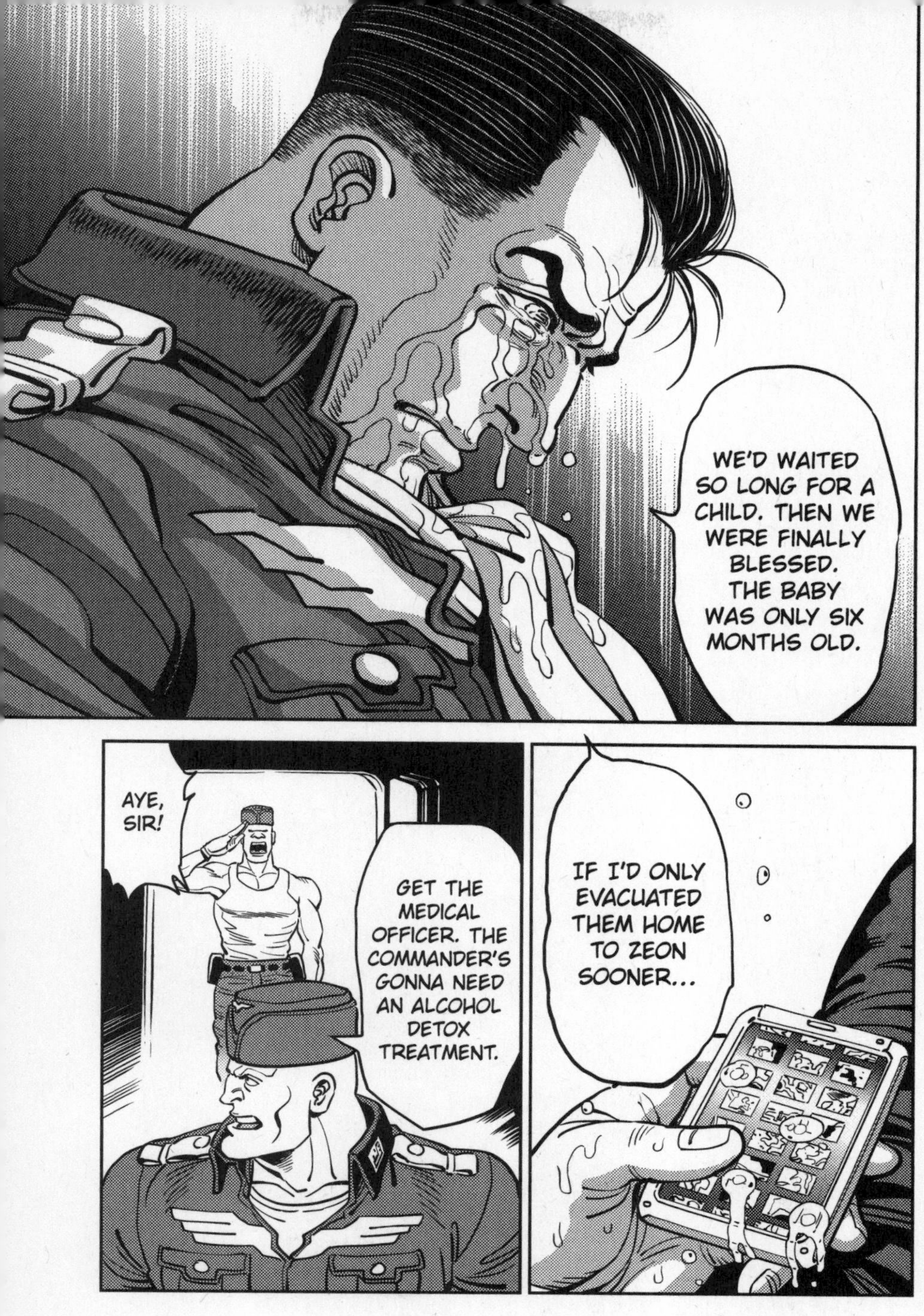
WE'D WAITED SO LONG FOR A CHILD. THEN WE WERE FINALLY BLESSED. THE BABY WAS ONLY SIX MONTHS OLD.
IF I'D ONLY EVACUATED THEM HOME TO ZEON SOONER...
GET THE MEDICAL OFFICER. THE COMMANDER'S GONNA NEED AN ALCOHOL DETOX TREATMENT.
AYE, SIR!

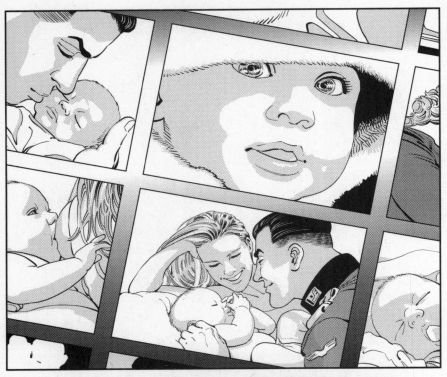

MY WIFE AND I DUG OUR BABY OUT OF THE RUBBLE...

HOW COULD THEY DO THIS TO A BABY... TO MY BABY...

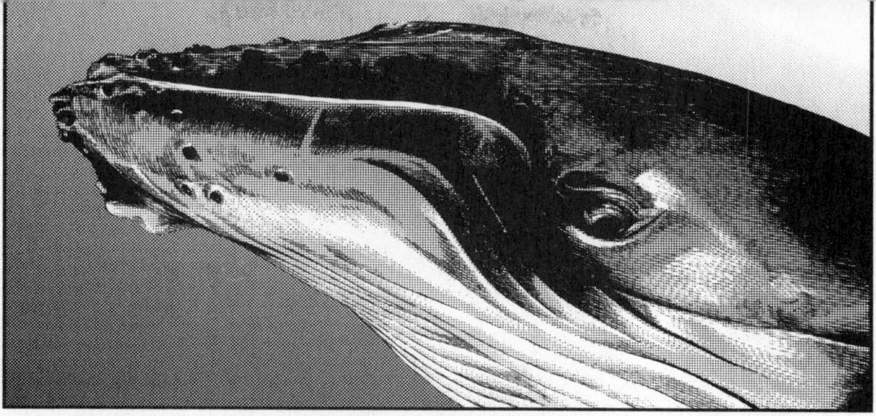
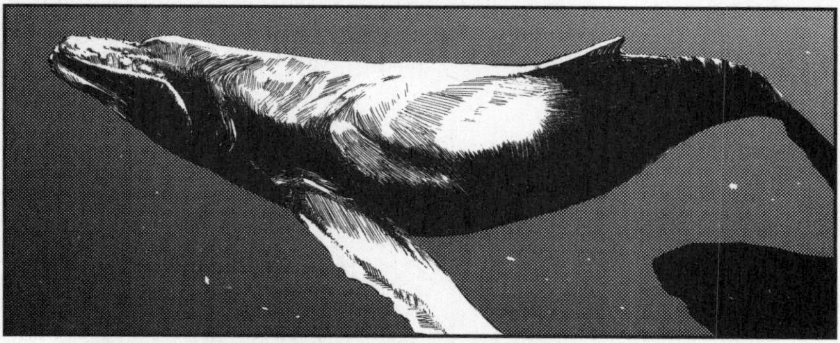
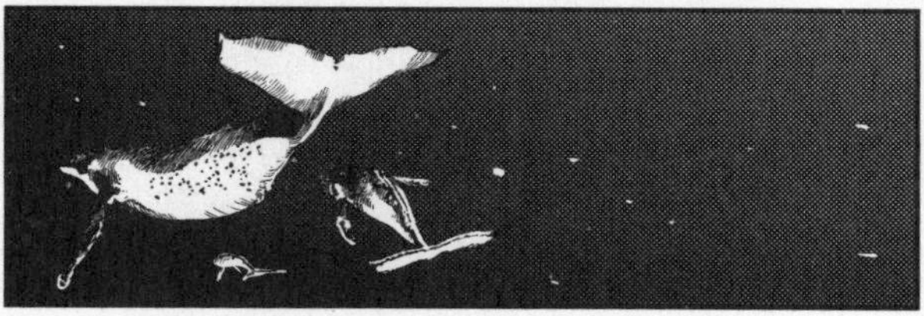
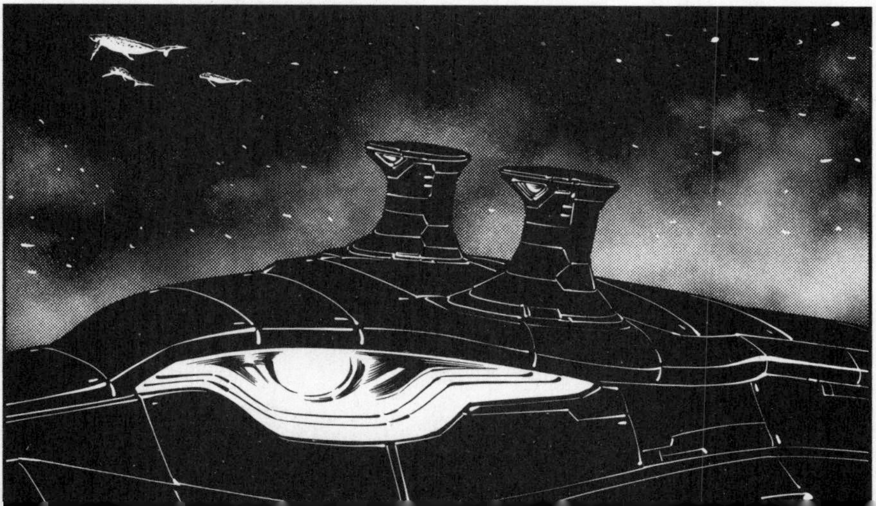

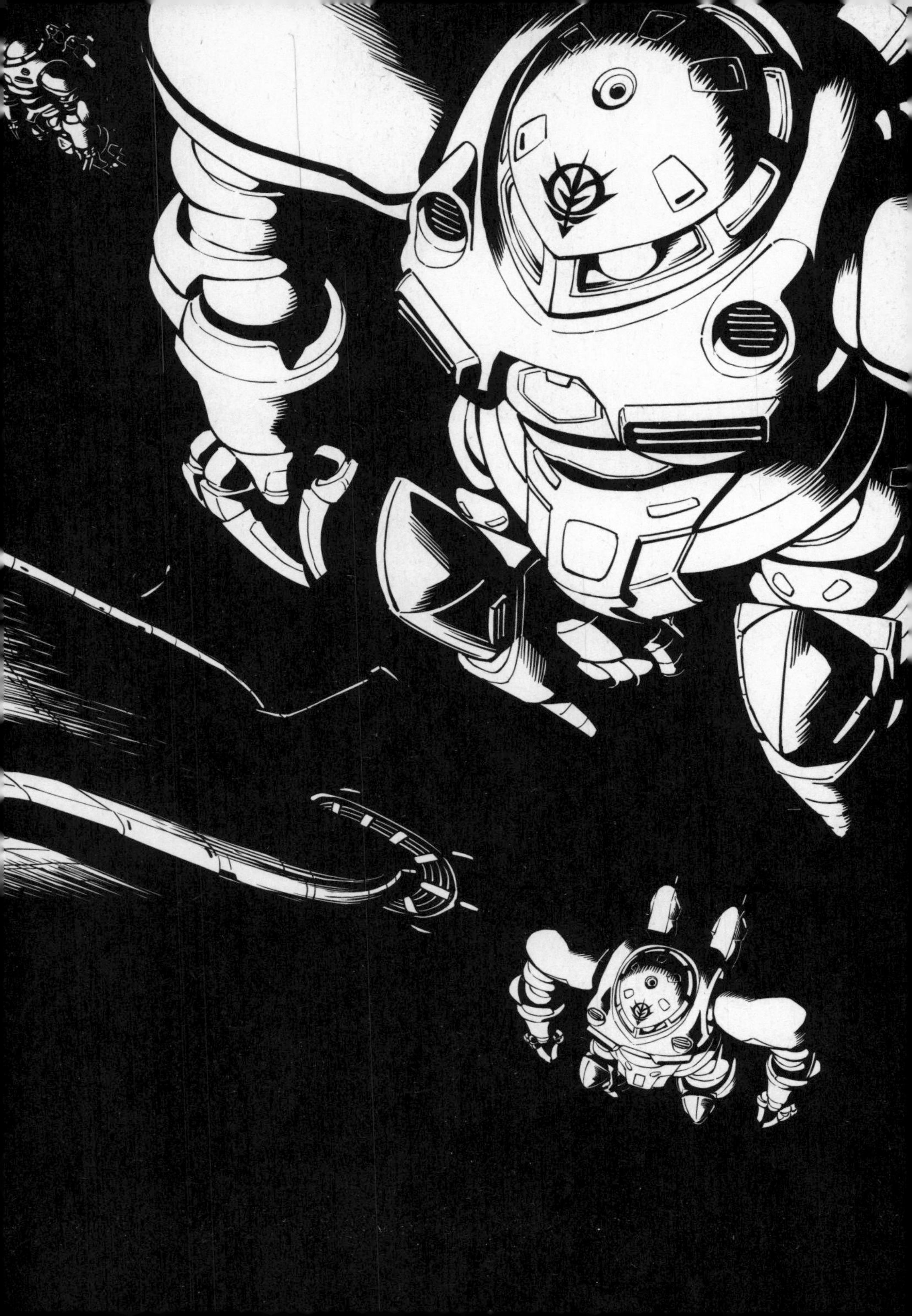

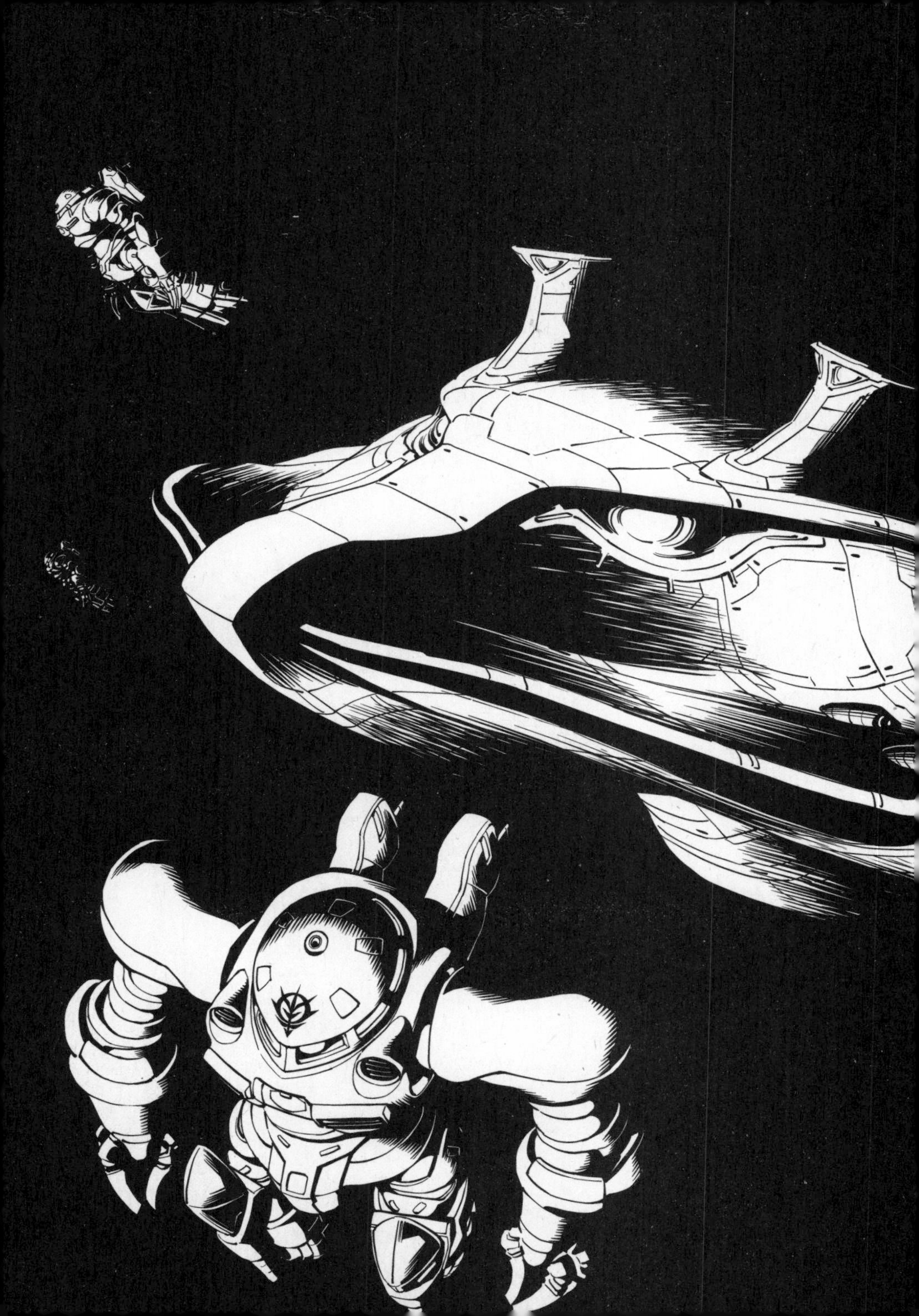

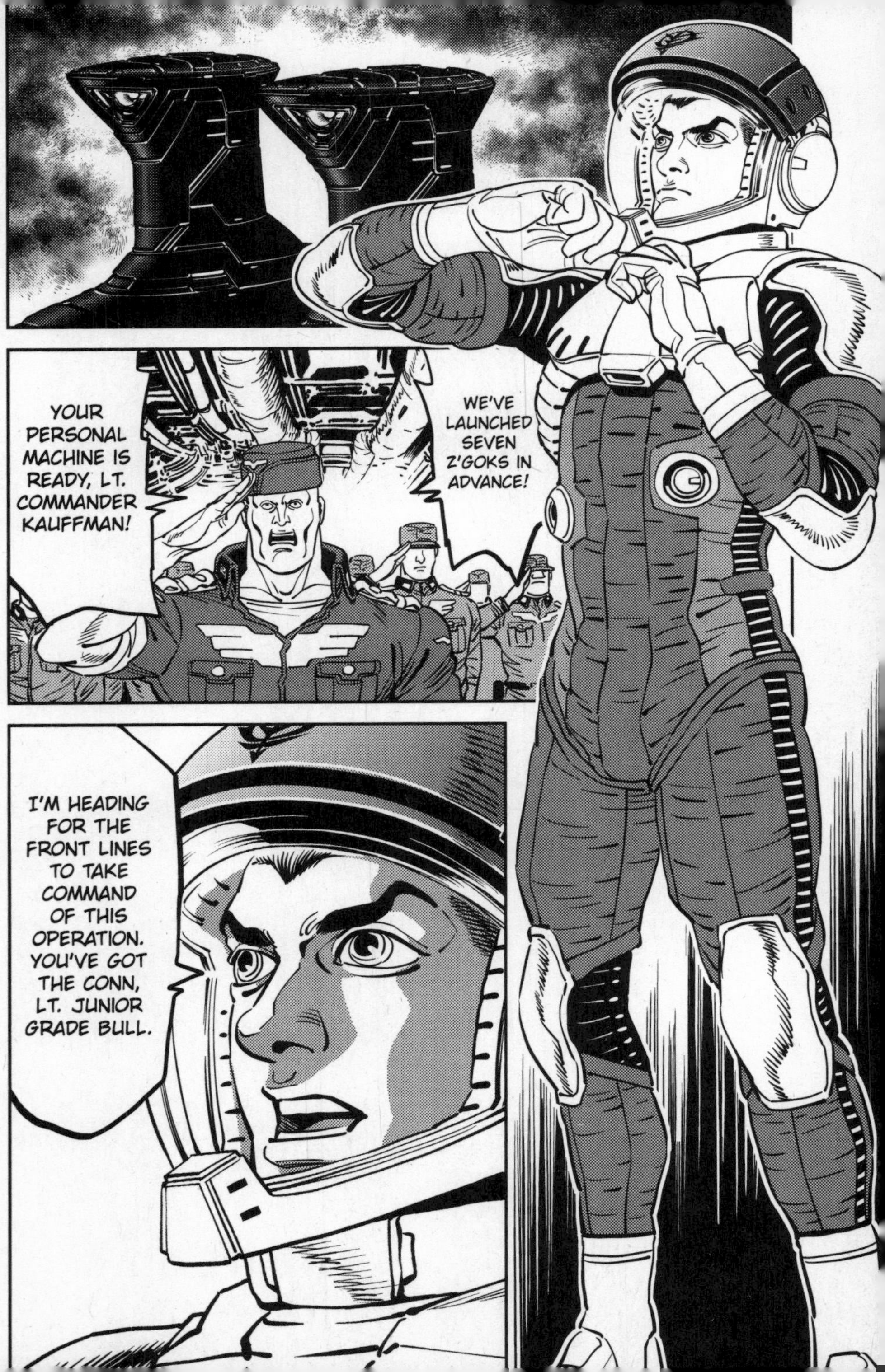
WE'VE LAUNCHED SEVEN Z'GOKS IN ADVANCE!
YOUR PERSONAL MACHINE IS READY, LT. COMMANDER KAUFFMAN!
I'M HEADING FOR THE FRONT LINES TO TAKE COMMAND OF THIS OPERATION. YOU'VE GOT THE CONN, LT. JUNIOR GRADE BULL.

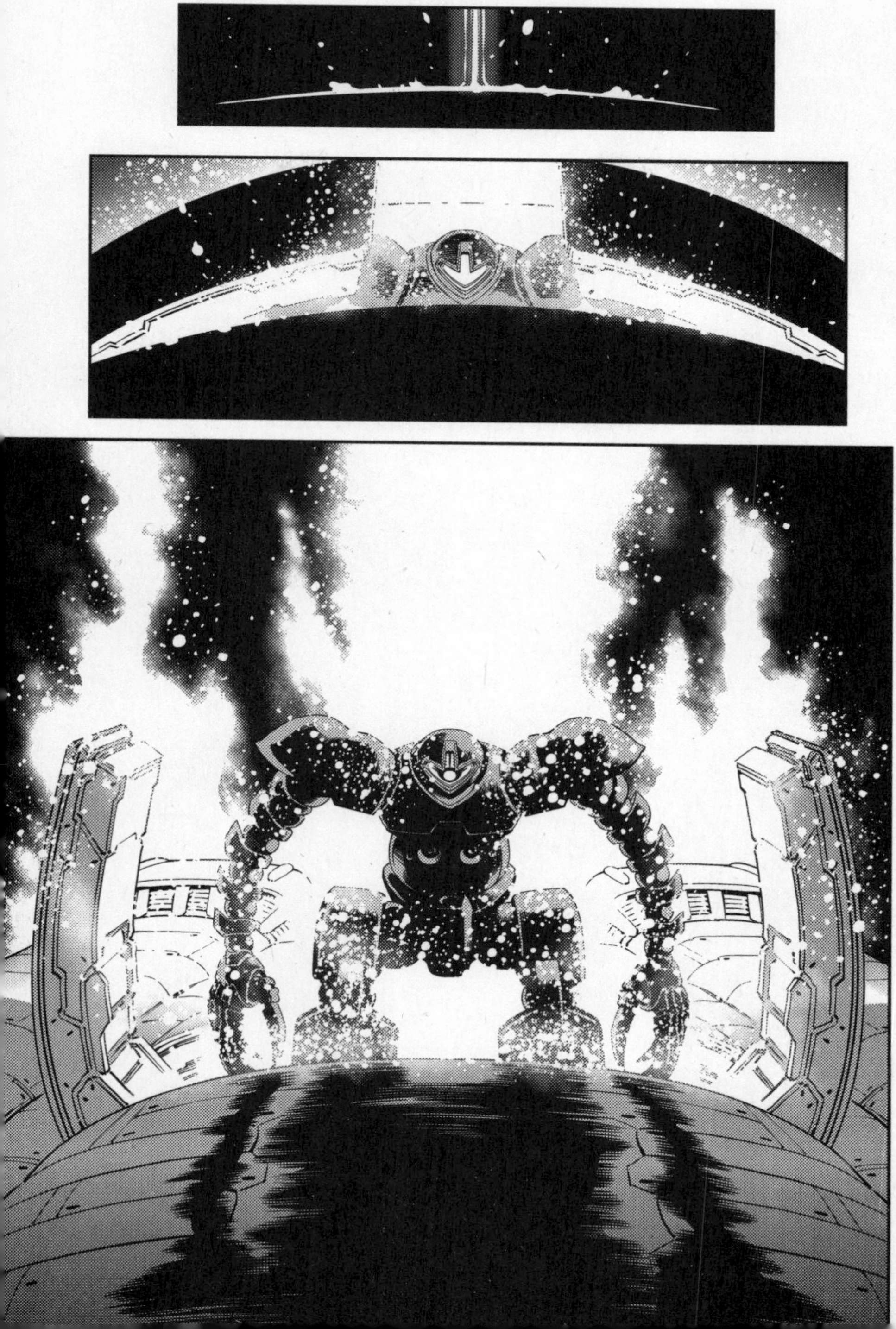

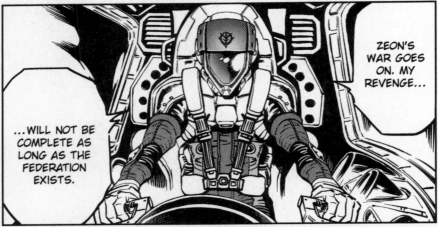

ZEON'S WAR GOES ON. MY REVENGE...

...WILL NOT BE COMPLETE AS LONG AS THE FEDERATION EXISTS.

FEDERATION *PIGS!* YOU'LL ALL TASTE THE SAME BITTER SUFFERING I HAVE!

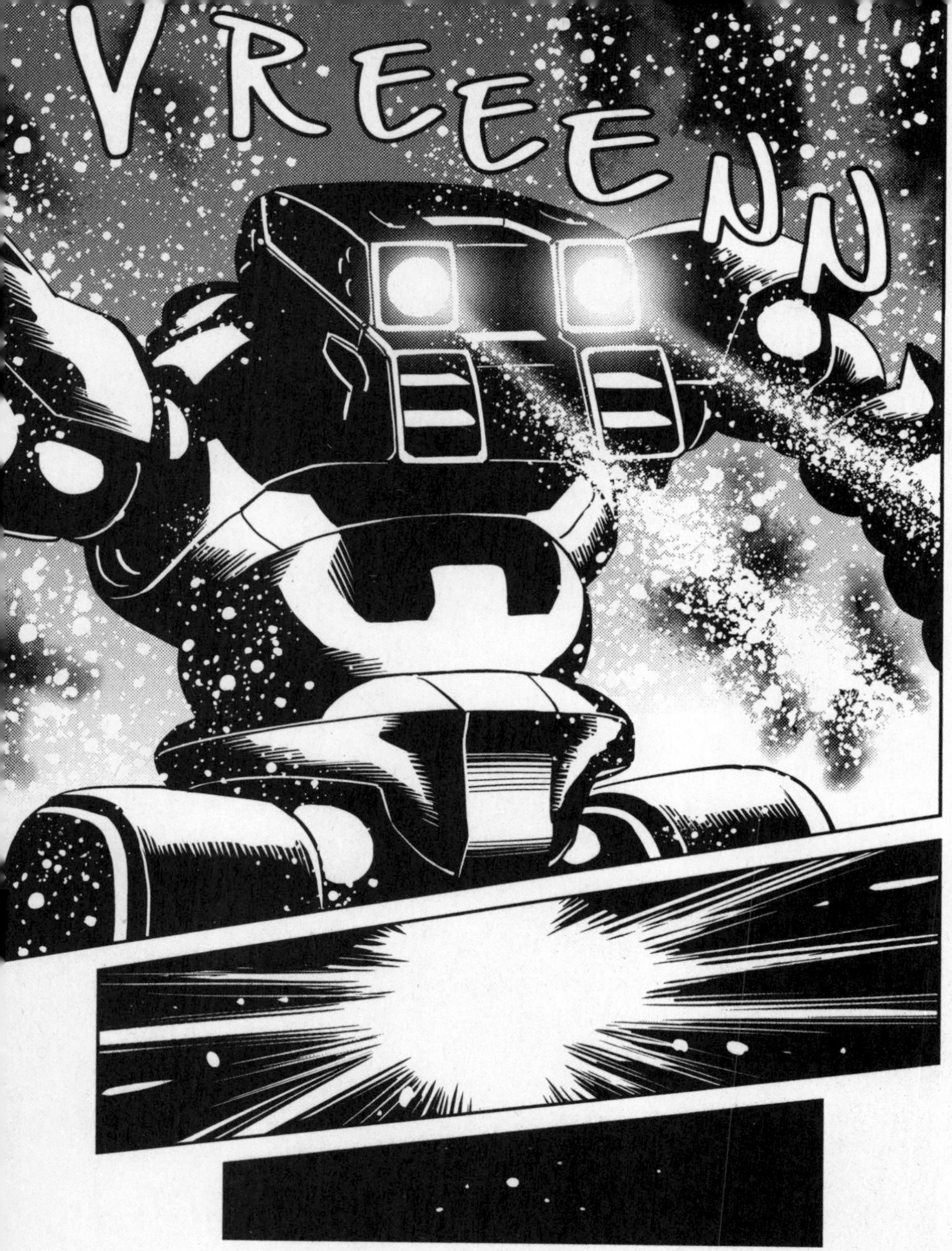
VREEENN

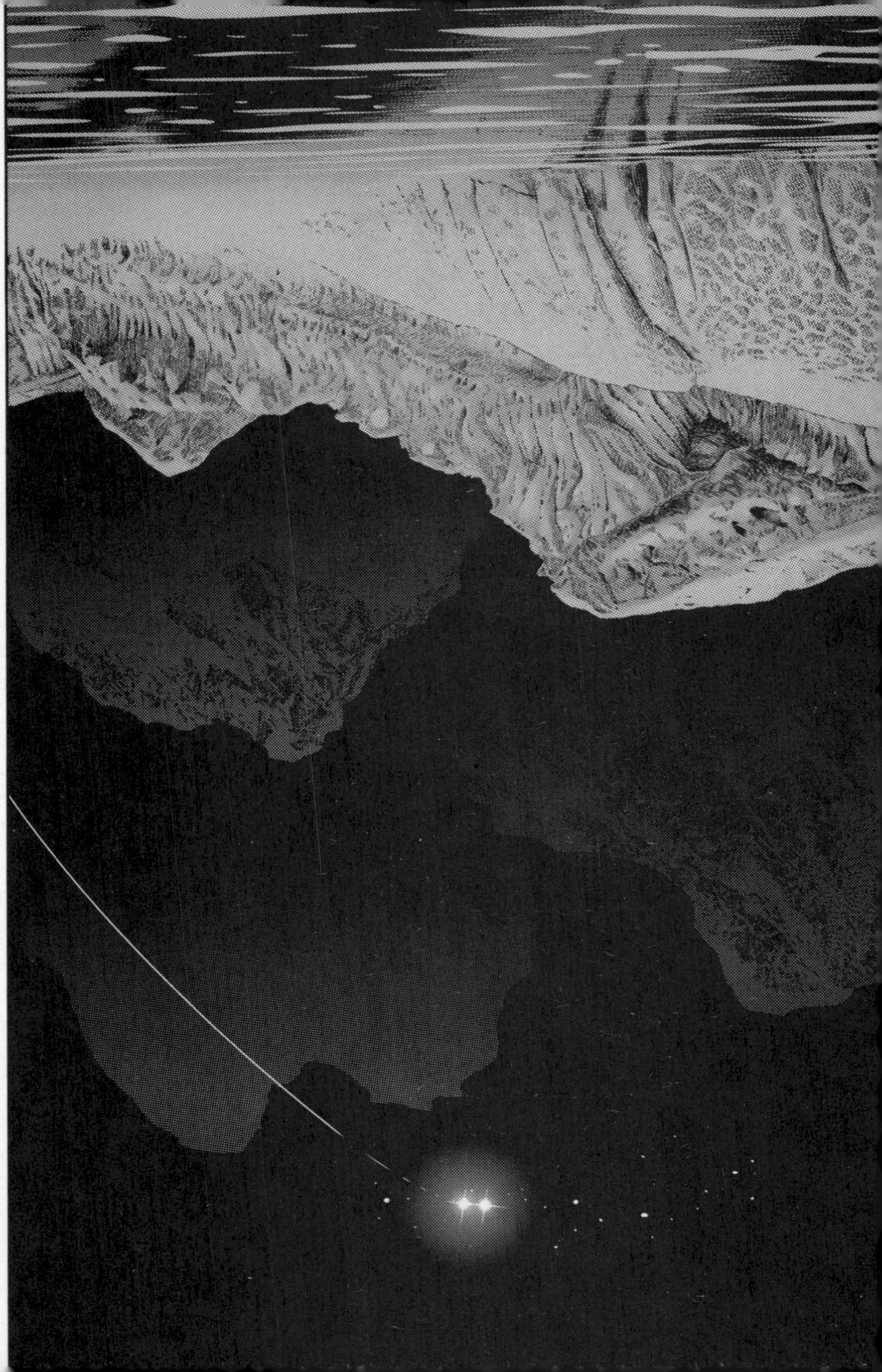

15 hours earlier...

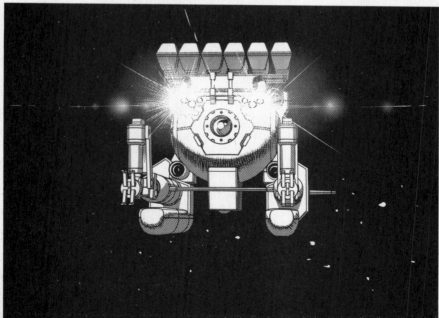

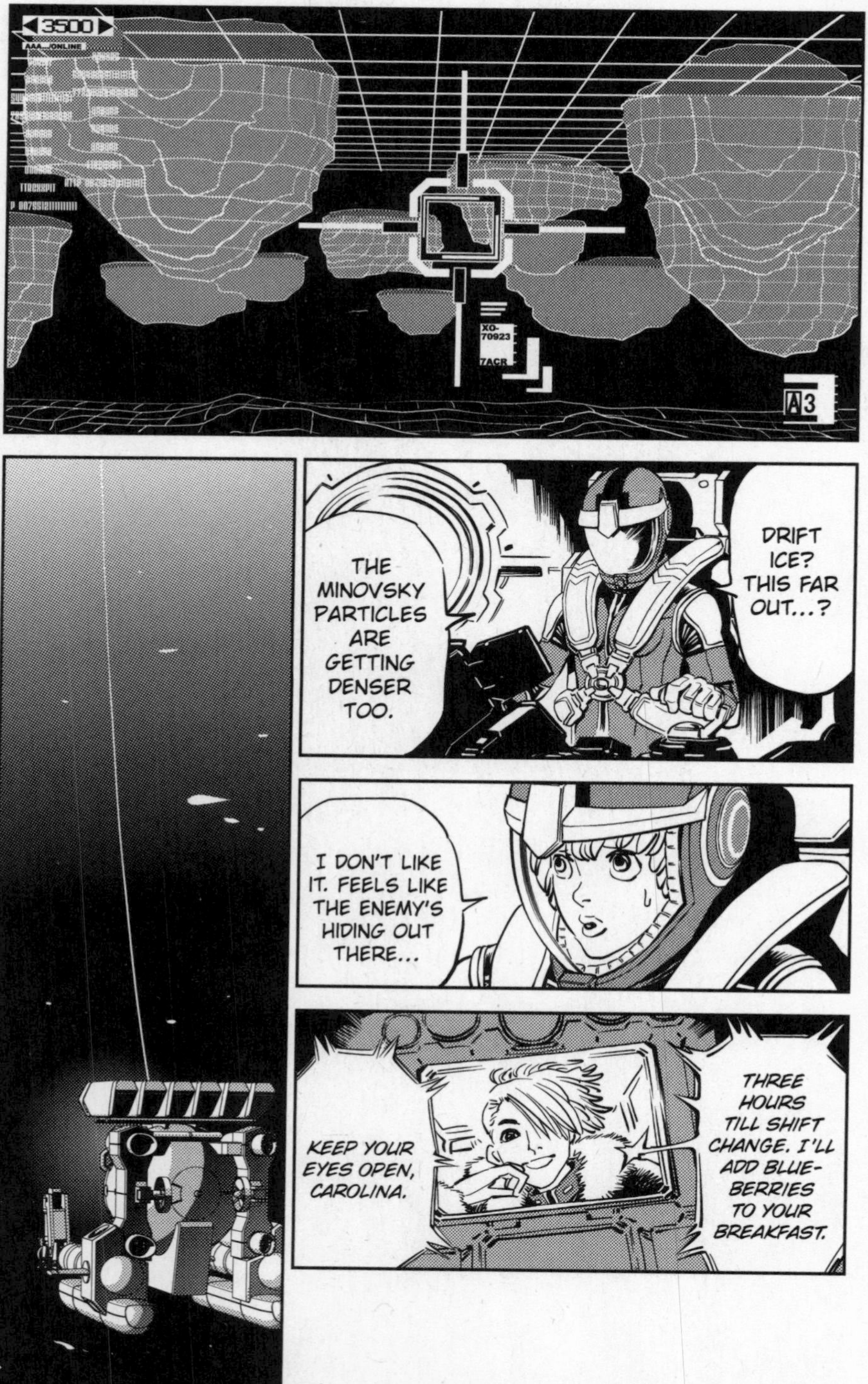
3500
XO-70923
7ACR
A3
DRIFT ICE? THIS FAR OUT...?
THE MINOVSKY PARTICLES ARE GETTING DENSER TOO.
I DON'T LIKE IT. FEELS LIKE THE ENEMY'S HIDING OUT THERE...
THREE HOURS TILL SHIFT CHANGE. I'LL ADD BLUE-BERRIES TO YOUR BREAKFAST.
KEEP YOUR EYES OPEN, CAROLINA.

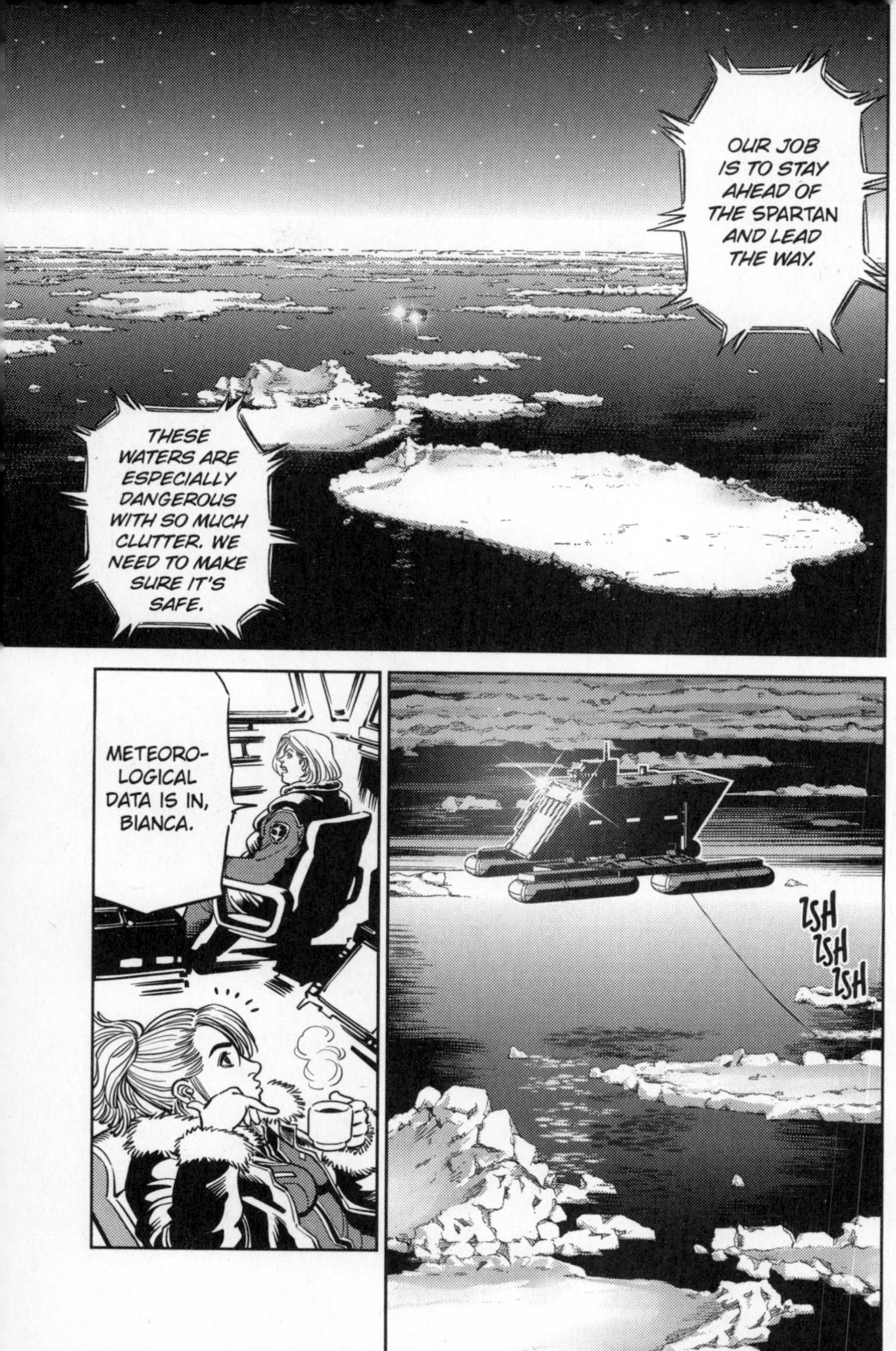
OUR JOB IS TO STAY AHEAD OF THE SPARTAN AND LEAD THE WAY.
THESE WATERS ARE ESPECIALLY DANGEROUS WITH SO MUCH CLUTTER. WE NEED TO MAKE SURE IT'S SAFE.
ZSH ZSH ZSH
METEORO-LOGICAL DATA IS IN, BIANCA.

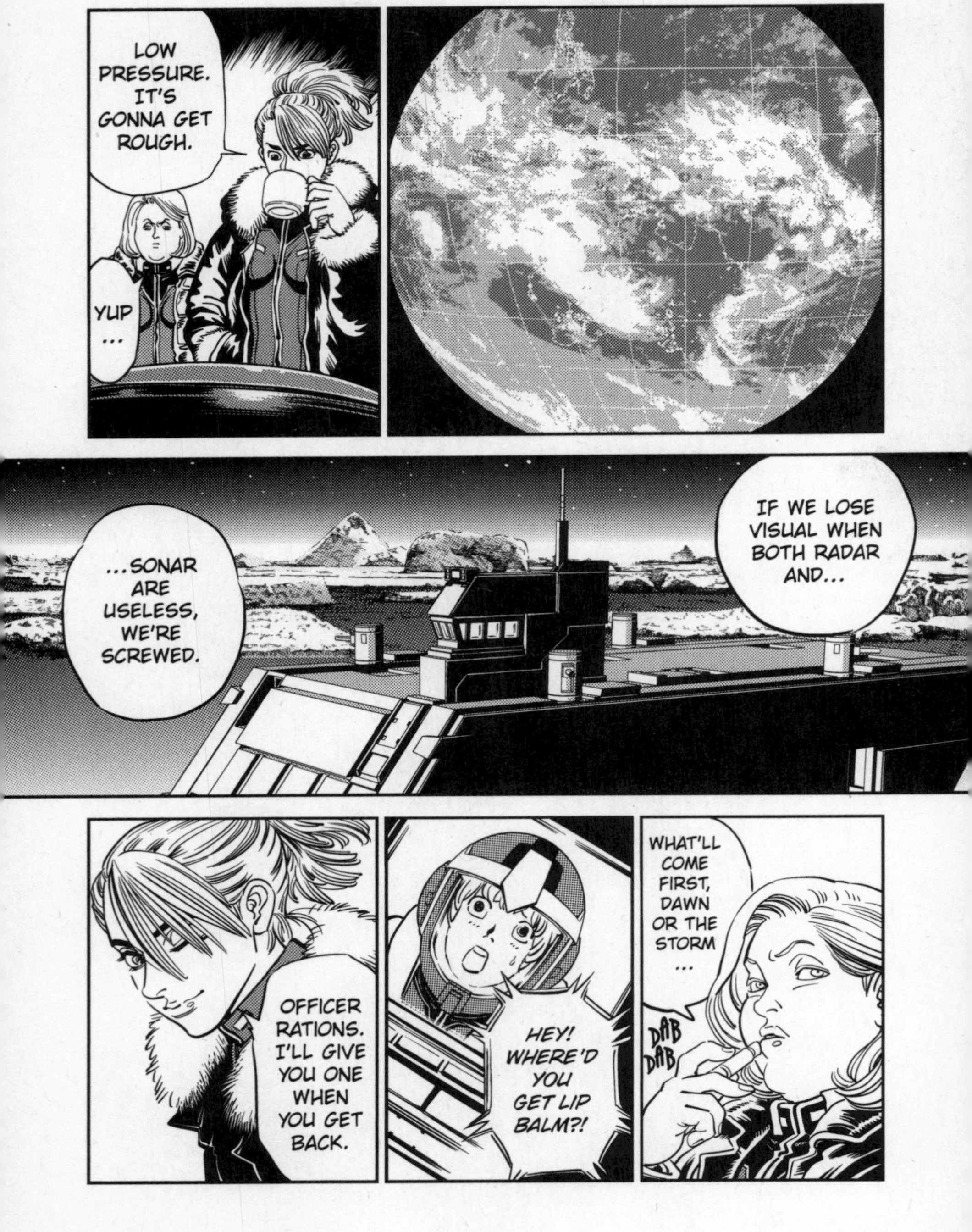
LOW PRESSURE. IT'S GONNA GET ROUGH.
YUP ...
IF WE LOSE VISUAL WHEN BOTH RADAR AND...
...SONAR ARE USELESS, WE'RE SCREWED.
WHAT'LL COME FIRST, DAWN OR THE STORM ...
DAB DAB
HEY! WHERE'D YOU GET LIP BALM?!
OFFICER RATIONS. I'LL GIVE YOU ONE WHEN YOU GET BACK.

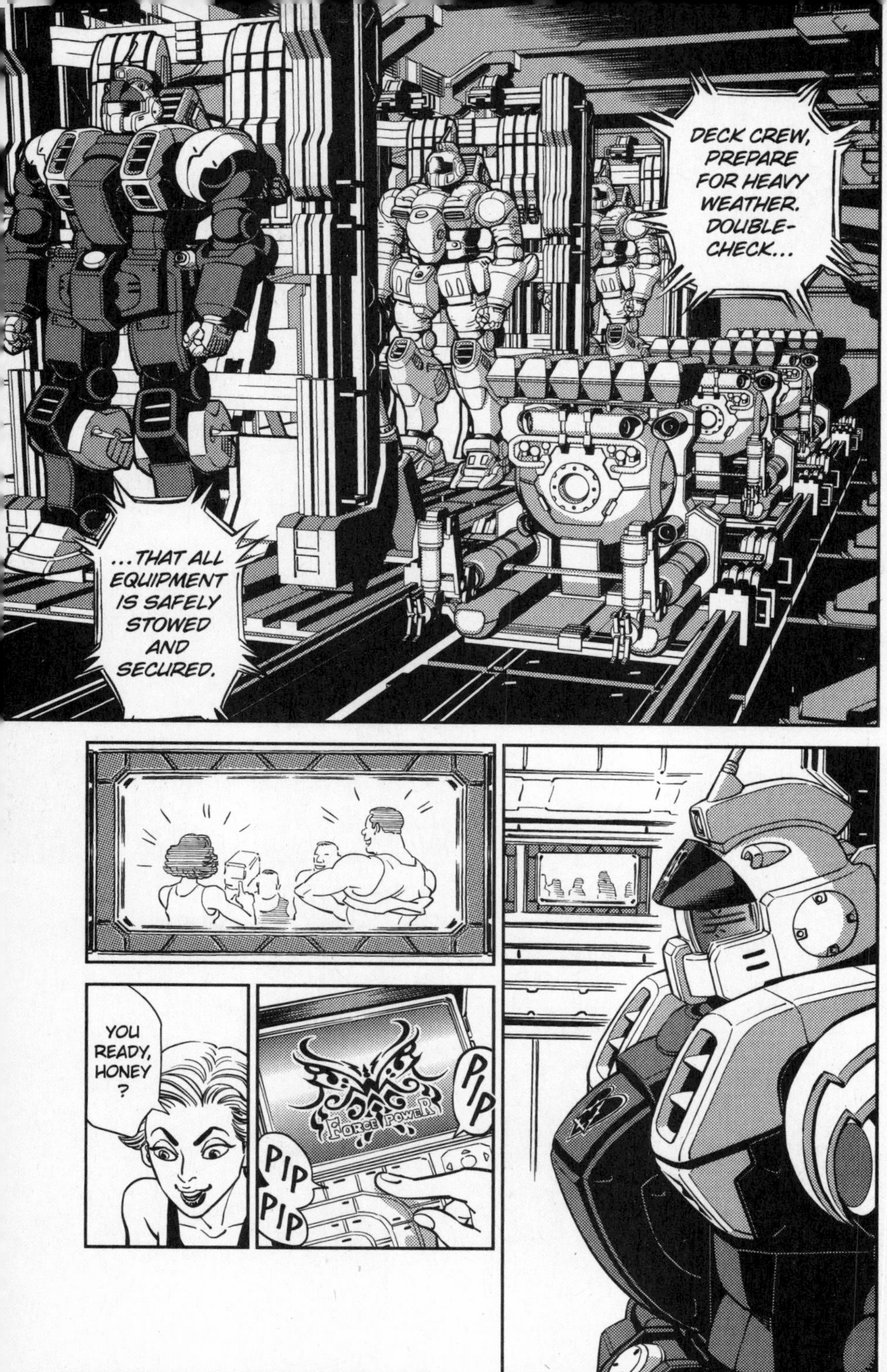
DECK CREW, PREPARE FOR HEAVY WEATHER. DOUBLE-CHECK...
...THAT ALL EQUIPMENT IS SAFELY STOWED AND SECURED.
PIP
FORCE POWER
PIP PIP
YOU READY, HONEY?

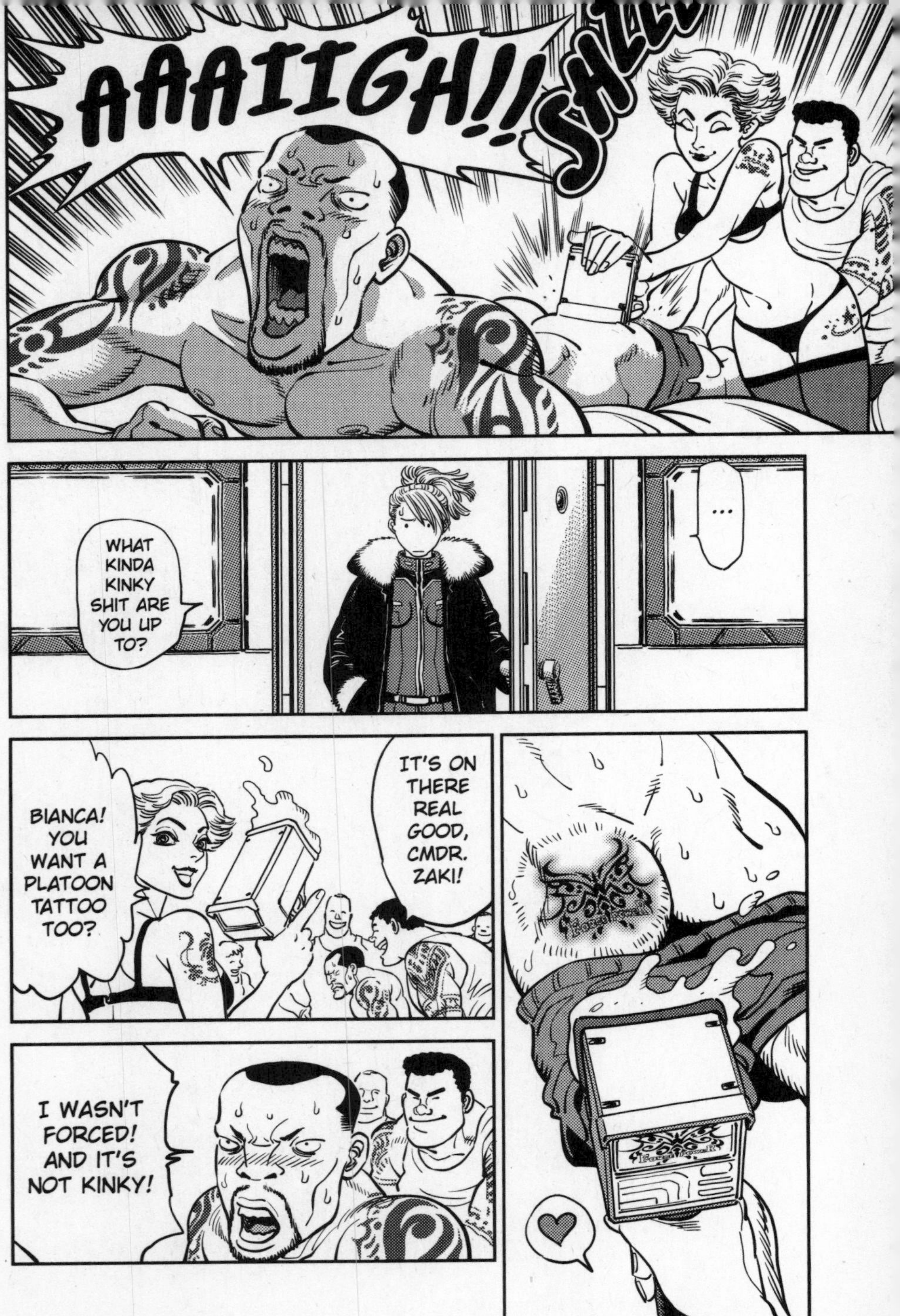
SHZZ
AAAIIGH!!!
...
WHAT KINDA KINKY SHIT ARE YOU UP TO?
IT'S ON THERE REAL GOOD, CMDR. ZAKI!
BIANCA! YOU WANT A PLATOON TATTOO TOO?
I WASN'T FORCED! AND IT'S NOT KINKY!

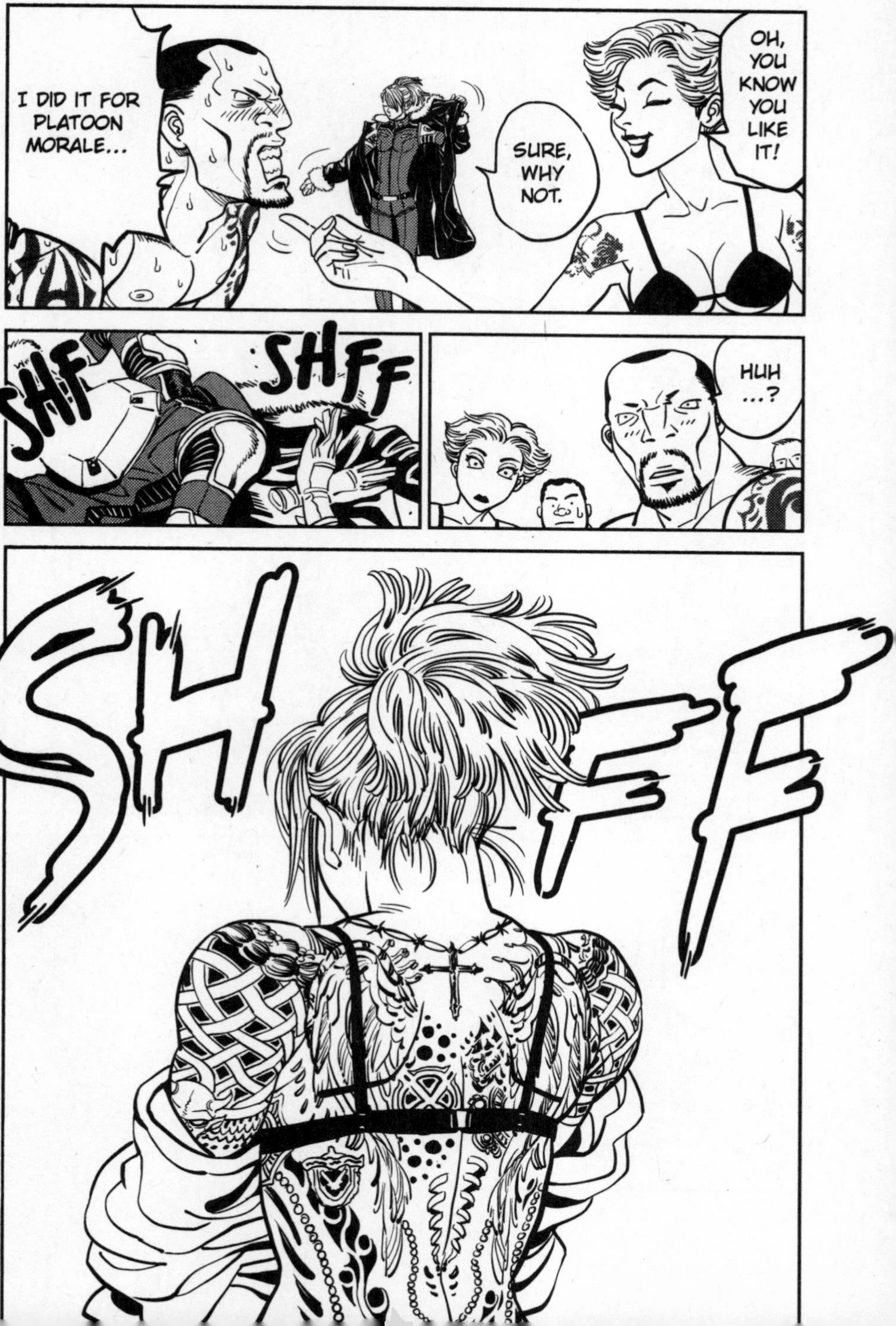
OH, YOU KNOW YOU LIKE IT!
SURE, WHY NOT.
I DID IT FOR PLATOON MORALE...
HUH ...?
SHFF
SHF
SHFF

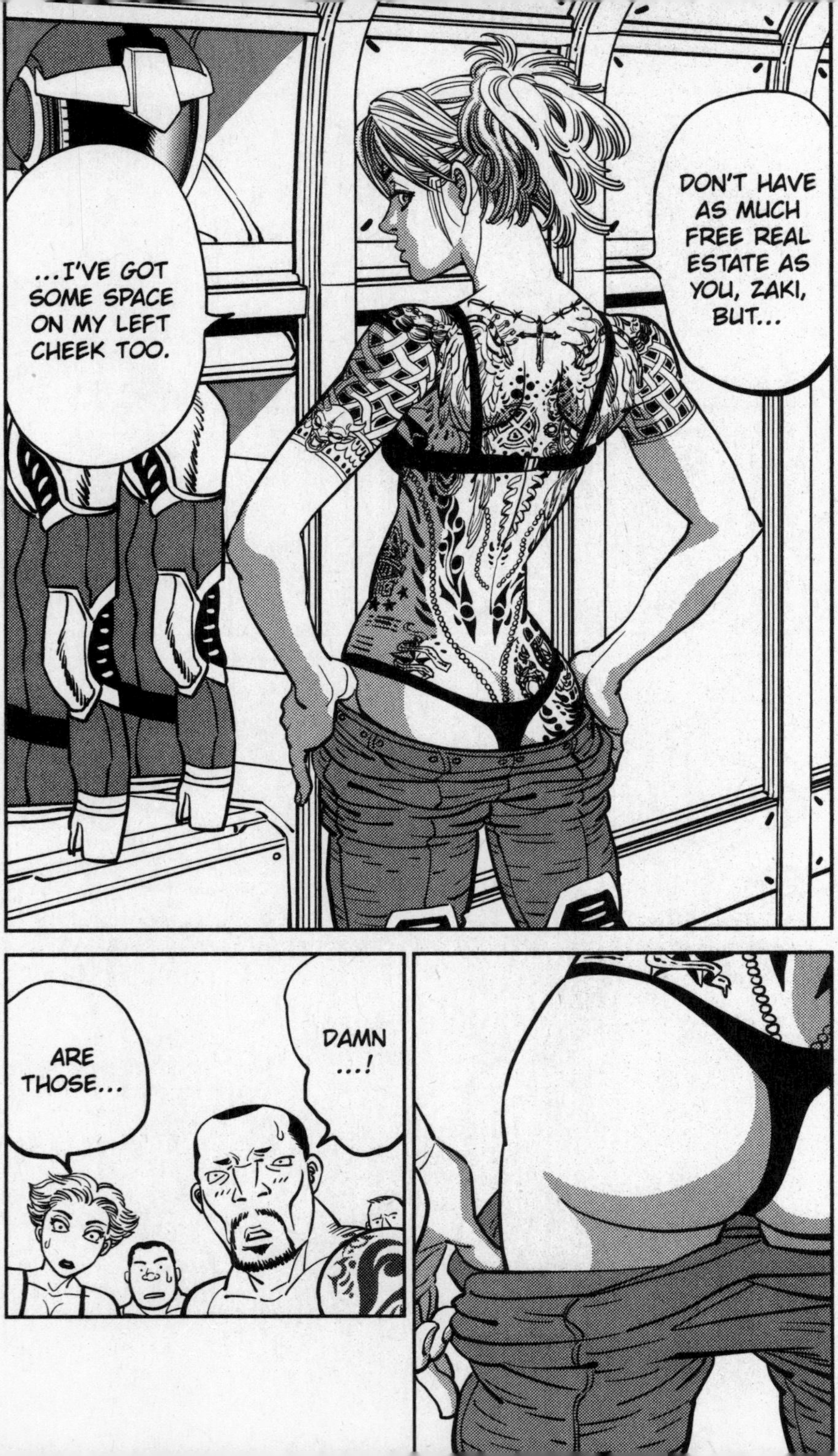
DON'T HAVE AS MUCH FREE REAL ESTATE AS YOU, ZAKI, BUT...
...I'VE GOT SOME SPACE ON MY LEFT CHEEK TOO.
DAMN ...!
ARE THOSE...

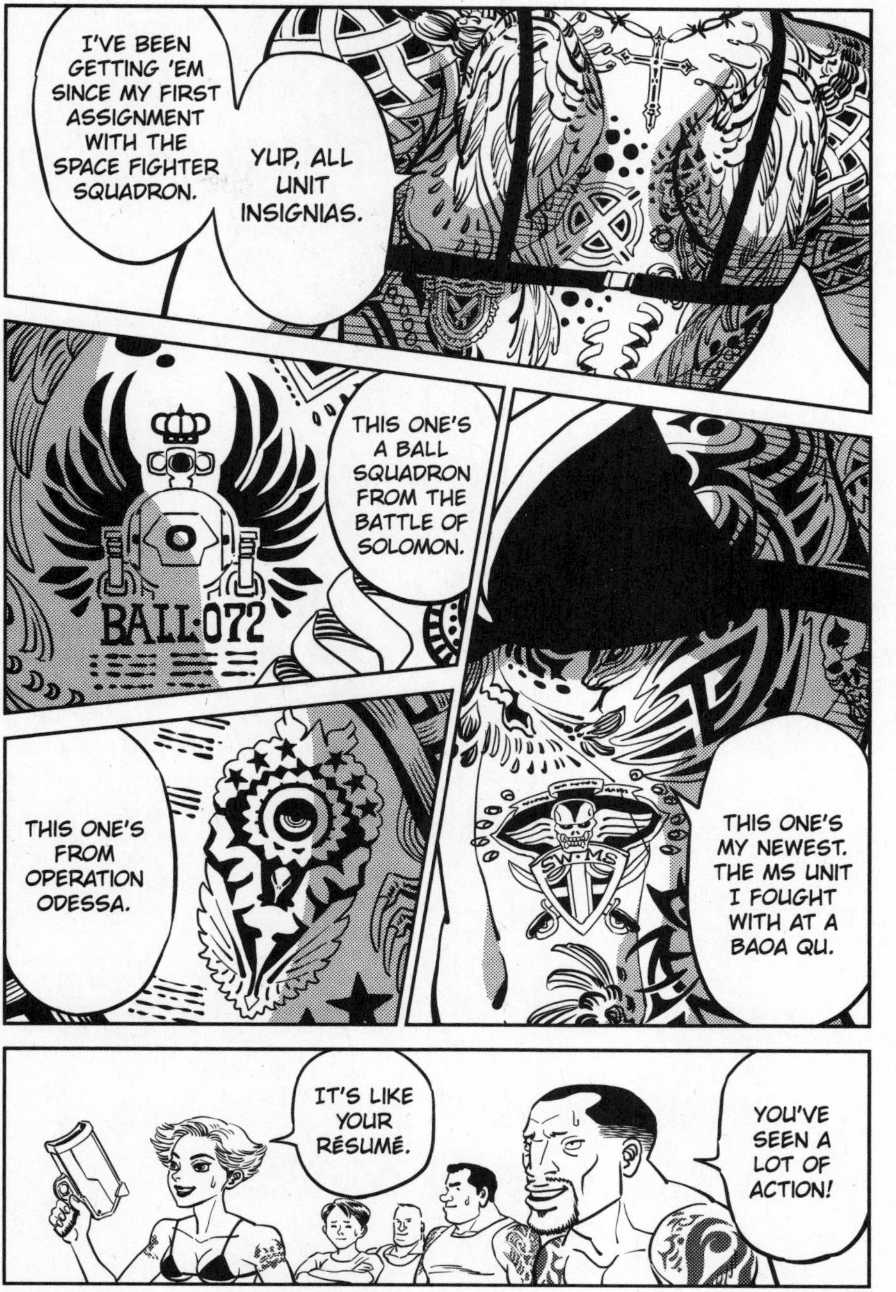
YUP, ALL UNIT INSIGNIAS.
I'VE BEEN GETTING 'EM SINCE MY FIRST ASSIGNMENT WITH THE SPACE FIGHTER SQUADRON.
THIS ONE'S MY NEWEST. THE MS UNIT I FOUGHT WITH AT A BAOA QU.
SW·MS
THIS ONE'S A BALL SQUADRON FROM THE BATTLE OF SOLOMON.
BALL·072
THIS ONE'S FROM OPERATION ODESSA.
YOU'VE SEEN A LOT OF ACTION!
IT'S LIKE YOUR RÉSUMÉ.

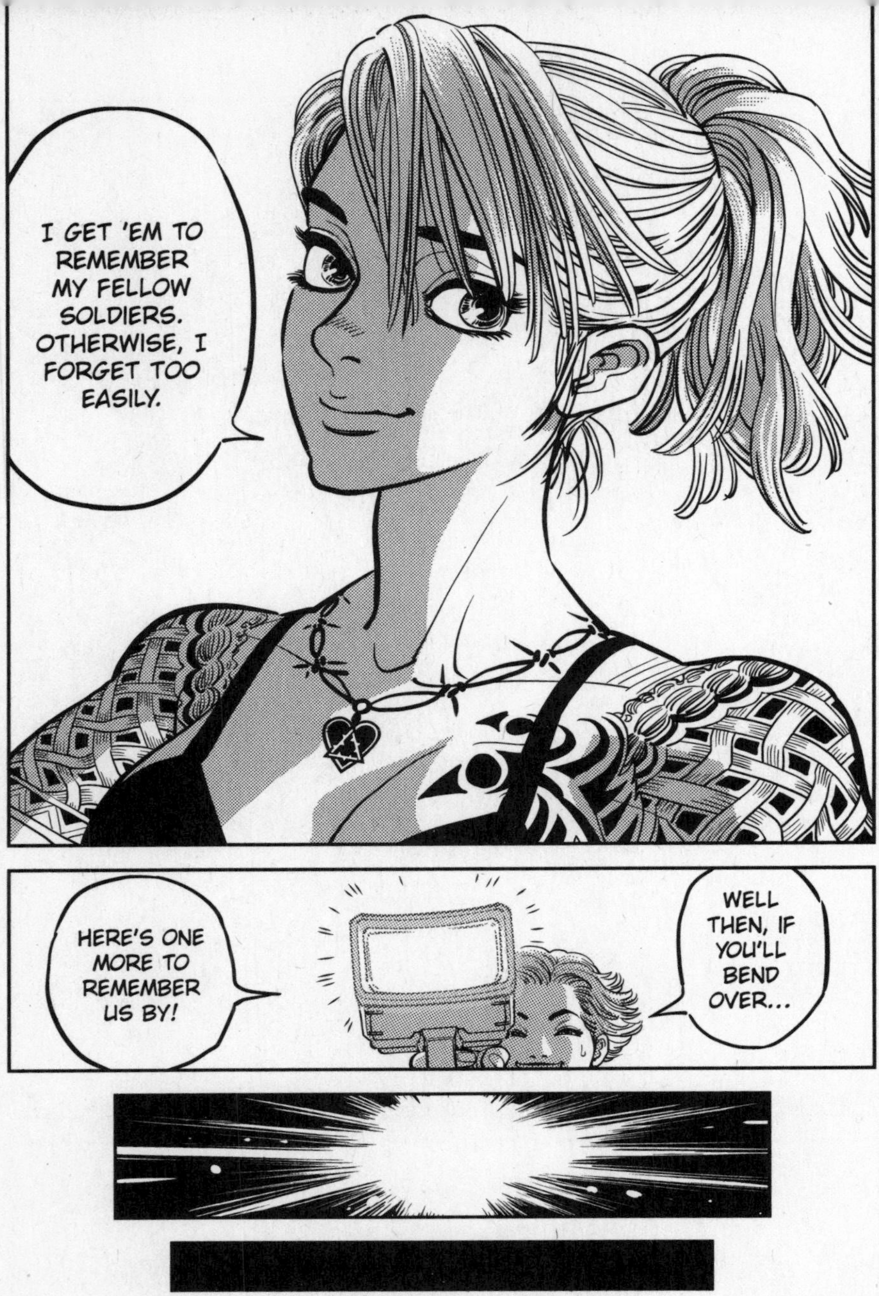
I GET 'EM TO REMEMBER MY FELLOW SOLDIERS. OTHERWISE, I FORGET TOO EASILY.
WELL THEN, IF YOU'LL BEND OVER...
HERE'S ONE MORE TO REMEMBER US BY!

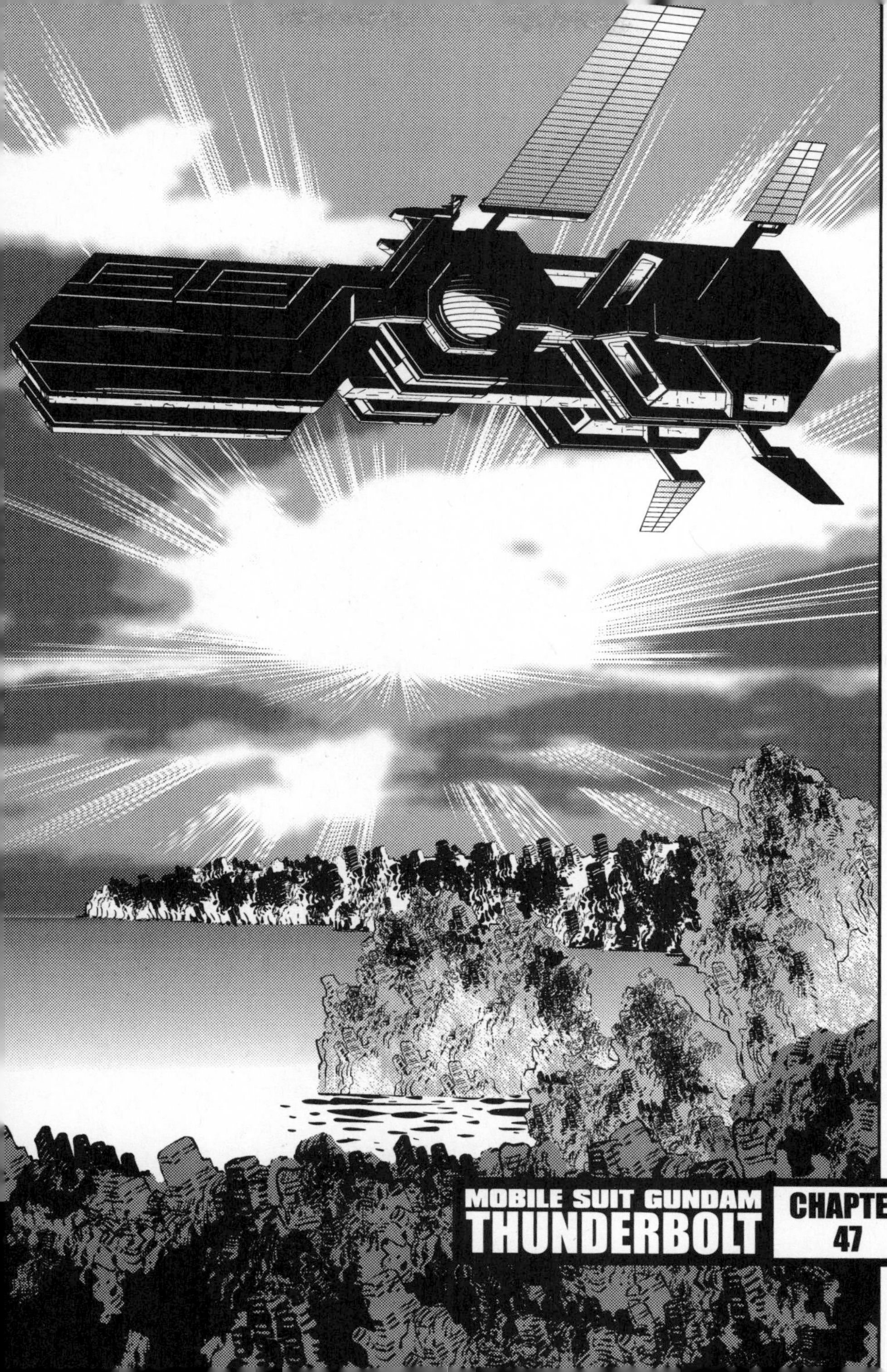
MOBILE SUIT GUNDAM
THUNDERBOLT
CHAPTER
47

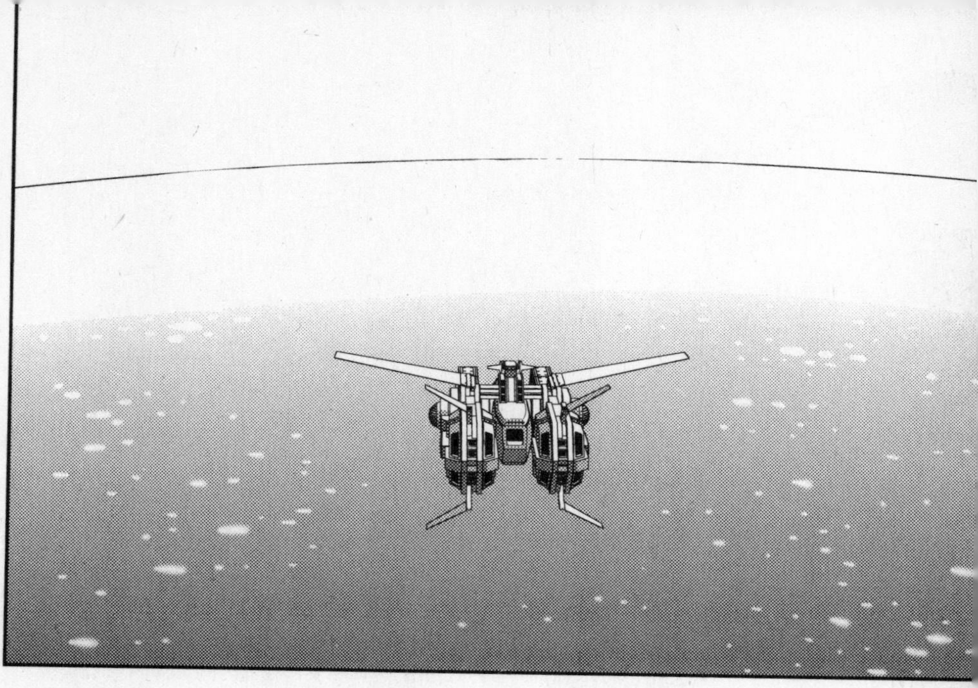

30 hours earlier…

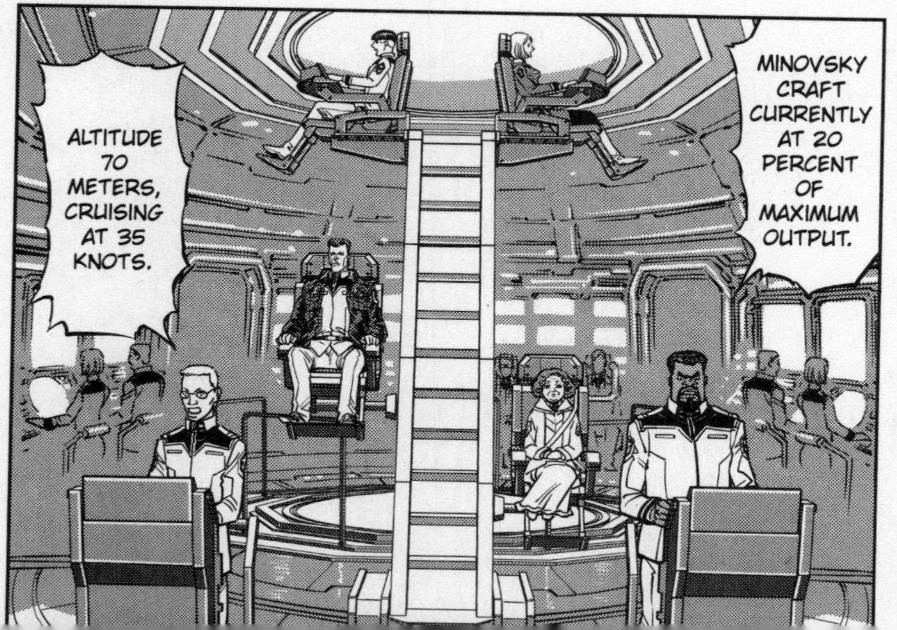
MINOVSKY CRAFT CURRENTLY AT 20 PERCENT OF MAXIMUM OUTPUT.
ALTITUDE 70 METERS, CRUISING AT 35 KNOTS.

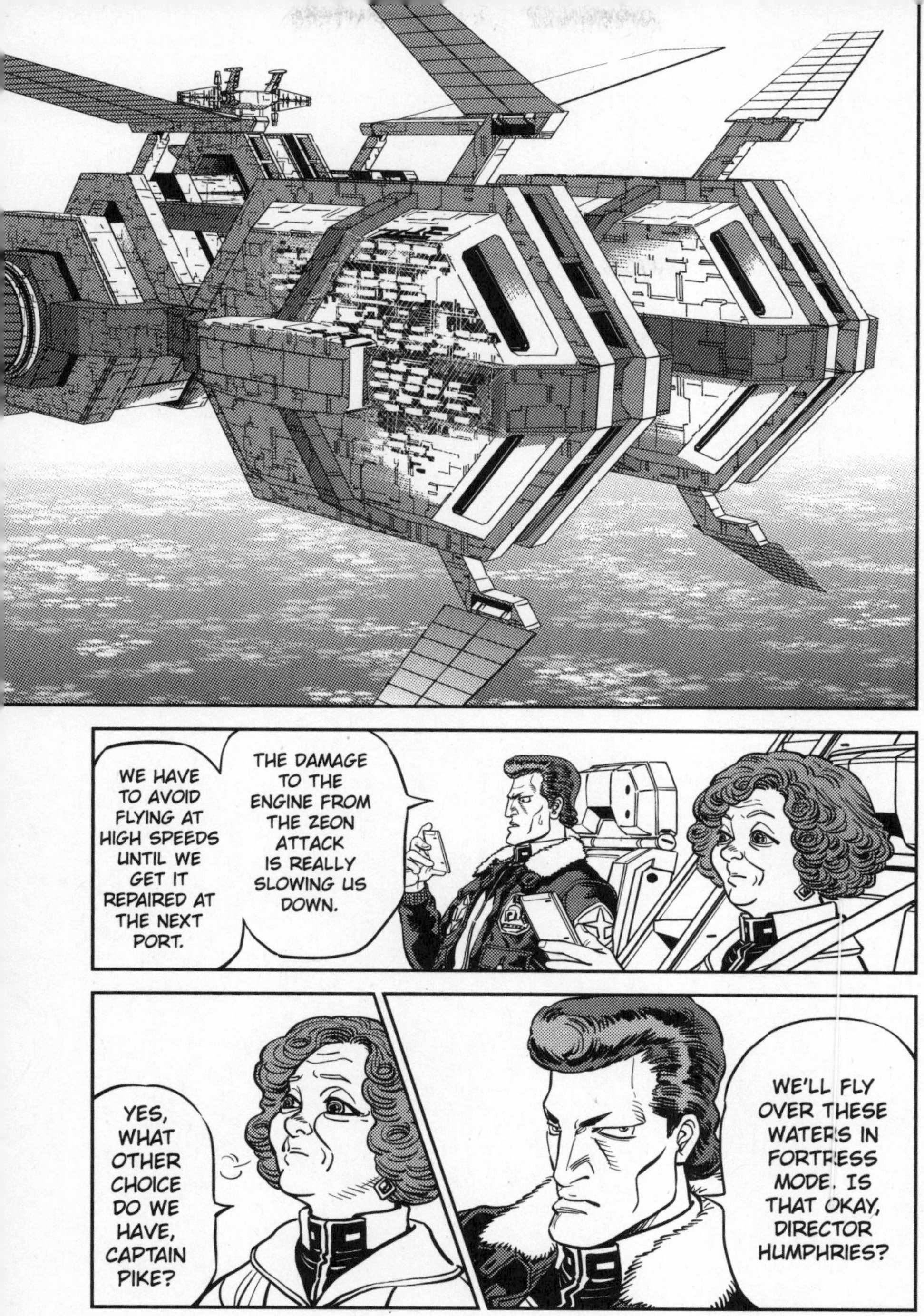
THE DAMAGE TO THE ENGINE FROM THE ZEON ATTACK IS REALLY SLOWING US DOWN.
WE HAVE TO AVOID FLYING AT HIGH SPEEDS UNTIL WE GET IT REPAIRED AT THE NEXT PORT.
WE'LL FLY OVER THESE WATERS IN FORTRESS MODE. IS THAT OKAY, DIRECTOR HUMPHRIES?
YES, WHAT OTHER CHOICE DO WE HAVE, CAPTAIN PIKE?

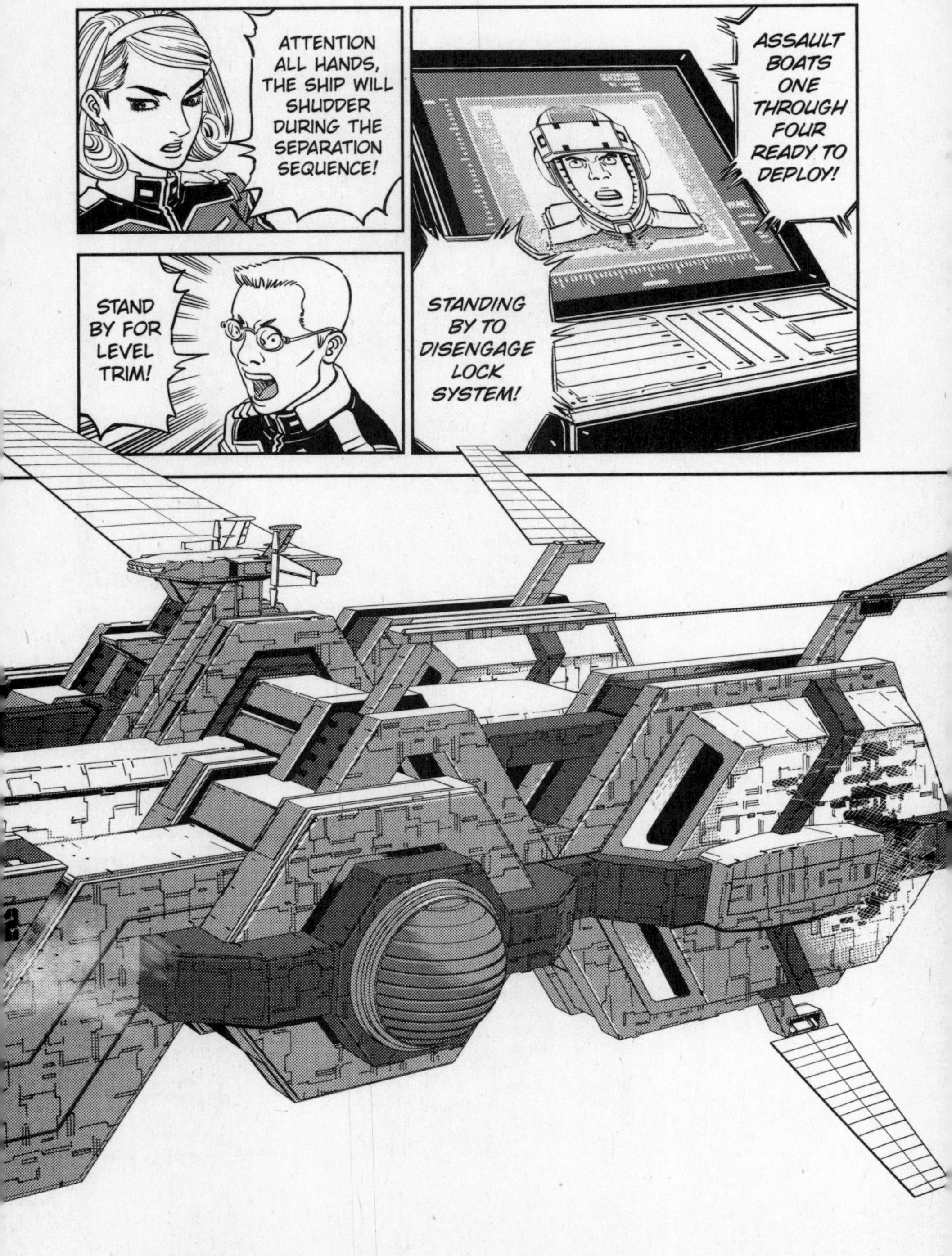
ASSAULT BOATS ONE THROUGH FOUR READY TO DEPLOY!
STANDING BY TO DISENGAGE LOCK SYSTEM!
ATTENTION ALL HANDS, THE SHIP WILL SHUDDER DURING THE SEPARATION SEQUENCE!
STAND BY FOR LEVEL TRIM!

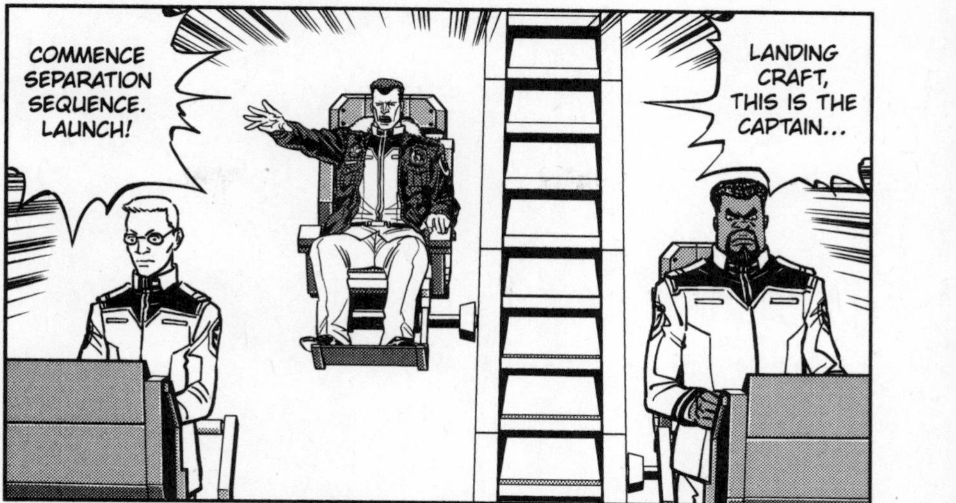
LANDING CRAFT, THIS IS THE CAPTAIN...
COMMENCE SEPARATION SEQUENCE. LAUNCH!

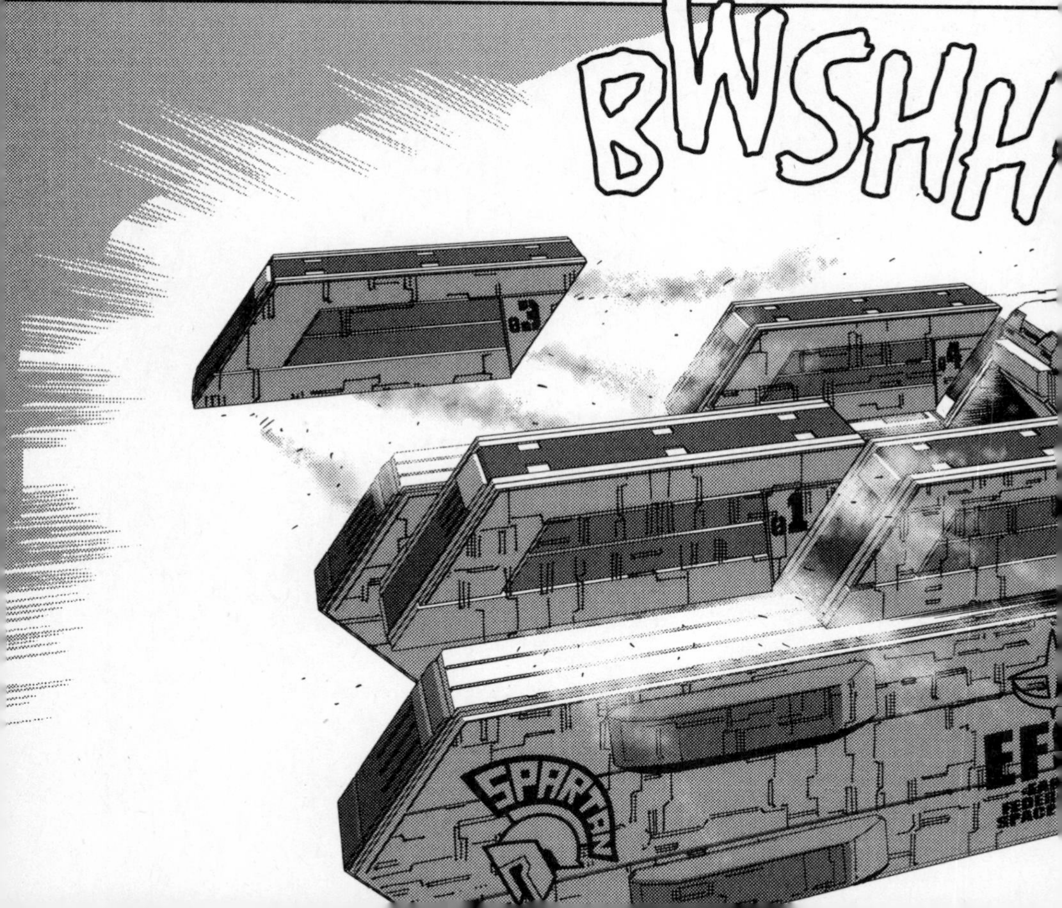
BWSHH
SPARTAN

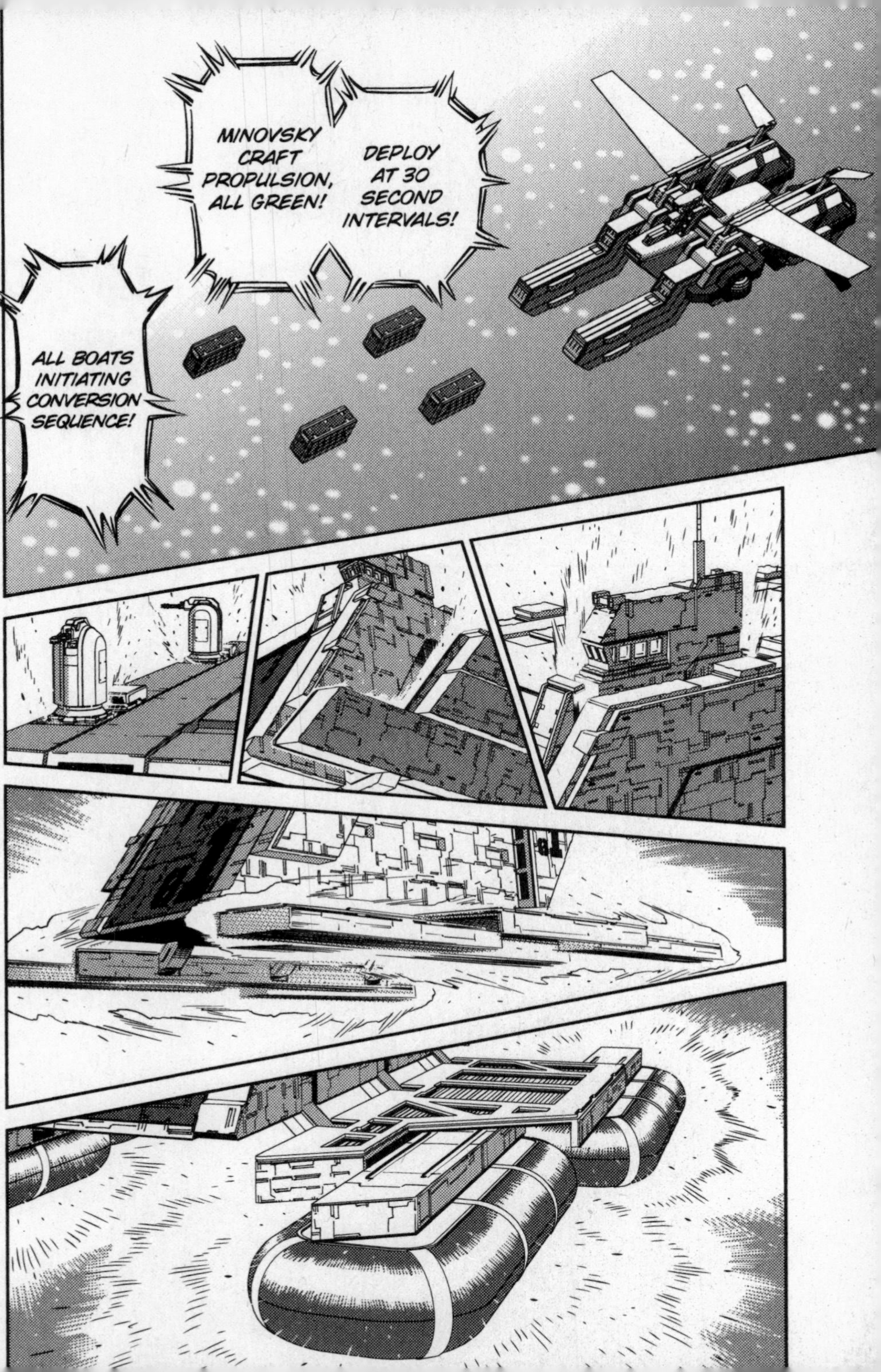
DEPLOY AT 30 SECOND INTERVALS!
MINOVSKY CRAFT PROPULSION, ALL GREEN!
ALL BOATS INITIATING CONVERSION SEQUENCE!

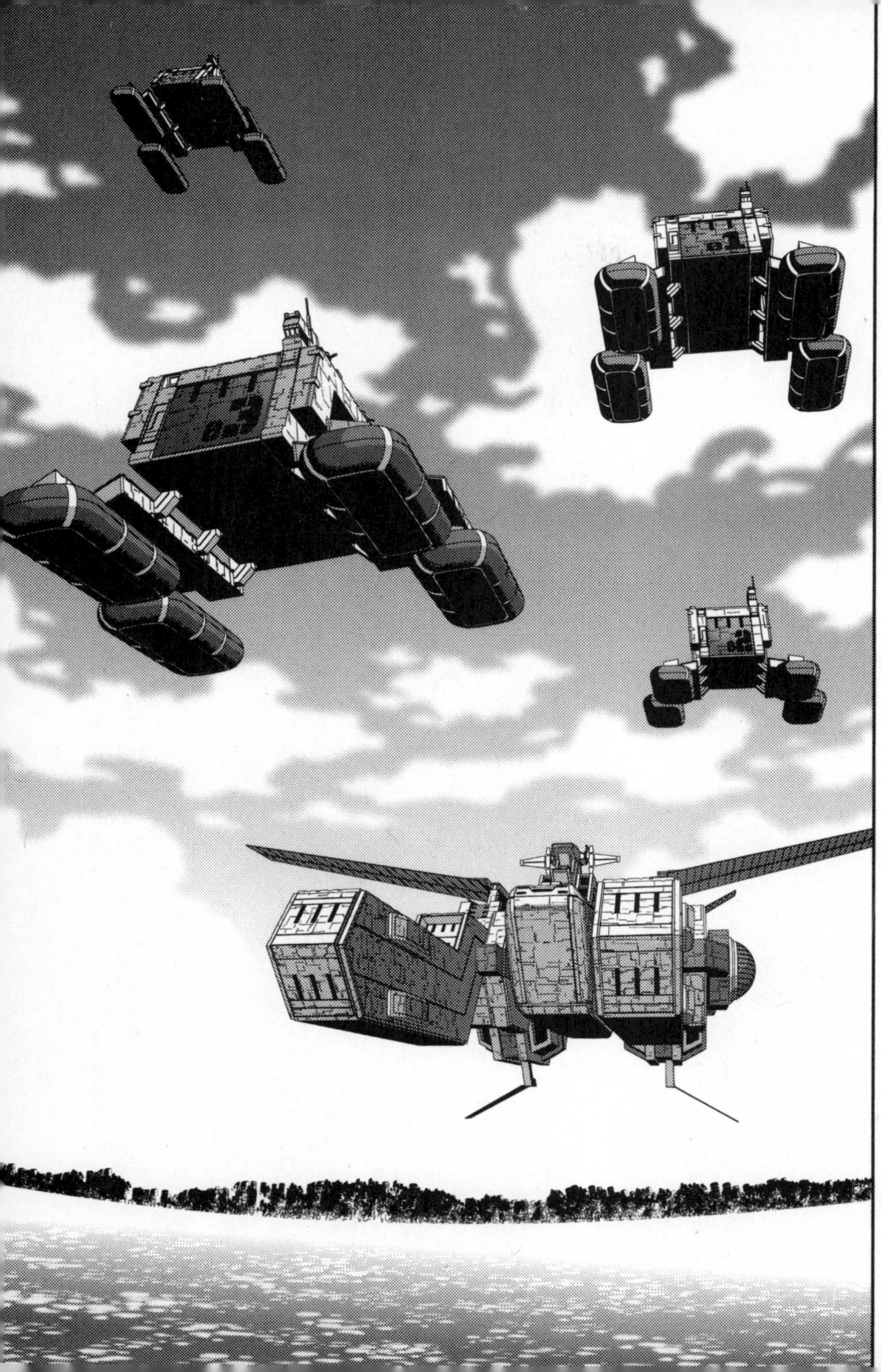

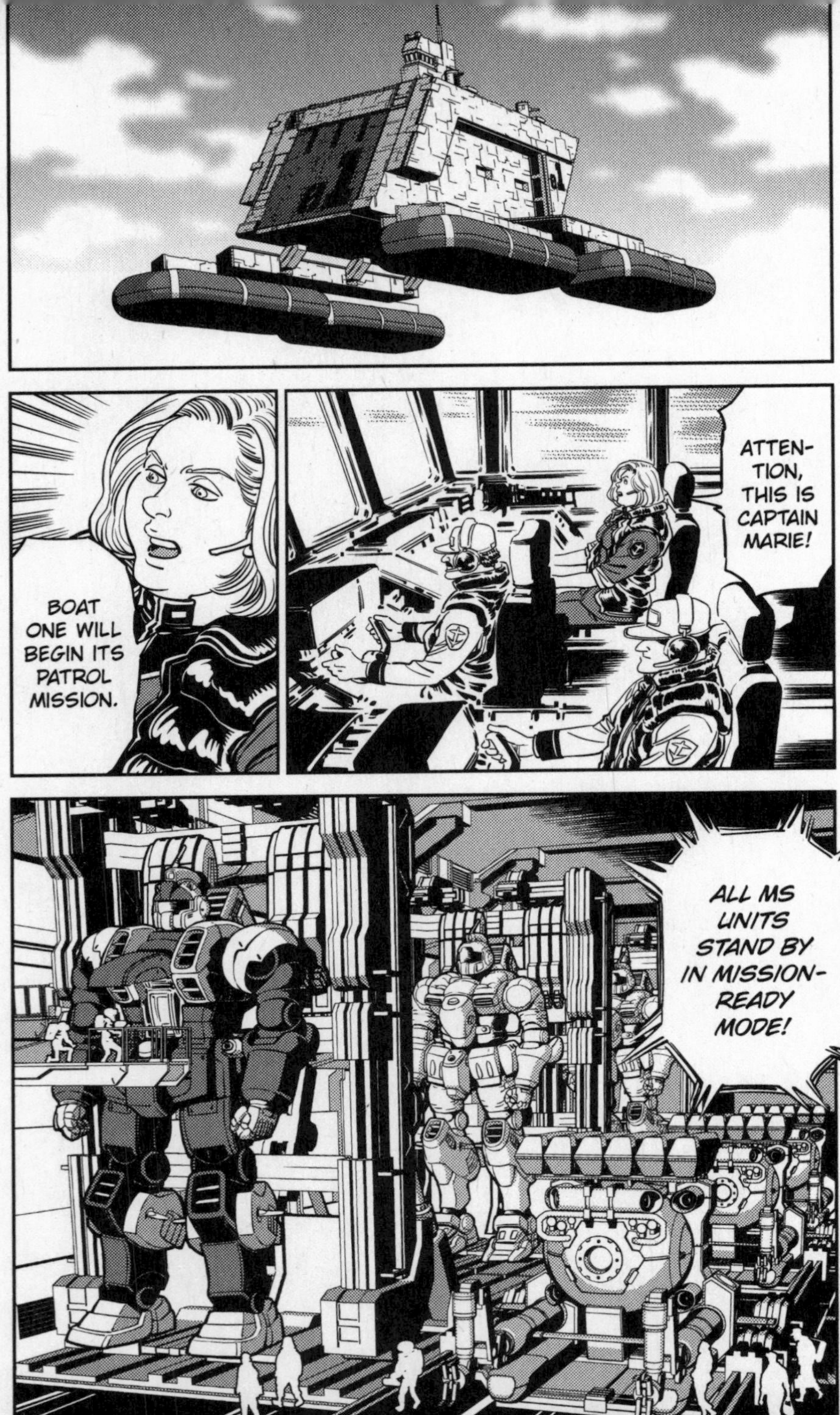
ATTEN-TION, THIS IS CAPTAIN MARIE!
BOAT ONE WILL BEGIN ITS PATROL MISSION.
ALL MS UNITS STAND BY IN MISSION-READY MODE!

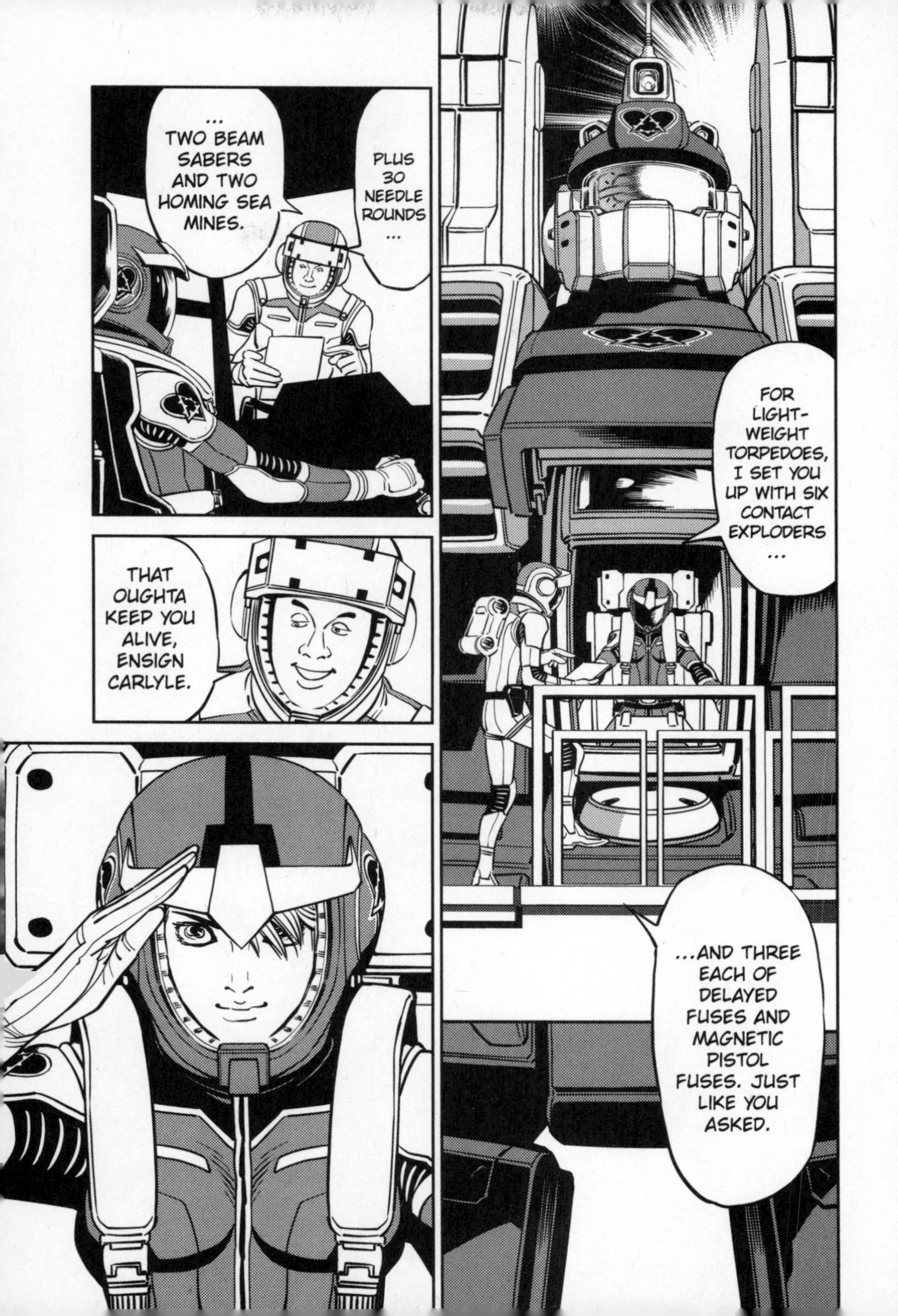
FOR LIGHT-WEIGHT TORPEDOES, I SET YOU UP WITH SIX CONTACT EXPLODERS ...
...AND THREE EACH OF DELAYED FUSES AND MAGNETIC PISTOL FUSES. JUST LIKE YOU ASKED.
PLUS 30 NEEDLE ROUNDS ...
... TWO BEAM SABERS AND TWO HOMING SEA MINES.
THAT OUGHTA KEEP YOU ALIVE, ENSIGN CARLYLE.

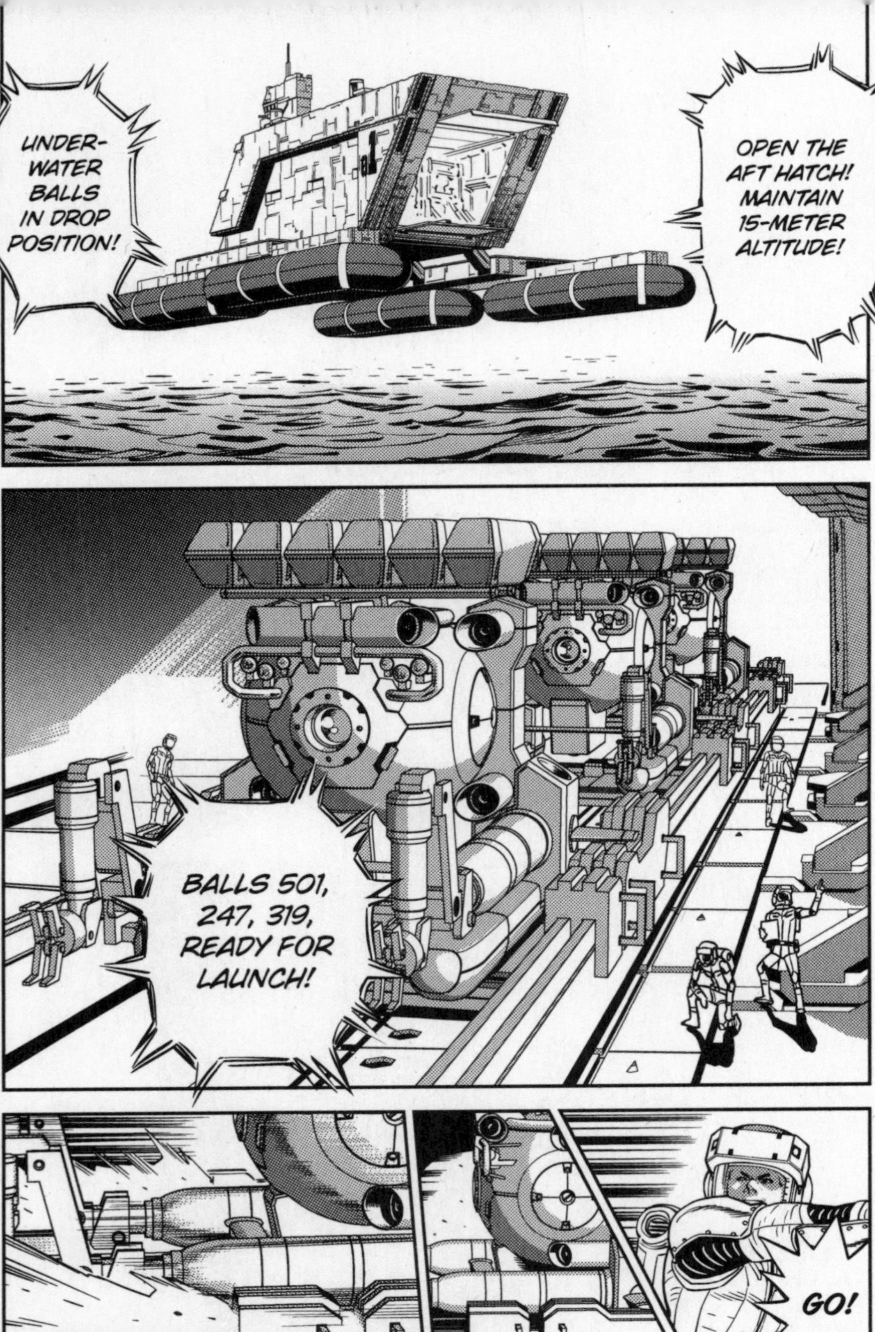
OPEN THE AFT HATCH! MAINTAIN 15-METER ALTITUDE!
UNDER-WATER BALLS IN DROP POSITION!
BALLS 501, 247, 319, READY FOR LAUNCH!
GO!

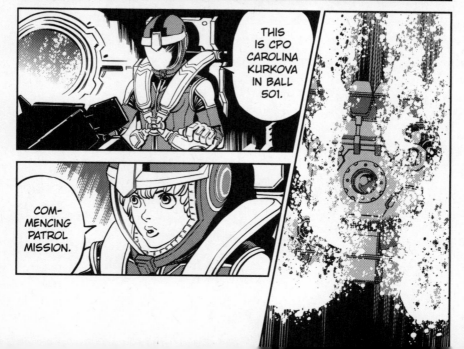

THIS IS CPO CAROLINA KURKOVA IN BALL 501.

COMMENCING PATROL MISSION.

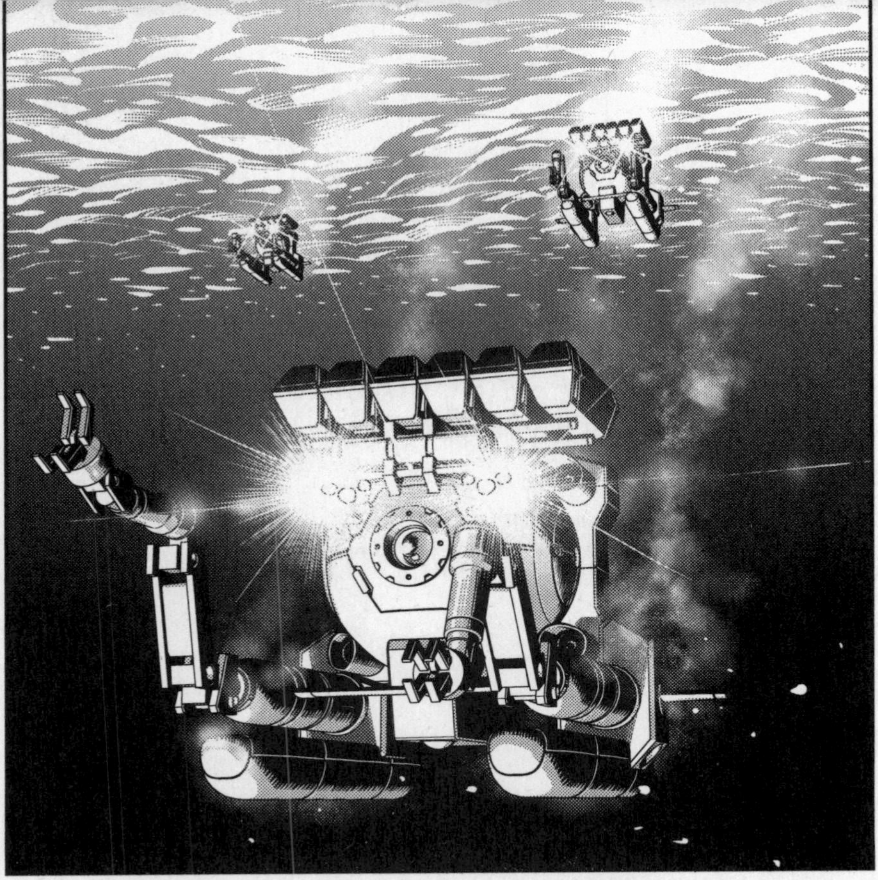

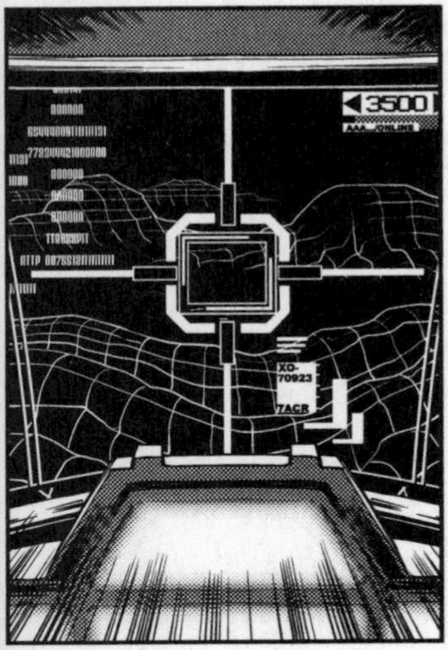
3500
XO-
70923
7ACR

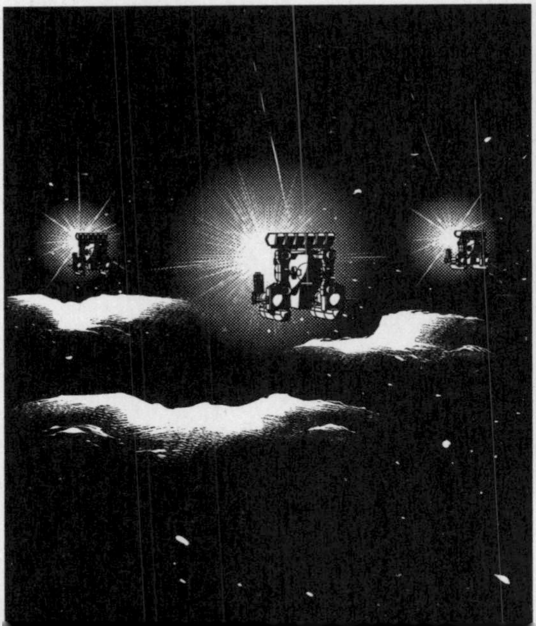

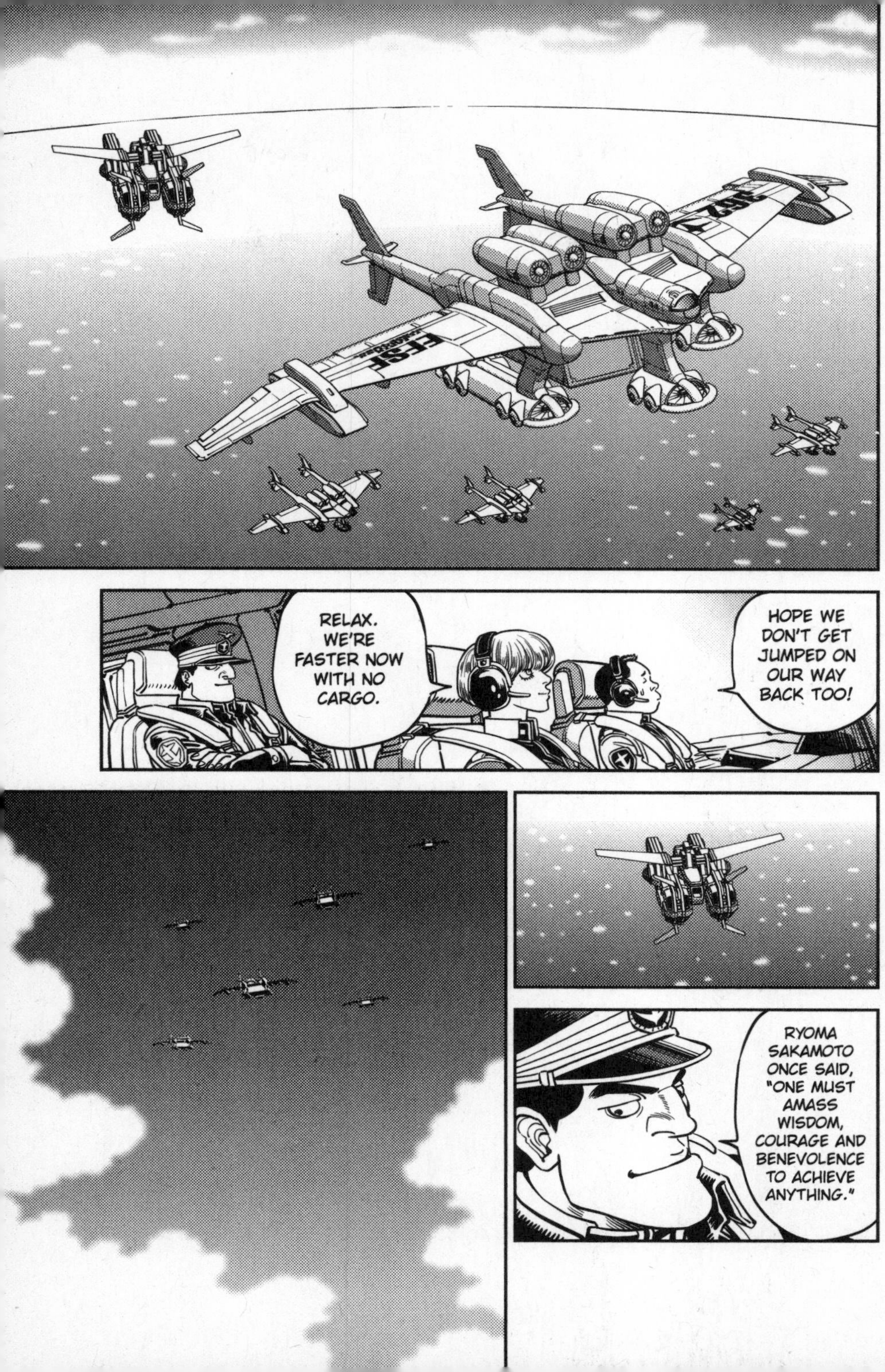
HOPE WE DON'T GET JUMPED ON OUR WAY BACK TOO!
RELAX. WE'RE FASTER NOW WITH NO CARGO.
RYOMA SAKAMOTO ONCE SAID, "ONE MUST AMASS WISDOM, COURAGE AND BENEVOLENCE TO ACHIEVE ANYTHING."

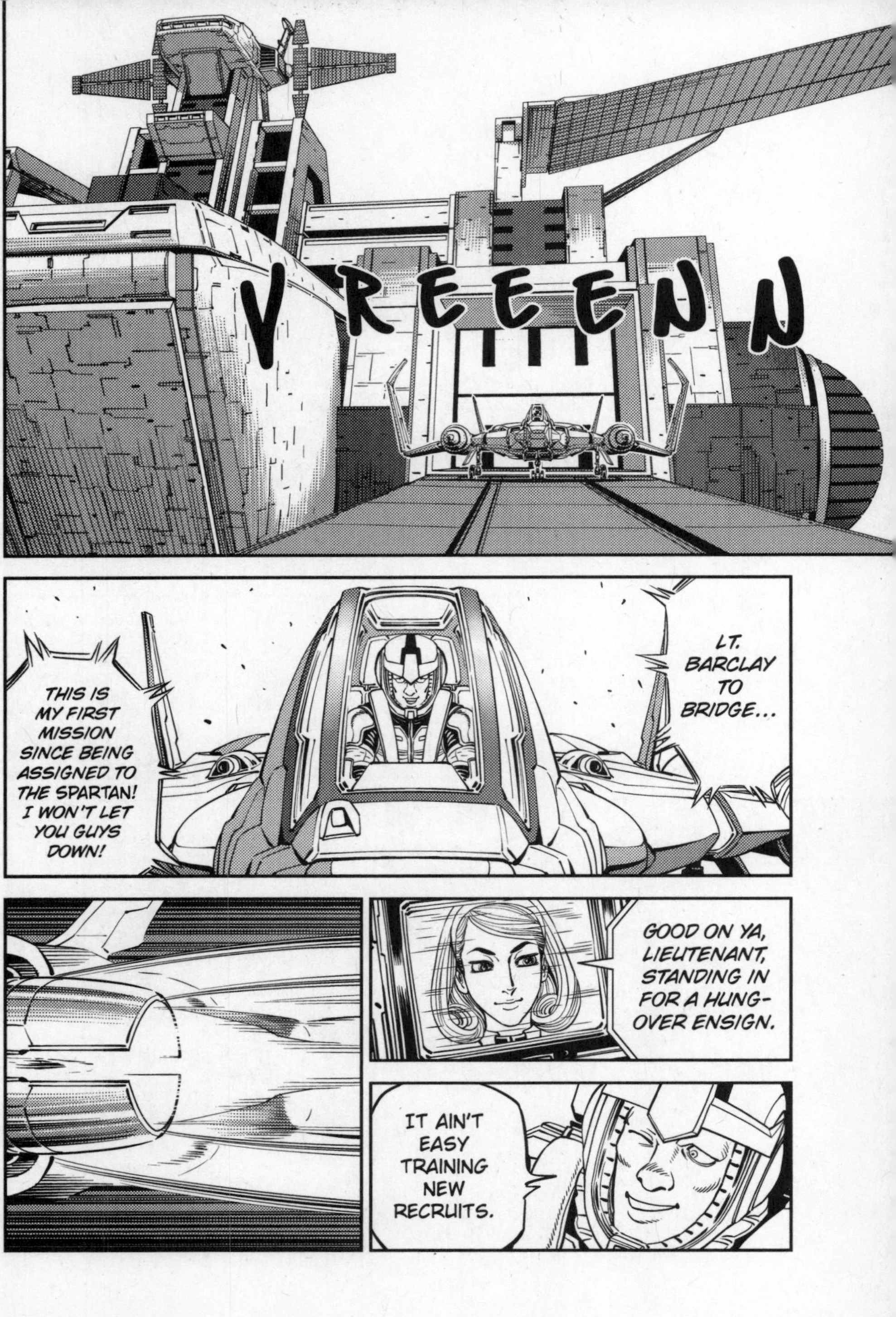
VREEENN
LT. BARCLAY TO BRIDGE...
THIS IS MY FIRST MISSION SINCE BEING ASSIGNED TO THE SPARTAN! I WON'T LET YOU GUYS DOWN!
GOOD ON YA, LIEUTENANT, STANDING IN FOR A HUNG-OVER ENSIGN.
IT AIN'T EASY TRAINING NEW RECRUITS.

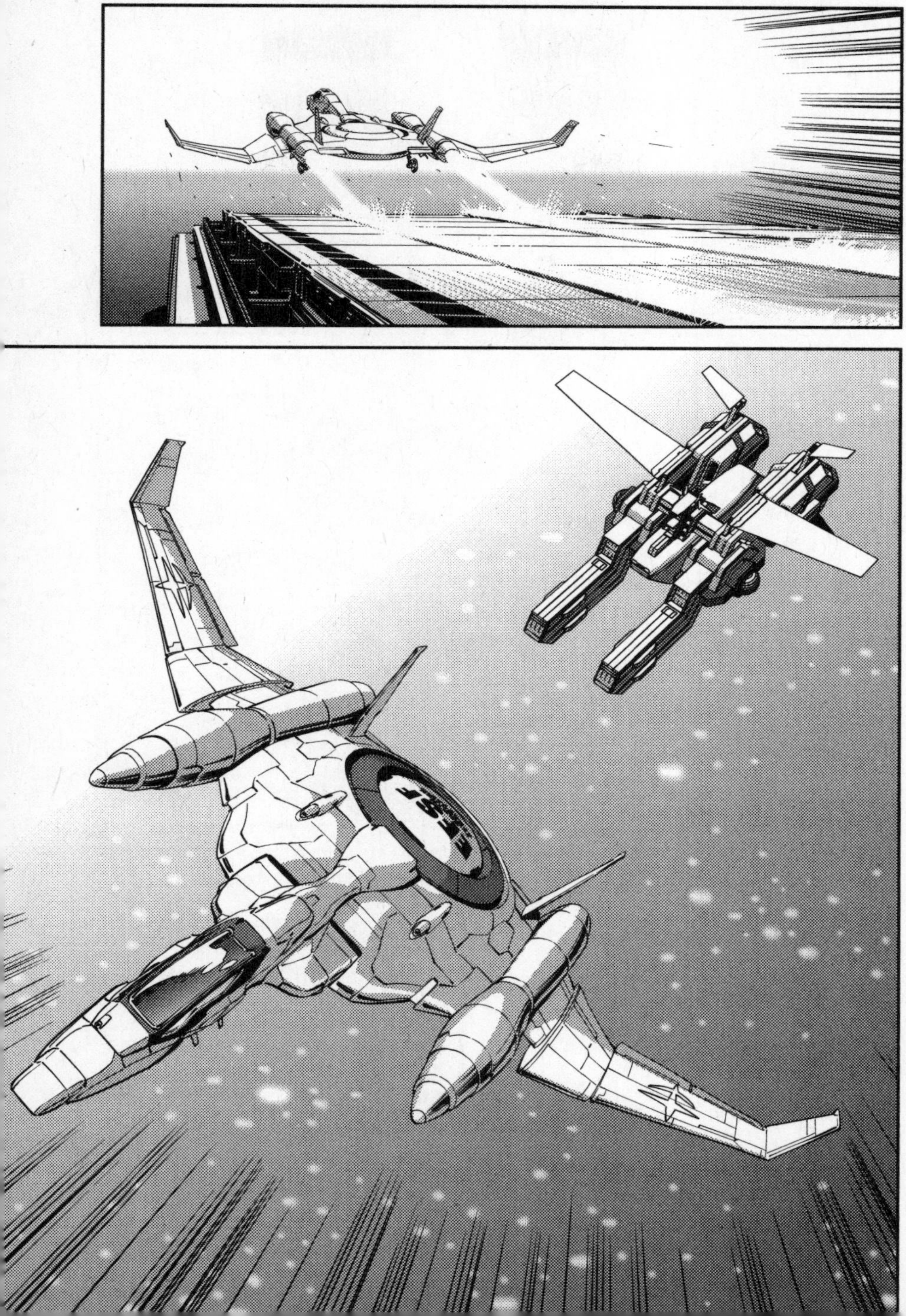

ALTITUDE 300 METERS. ACTIVATING RADOME.

HMMMM

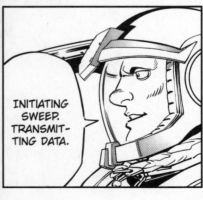

INITIATING SWEEP. TRANSMITTING DATA.

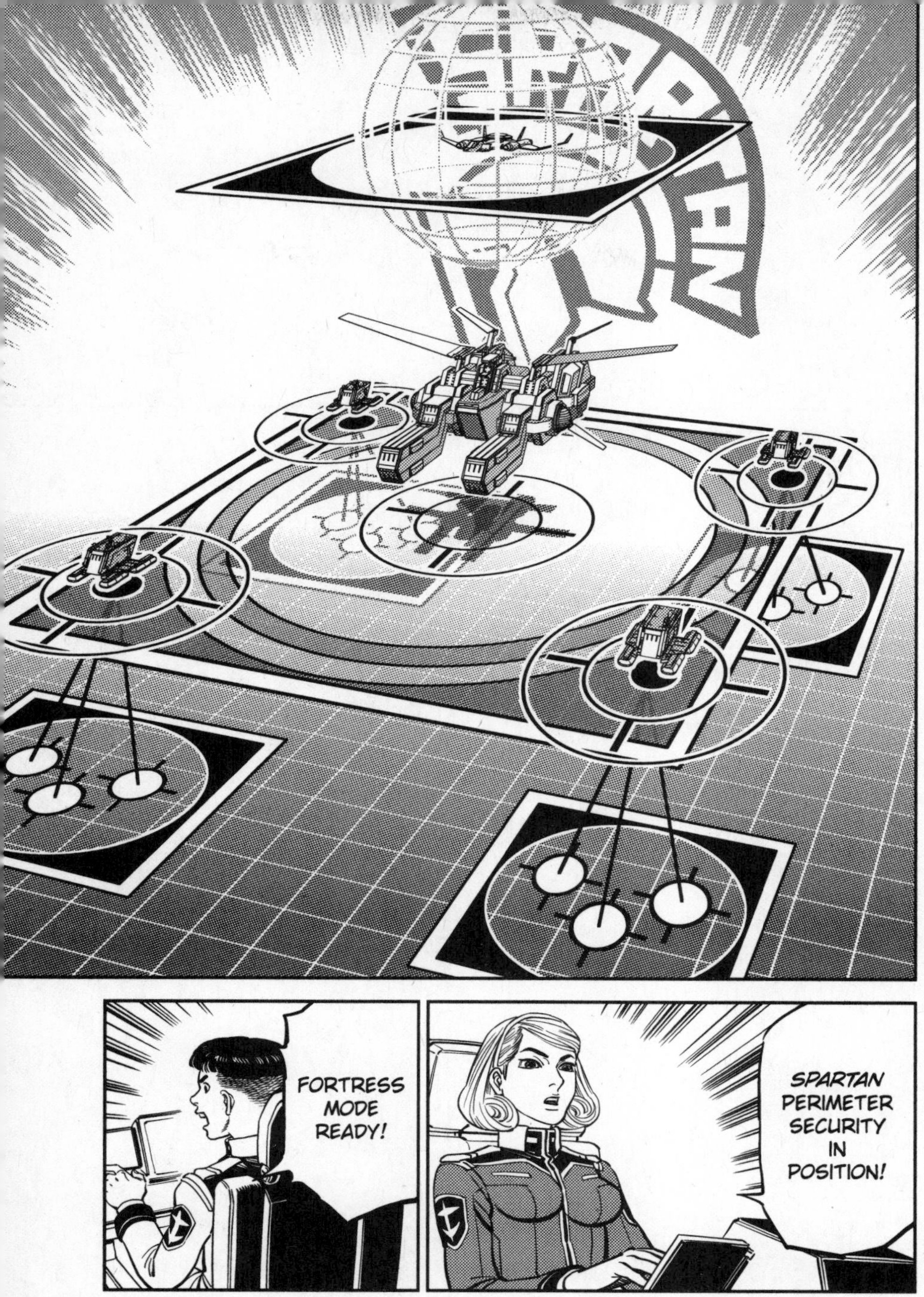
SPARTAN PERIMETER SECURITY IN POSITION!
FORTRESS MODE READY!

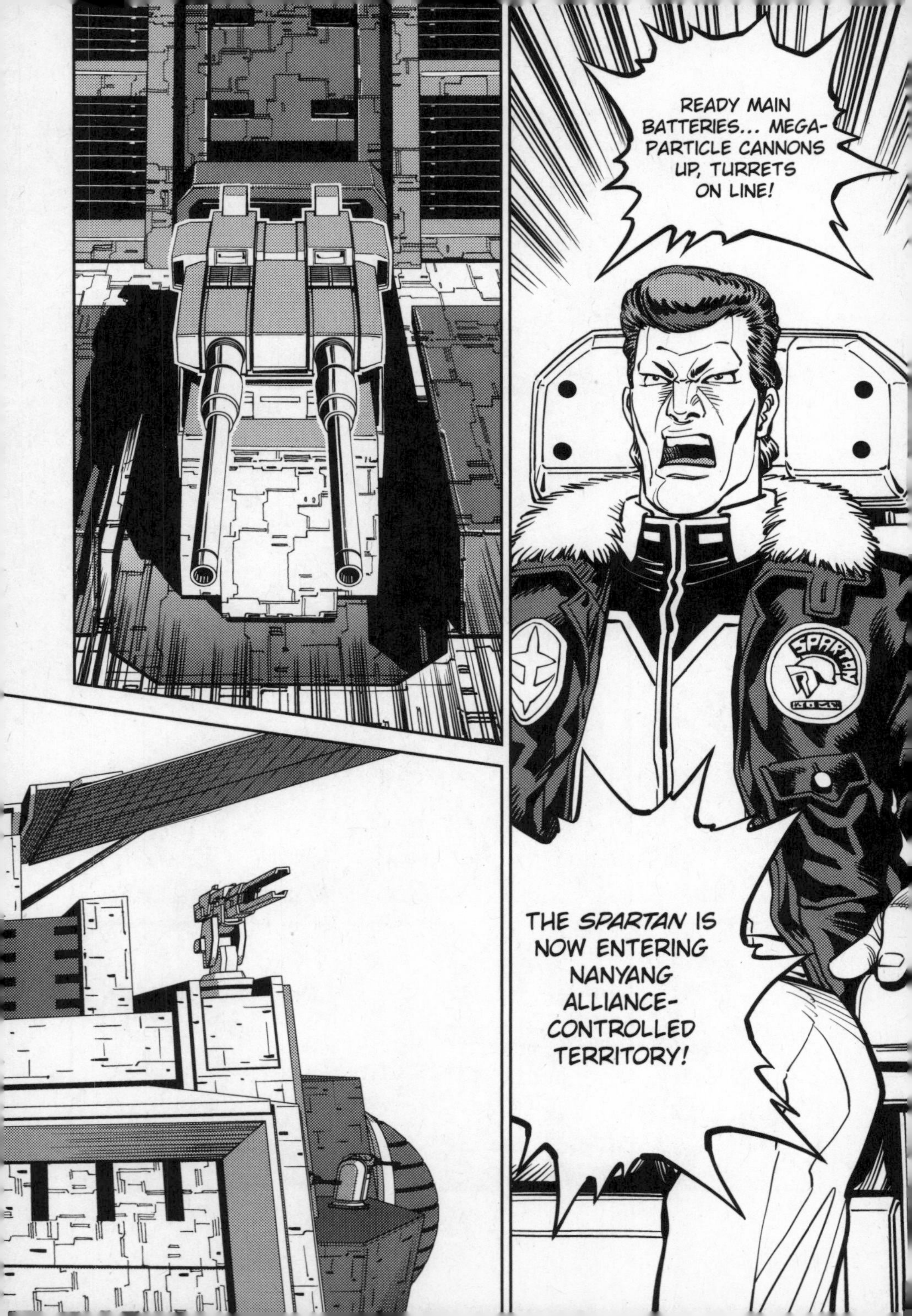
READY MAIN BATTERIES... MEGA-PARTICLE CANNONS UP, TURRETS ON LINE!
SPARTAN
THE *SPARTAN* IS NOW ENTERING NANYANG ALLIANCE-CONTROLLED TERRITORY!

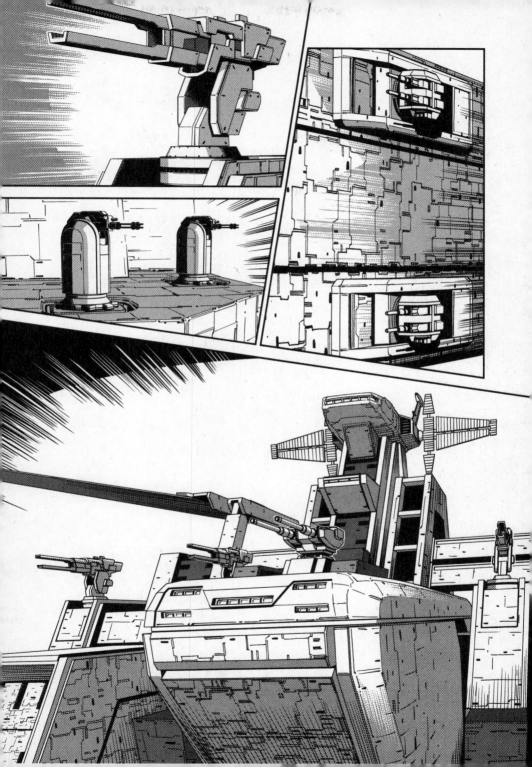

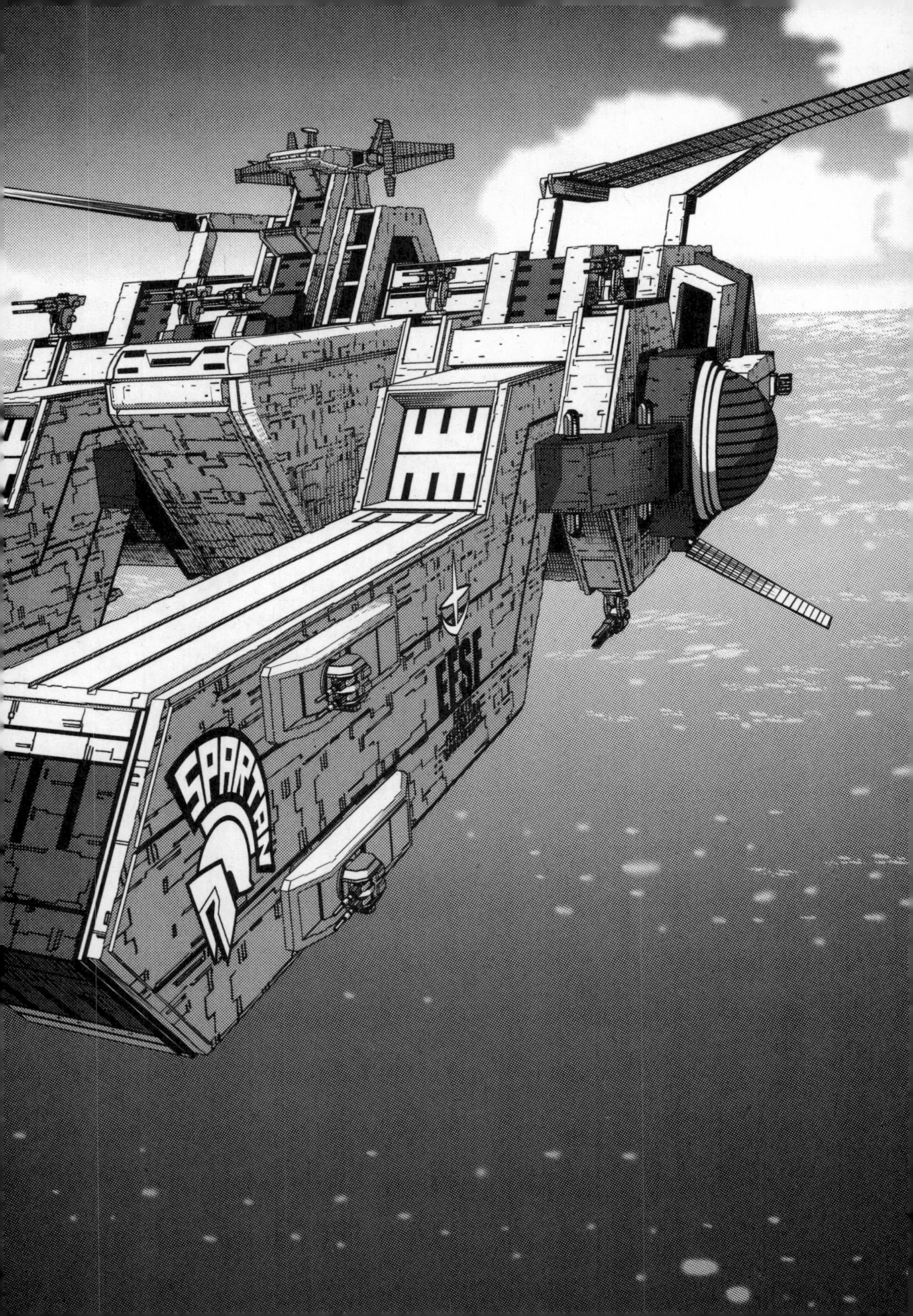
SPARTAN
EFSF

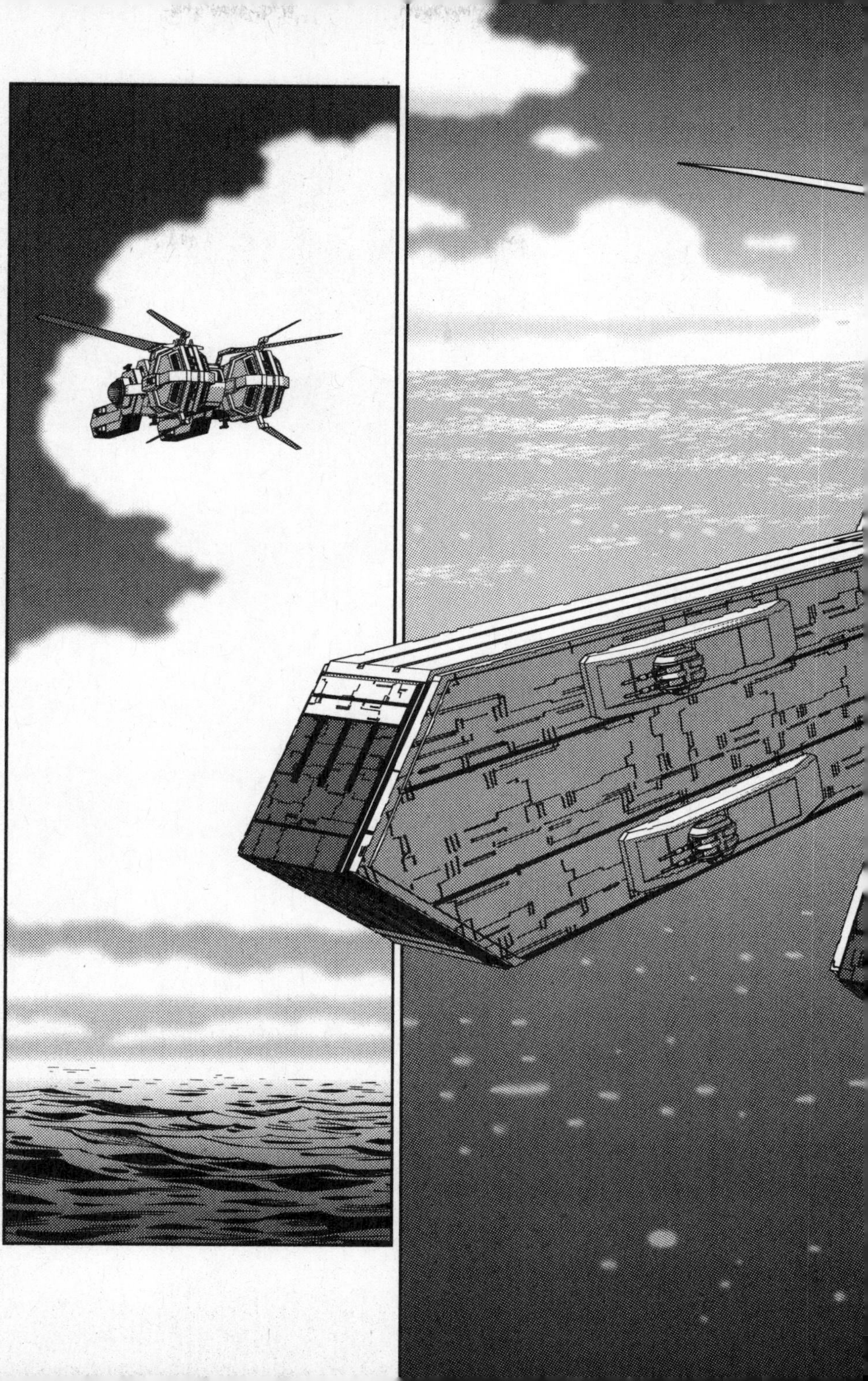

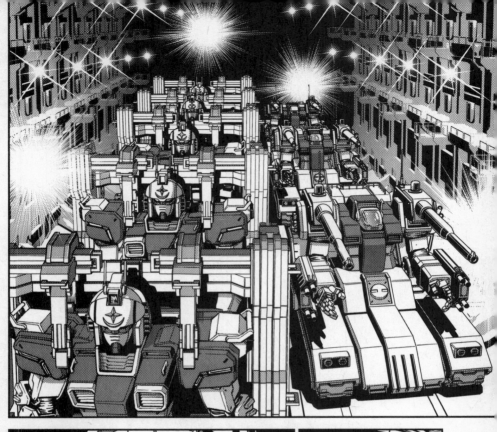

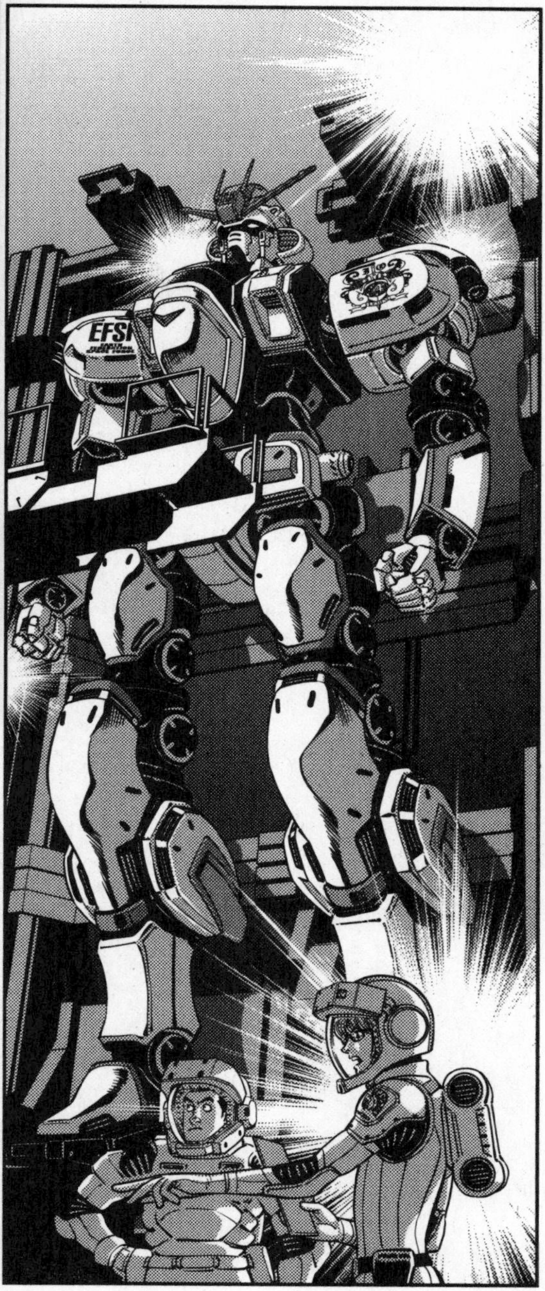
EFSF
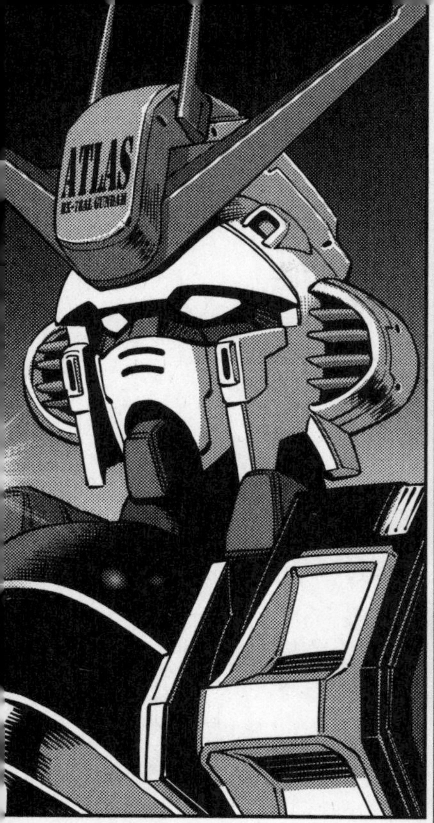
ATLAS
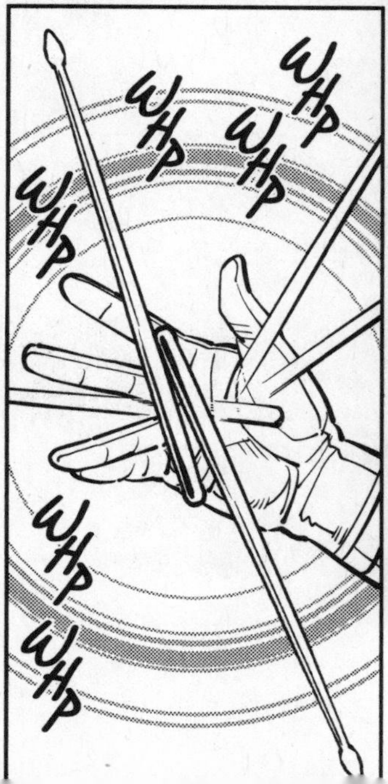
WHP
WHP
WHP
WHP
WHP
WHP

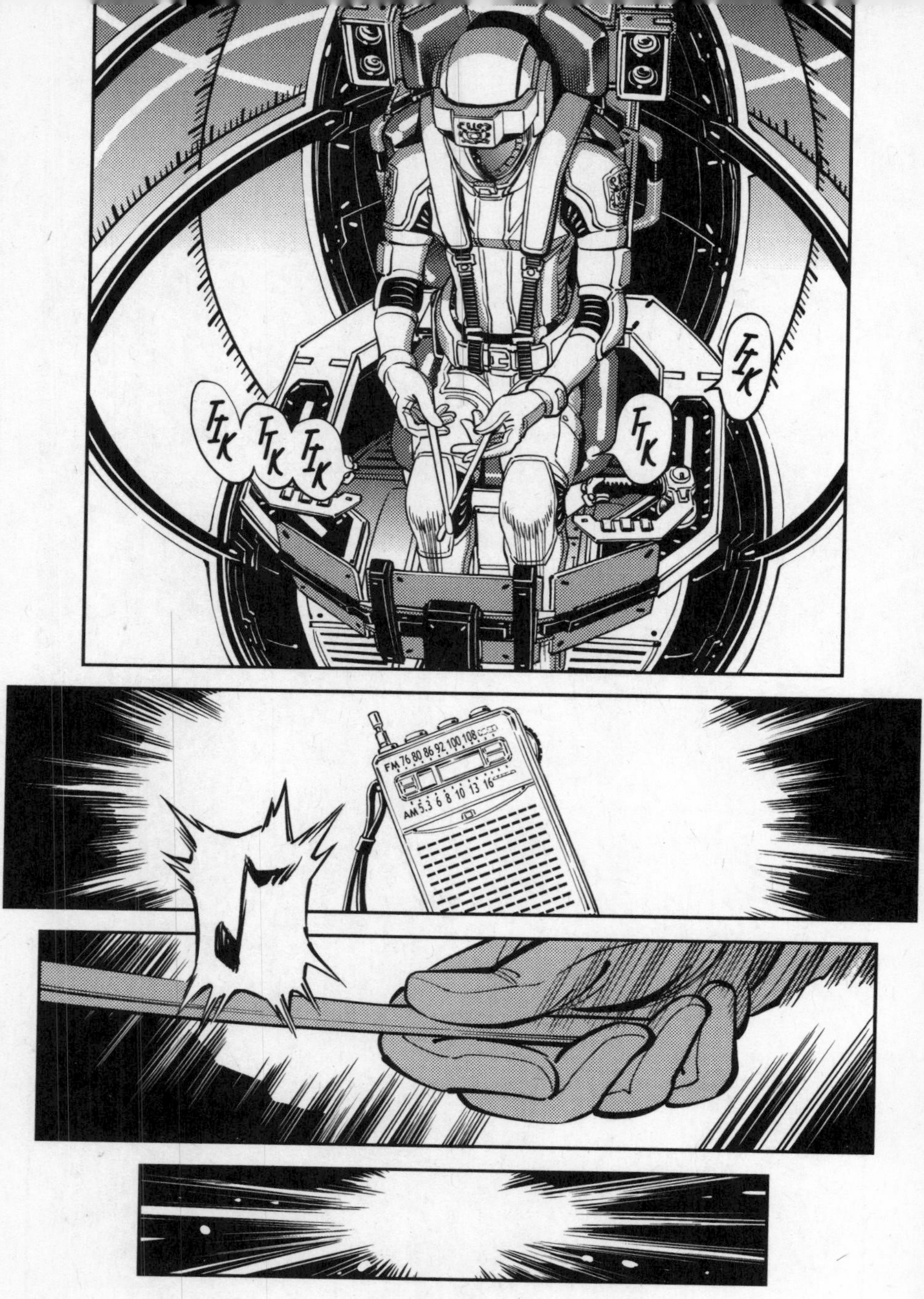
TIK
TIK
TIK
TIK
TIK
FM 76 80 86 92 100 108
AM 5.3 6 8 10 13 16

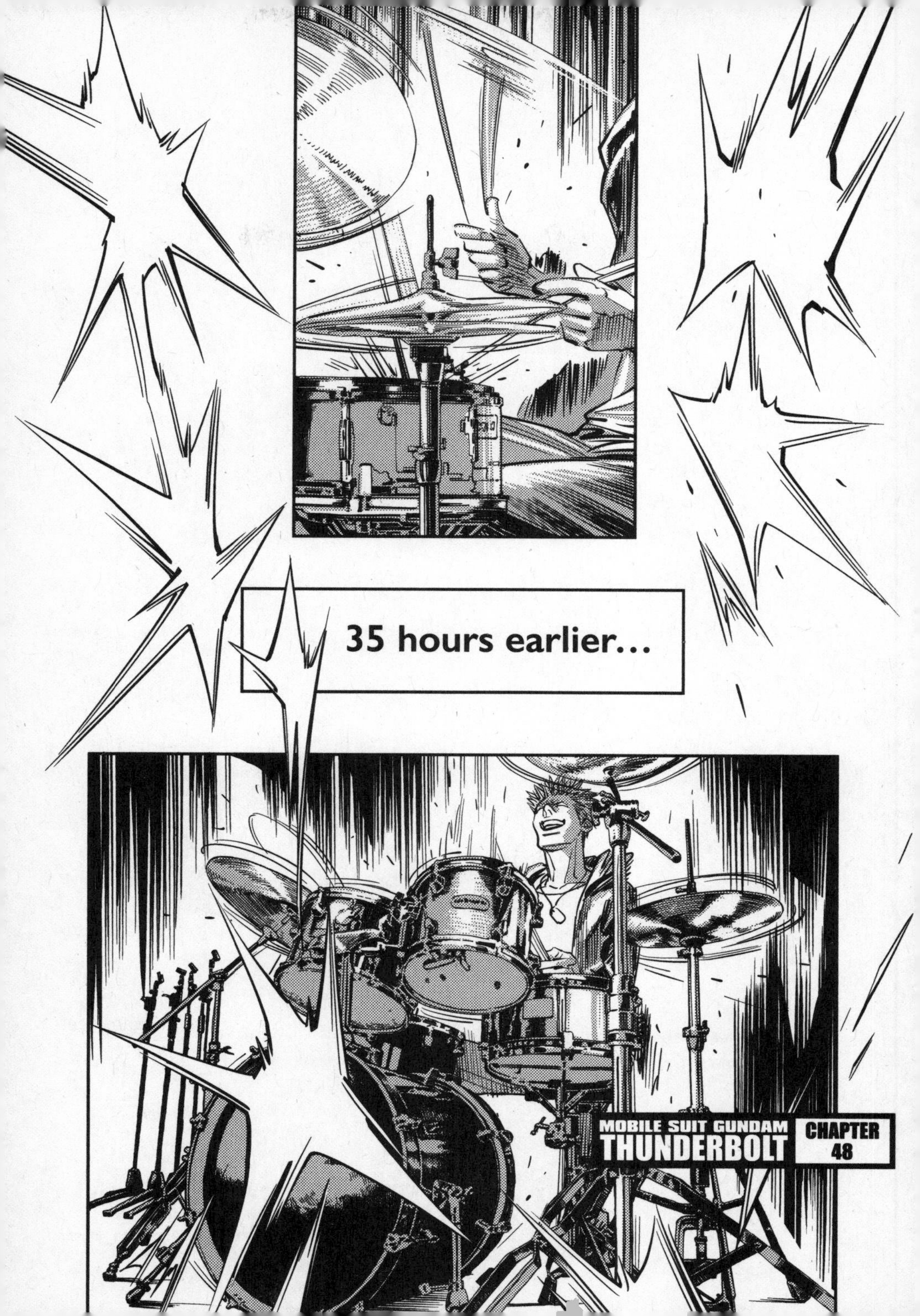
35 hours earlier...
MOBILE SUIT GUNDAM
THUNDERBOLT
CHAPTER
48

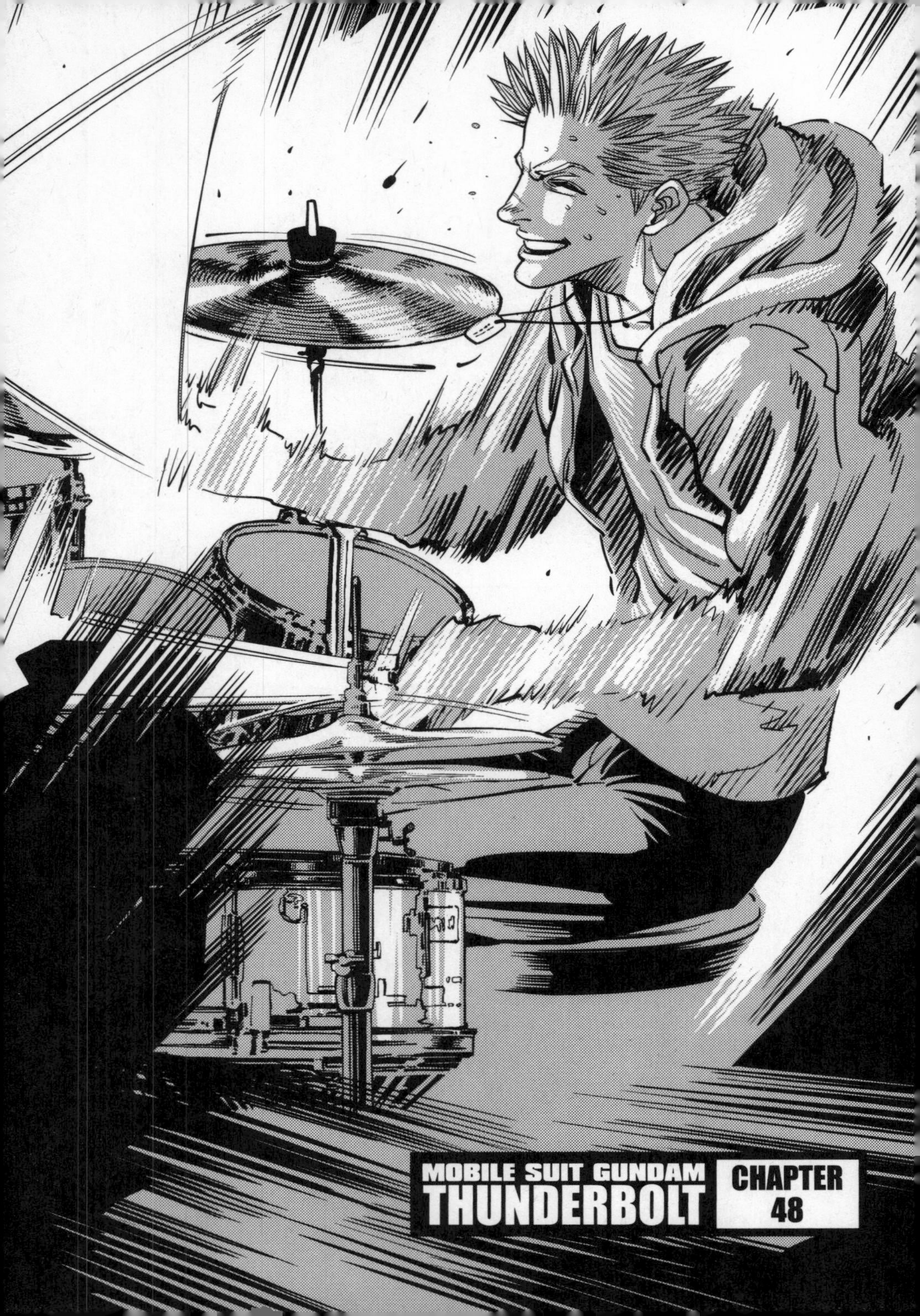
MOBILE SUIT GUNDAM
THUNDERBOLT
CHAPTER
48

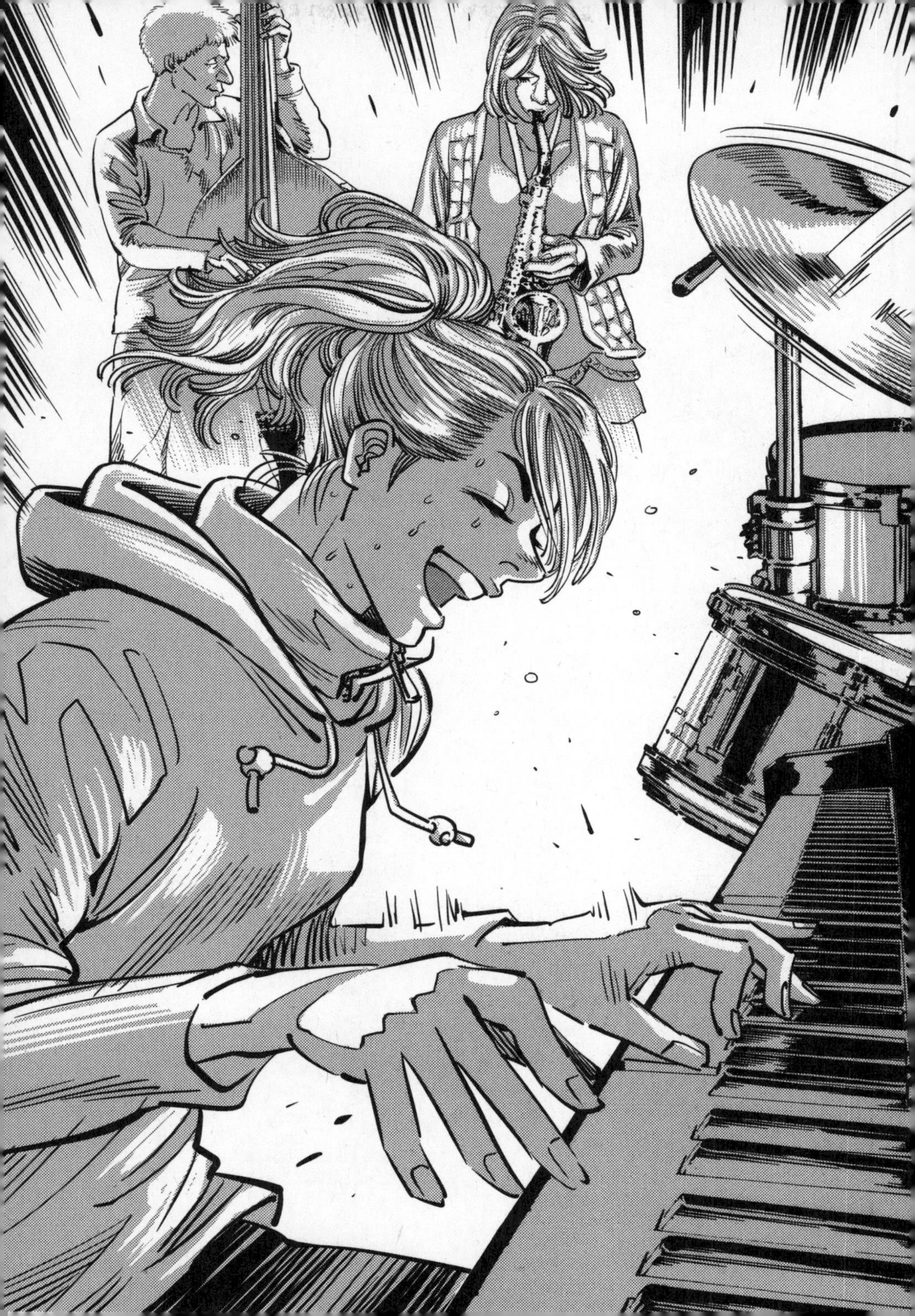

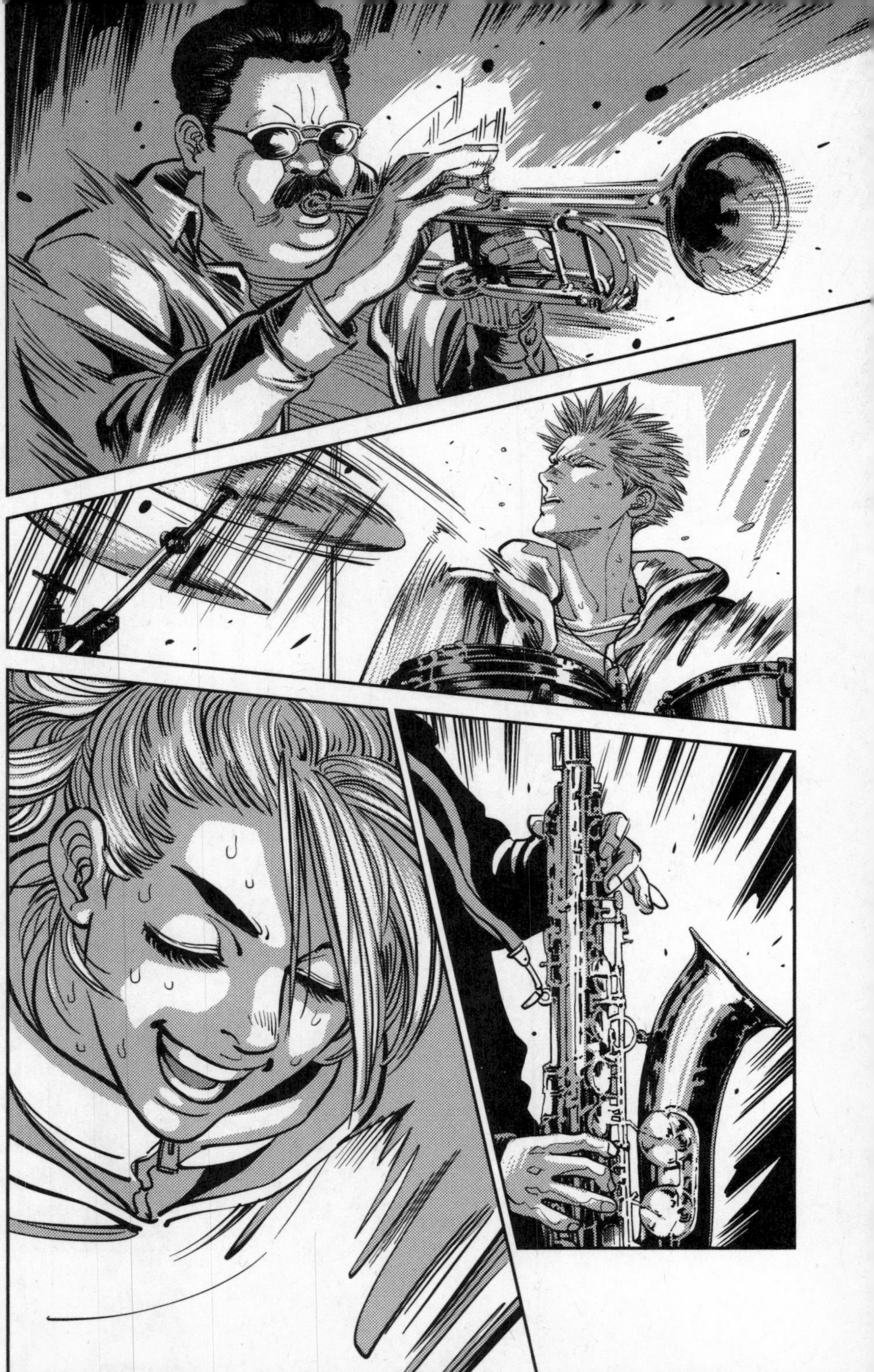

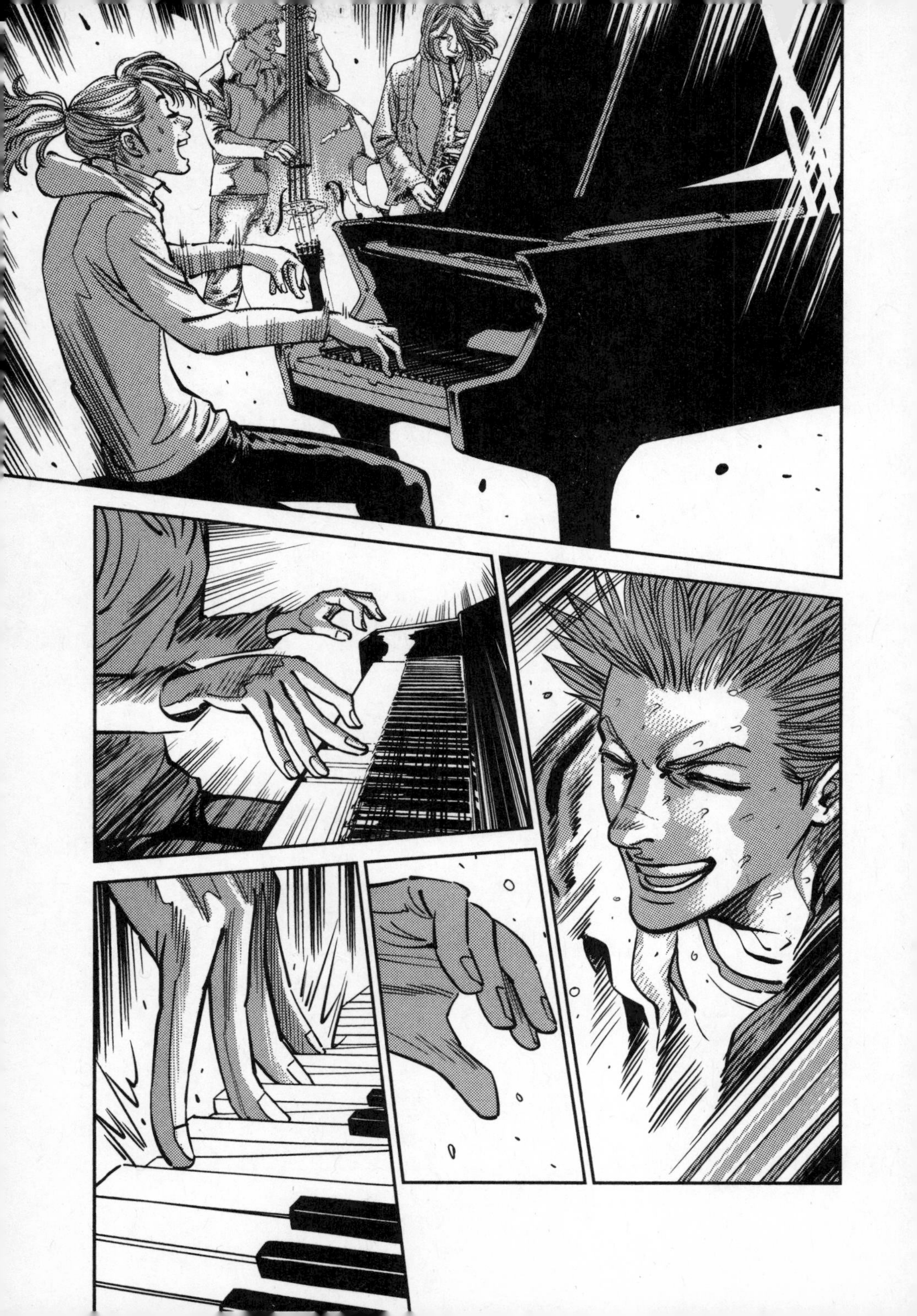

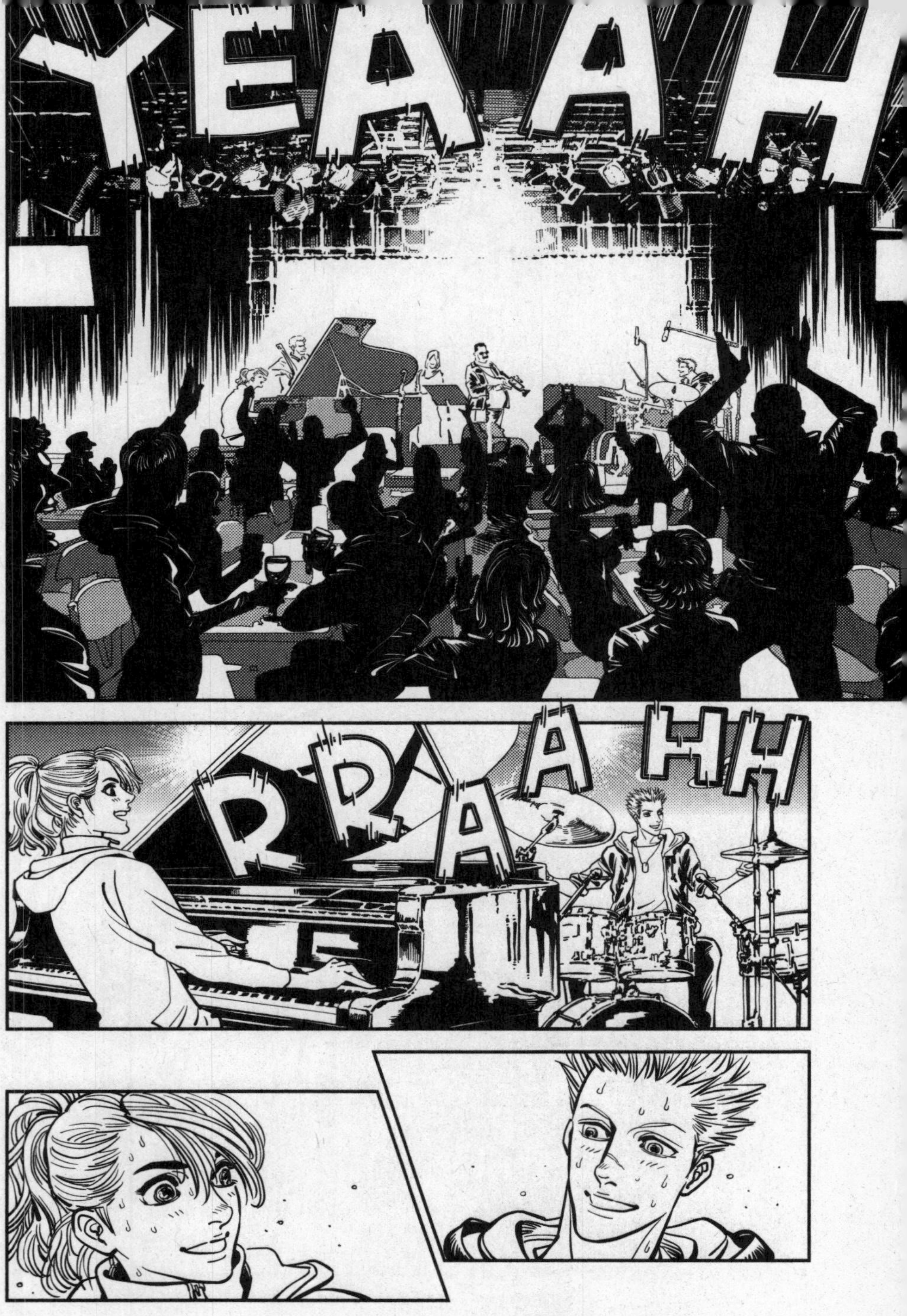
YEAAH
RRAAHH

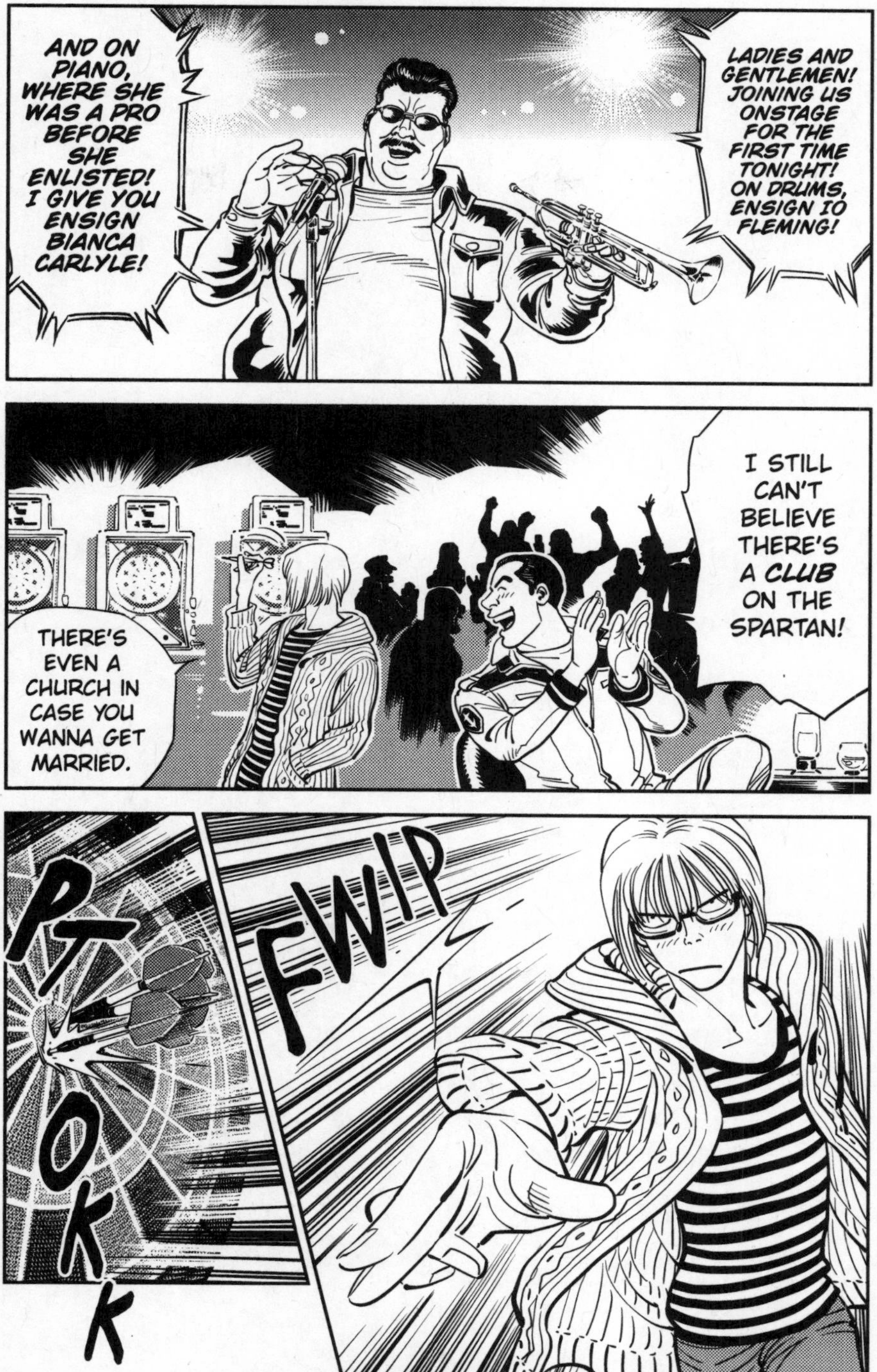
LADIES AND GENTLEMEN! JOINING US ONSTAGE FOR THE FIRST TIME TONIGHT! ON DRUMS, ENSIGN IO FLEMING!
AND ON PIANO, WHERE SHE WAS A PRO BEFORE SHE ENLISTED! I GIVE YOU ENSIGN BIANCA CARLYLE!
I STILL CAN'T BELIEVE THERE'S A *CLUB* ON THE SPARTAN!
THERE'S EVEN A CHURCH IN CASE YOU WANNA GET MARRIED.
FWIP
PTOKK

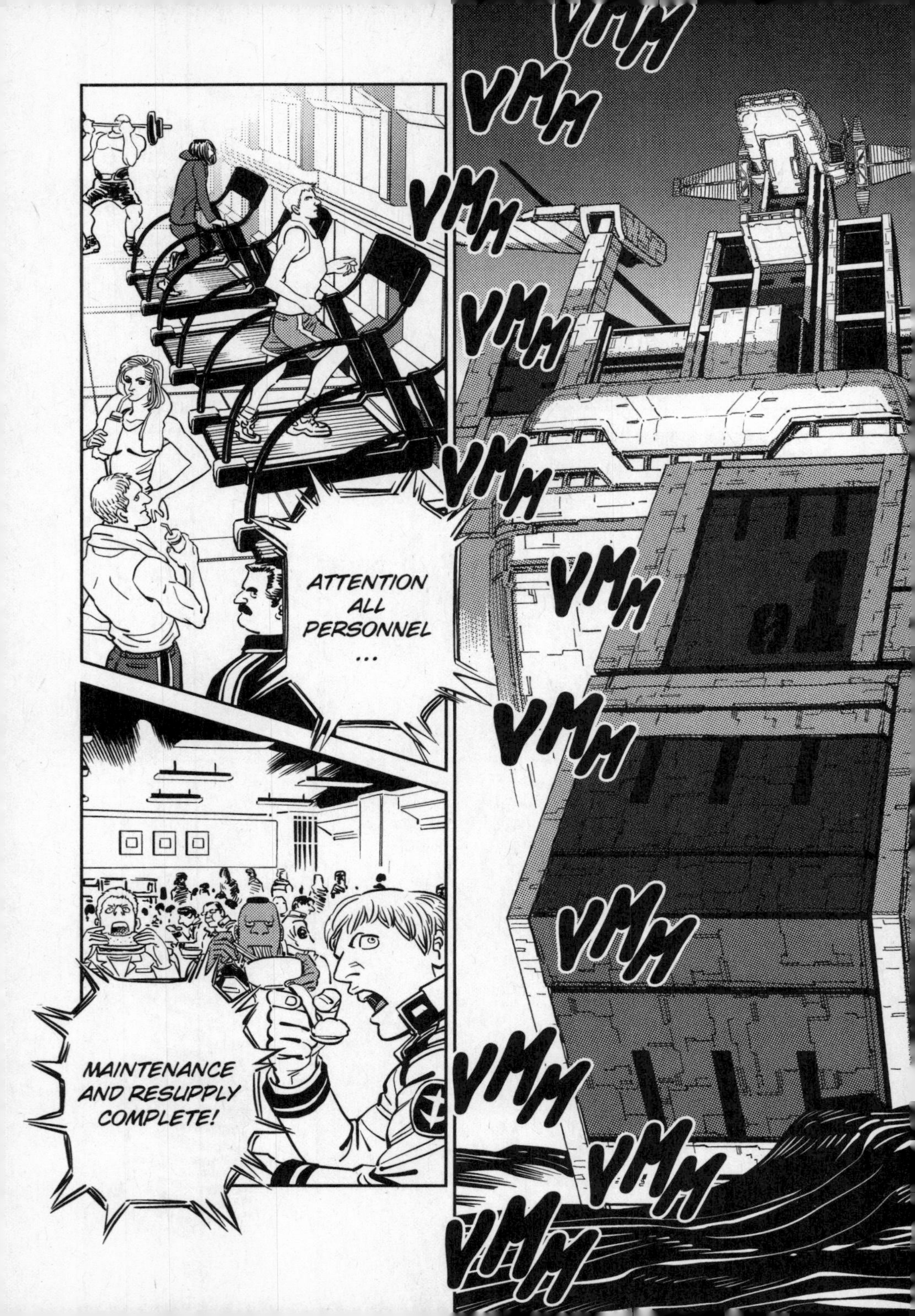

VMM
VMM
VMM
VMM
VMM
VMM
VMM
VMM
VMM
VMM
VMM
ATTENTION ALL PERSONNEL ...
MAINTENANCE AND RESUPPLY COMPLETE!

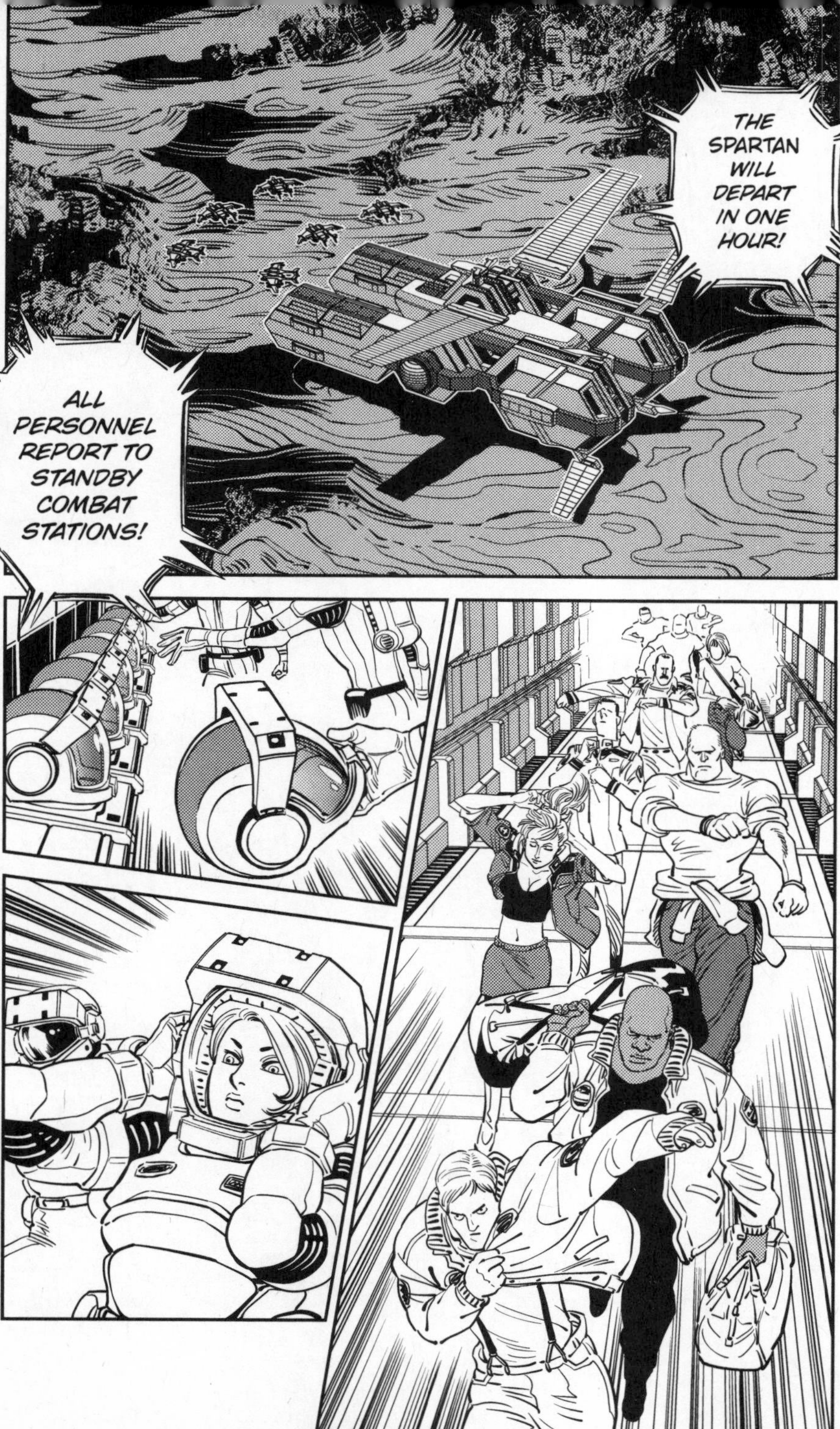
THE SPARTAN WILL DEPART IN ONE HOUR!
ALL PERSONNEL REPORT TO STANDBY COMBAT STATIONS!

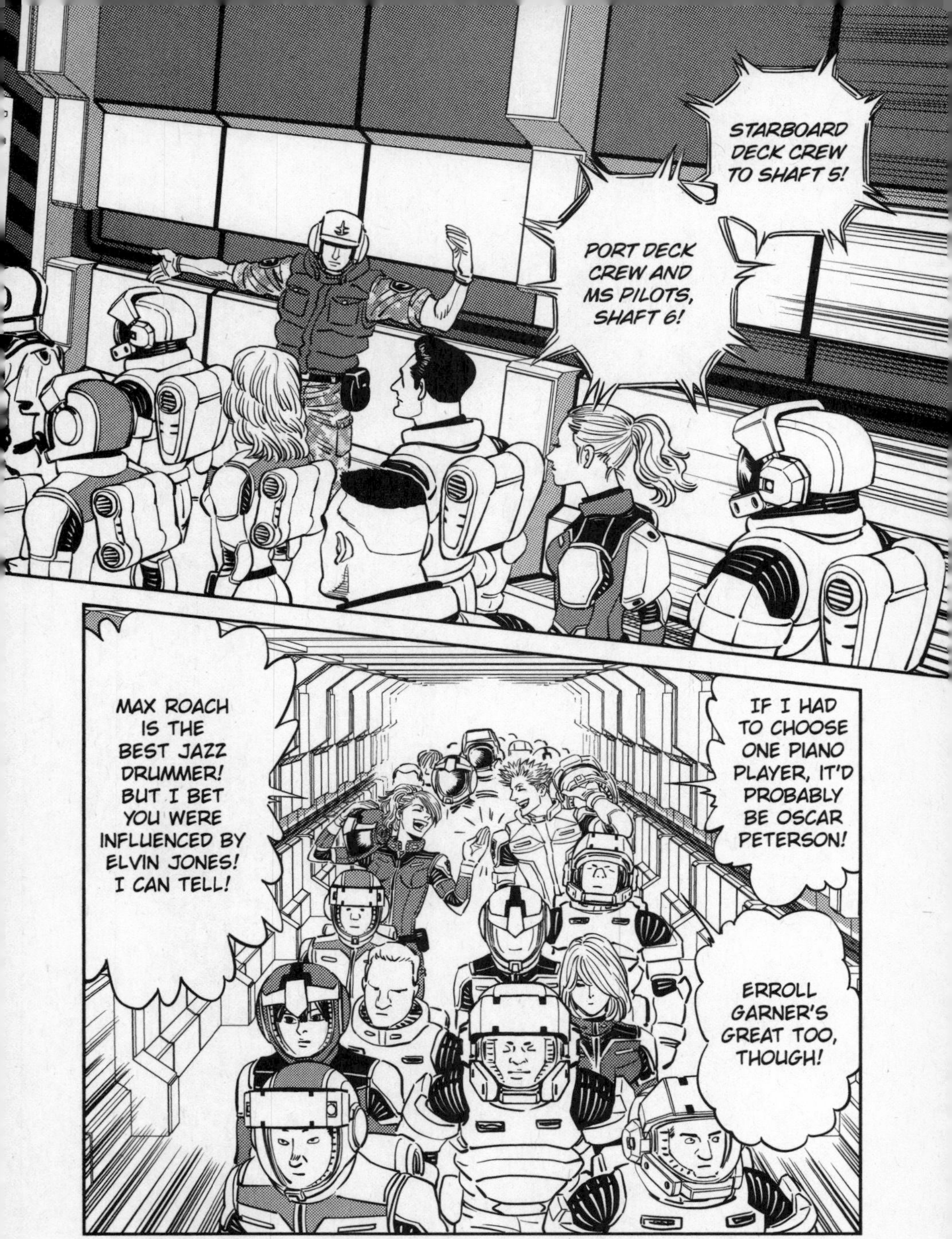
STARBOARD DECK CREW TO SHAFT 5!
PORT DECK CREW AND MS PILOTS, SHAFT 6!
IF I HAD TO CHOOSE ONE PIANO PLAYER, IT'D PROBABLY BE OSCAR PETERSON!
MAX ROACH IS THE BEST JAZZ DRUMMER! BUT I BET YOU WERE INFLUENCED BY ELVIN JONES! I CAN TELL!
ERROLL GARNER'S GREAT TOO, THOUGH!

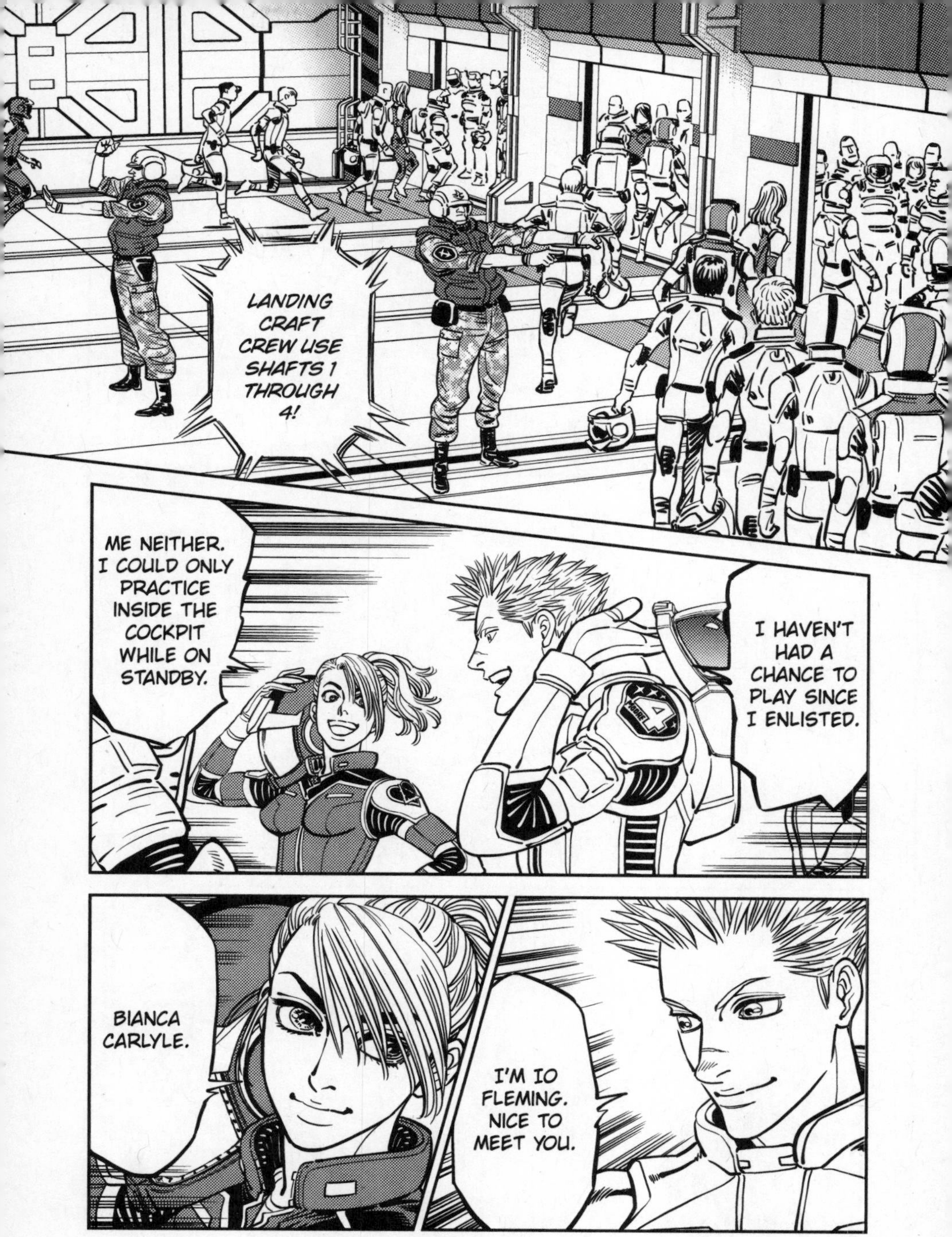
LANDING CRAFT CREW USE SHAFTS 1 THROUGH 4!
I HAVEN'T HAD A CHANCE TO PLAY SINCE I ENLISTED.
ME NEITHER. I COULD ONLY PRACTICE INSIDE THE COCKPIT WHILE ON STANDBY.
I'M IO FLEMING. NICE TO MEET YOU.
BIANCA CARLYLE.

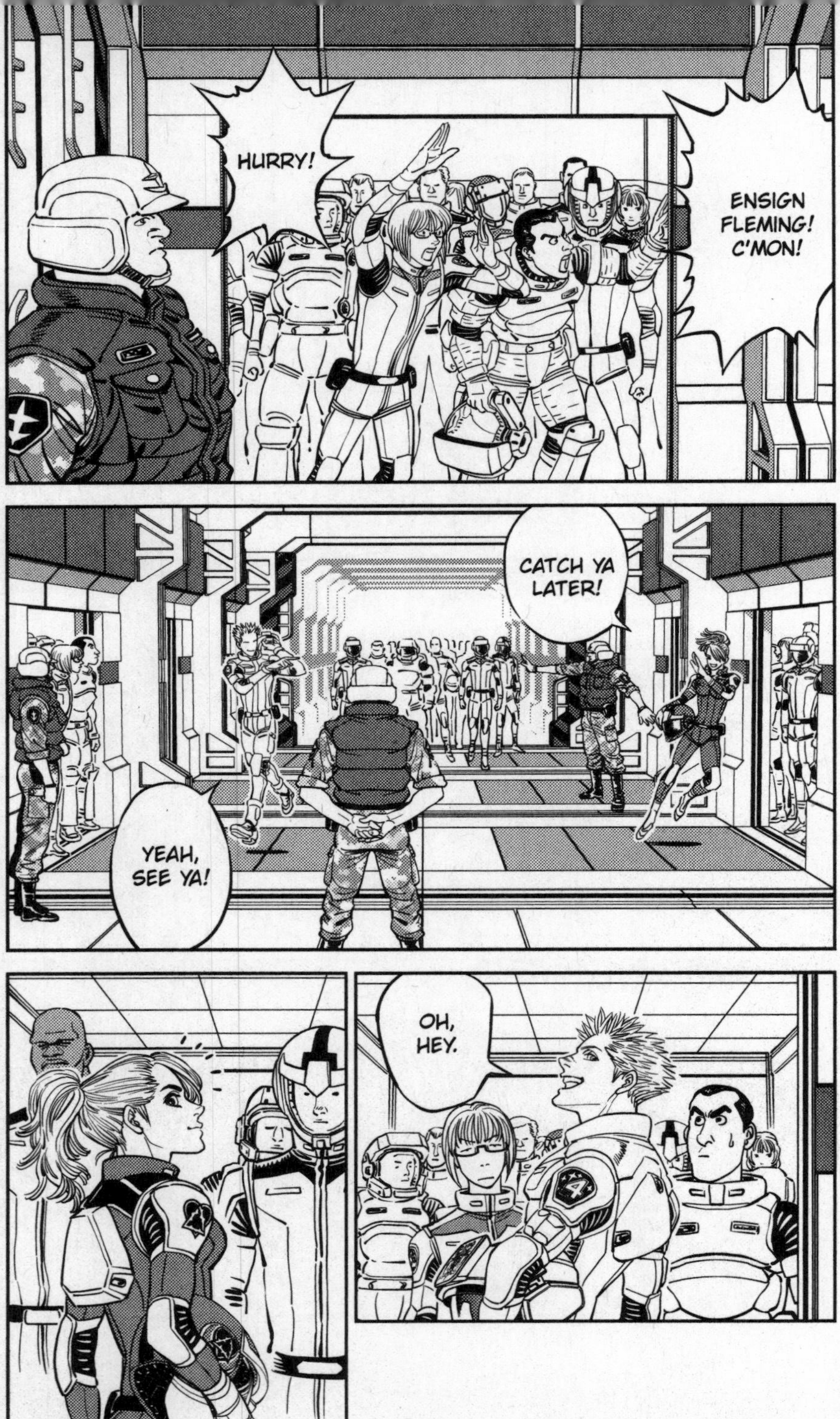
ENSIGN FLEMING! C'MON!
HURRY!
CATCH YA LATER!
YEAH, SEE YA!
OH, HEY.

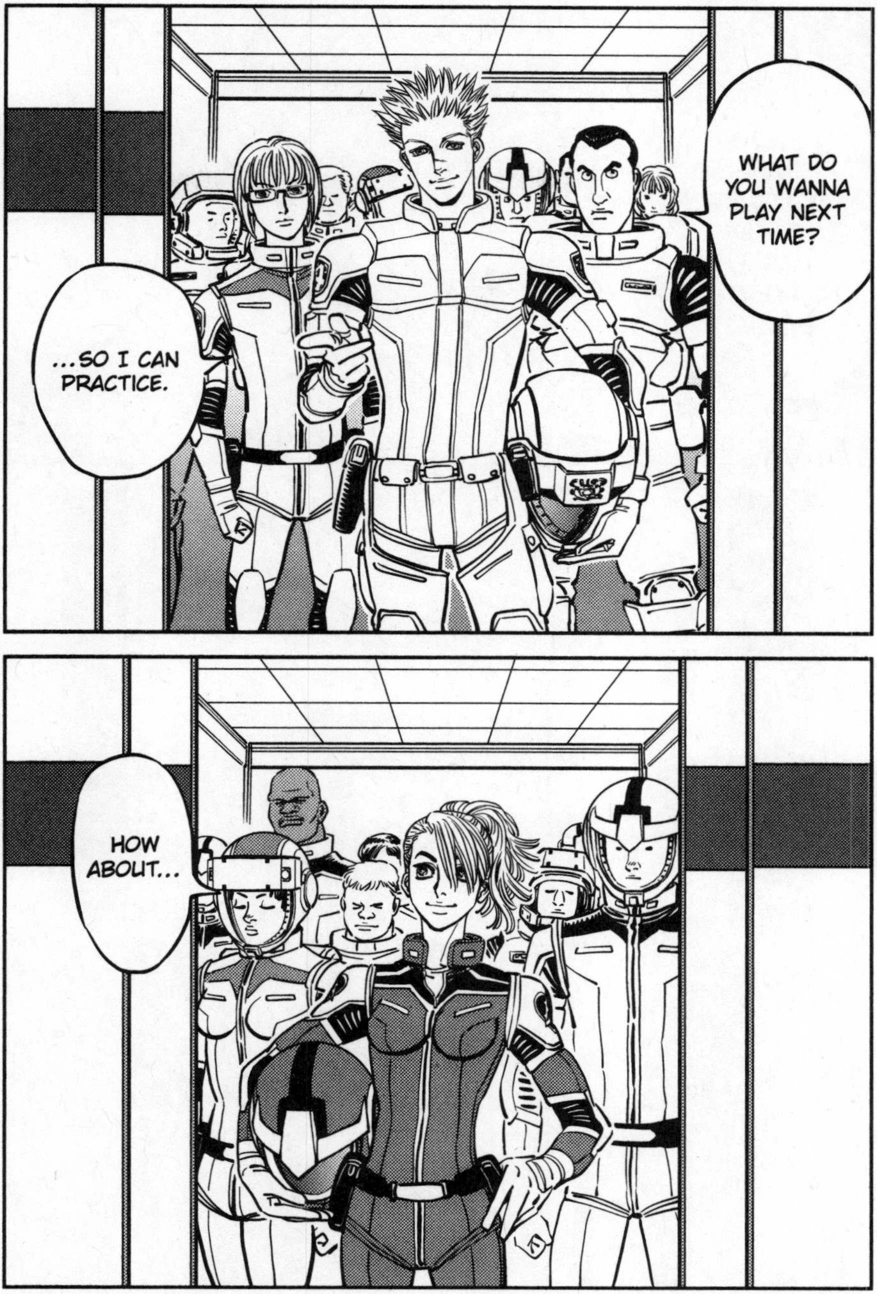
WHAT DO YOU WANNA PLAY NEXT TIME?
...SO I CAN PRACTICE.
HOW ABOUT...

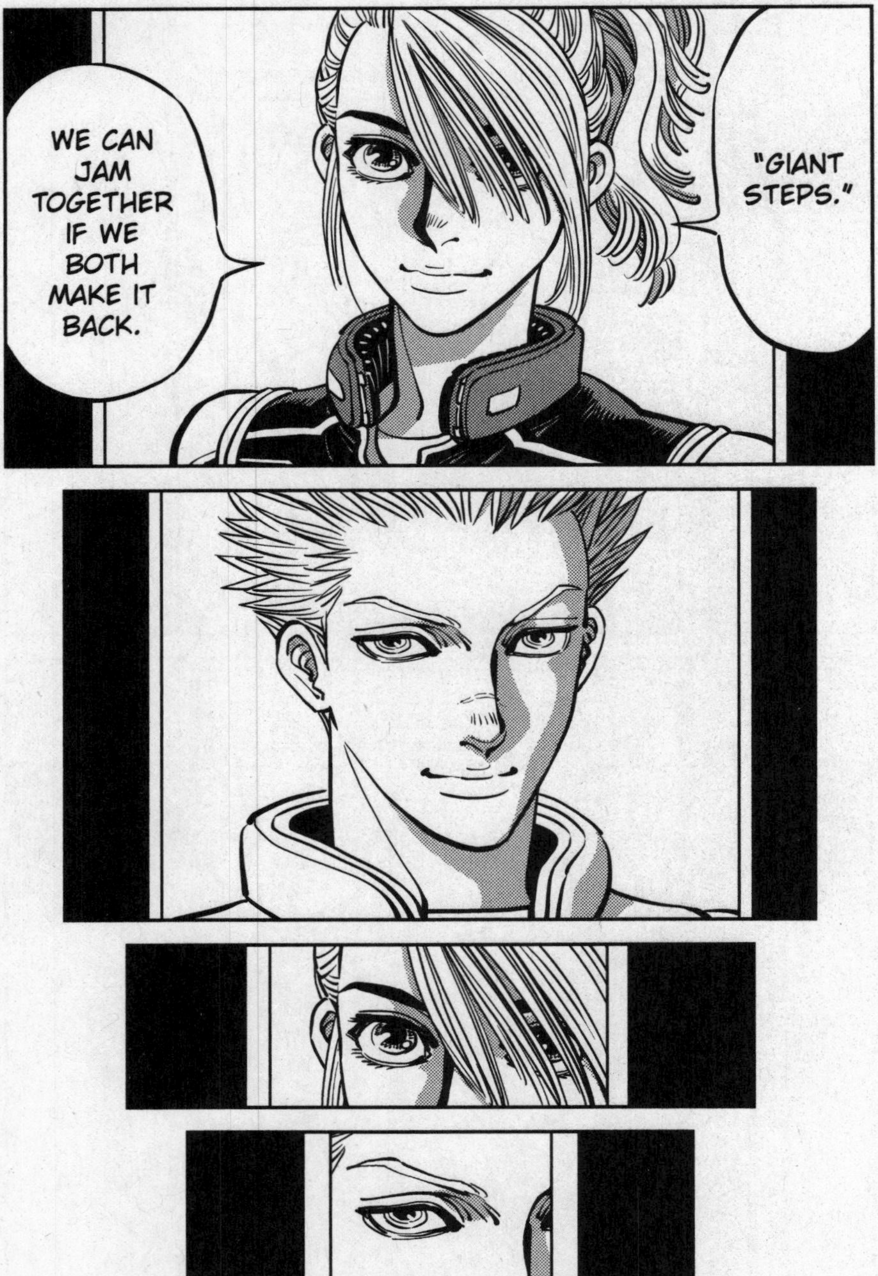
"GIANT STEPS."
WE CAN JAM TOGETHER IF WE BOTH MAKE IT BACK.

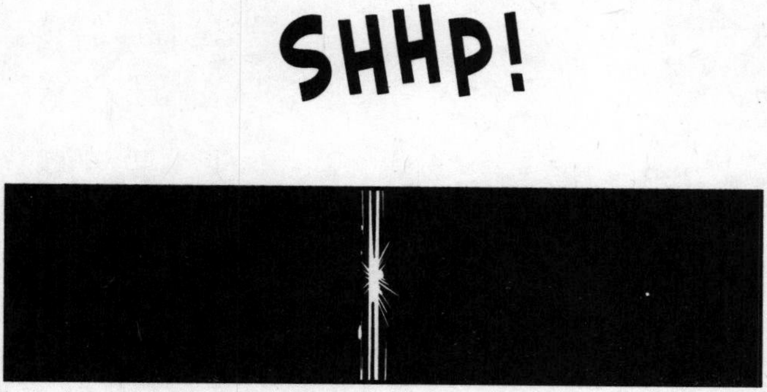
SHHP!

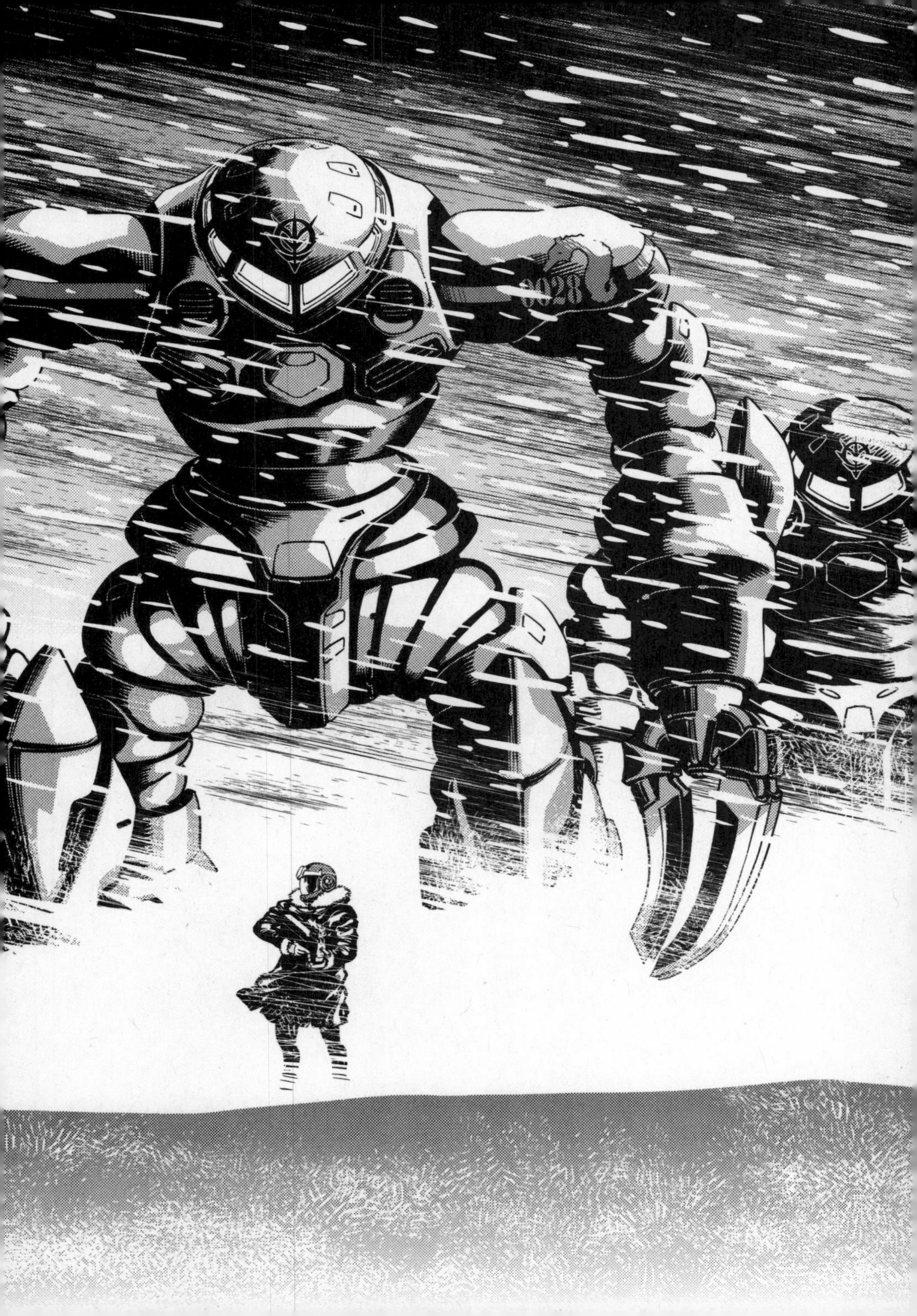
0028

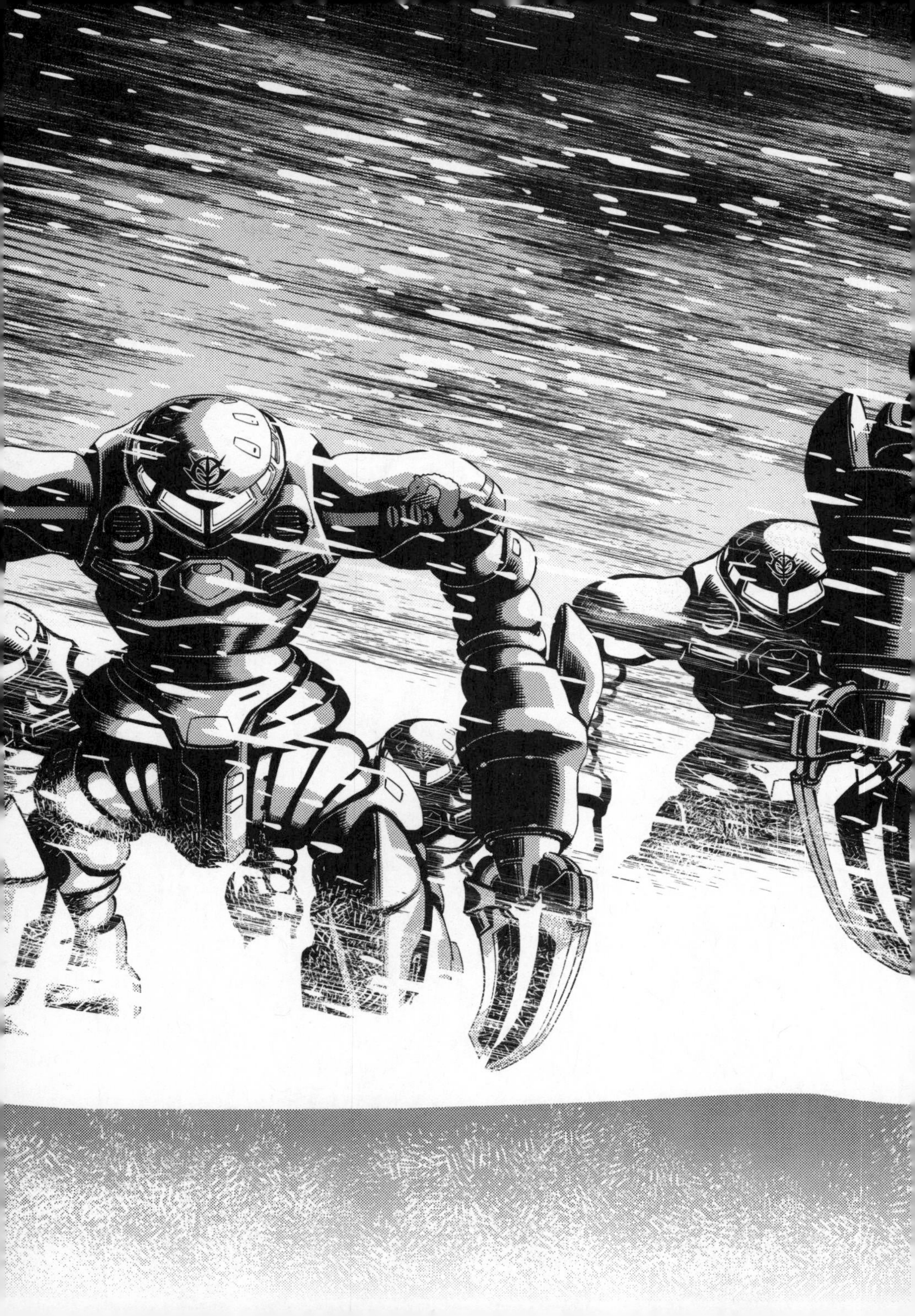
0105

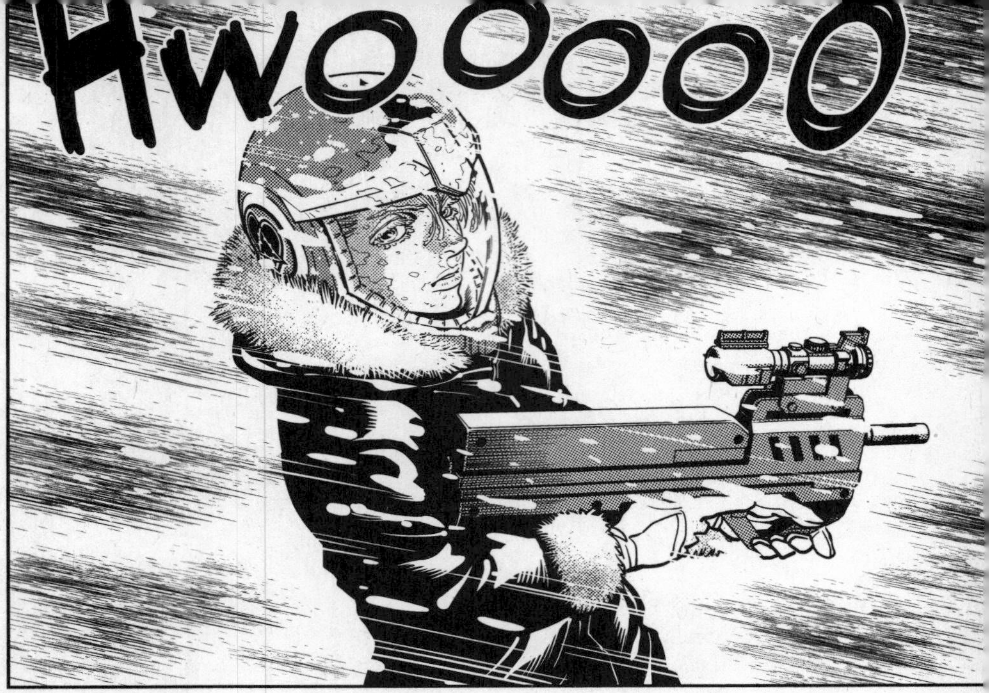
HWOOOOO

The present

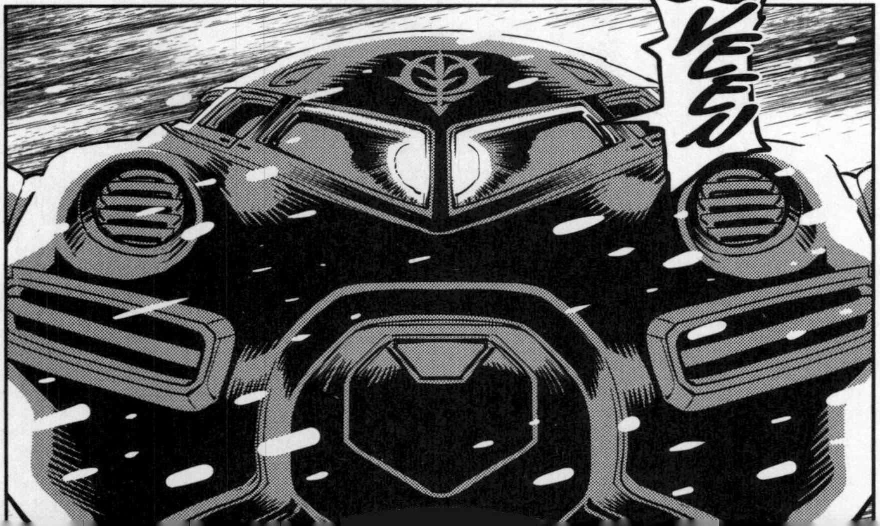
VEEN

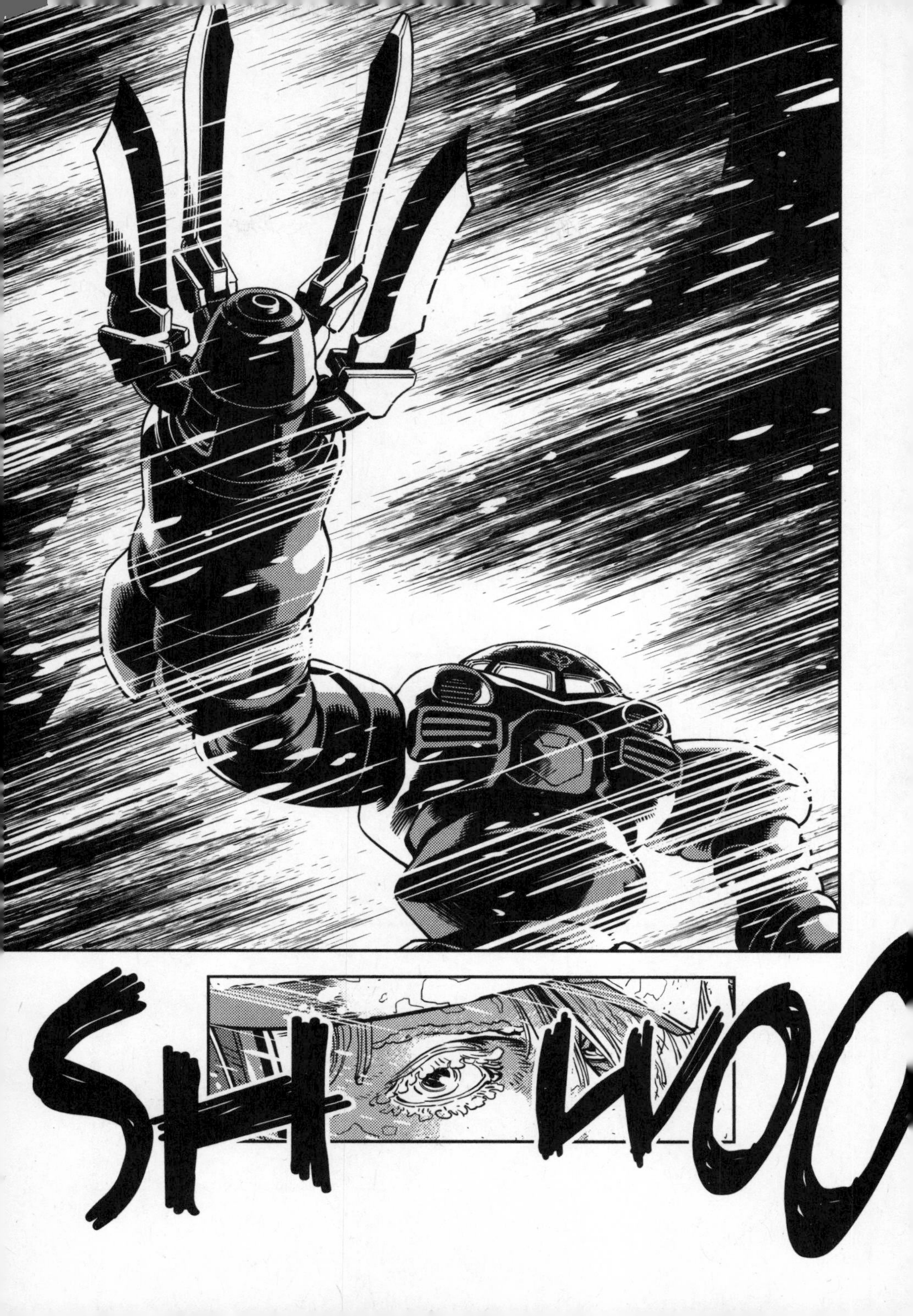
SHWOO

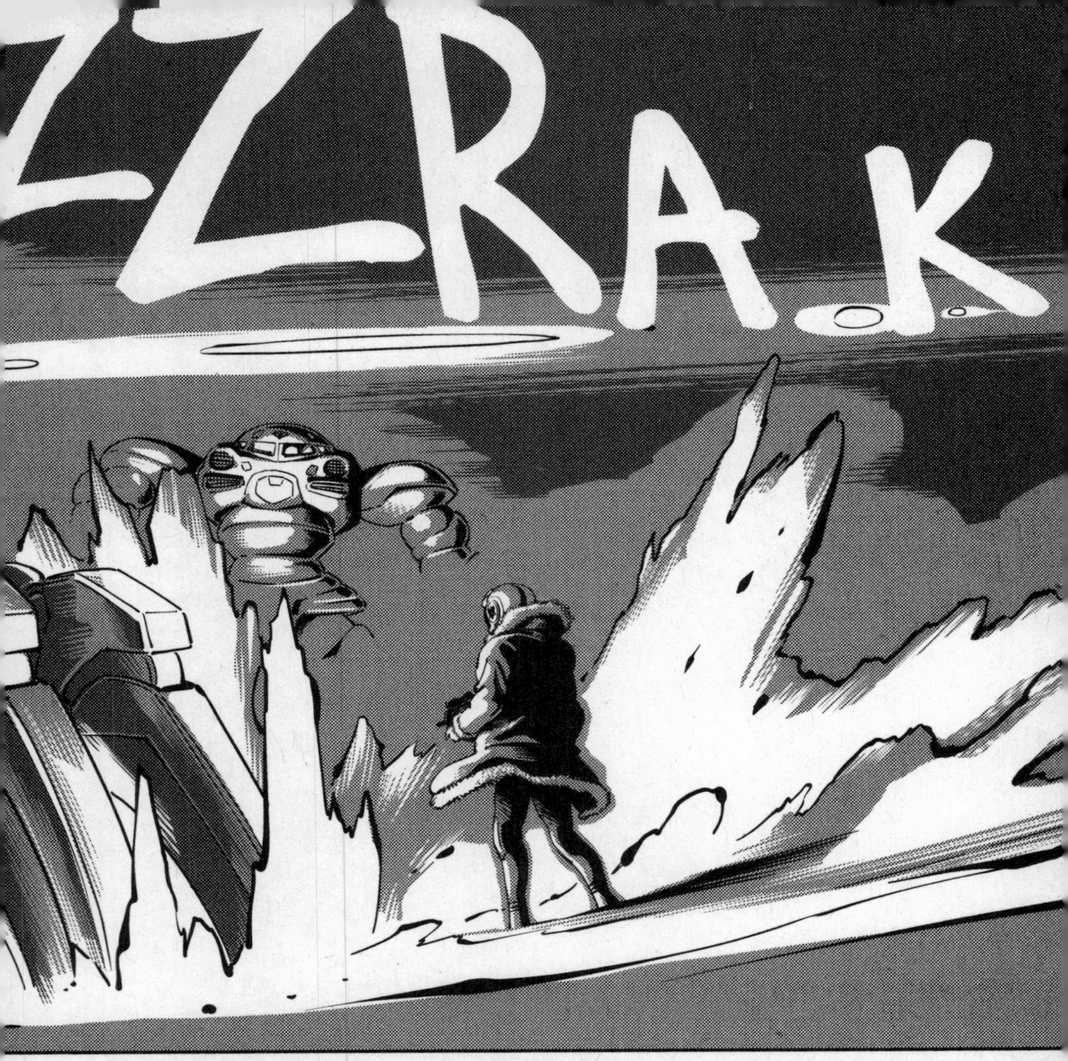
ZZRAK
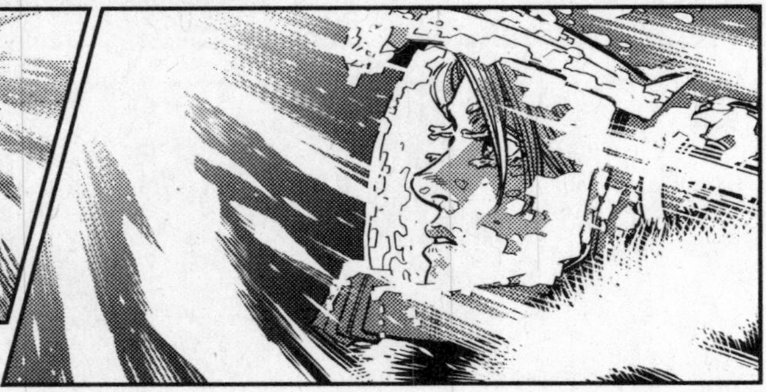
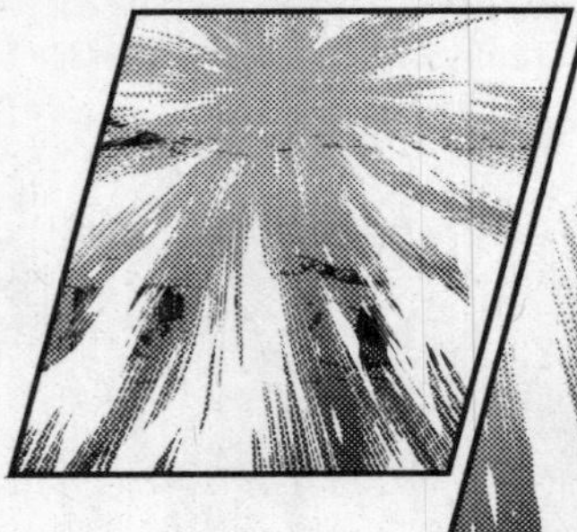

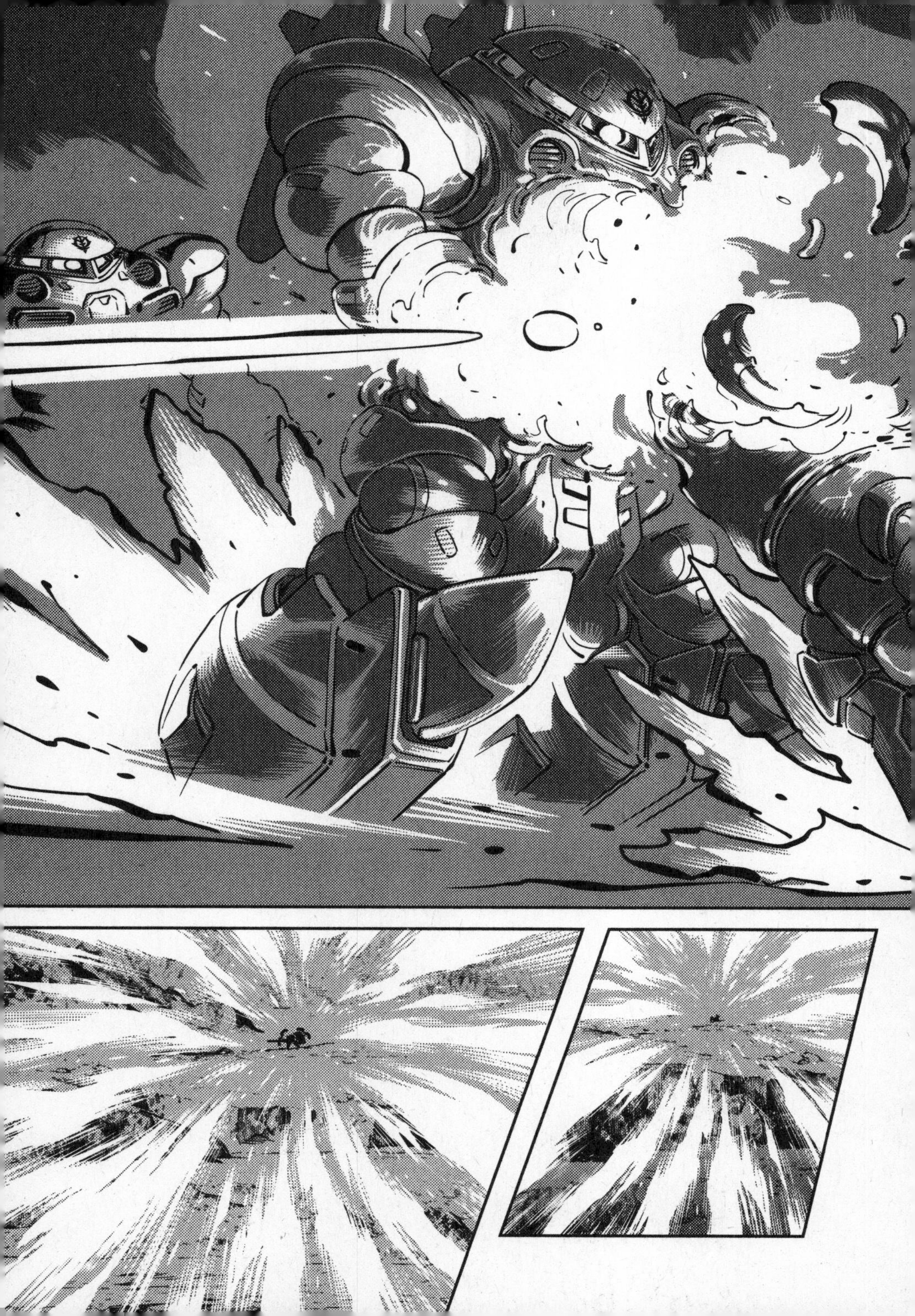

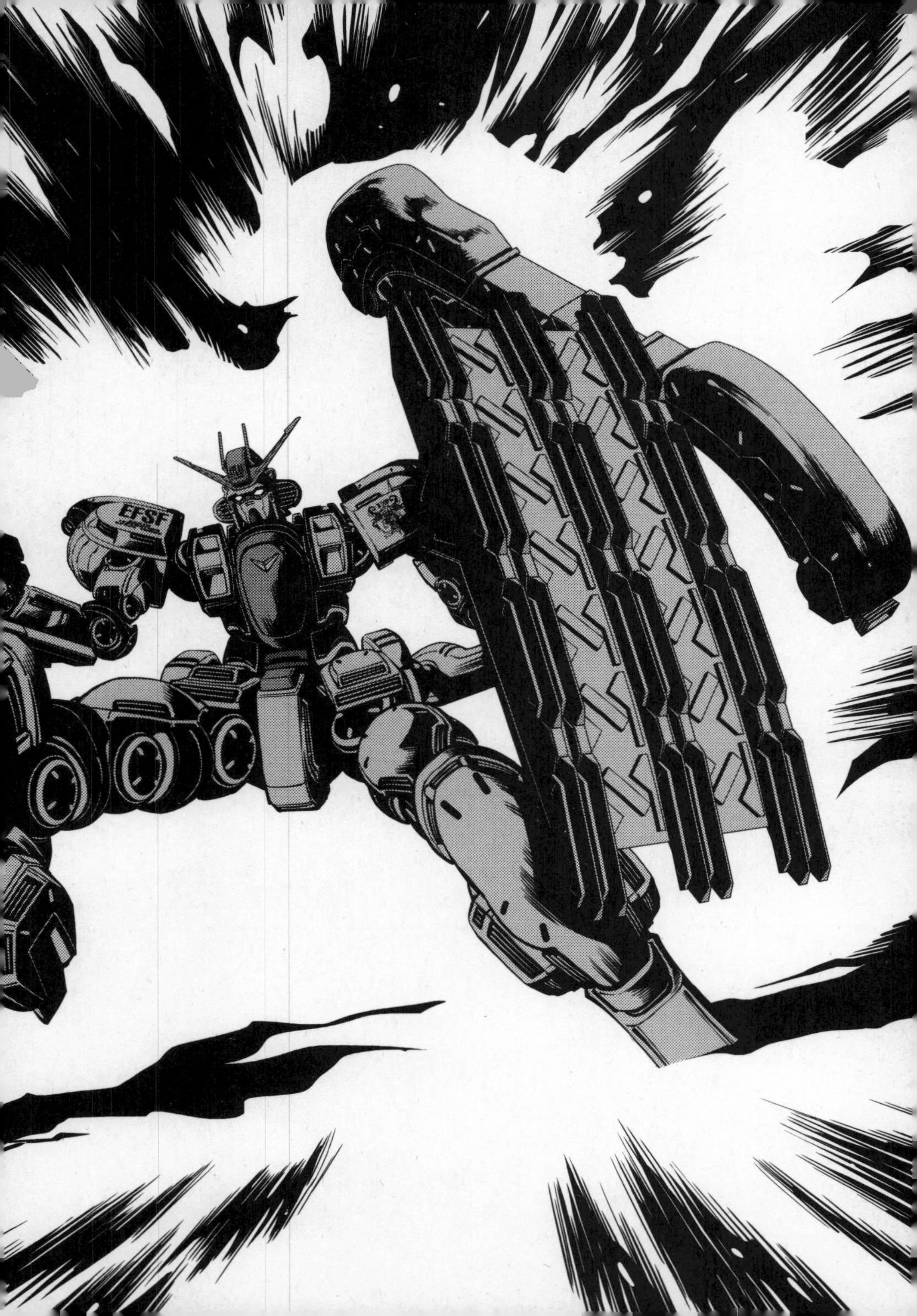
EFSF

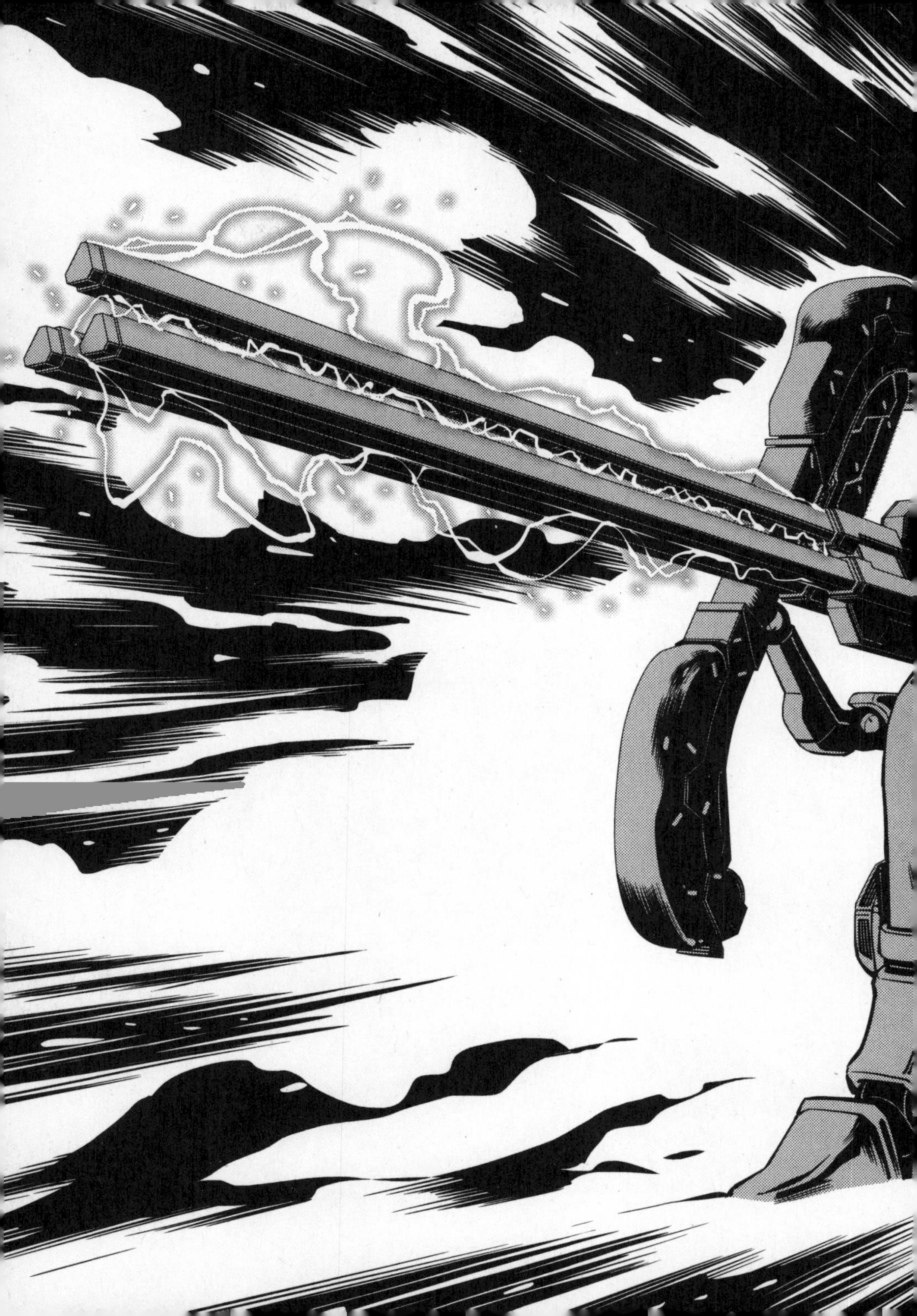

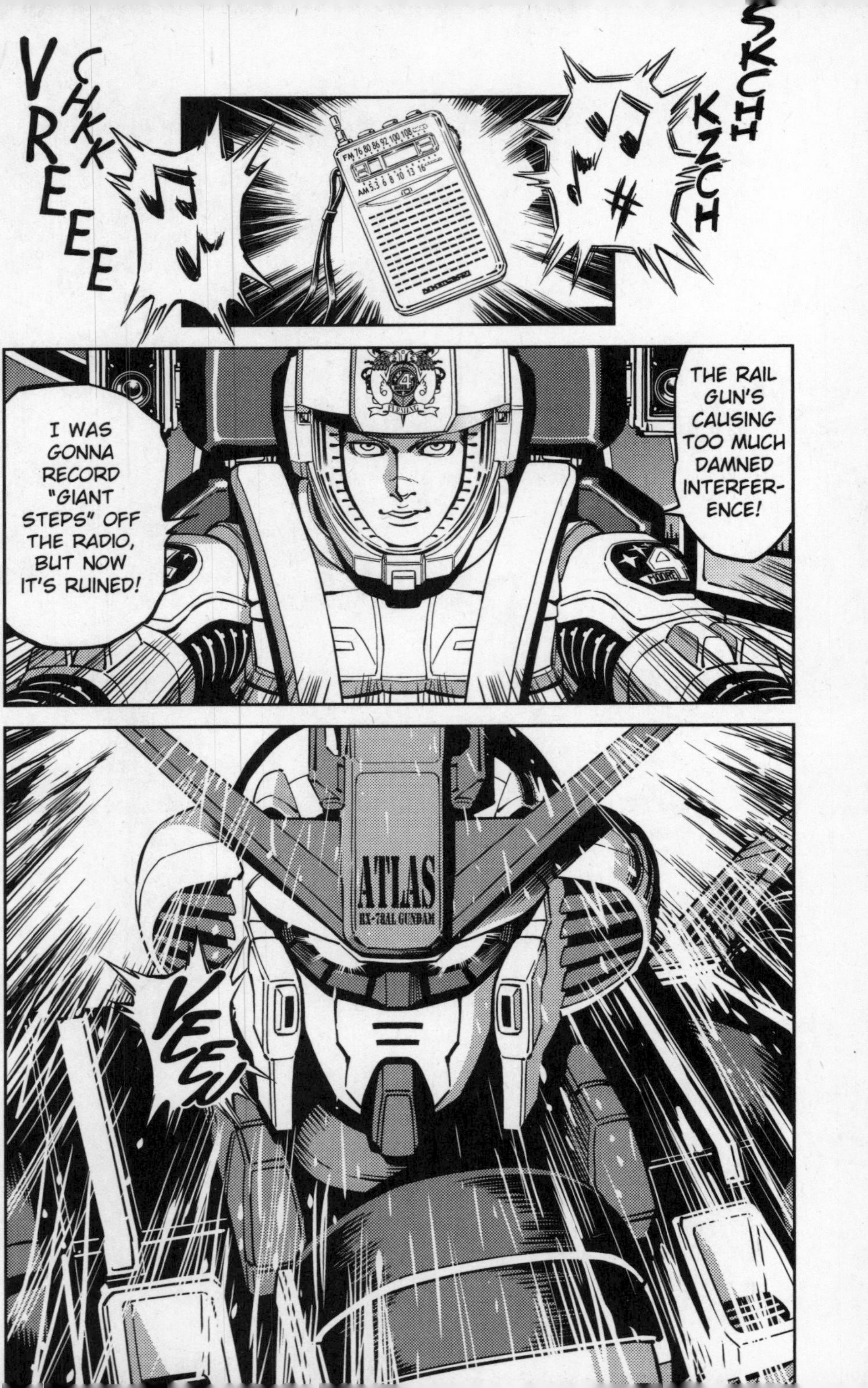
SKCHH
KZCH
FM 76 80 86 92 100 108
AM 5.3 6 8 10 13 16
CHKK
VREEEE
THE RAIL GUN'S CAUSING TOO MUCH DAMNED INTERFERENCE!
I WAS GONNA RECORD "GIANT STEPS" OFF THE RADIO, BUT NOW IT'S RUINED!
ATLAS
RX-78AL GUNDAM
VEEW

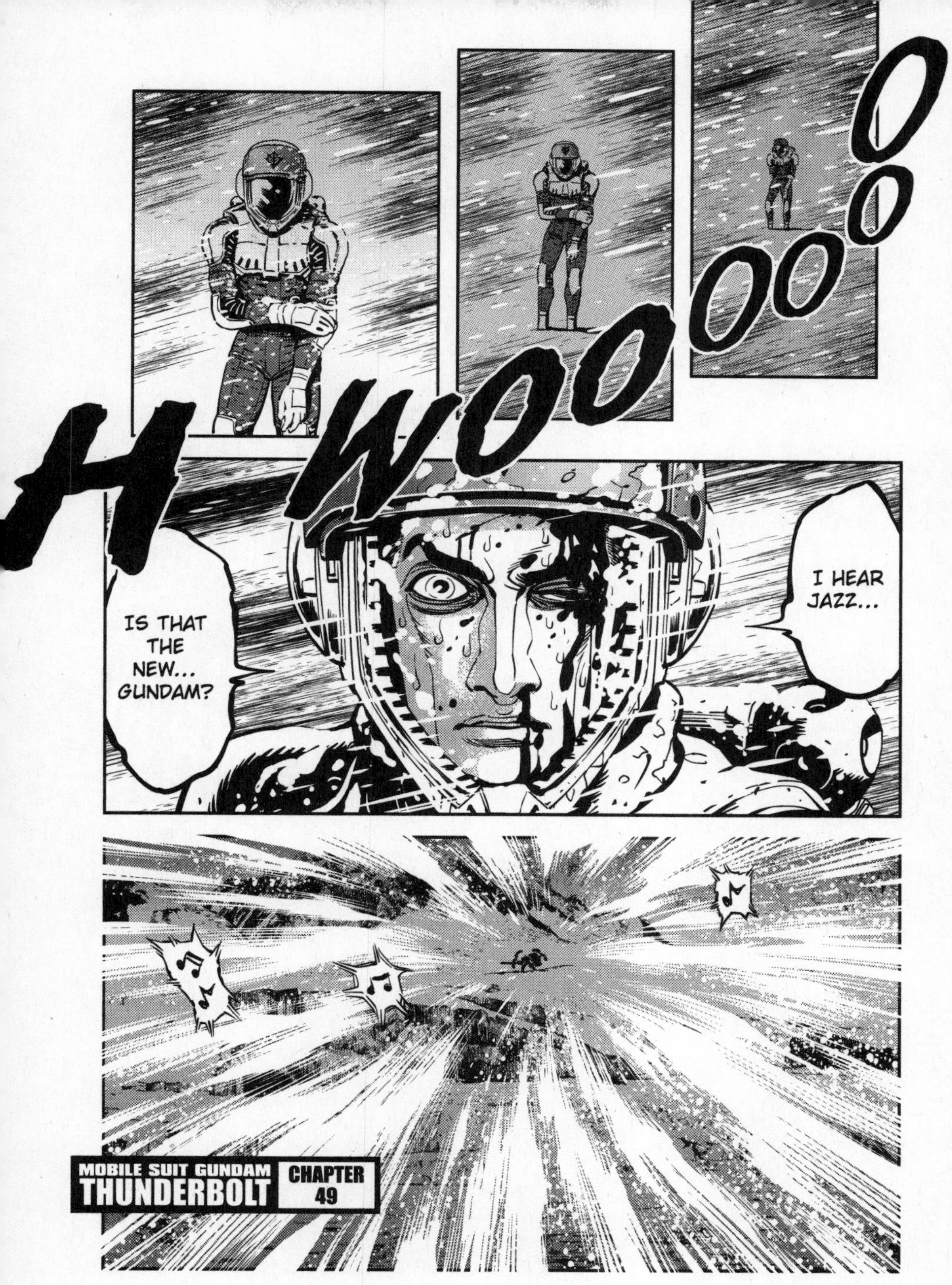
HWOOOOOOOOO
I HEAR JAZZ...
IS THAT THE NEW... GUNDAM?
MOBILE SUIT GUNDAM THUNDERBOLT
CHAPTER 49

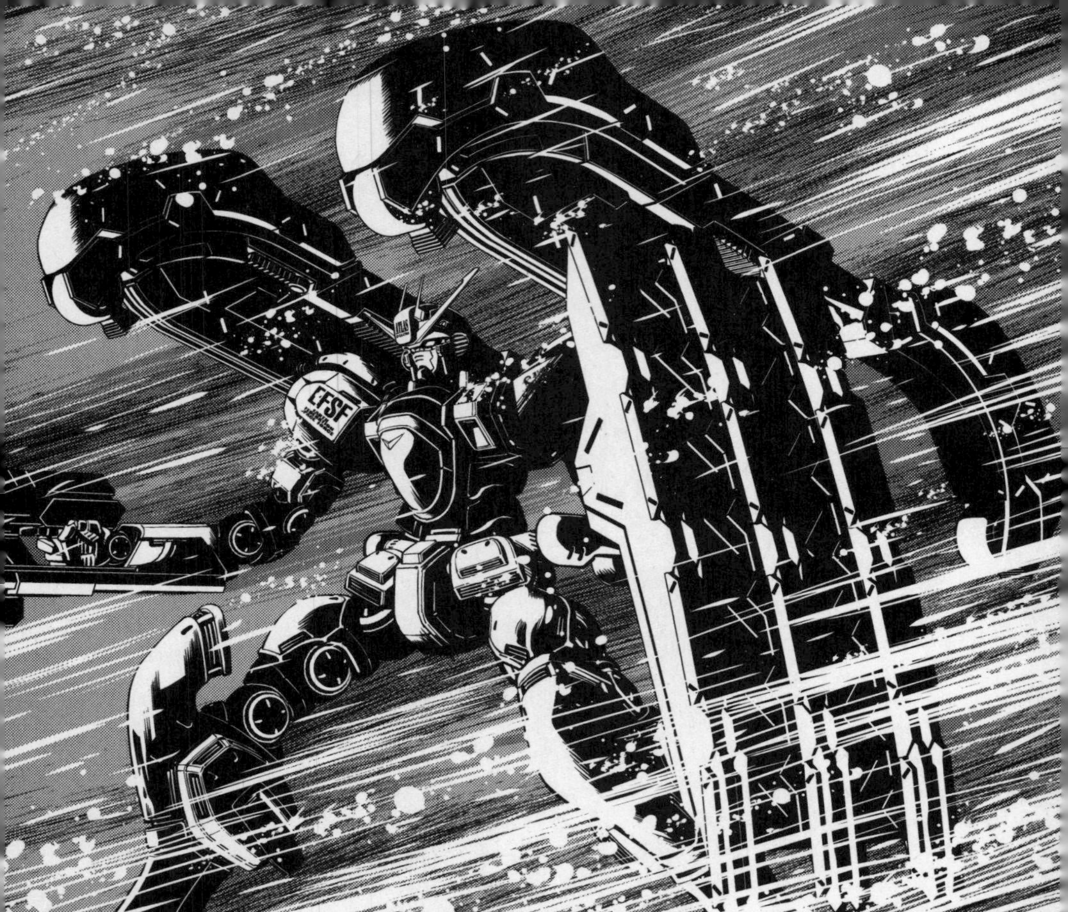
EFSF

MOBILE SUIT GUNDAM
THUNDERBOLT

CHAPTER
49

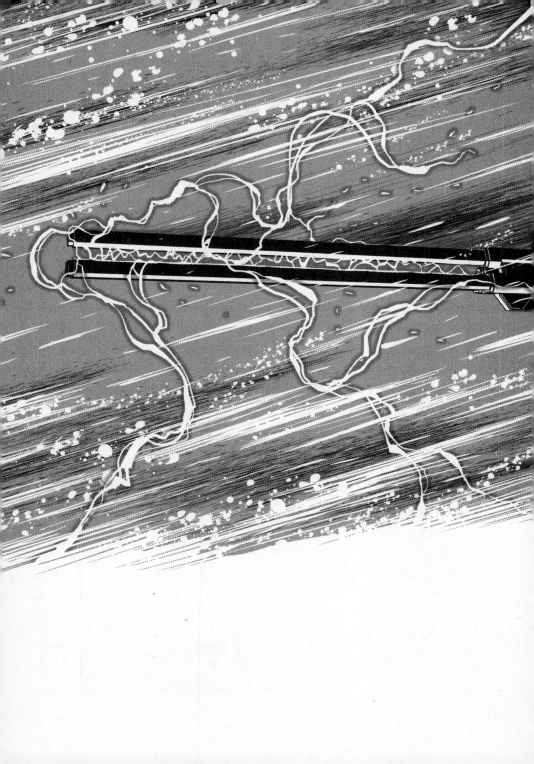

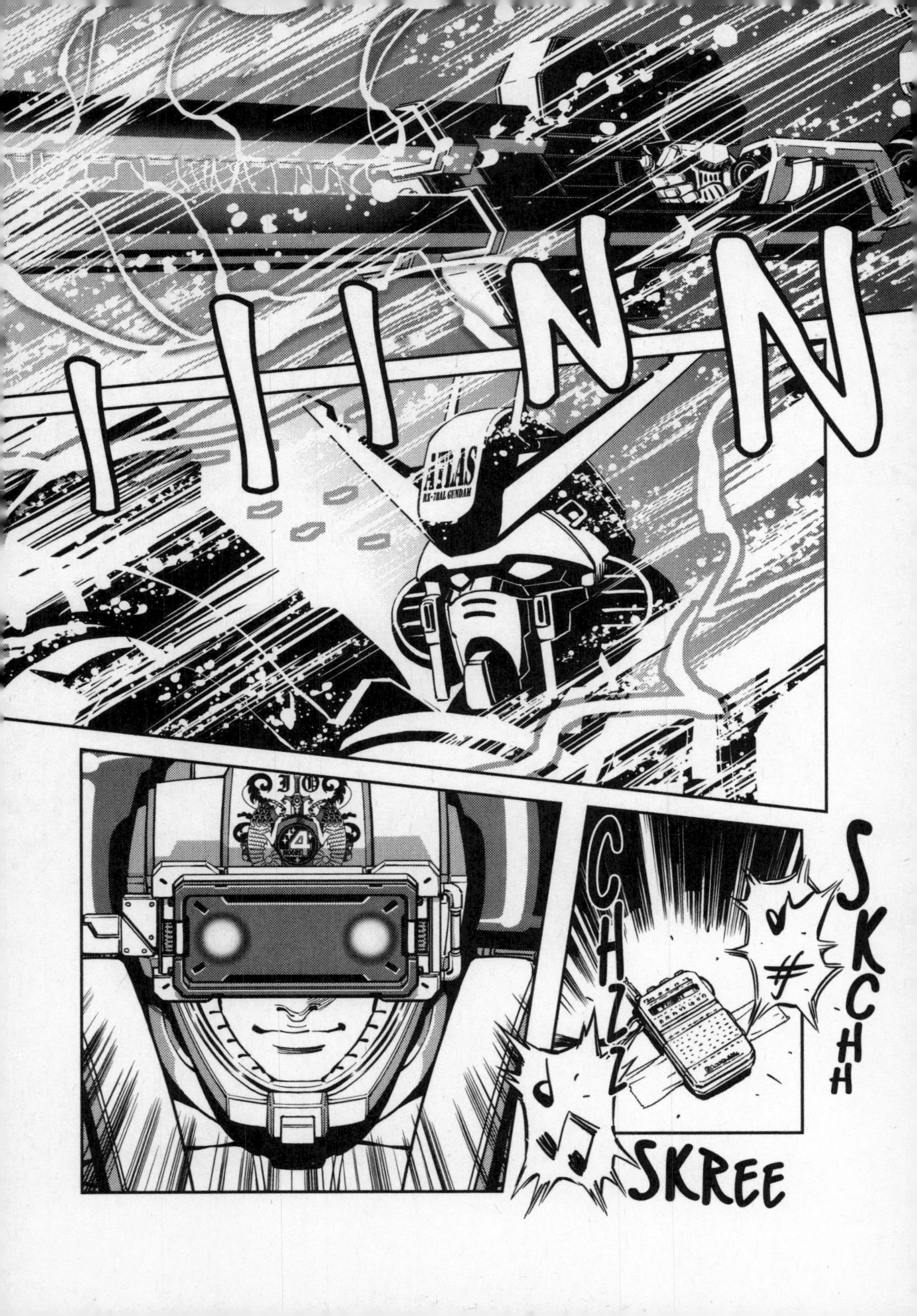
IIINN
ATLAS
RX-78AL GUNDAM
SKCHH
CHZZZ
SKREE

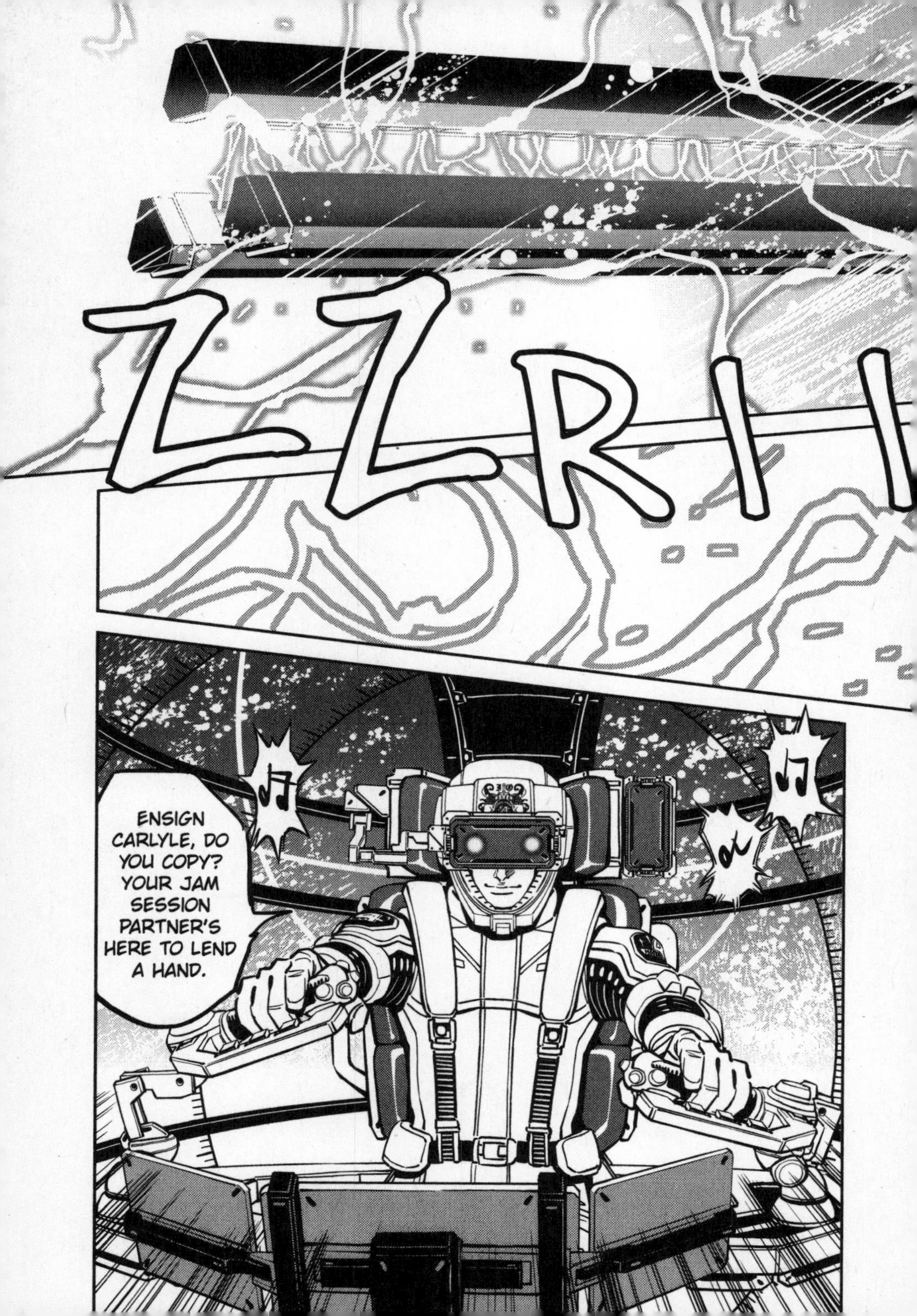
ZZRII
ENSIGN CARLYLE, DO YOU COPY? YOUR JAM SESSION PARTNER'S HERE TO LEND A HAND.

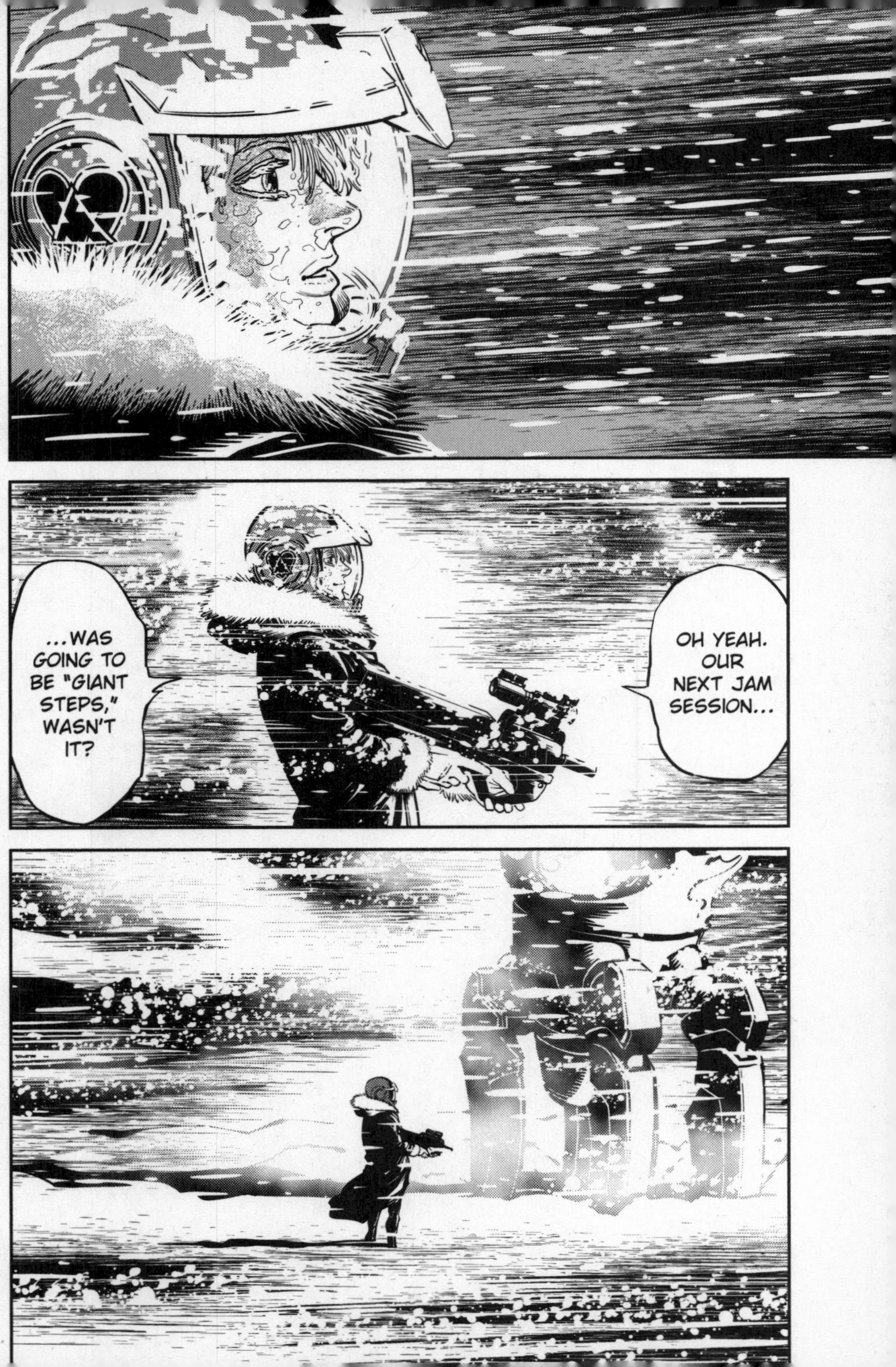
OH YEAH. OUR NEXT JAM SESSION...
...WAS GOING TO BE "GIANT STEPS," WASN'T IT?

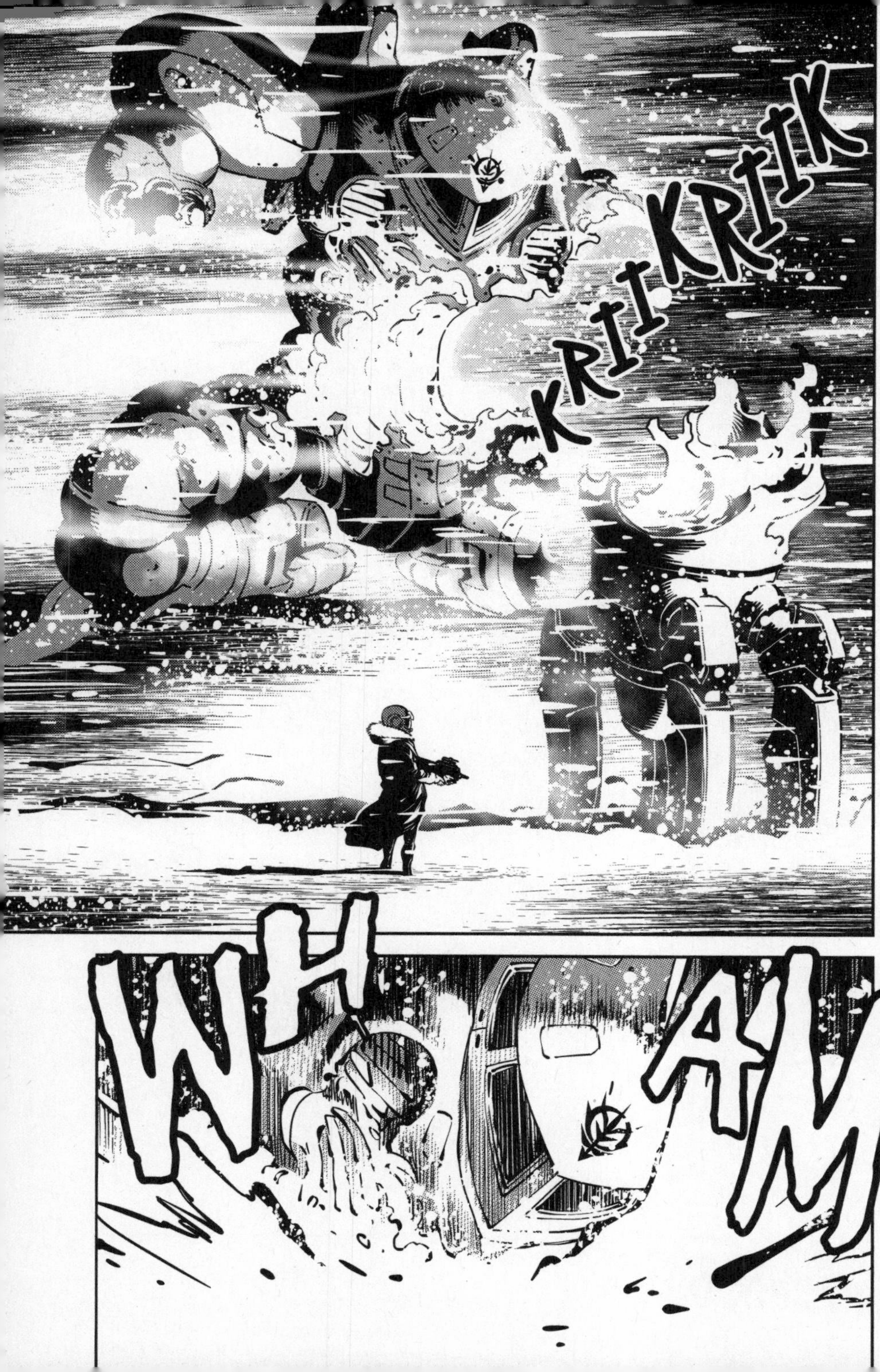
KRIIKRIIKRIIK
WHAM

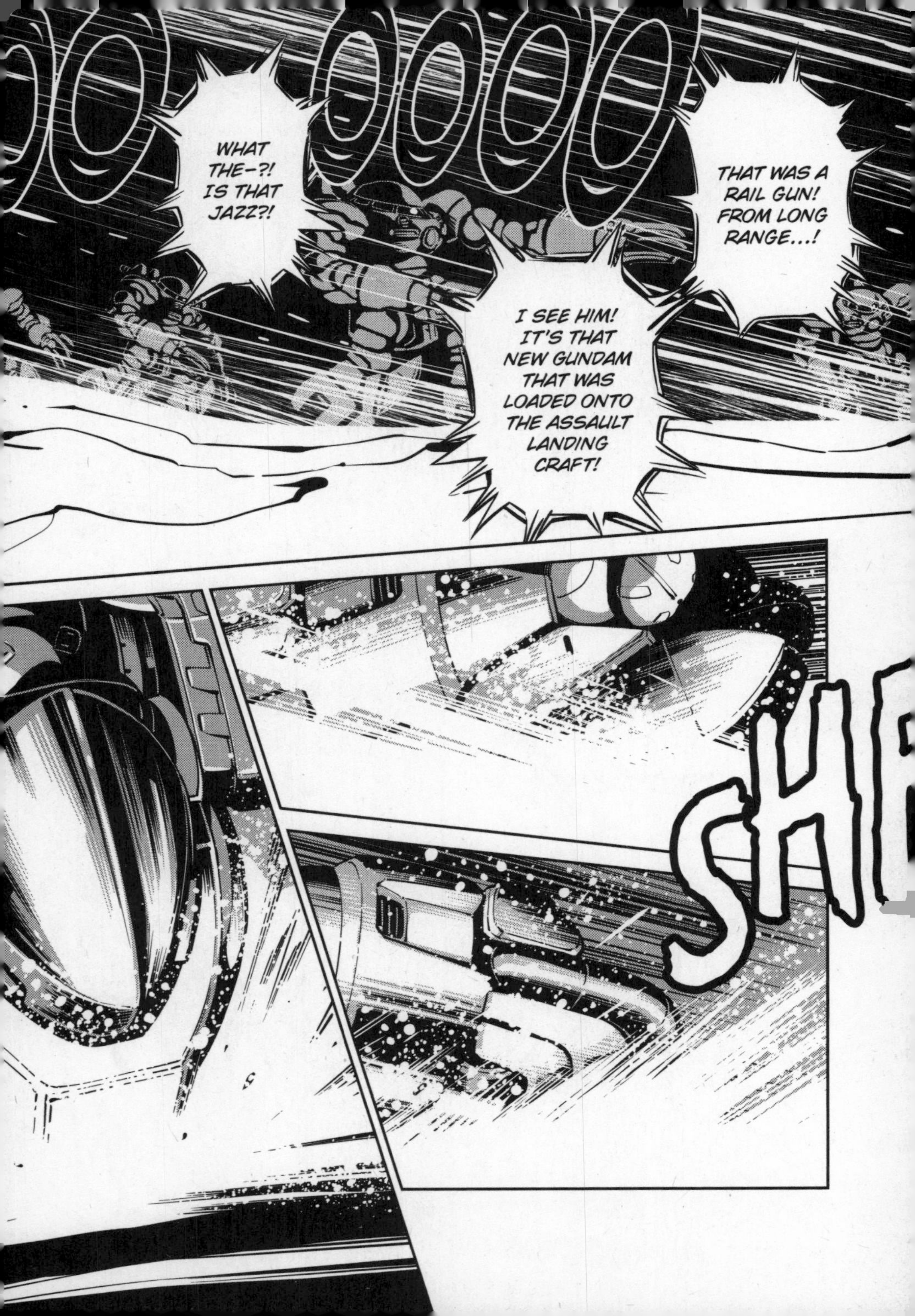
THAT WAS A RAIL GUN! FROM LONG RANGE...!
WHAT THE-?! IS THAT JAZZ?!
I SEE HIM! IT'S THAT NEW GUNDAM THAT WAS LOADED ONTO THE ASSAULT LANDING CRAFT!
SH

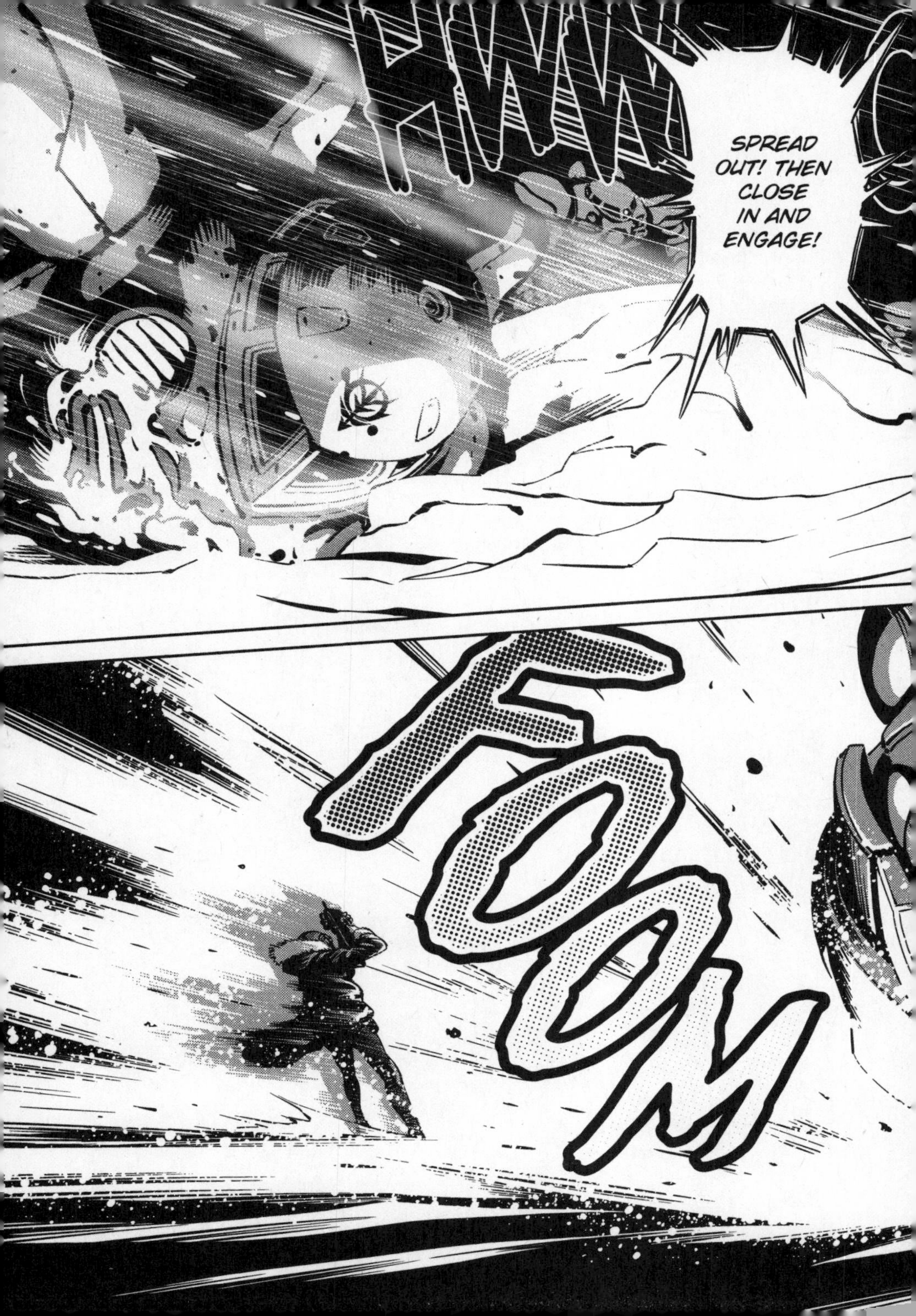
SPREAD OUT! THEN CLOSE IN AND ENGAGE!
FOOM

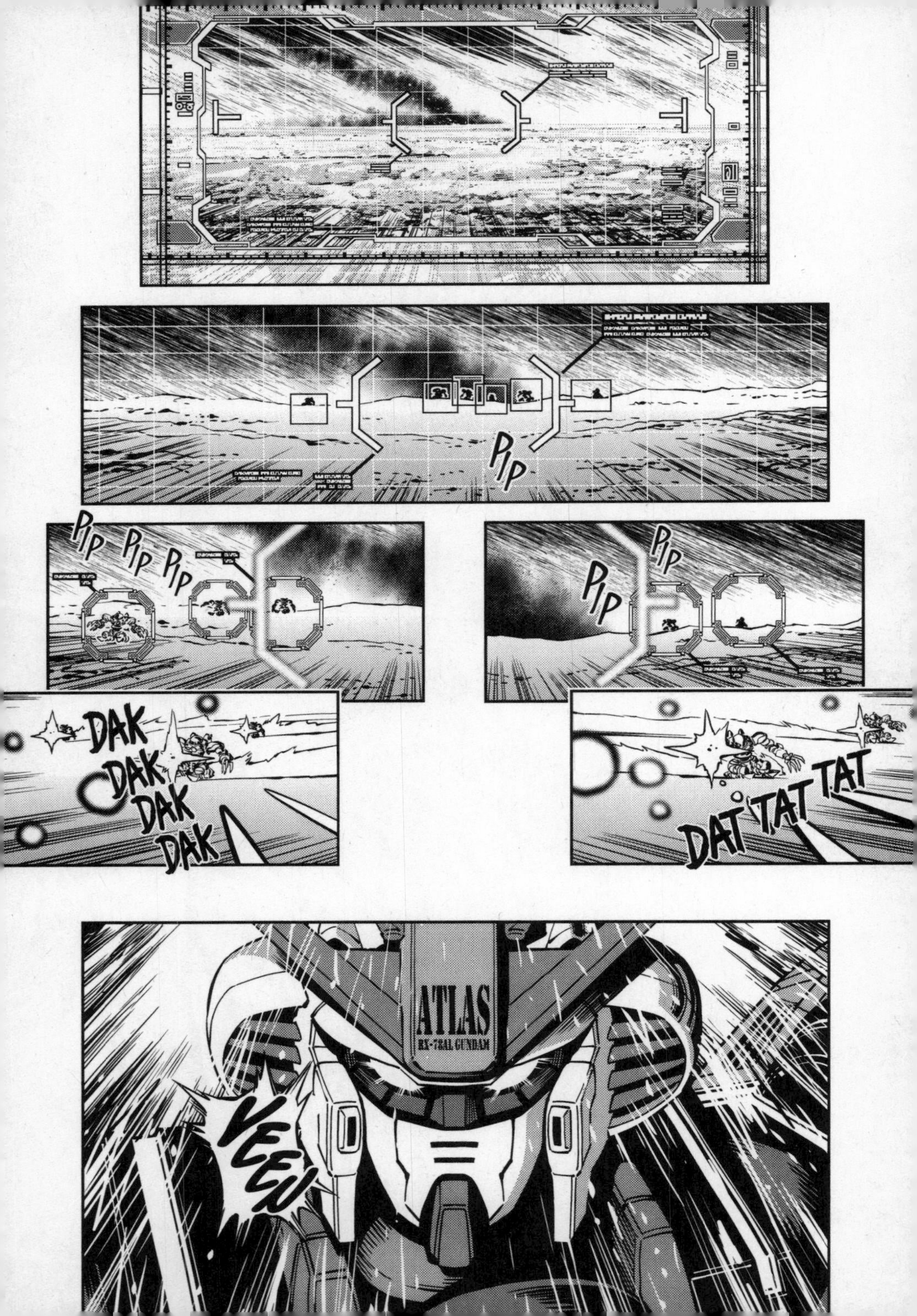
PIP
PIP PIP
PIP PIP PIP
DAT TAT TAT
DAK DAK DAK DAK
ATLAS
RX-78AL GUNDAM
VEEN

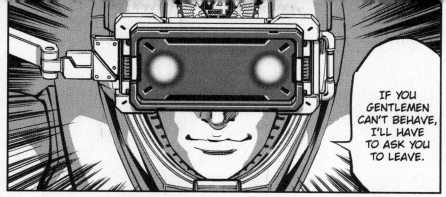

IF YOU GENTLEMEN CAN'T BEHAVE, I'LL HAVE TO ASK YOU TO LEAVE.

ZZRIIIN

KTNG

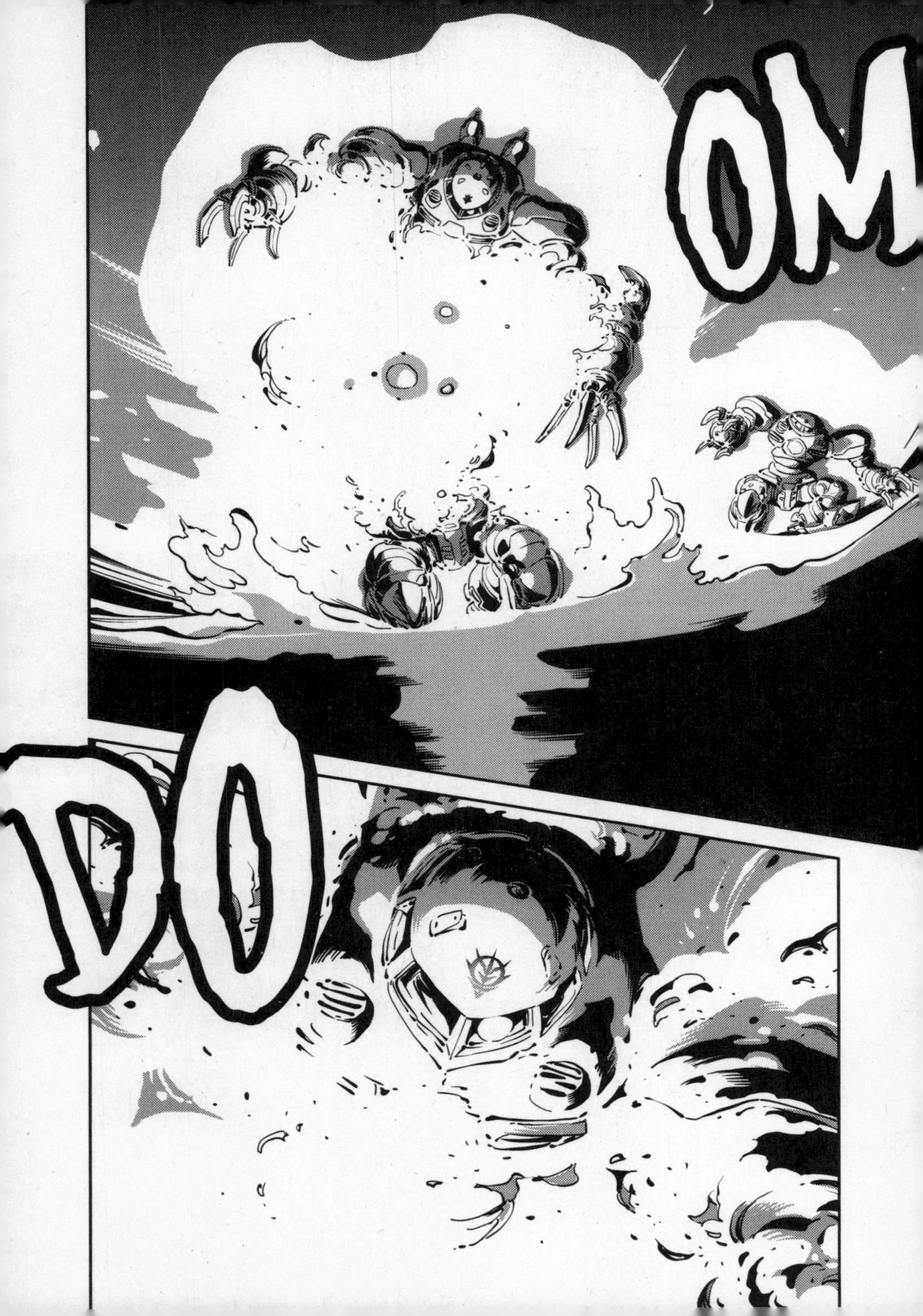
OM
DO

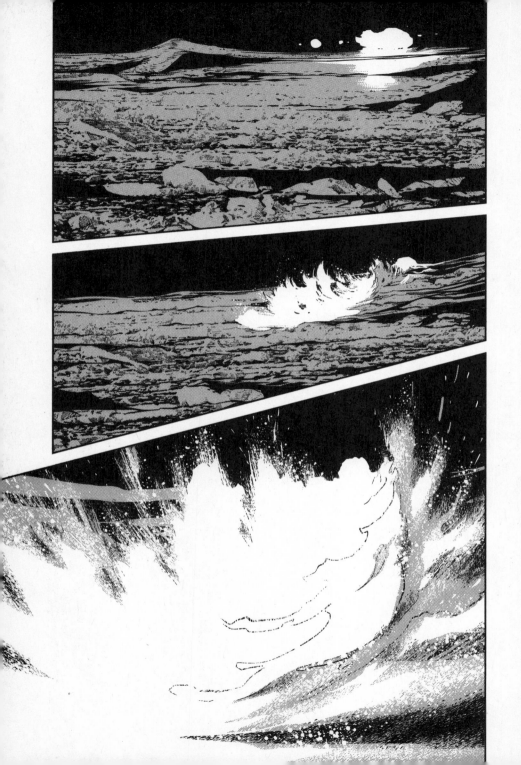

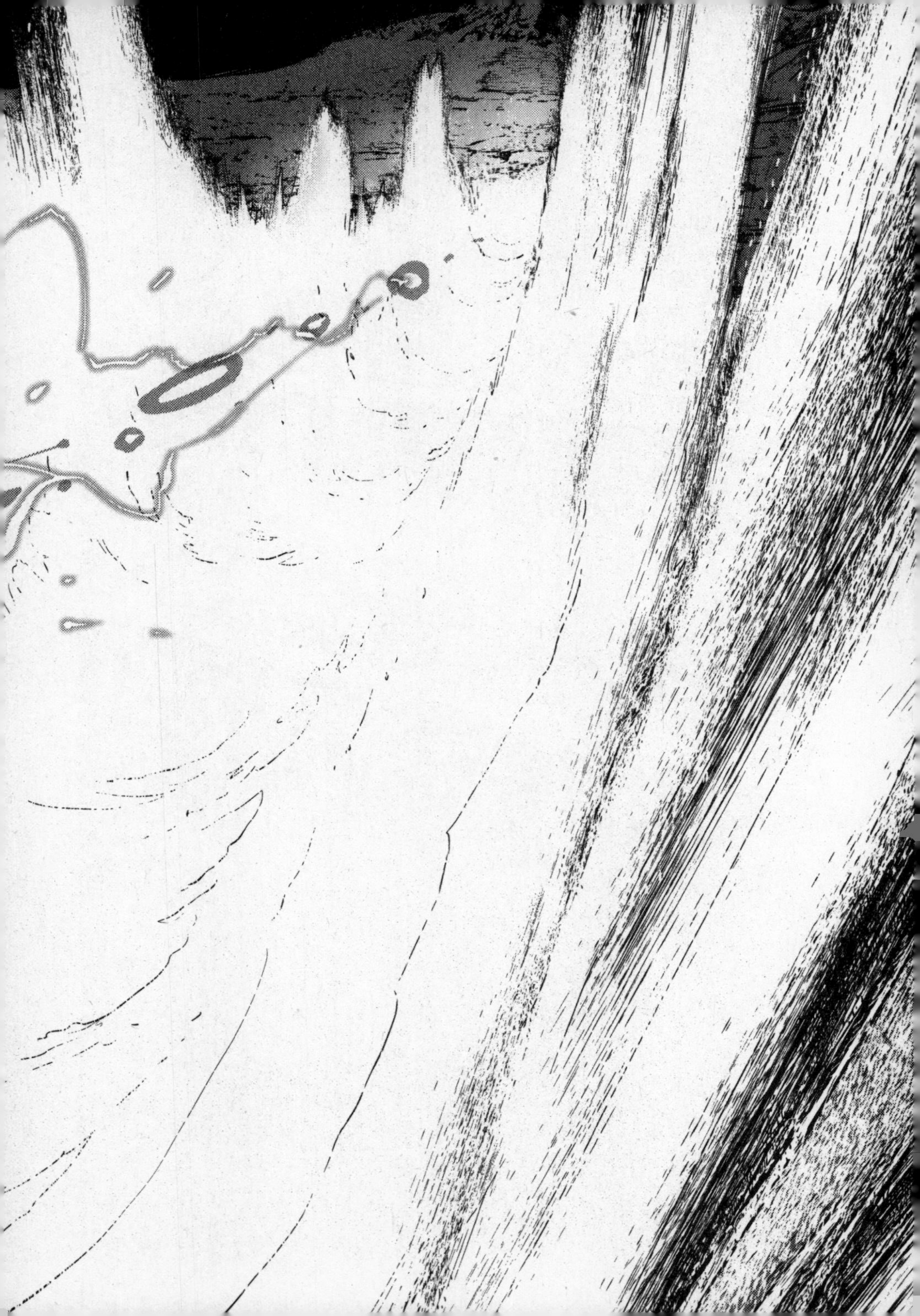

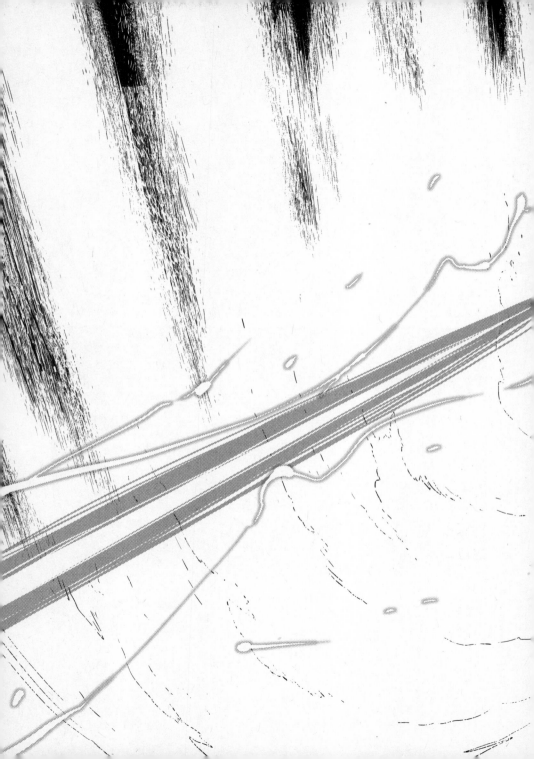

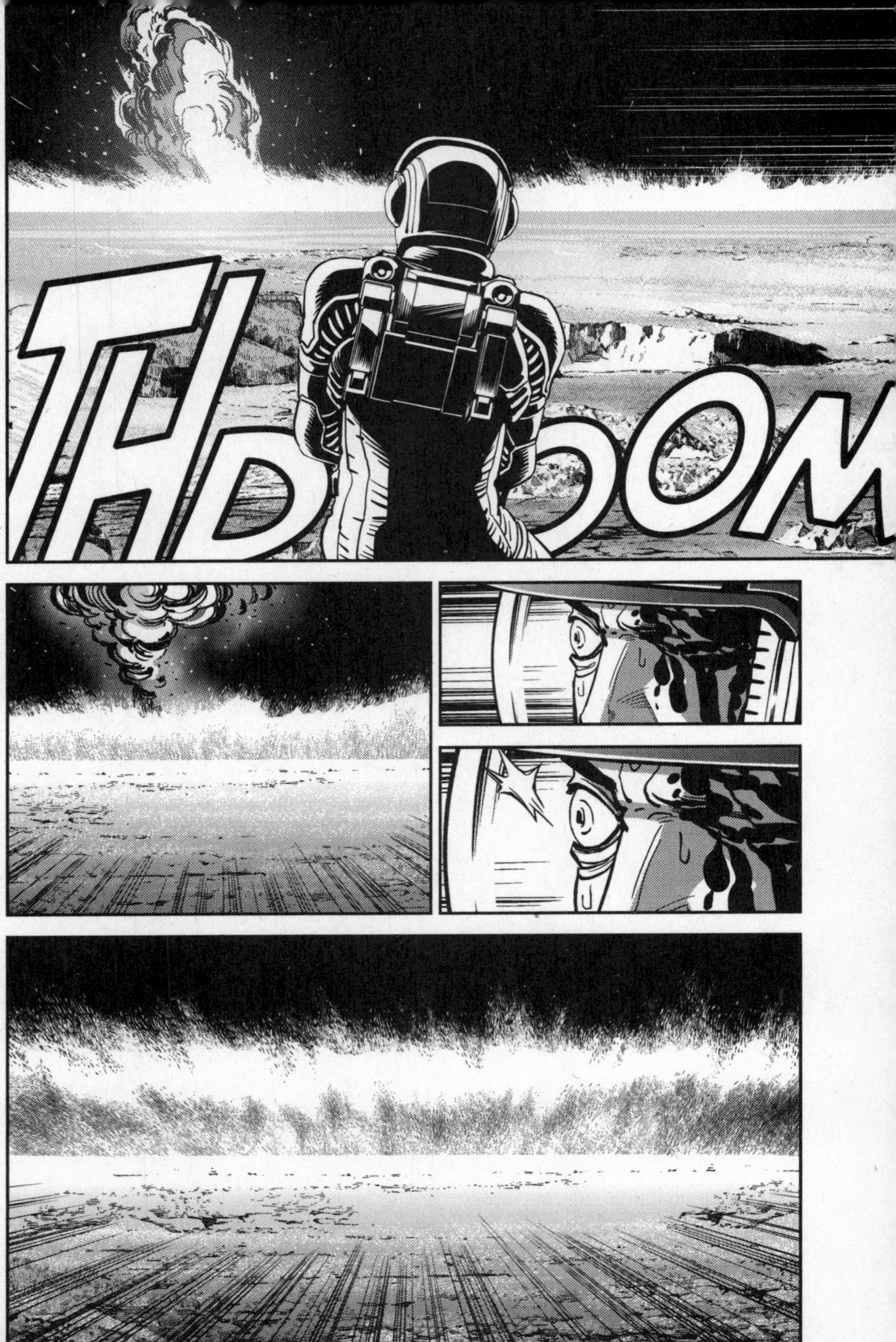
THD OOM

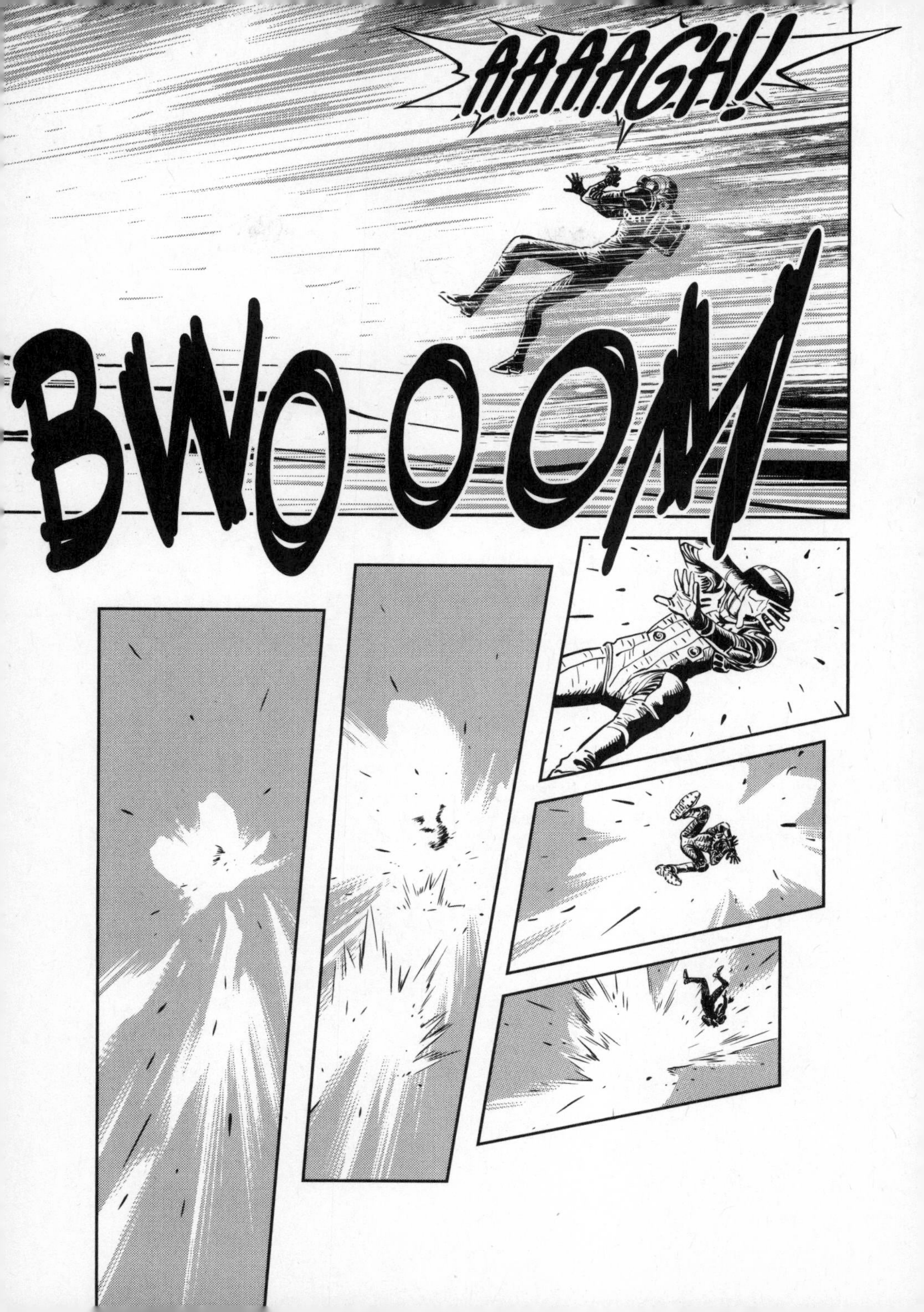
AAAAGH!
BWOOOM

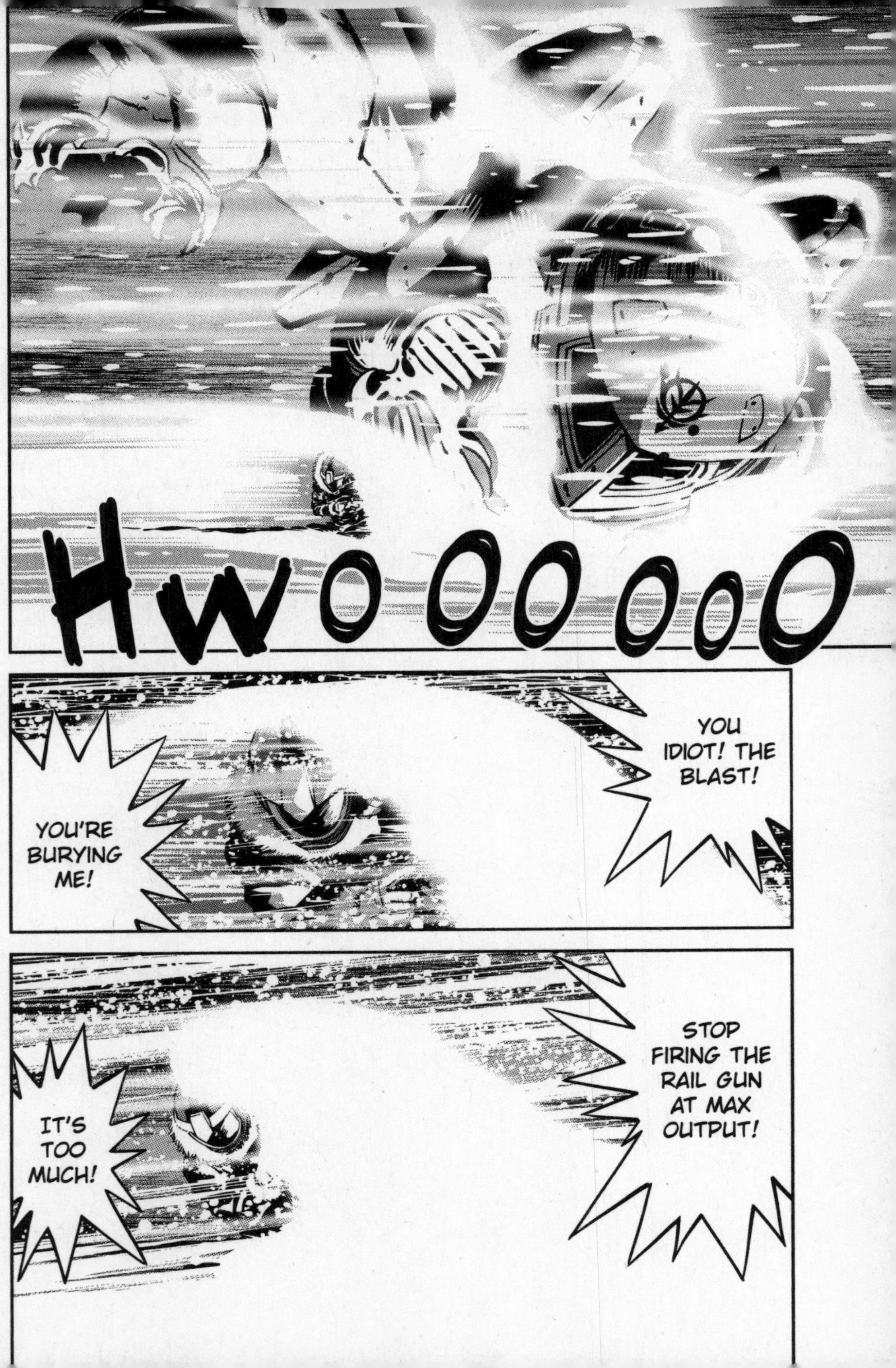
HWOOOOOO
YOU IDIOT! THE BLAST!
YOU'RE BURYING ME!
STOP FIRING THE RAIL GUN AT MAX OUTPUT!
IT'S TOO MUCH!

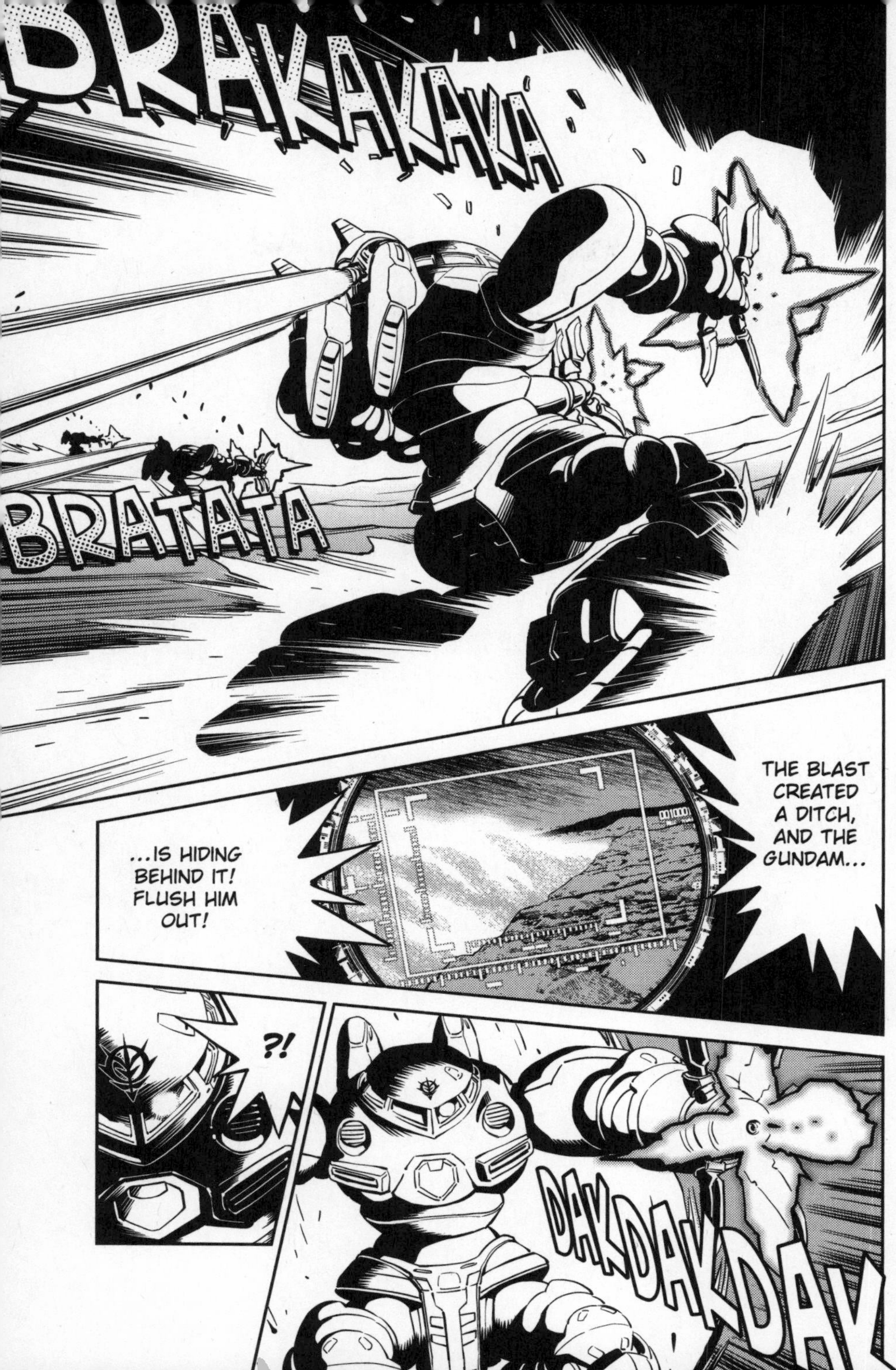
BRAKAKAKA
BRATATA
THE BLAST CREATED A DITCH, AND THE GUNDAM...
...IS HIDING BEHIND IT! FLUSH HIM OUT!
DAKDAKDAK
?!

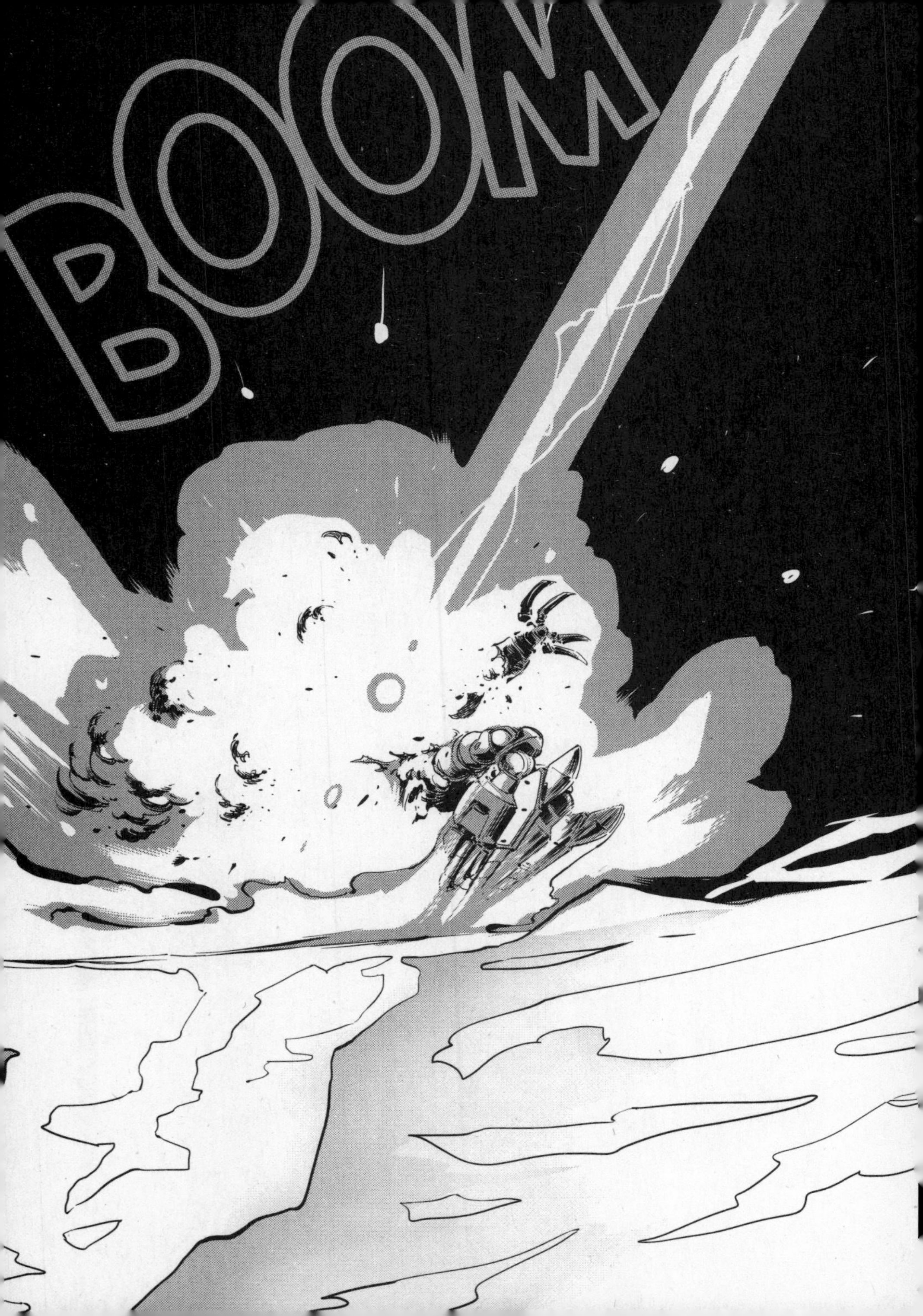
BOOM

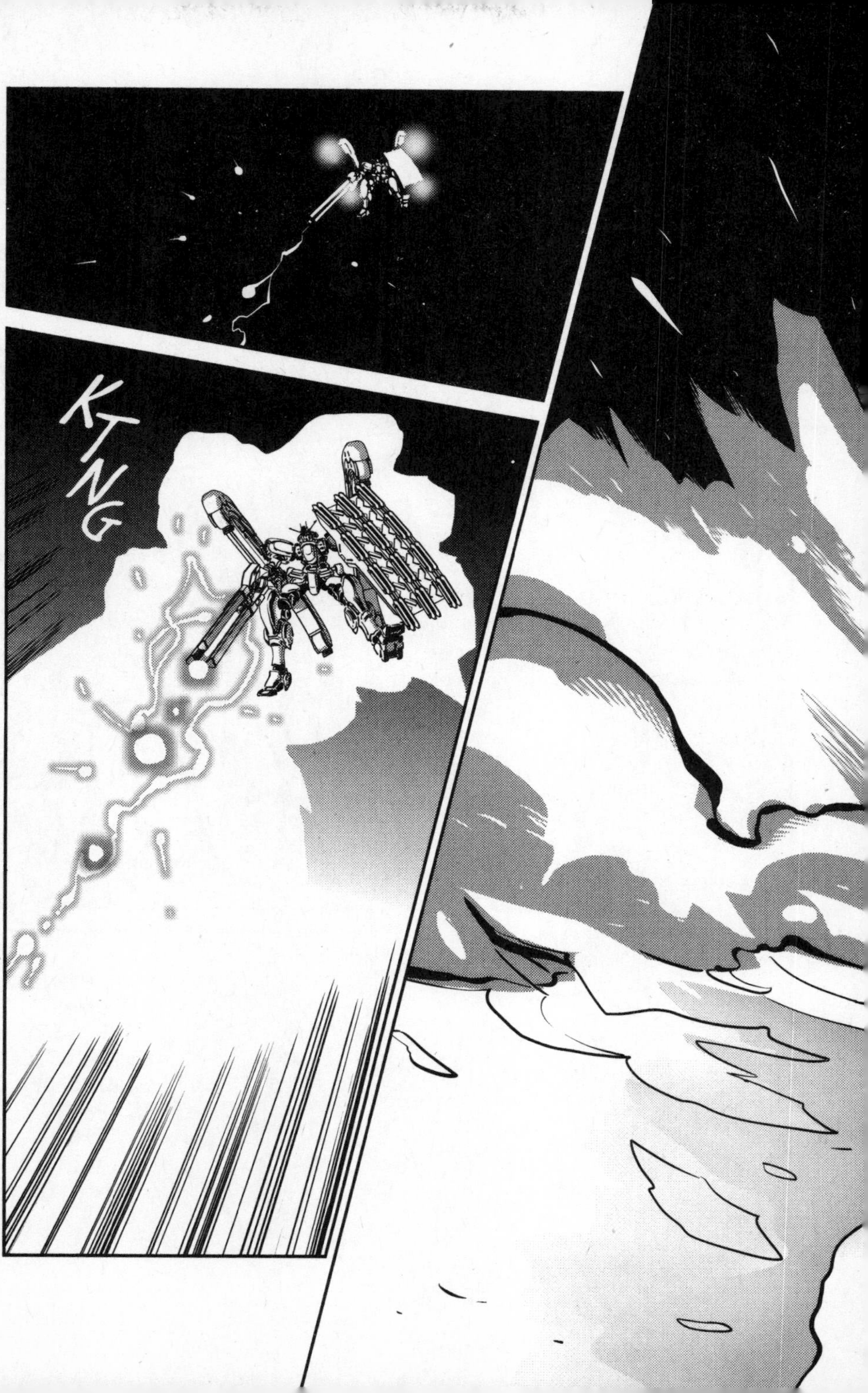
KTING

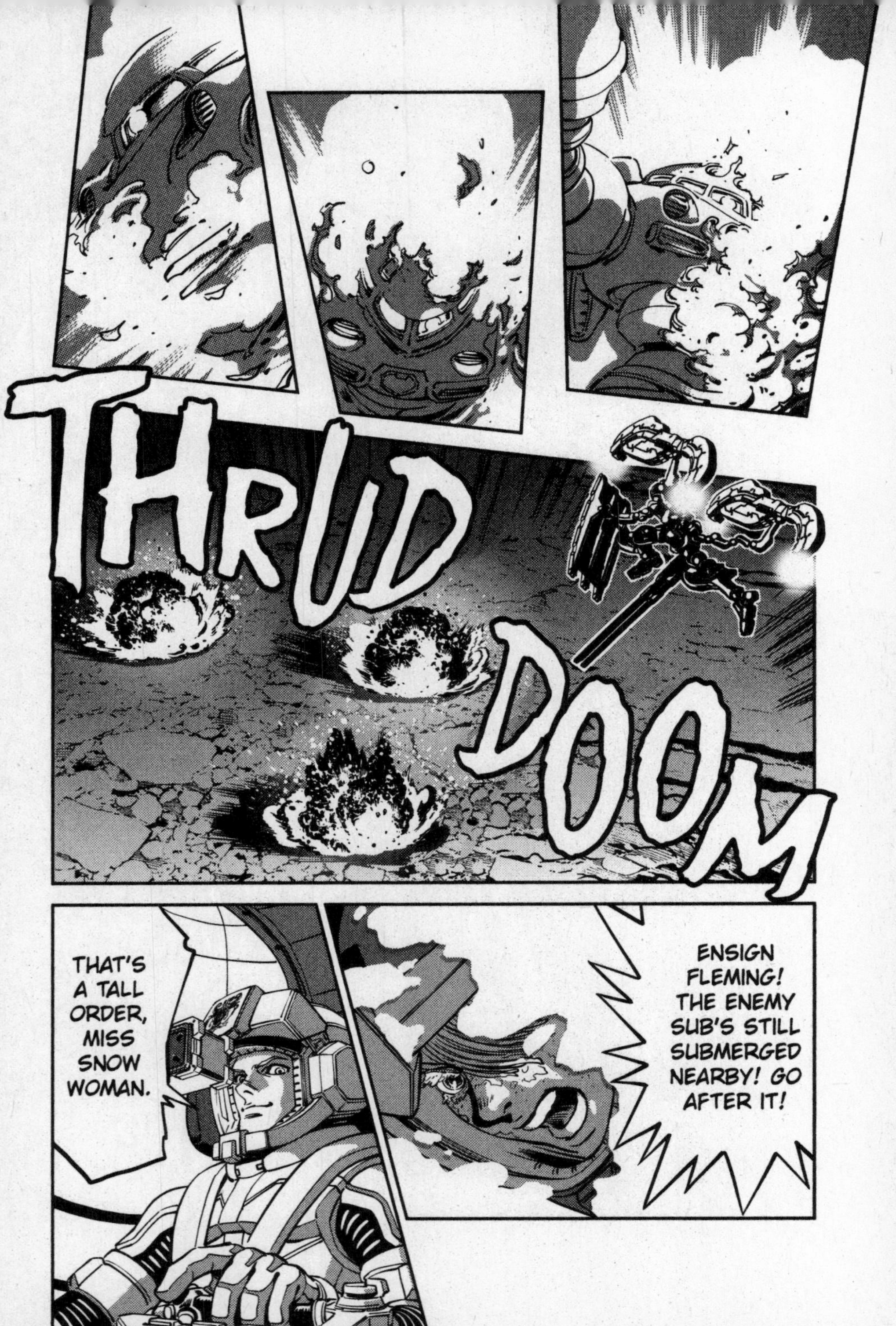
THRUD
DOOM
ENSIGN FLEMING! THE ENEMY SUB'S STILL SUBMERGED NEARBY! GO AFTER IT!
THAT'S A TALL ORDER, MISS SNOW WOMAN.

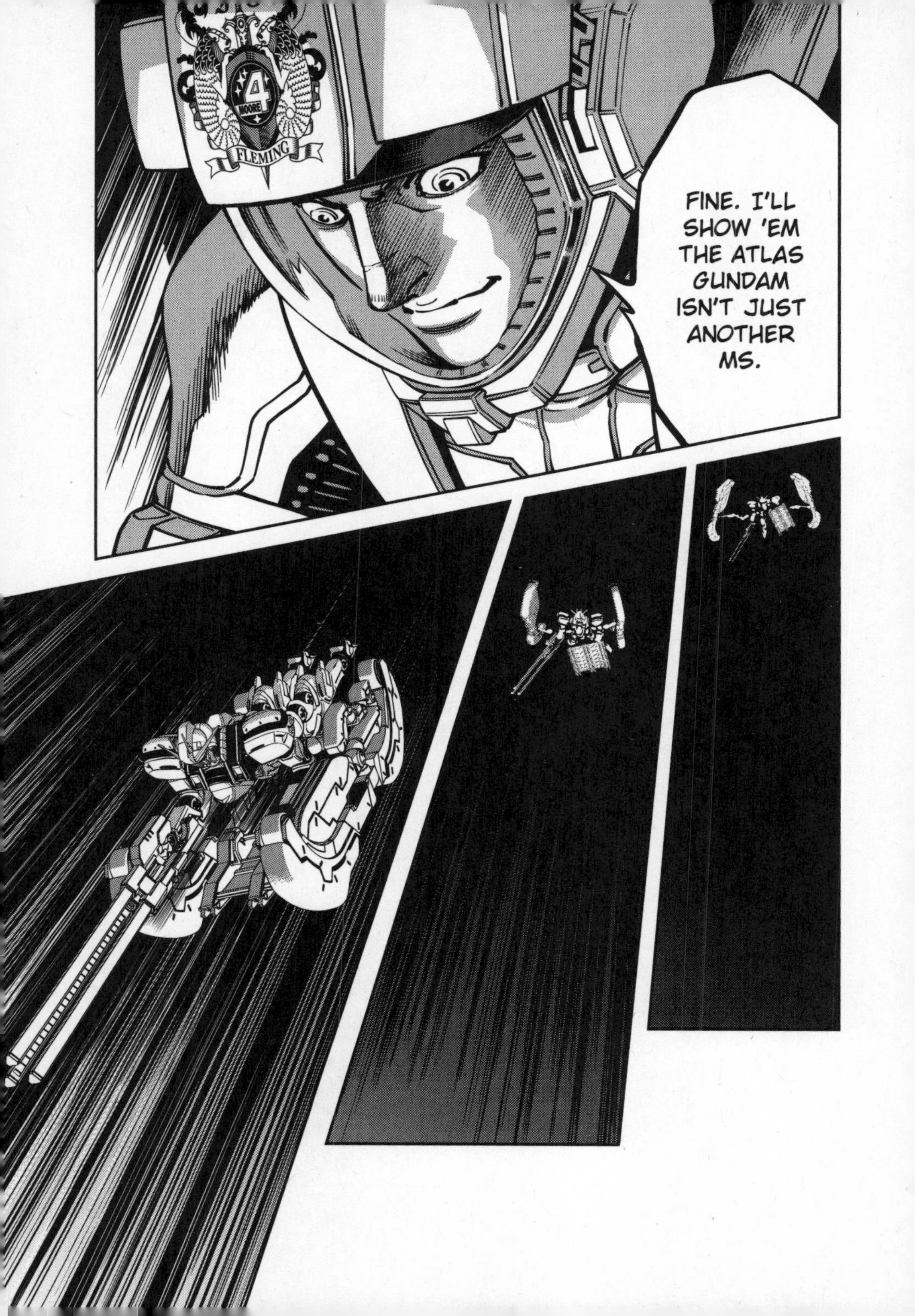
4
MOORE
FLEMING
FINE. I'LL SHOW 'EM THE ATLAS GUNDAM ISN'T JUST ANOTHER MS.

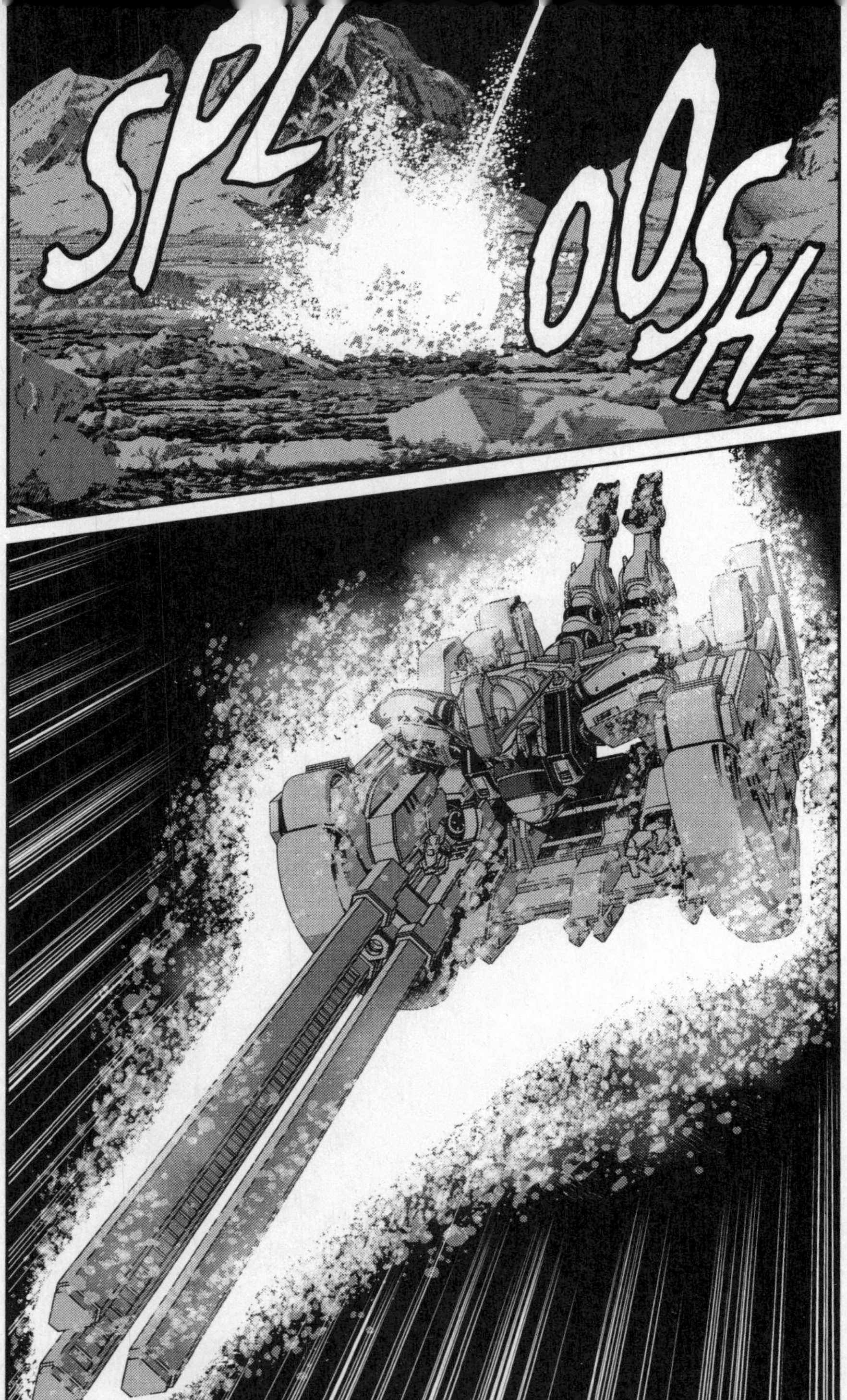
SPLOOSH

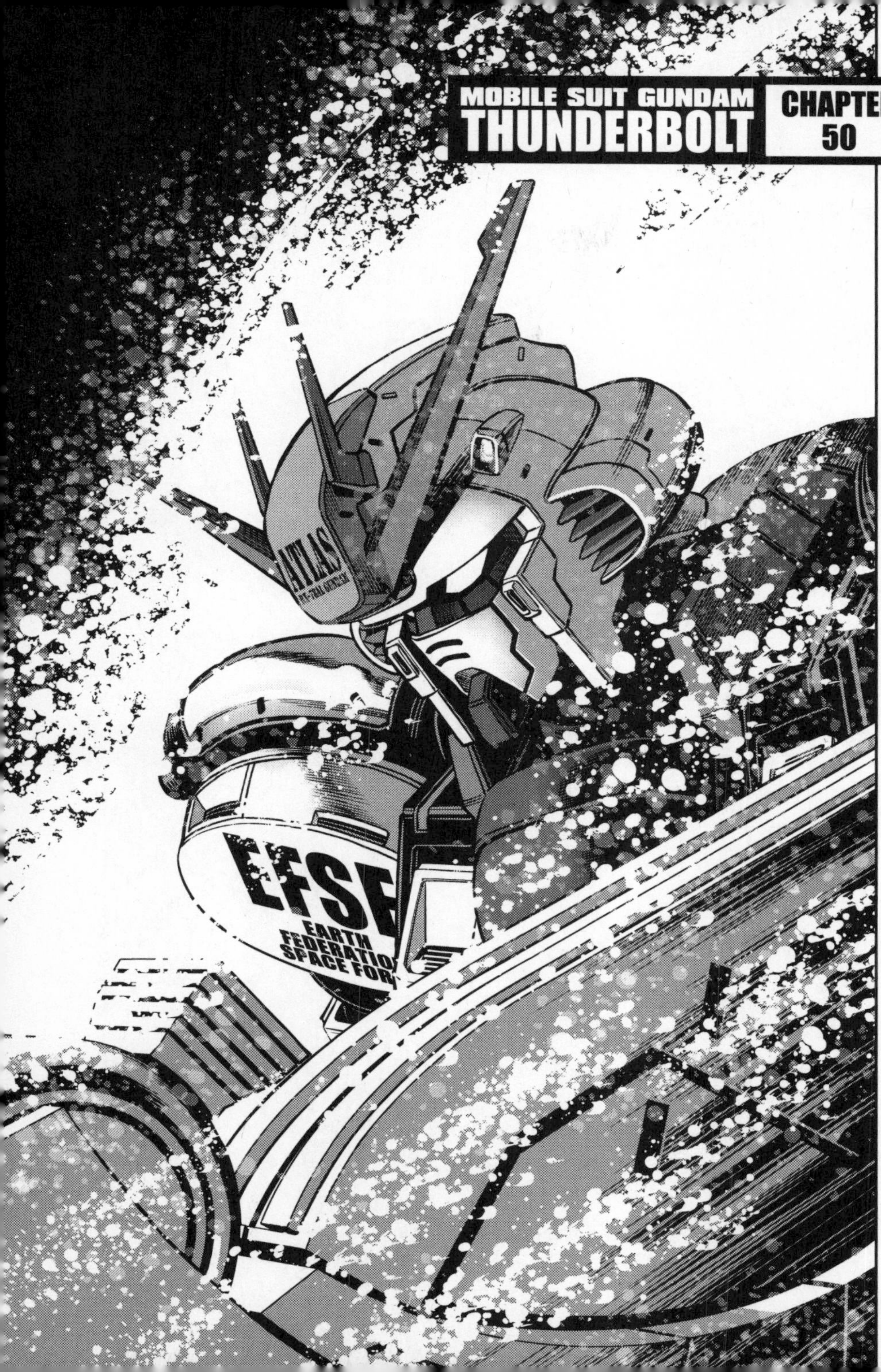
MOBILE SUIT GUNDAM
THUNDERBOLT
CHAPTER
50
ATLAS
EFSE
EARTH
FEDERATIO
SPACE FOR

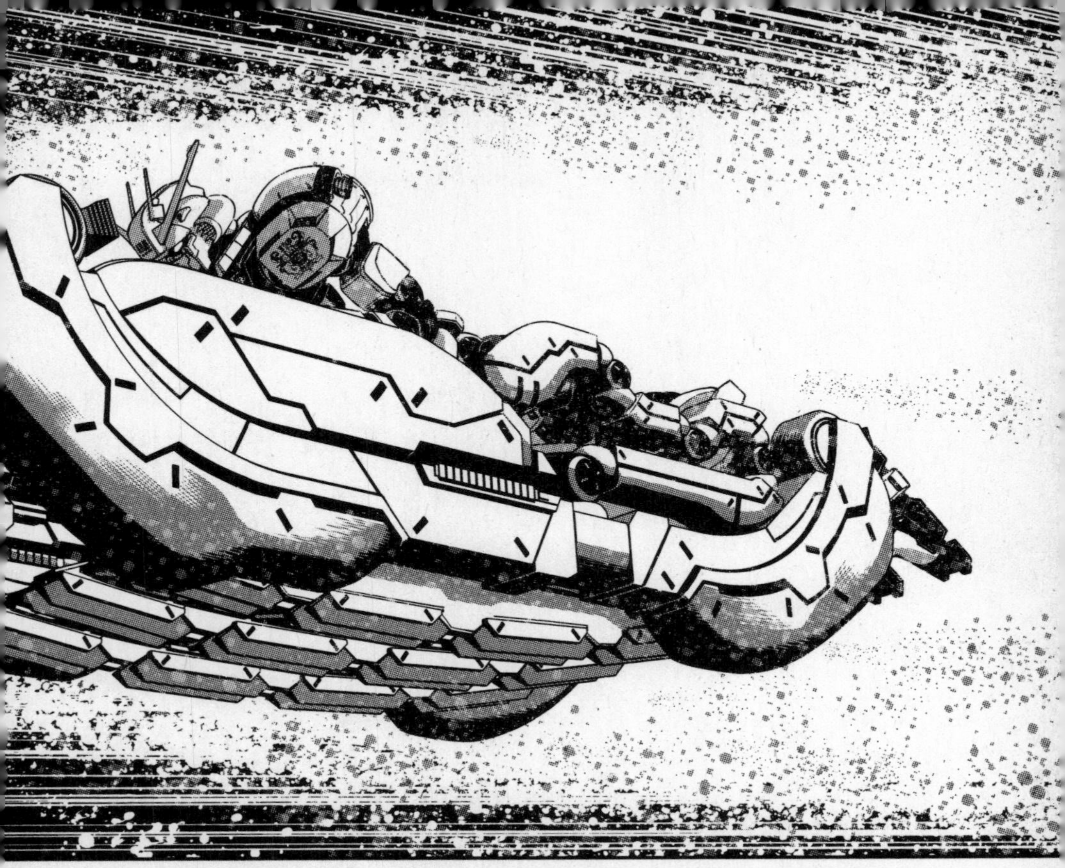

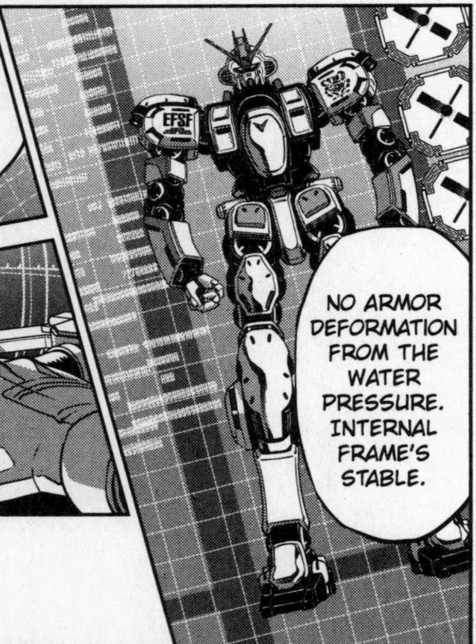
NO ARMOR DEFORMATION FROM THE WATER PRESSURE. INTERNAL FRAME'S STABLE.

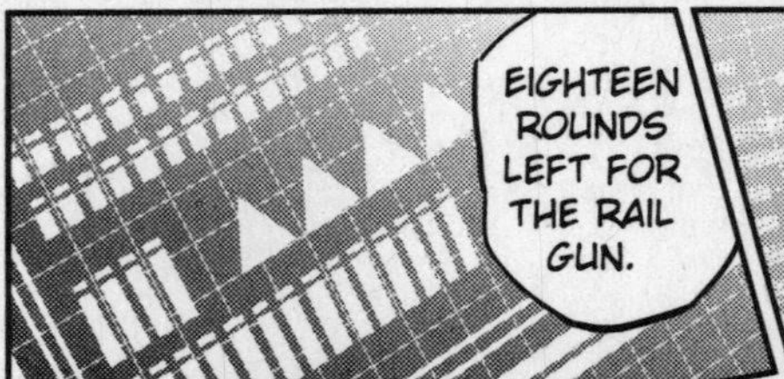
EIGHTEEN ROUNDS LEFT FOR THE RAIL GUN.

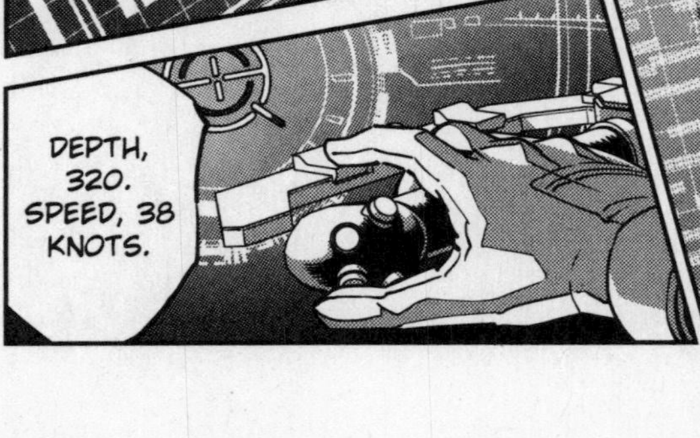
DEPTH, 320. SPEED, 38 KNOTS.

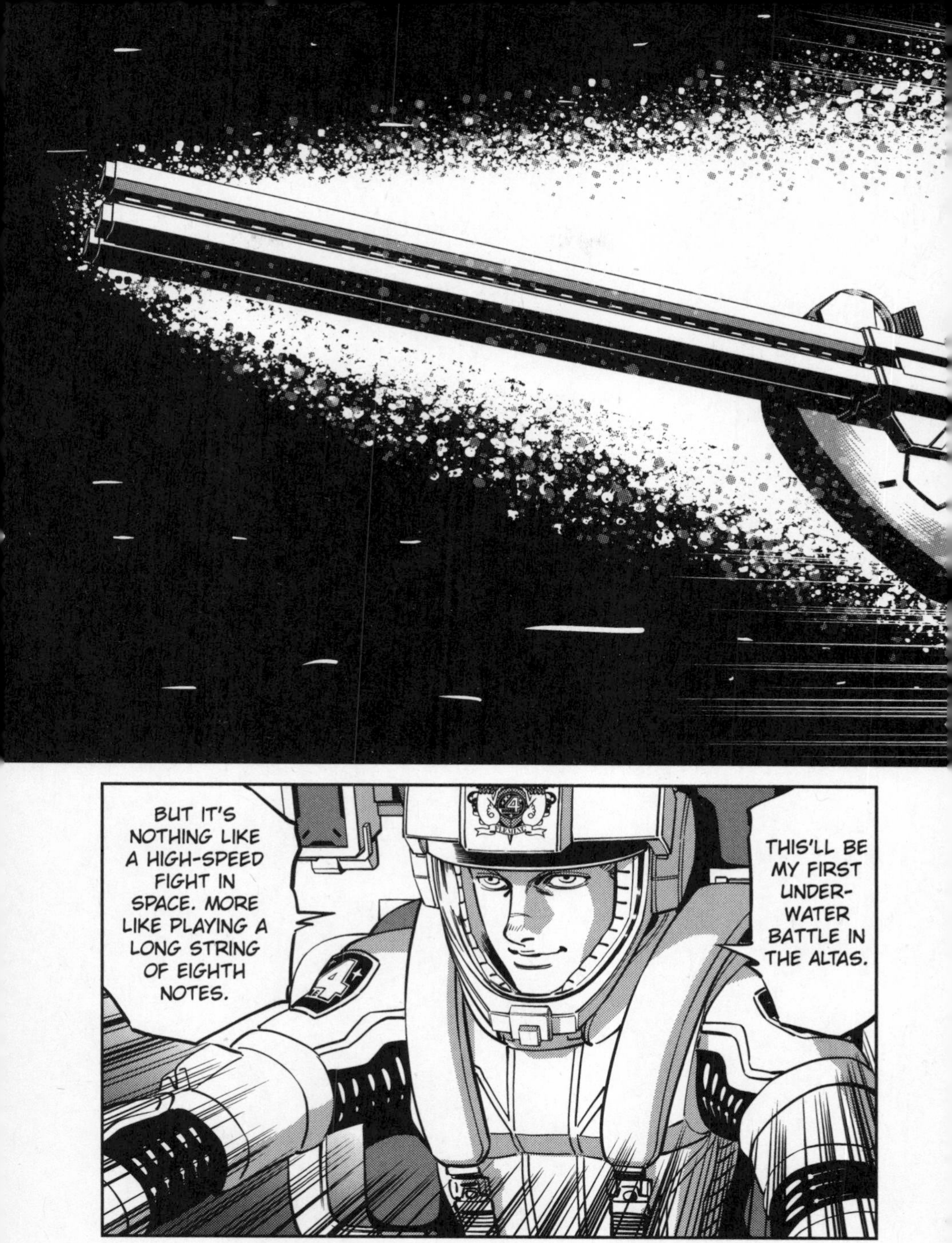
THIS'LL BE MY FIRST UNDER-WATER BATTLE IN THE ALTAS.
BUT IT'S NOTHING LIKE A HIGH-SPEED FIGHT IN SPACE. MORE LIKE PLAYING A LONG STRING OF EIGHTH NOTES.

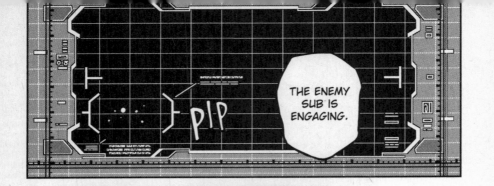

THE ENEMY SUB IS ENGAGING.

PIP

SHWA AA AAA

A

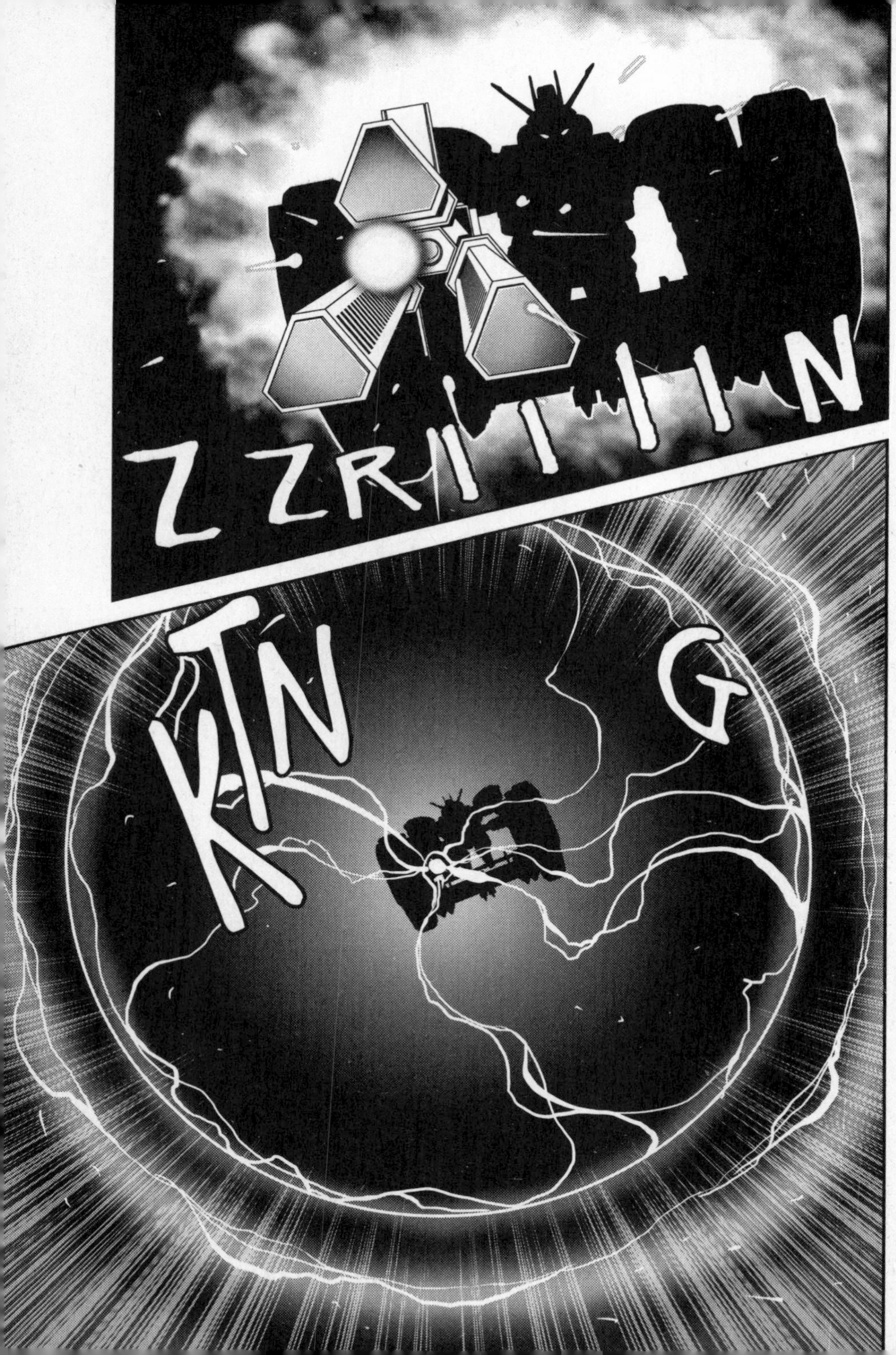
ZZRIIIIIIN
KTN G

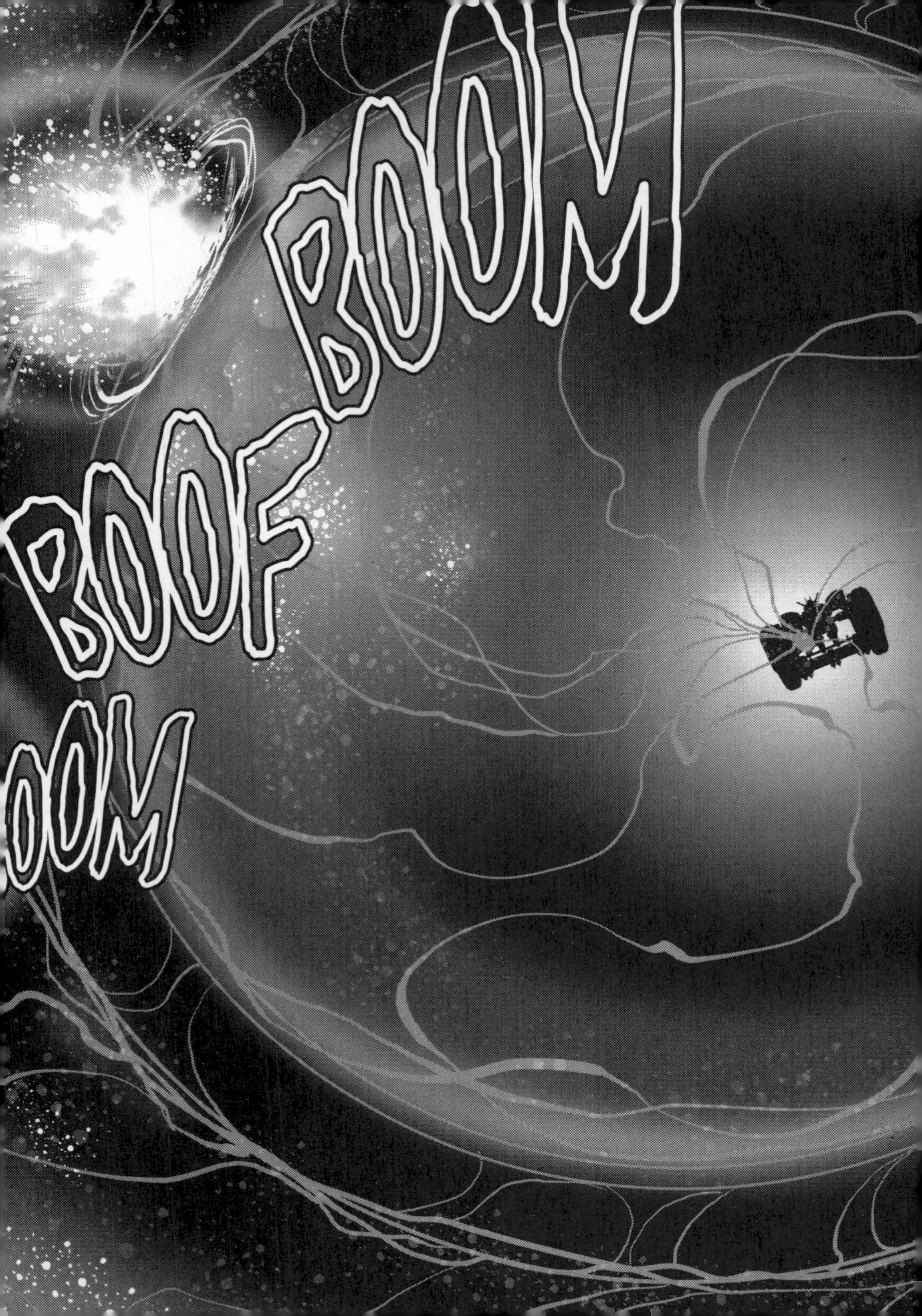
BOOM
BOOF
OOM

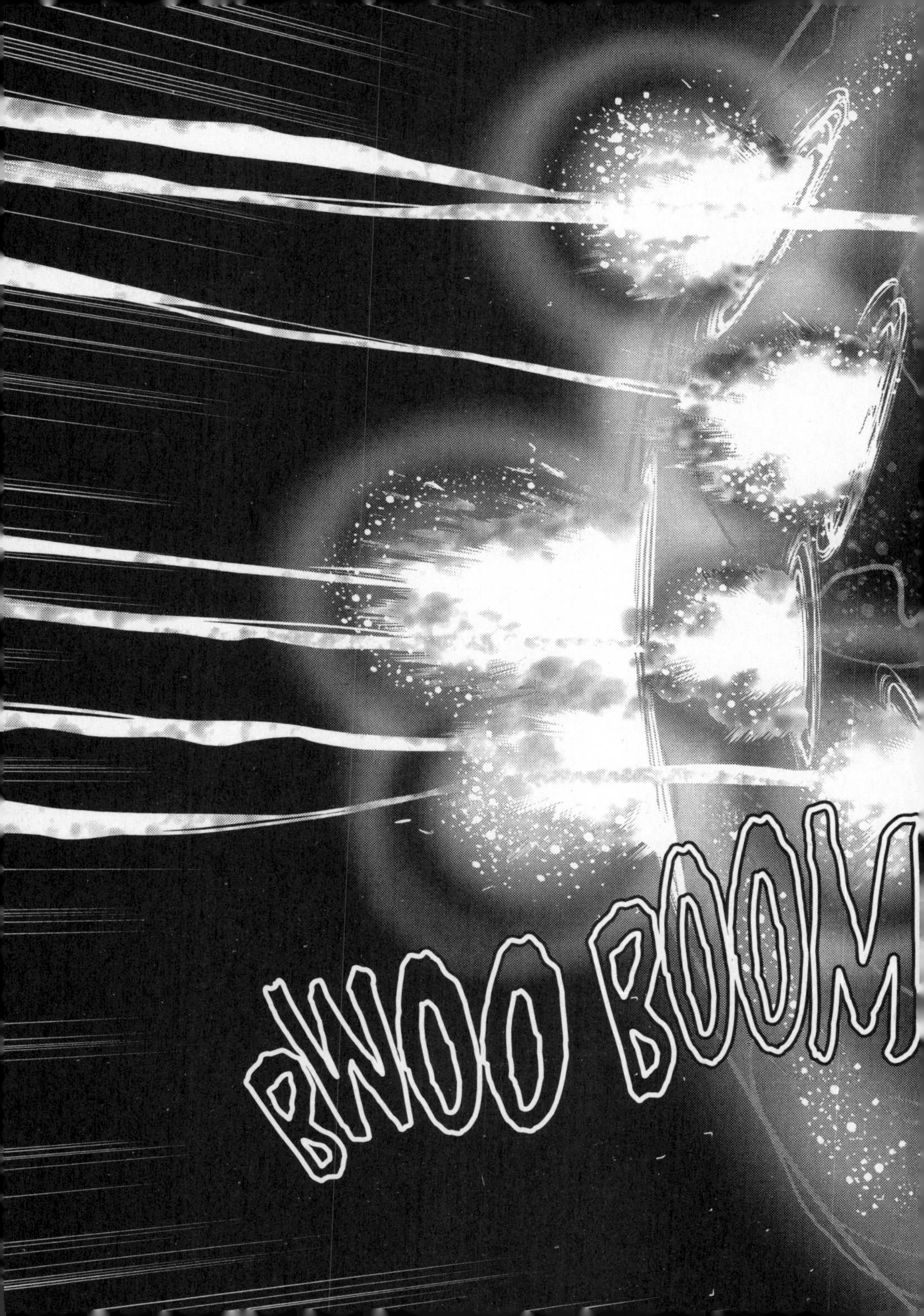
BWOO BOOM

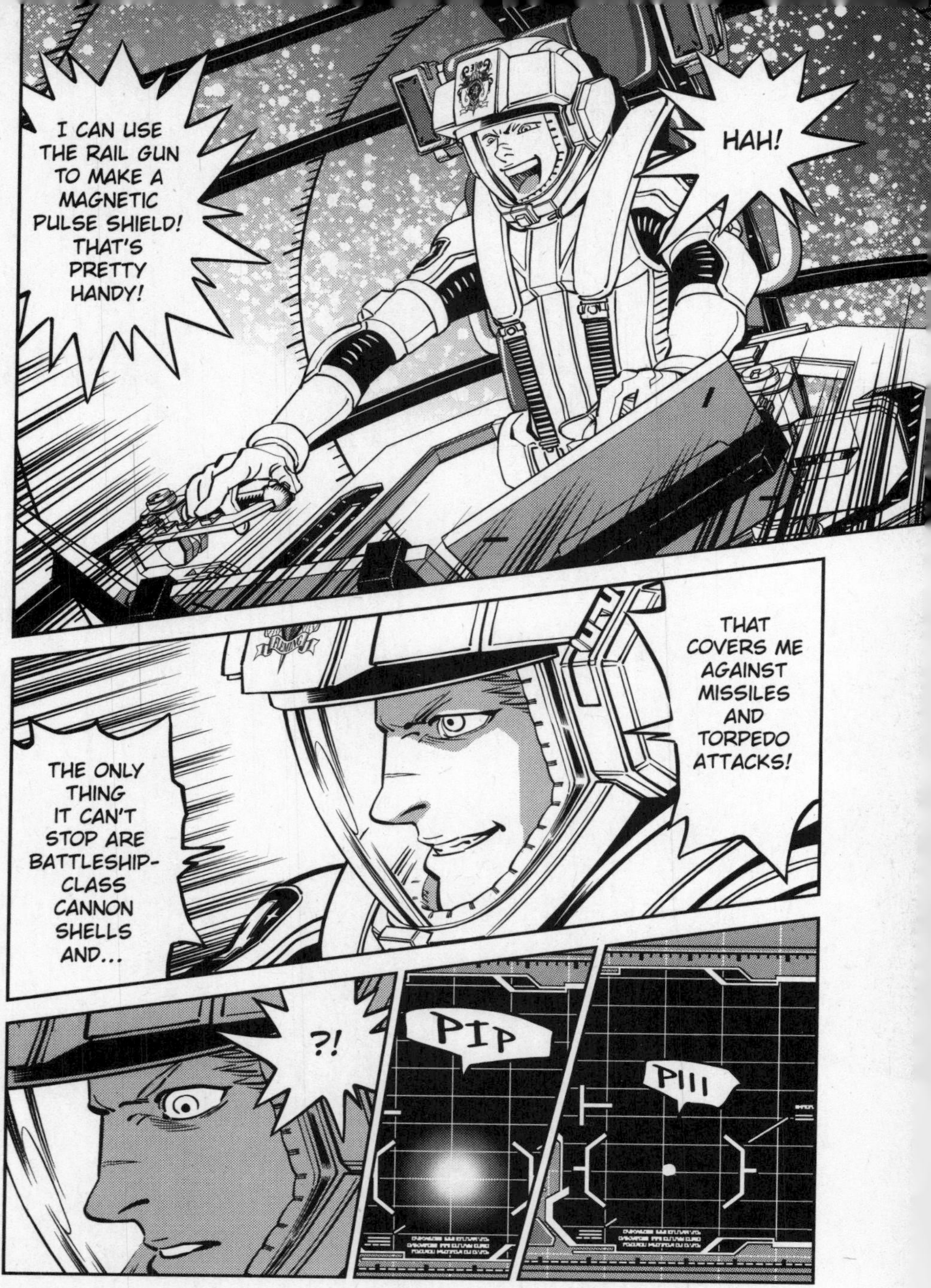
HAH!
I CAN USE THE RAIL GUN TO MAKE A MAGNETIC PULSE SHIELD! THAT'S PRETTY HANDY!
THAT COVERS ME AGAINST MISSILES AND TORPEDO ATTACKS!
THE ONLY THING IT CAN'T STOP ARE BATTLESHIP-CLASS CANNON SHELLS AND...
PIII
PIP
?!

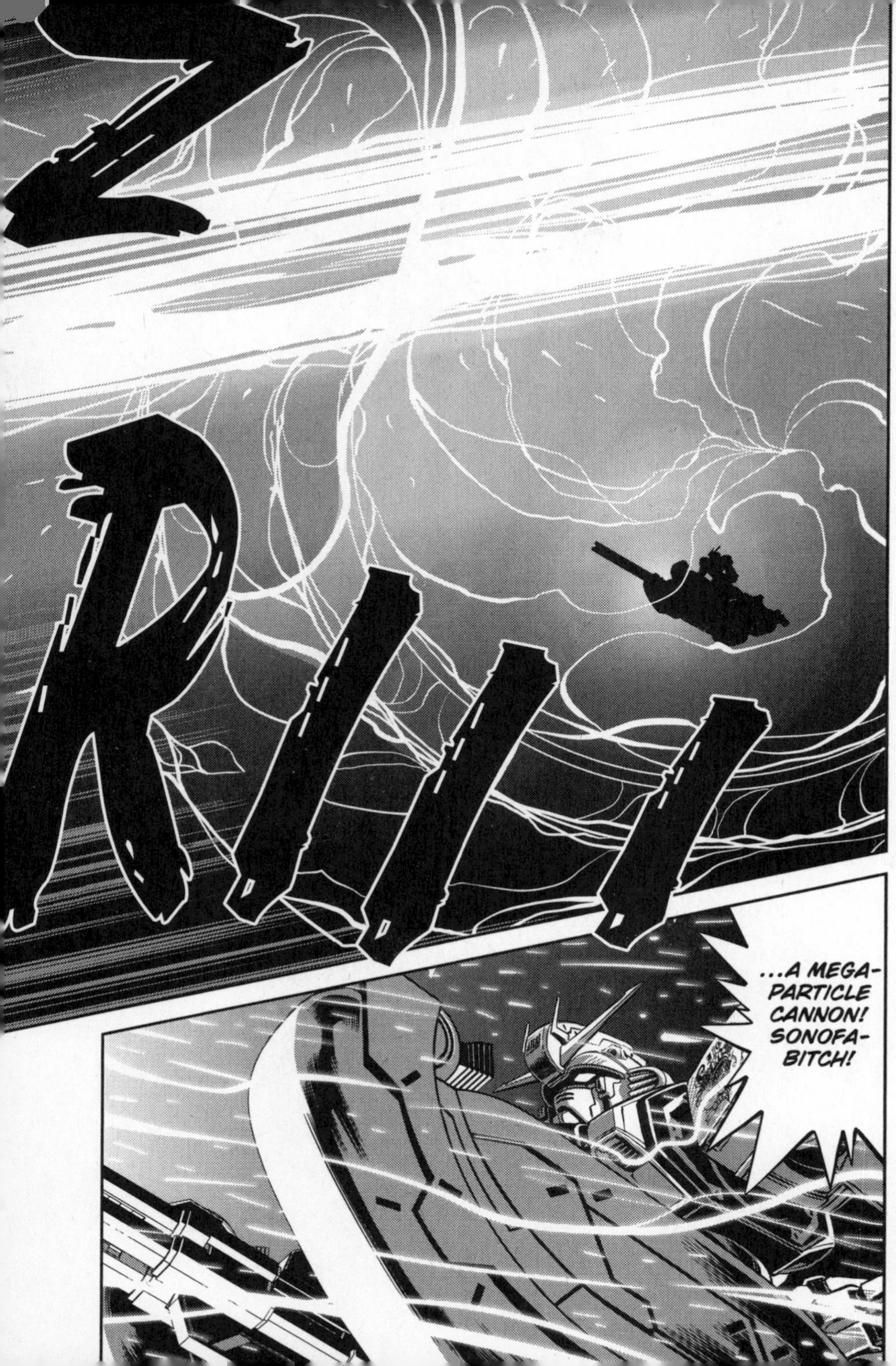
ZRIII
...A MEGA-PARTICLE CANNON! SONOFA-BITCH!

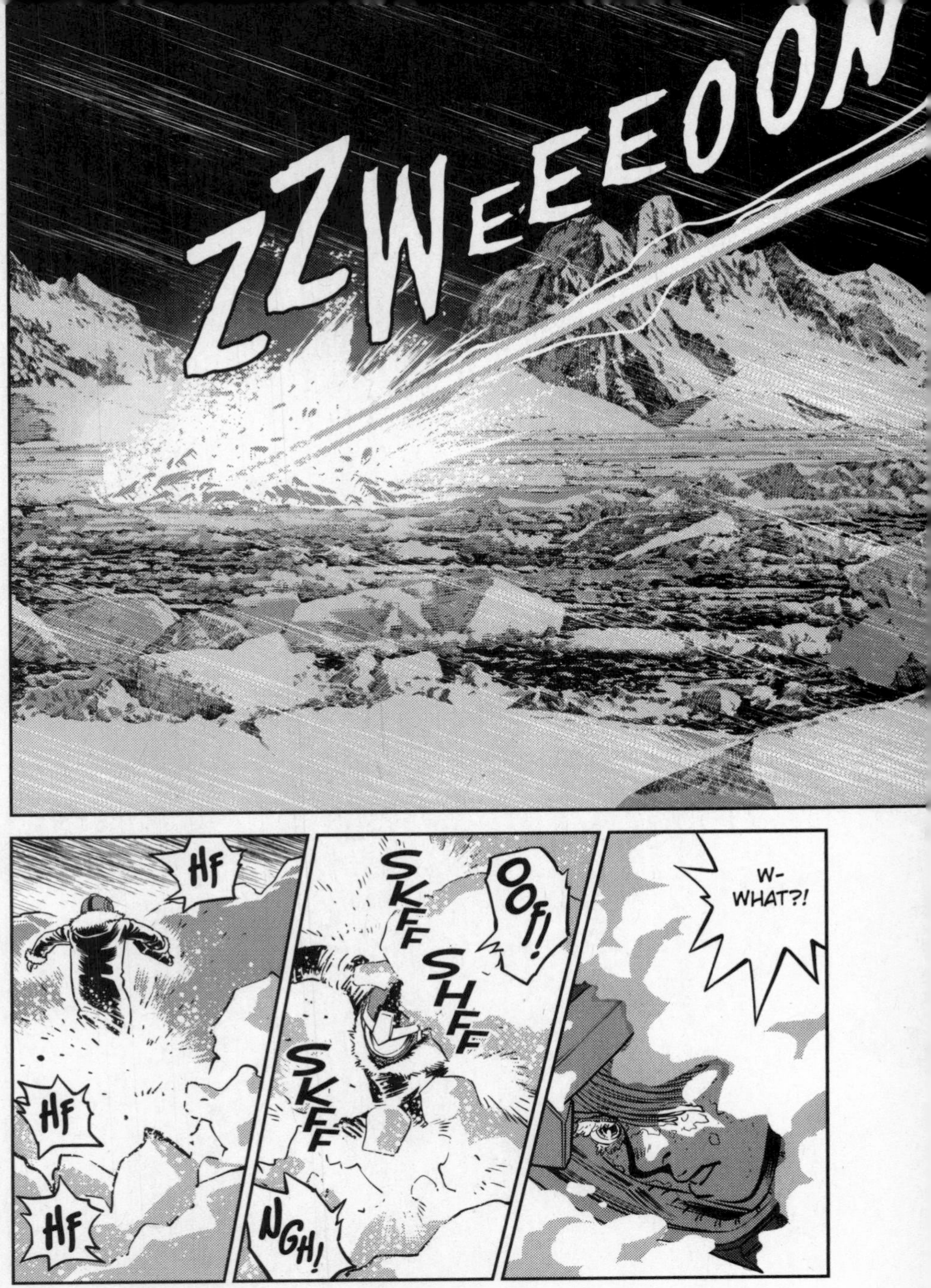
ZZWEEEOON
W-
WHAT?!
OOF!
SKFF
SHFFF
SKFF
NGH!
HF
HF
HF

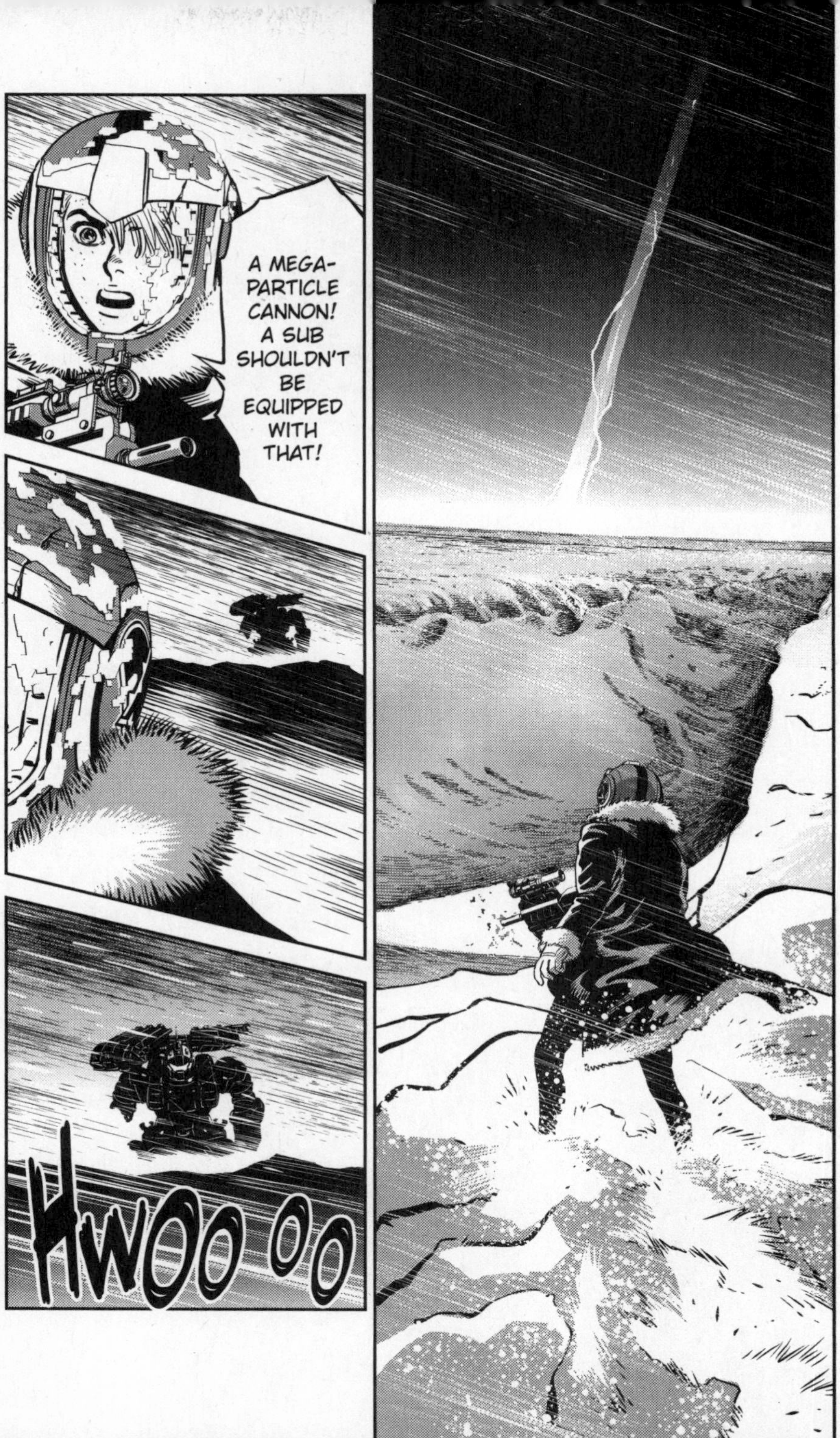
A MEGA-PARTICLE CANNON! A SUB SHOULDN'T BE EQUIPPED WITH THAT!
HWOO OO

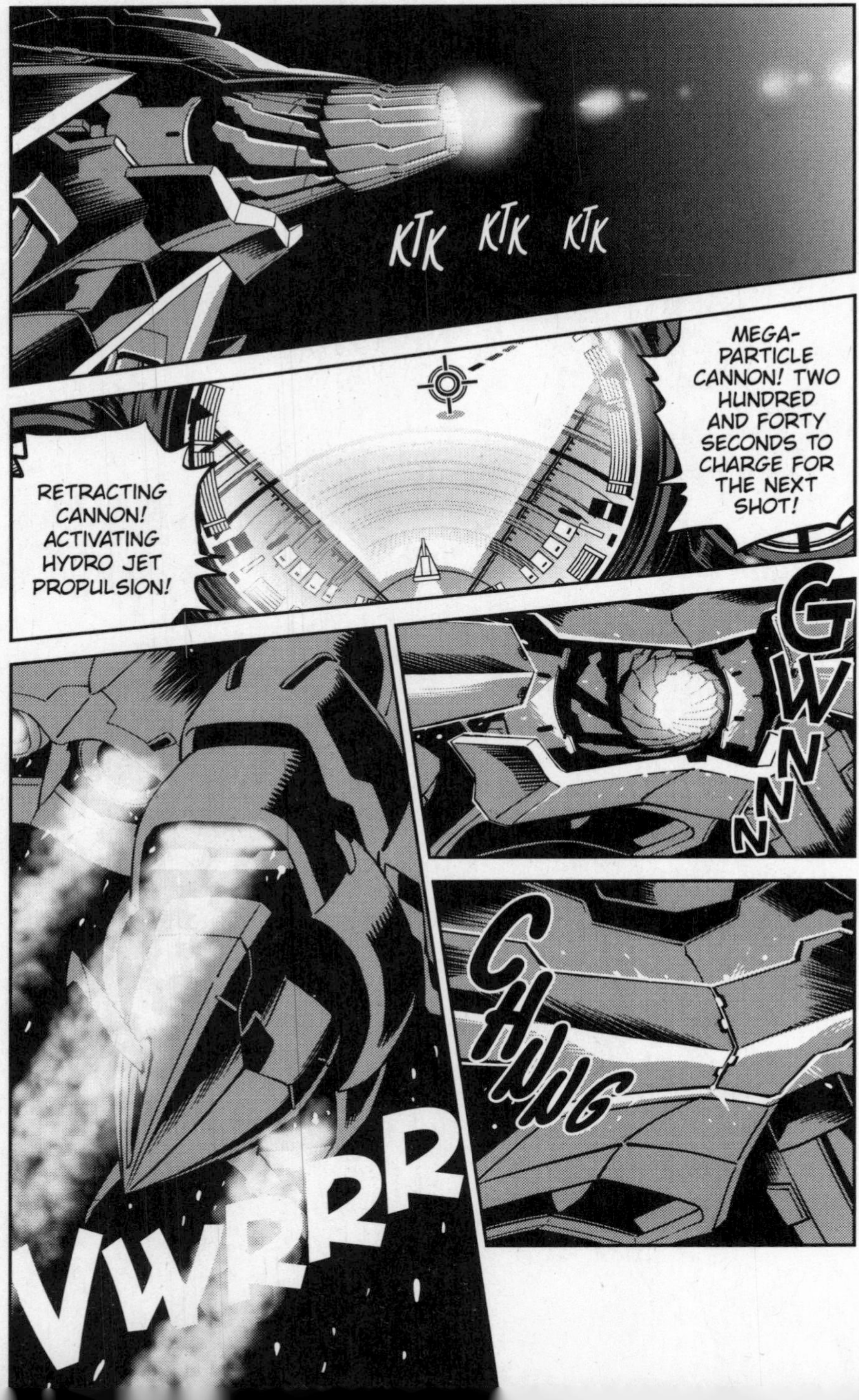
KTK KTK KTK
MEGA-PARTICLE CANNON! TWO HUNDRED AND FORTY SECONDS TO CHARGE FOR THE NEXT SHOT!
RETRACTING CANNON! ACTIVATING HYDRO JET PROPULSION!
GWNNNN
CHUNG
VWRRR

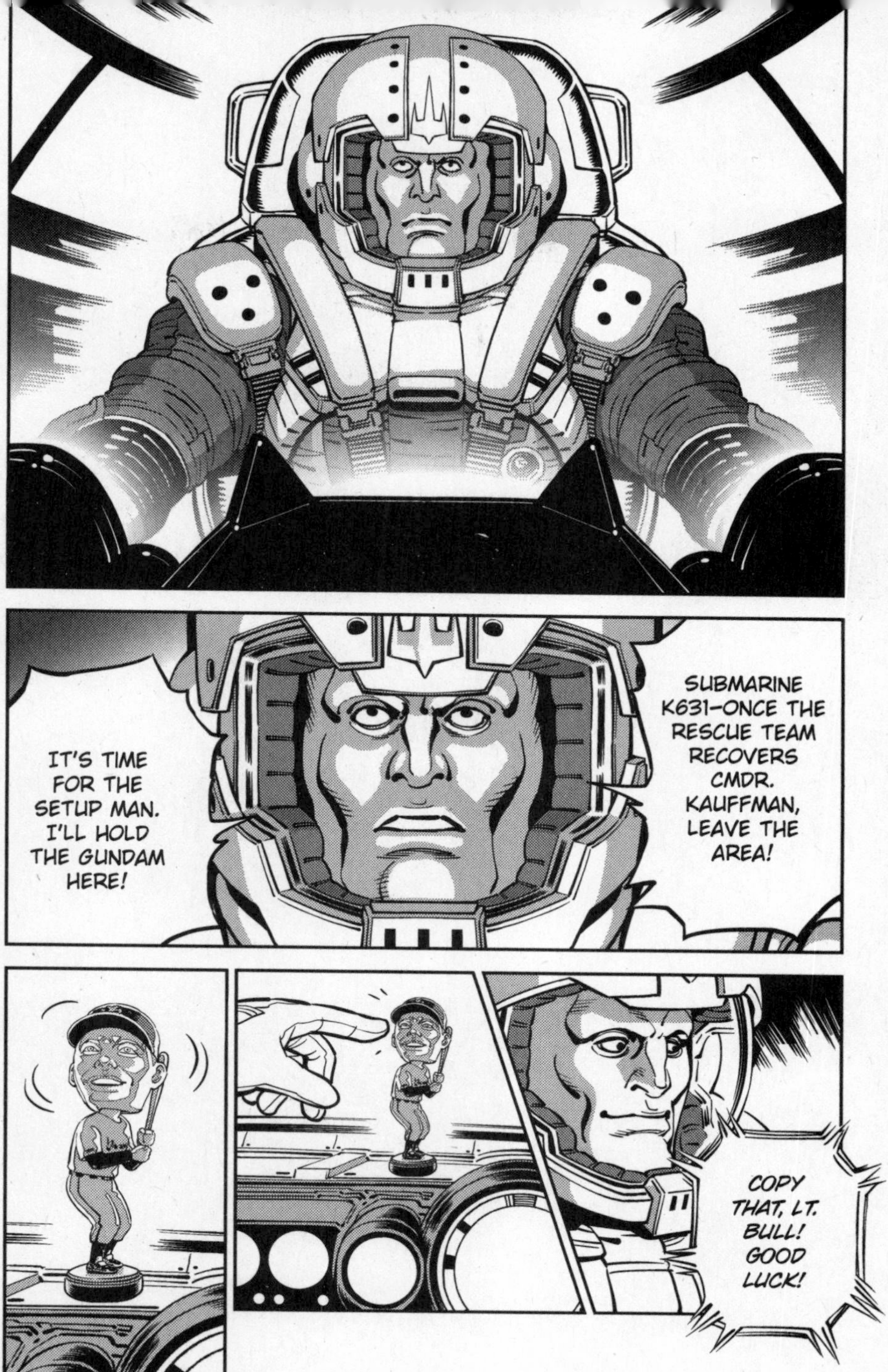
SUBMARINE K631—ONCE THE RESCUE TEAM RECOVERS CMDR. KAUFFMAN, LEAVE THE AREA!
IT'S TIME FOR THE SETUP MAN. I'LL HOLD THE GUNDAM HERE!
COPY THAT, LT. BULL! GOOD LUCK!

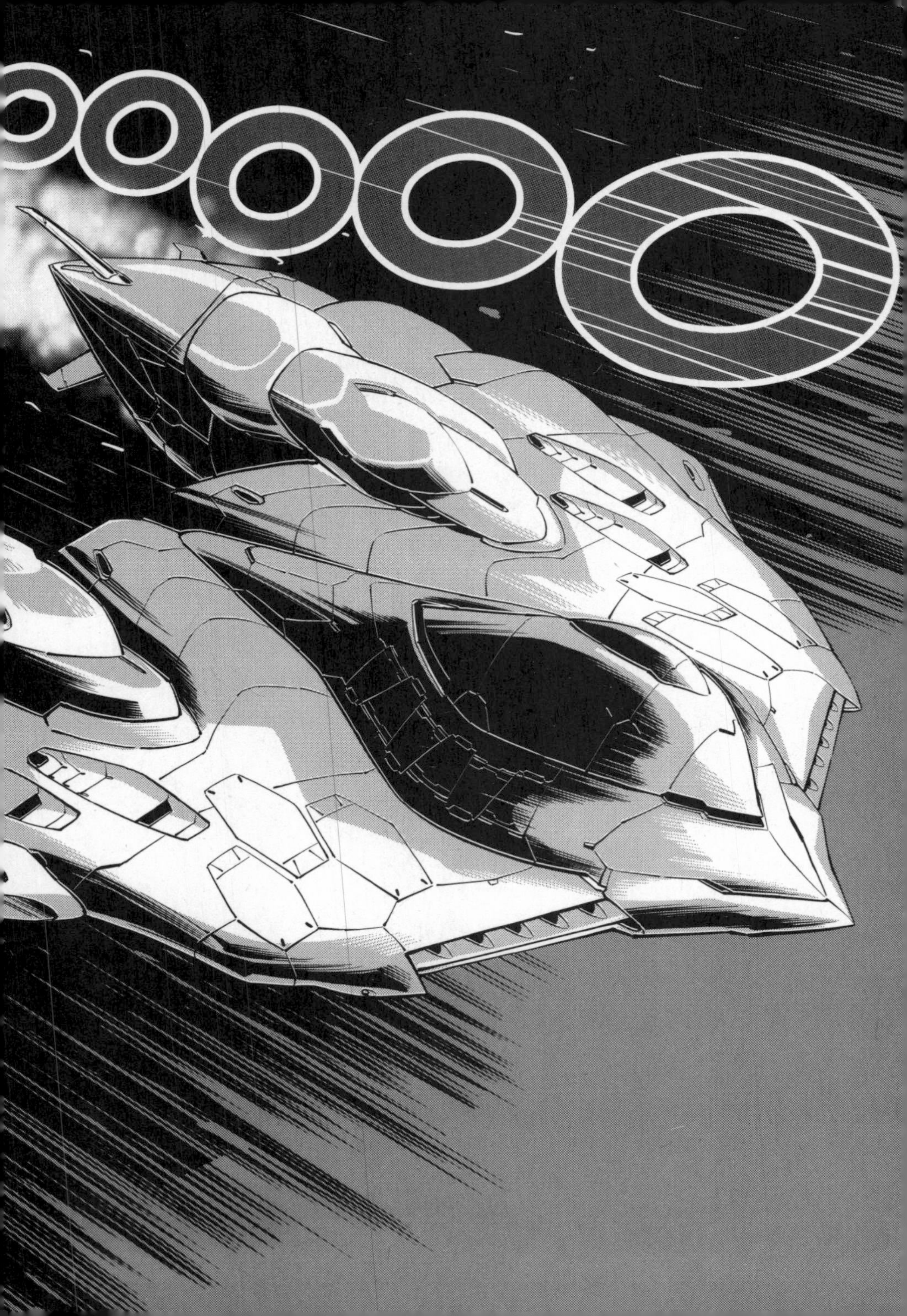

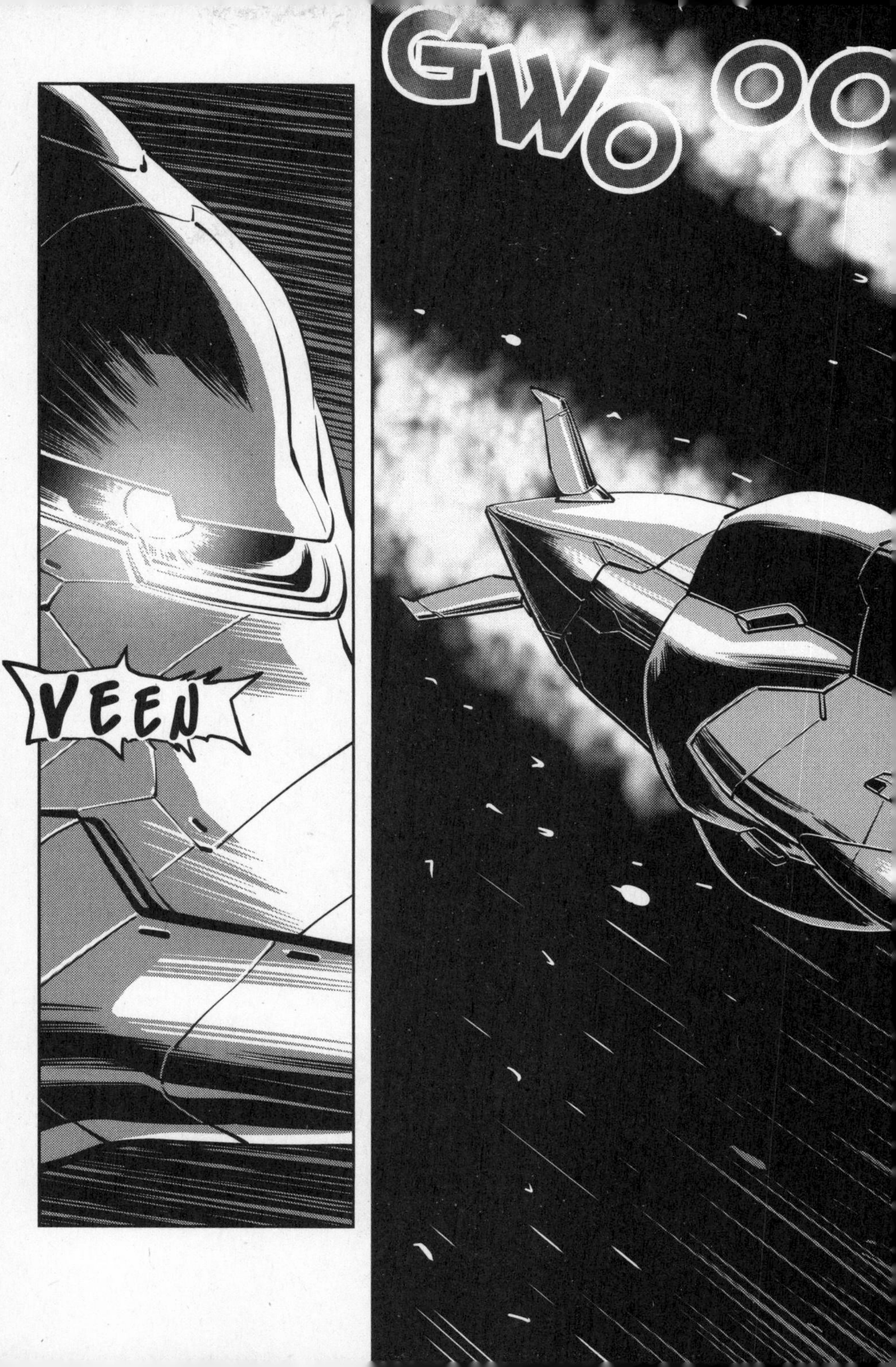
GWO OO
VEEN

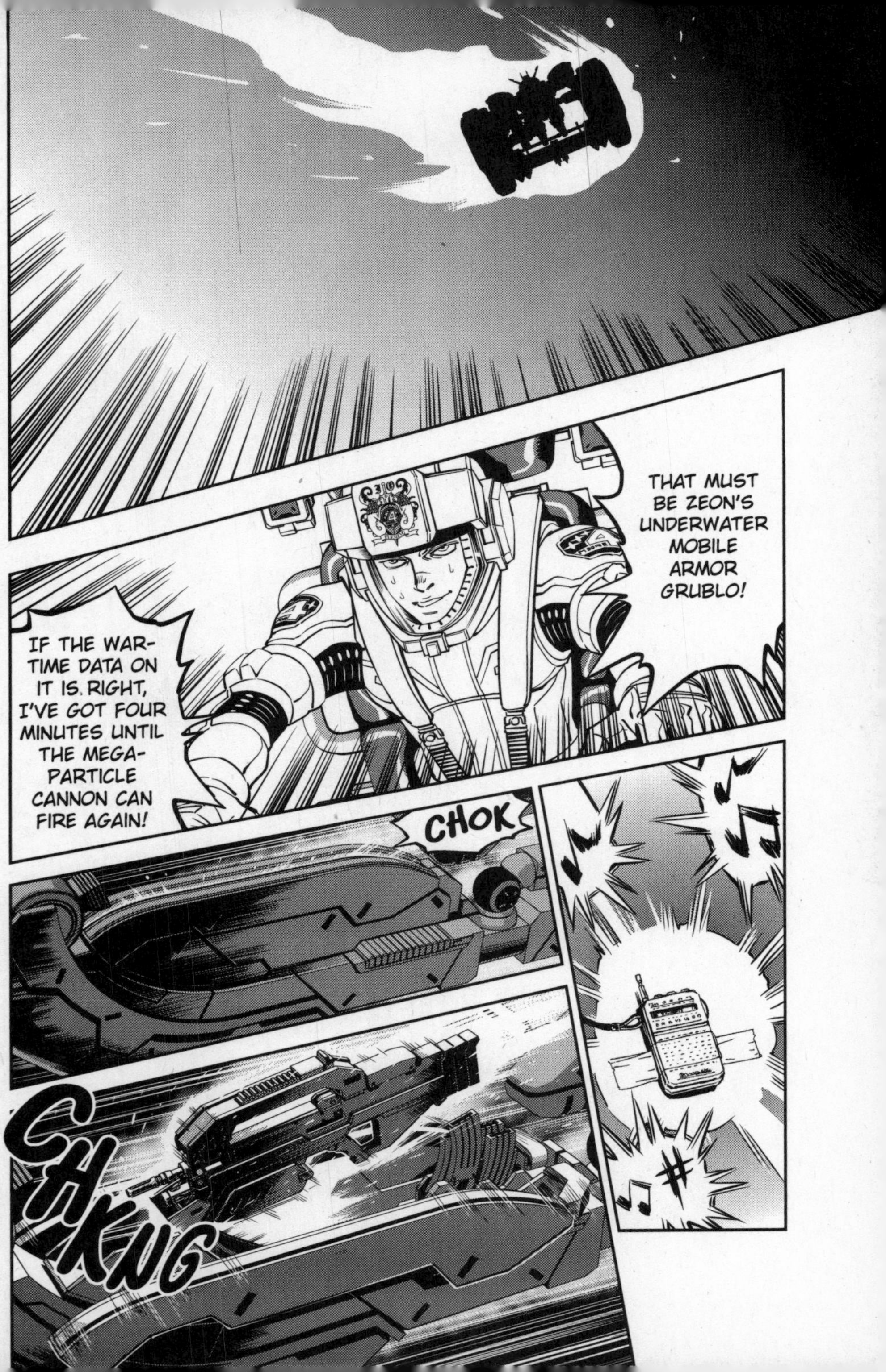
THAT MUST BE ZEON'S UNDERWATER MOBILE ARMOR GRUBLO!
IF THE WAR-TIME DATA ON IT IS. RIGHT, I'VE GOT FOUR MINUTES UNTIL THE MEGA-PARTICLE CANNON CAN FIRE AGAIN!
CHOK
CHKNG

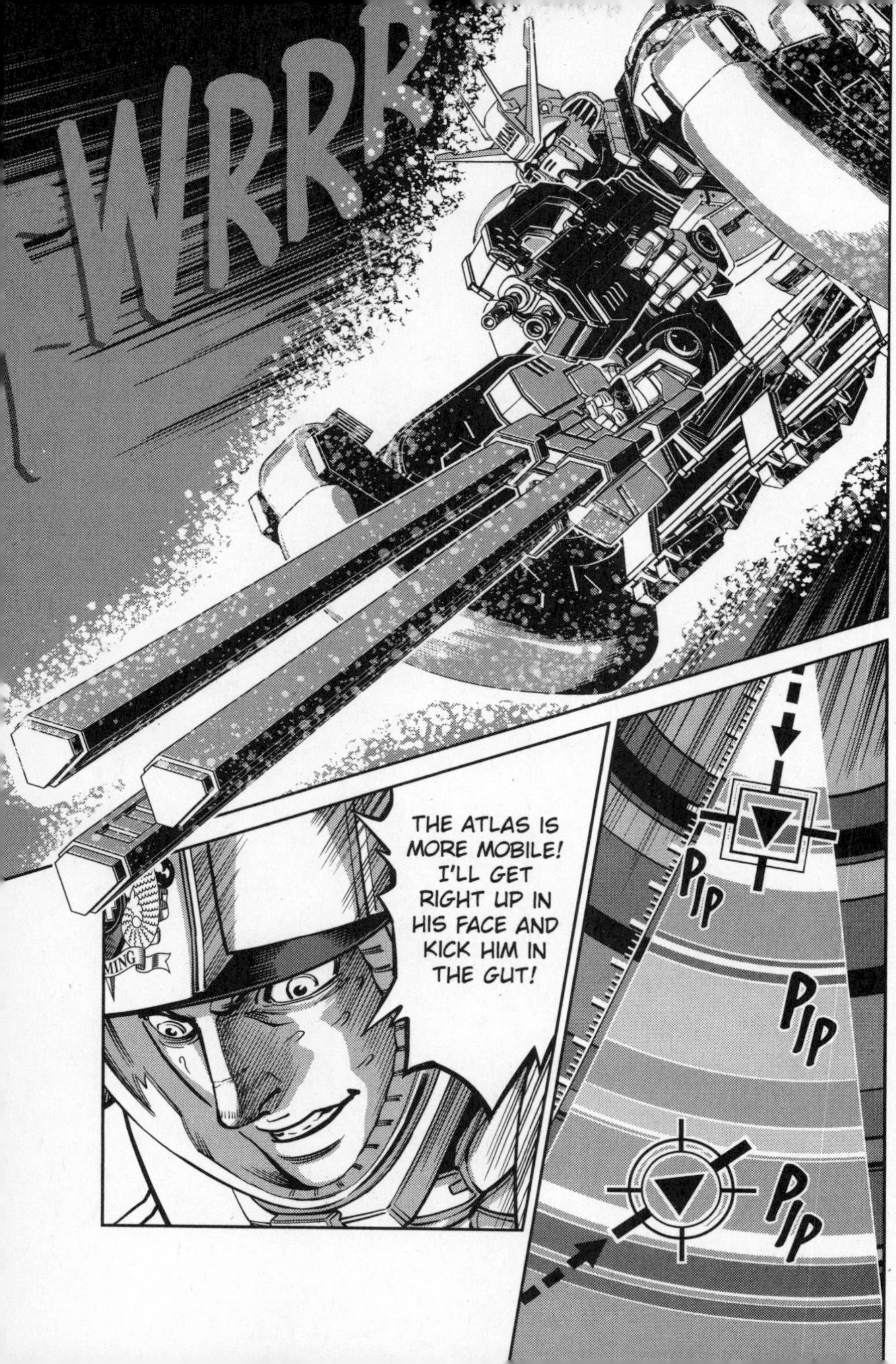
WRRR
THE ATLAS IS MORE MOBILE! I'LL GET RIGHT UP IN HIS FACE AND KICK HIM IN THE GUT!
PIP
PIP
PIP

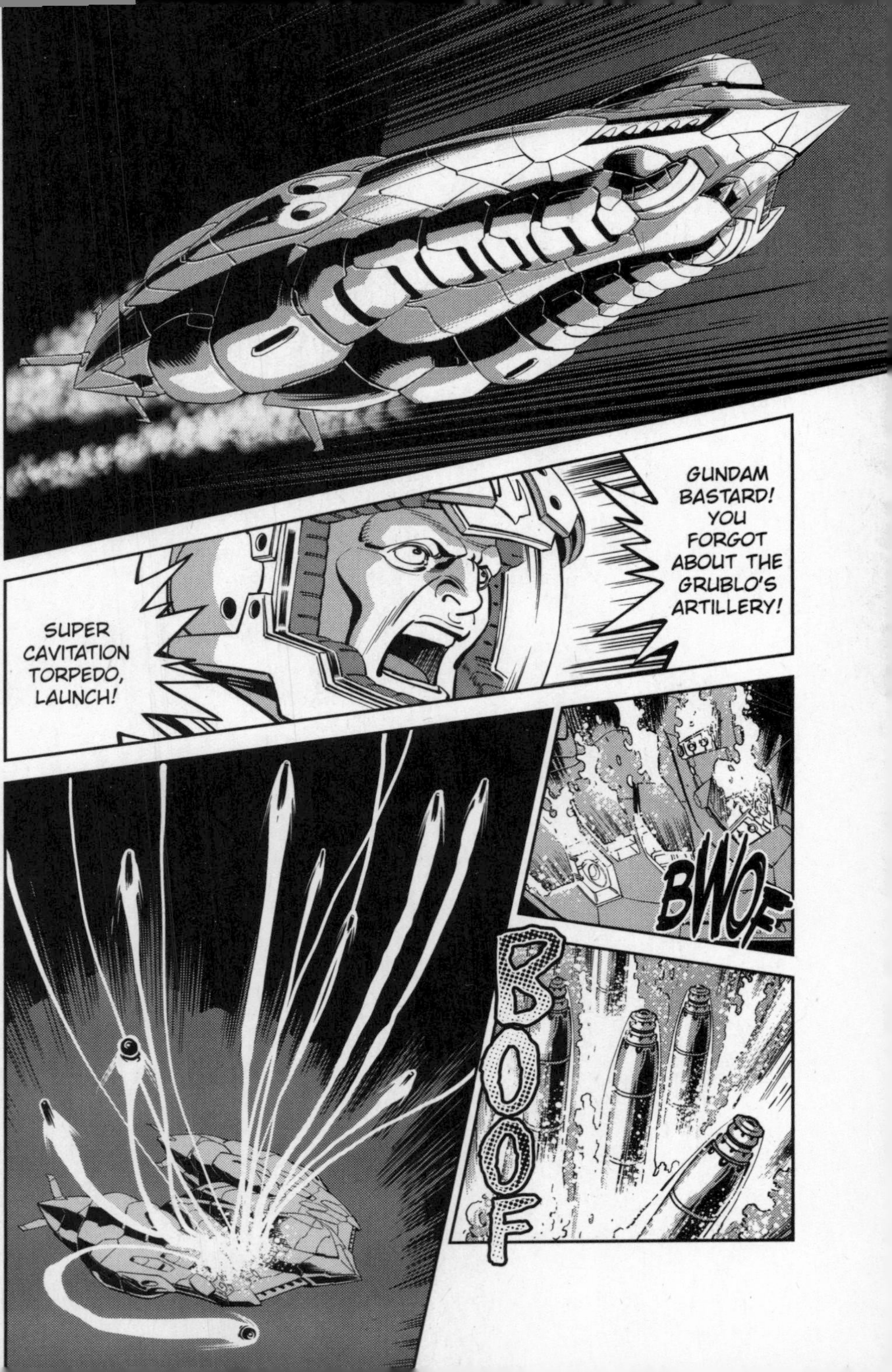
GUNDAM BASTARD! YOU FORGOT ABOUT THE GRUBLO'S ARTILLERY!
SUPER CAVITATION TORPEDO, LAUNCH!
BWOF
BOOOF

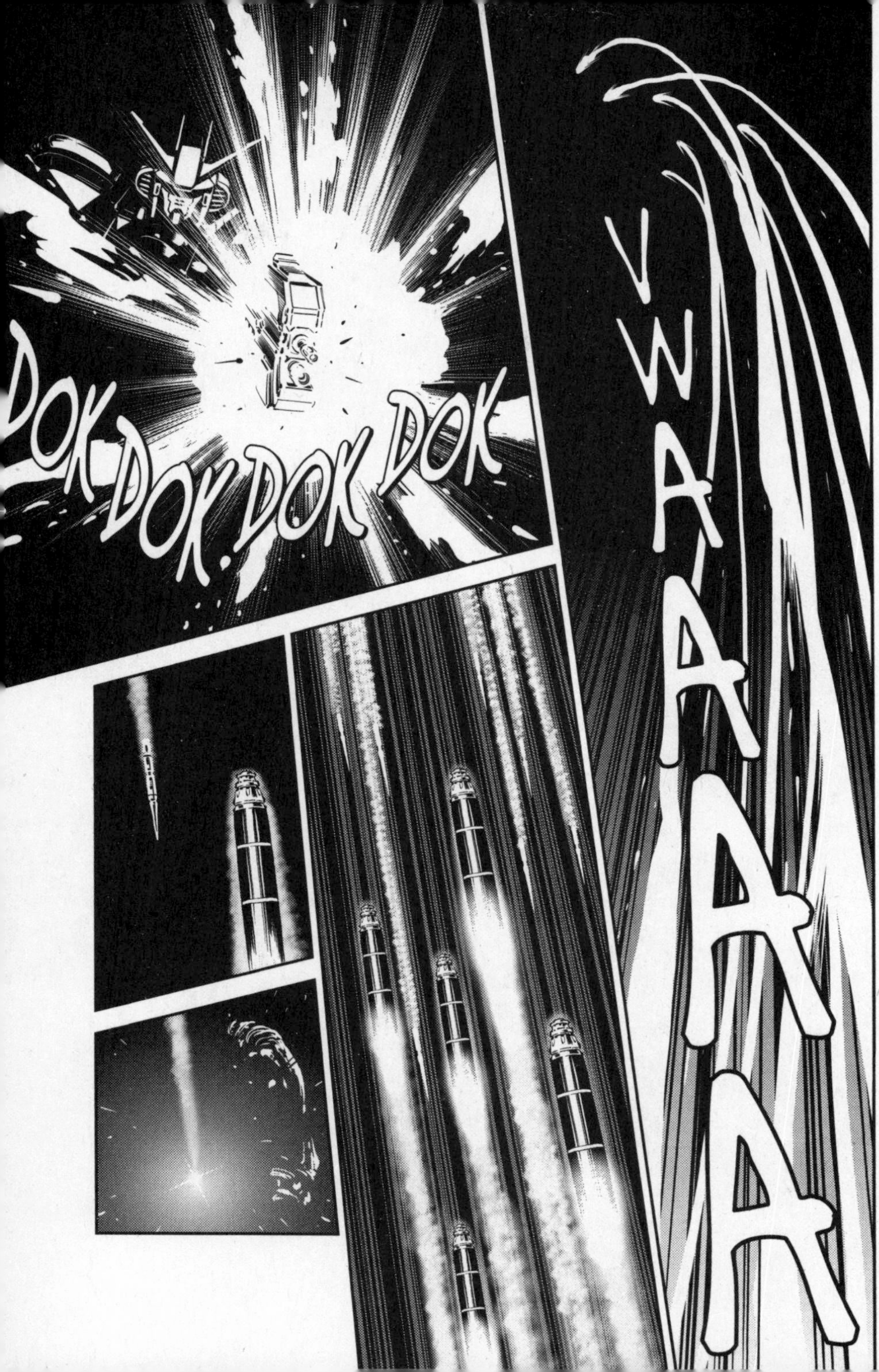
VWAAAA
DOK DOK DOK DOK

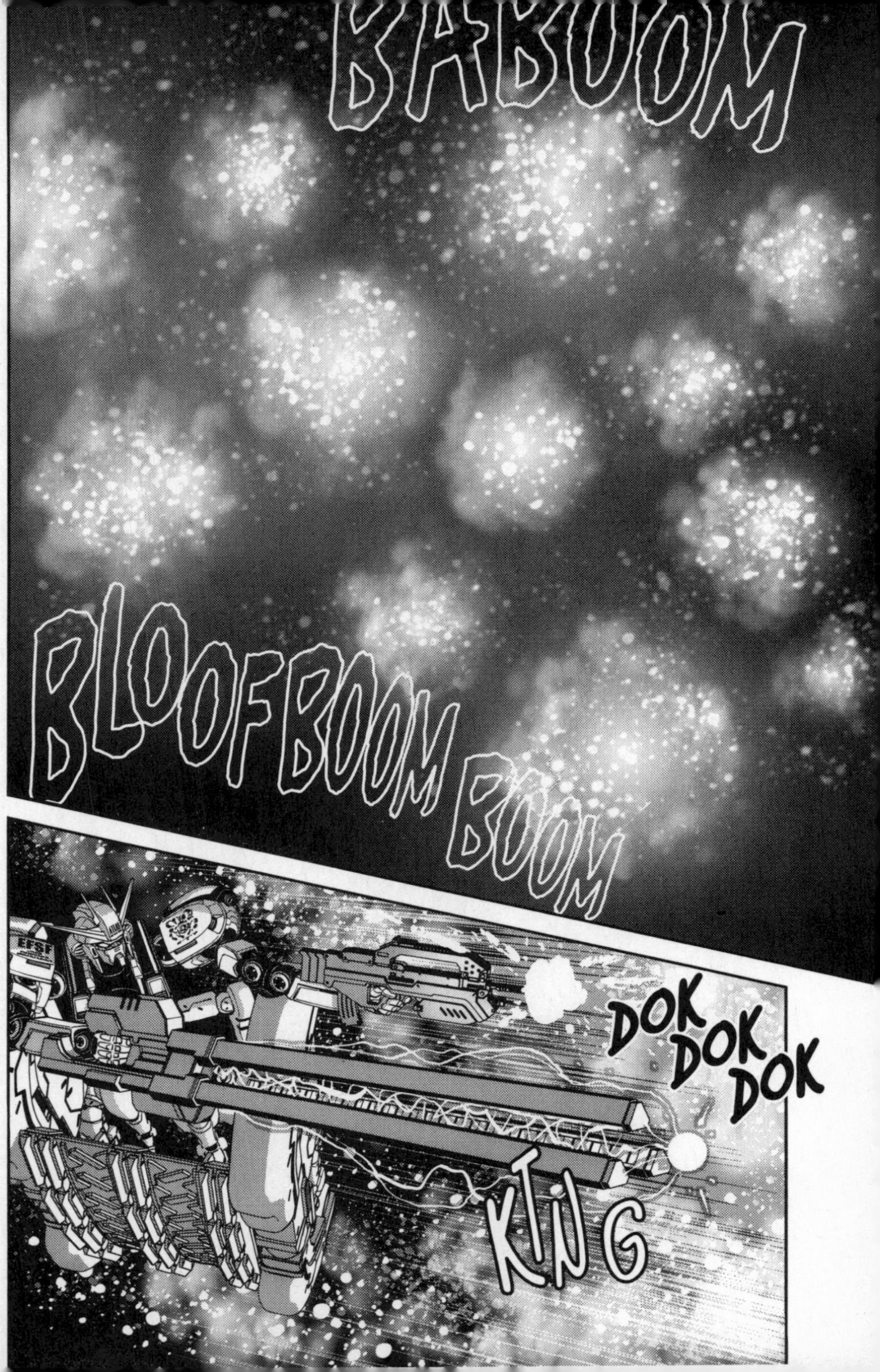
BABOOM
BLOOF BOOM BOOM
EFSF
DOK DOK DOK
KTING

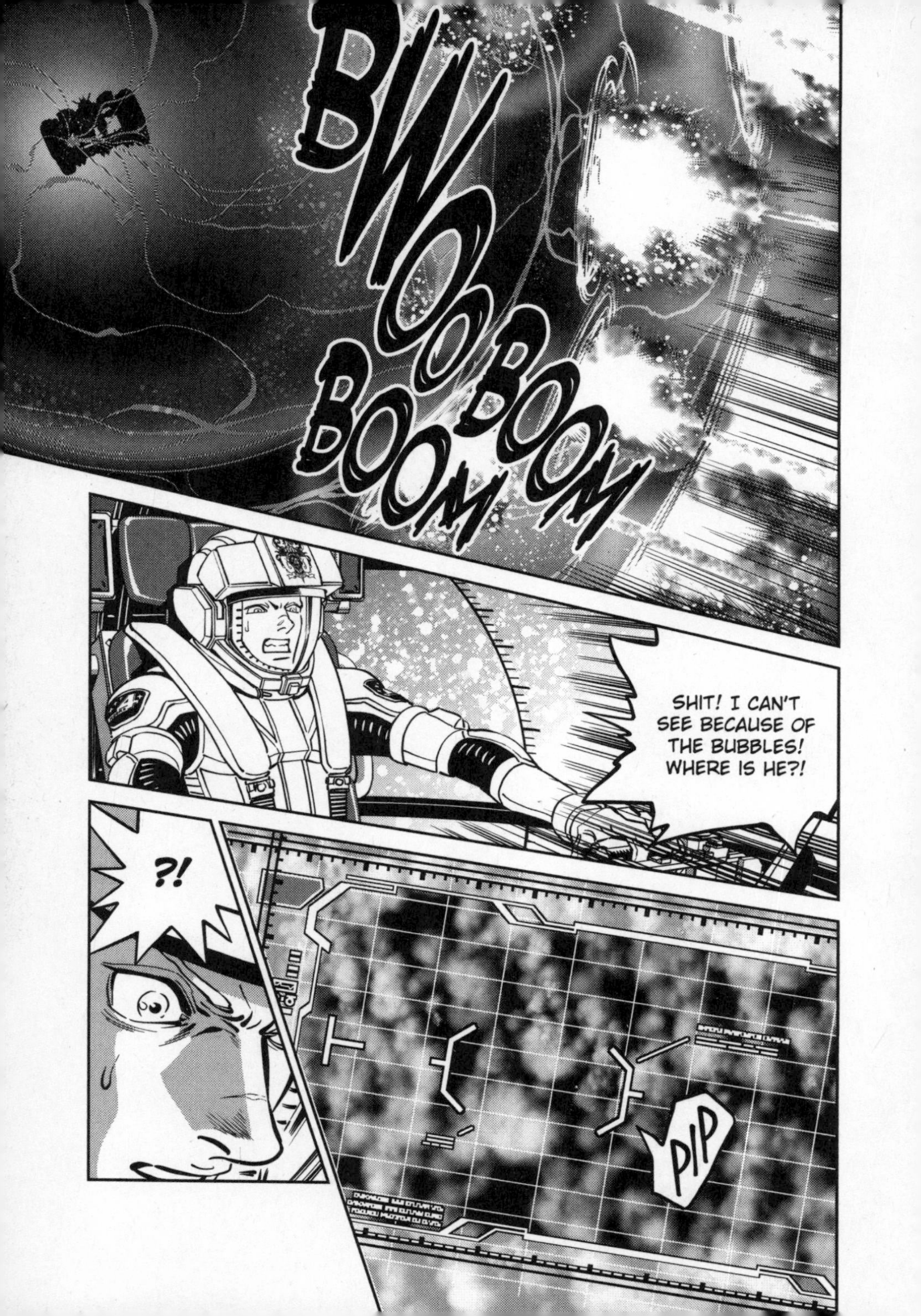
BWOOOBOOM
BOOM
SHIT! I CAN'T SEE BECAUSE OF THE BUBBLES! WHERE IS HE?!
PIP
?!

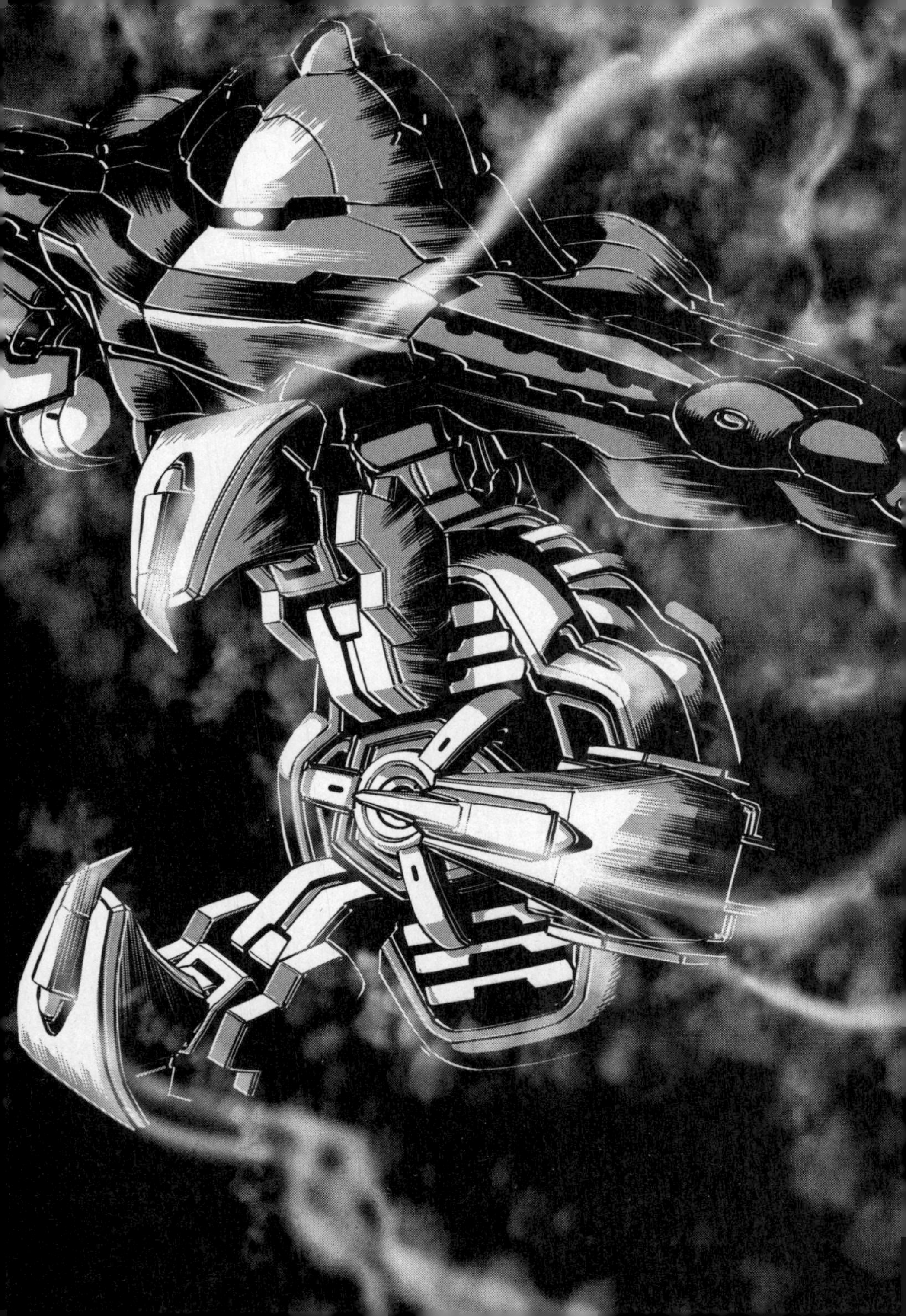

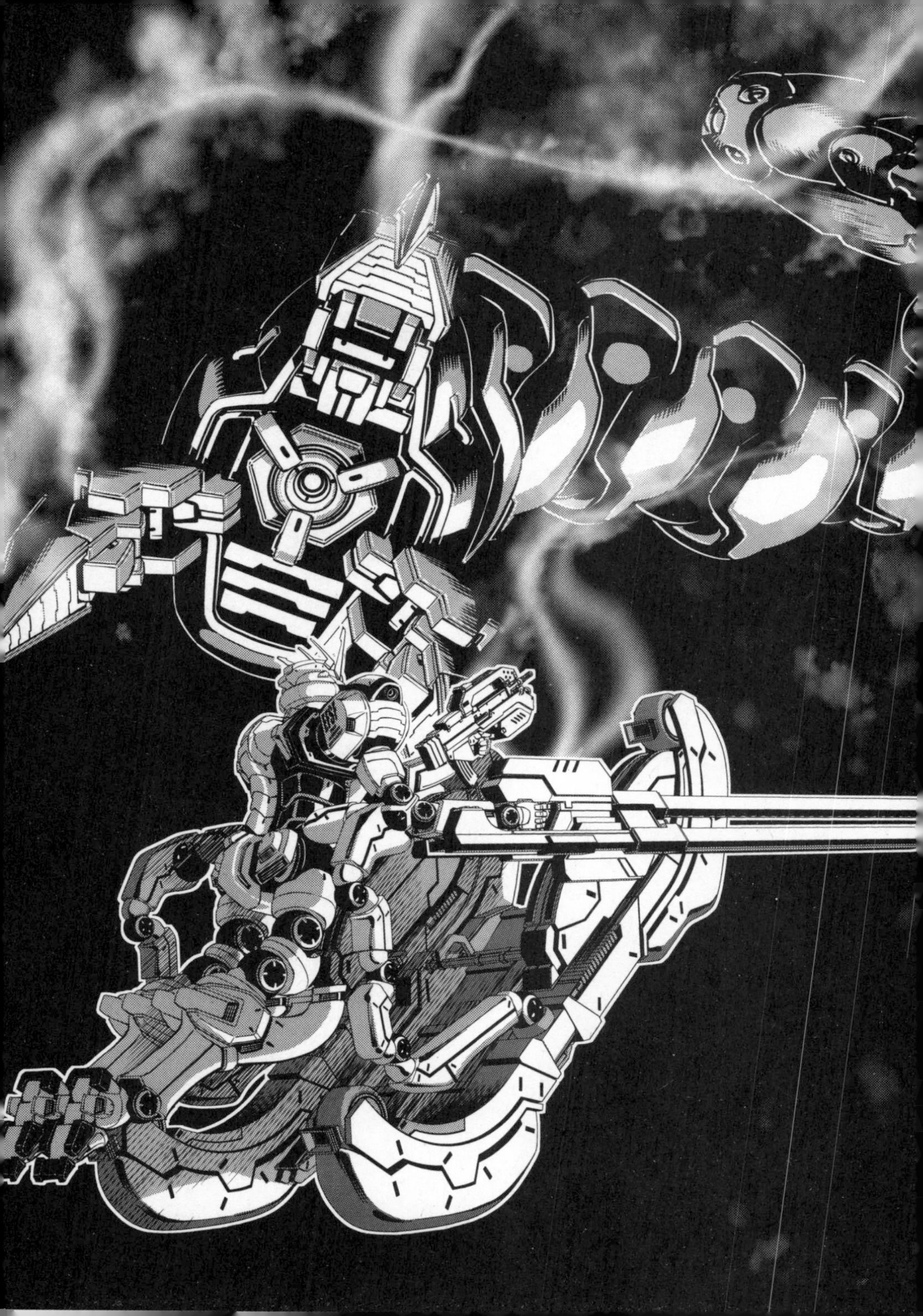

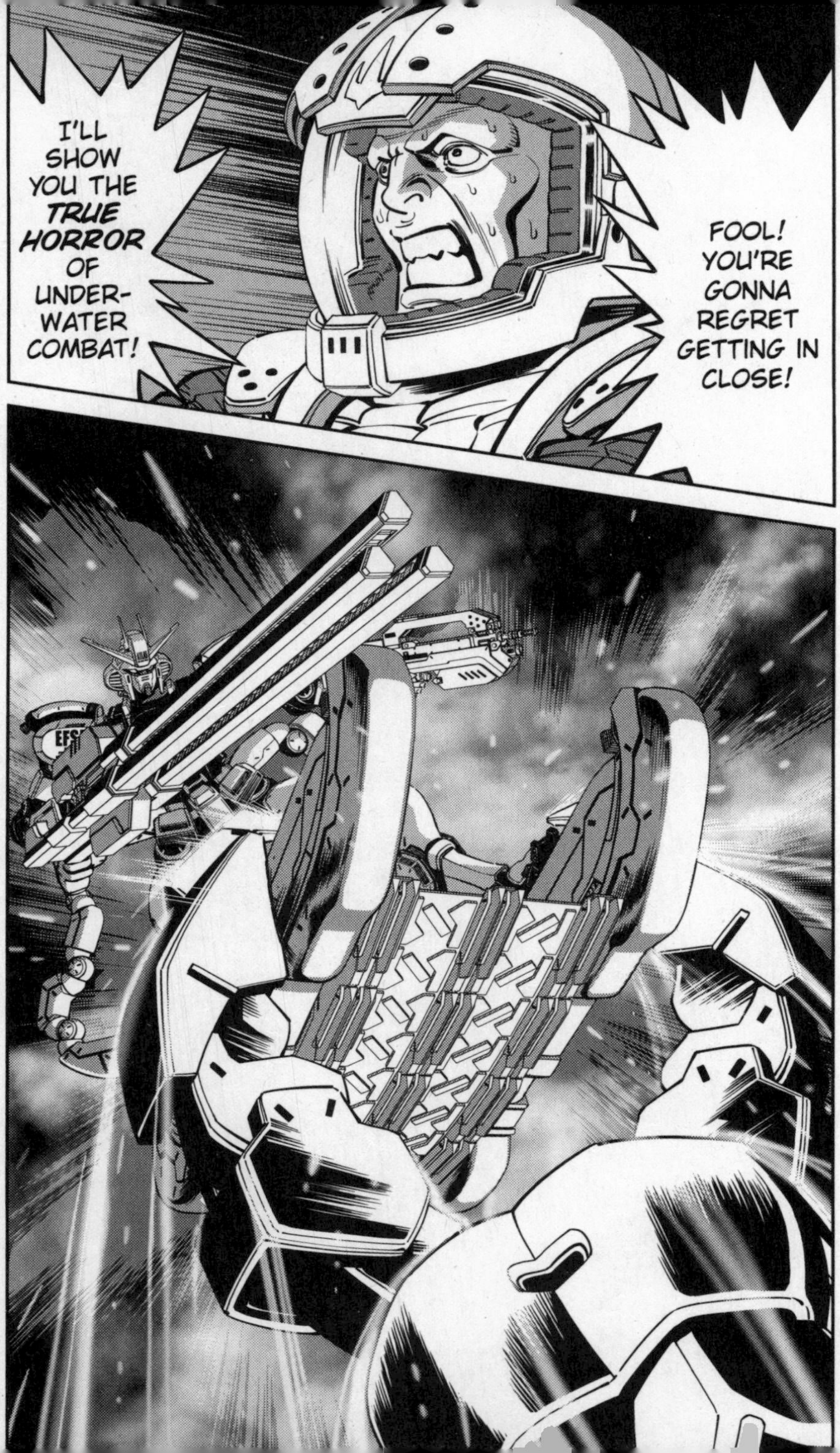
FOOL! YOU'RE GONNA REGRET GETTING IN CLOSE!
I'LL SHOW YOU THE ***TRUE HORROR*** OF UNDER-WATER COMBAT!
EFS

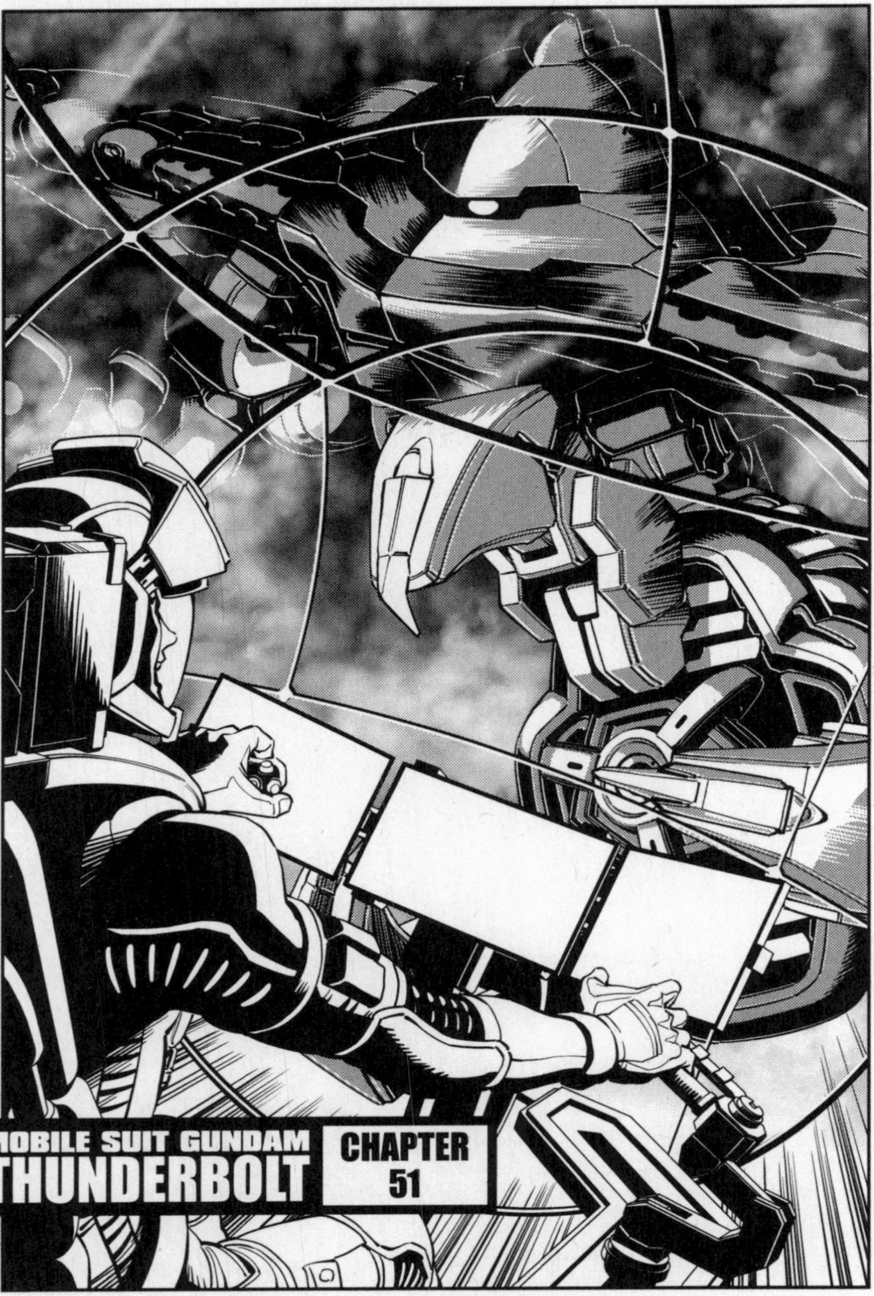
MOBILE SUIT GUNDAM
THUNDERBOLT
CHAPTER
51

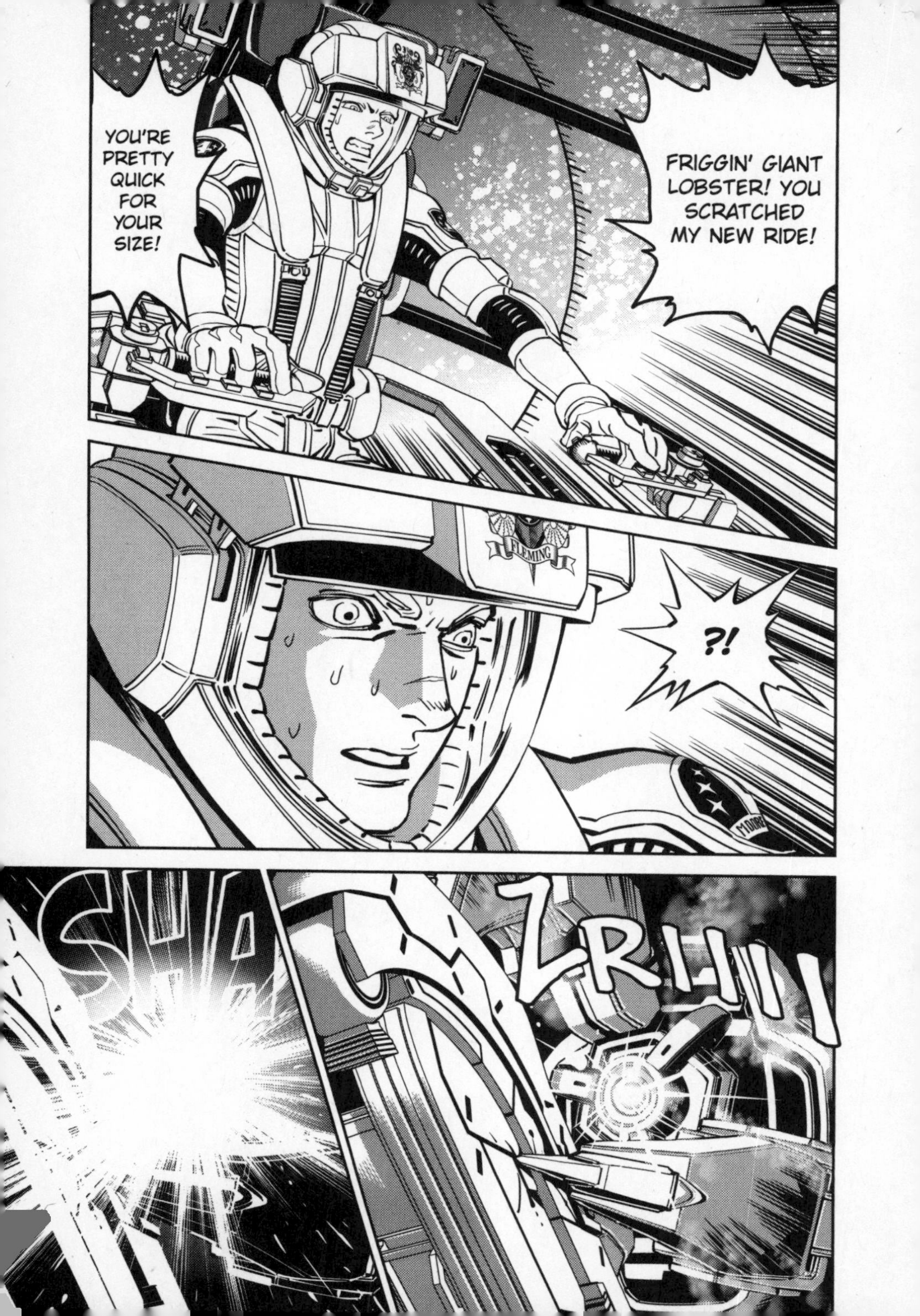
FRIGGIN' GIANT LOBSTER! YOU SCRATCHED MY NEW RIDE!
YOU'RE PRETTY QUICK FOR YOUR SIZE!
FLEMING
?!
ZRIIIII
SHA

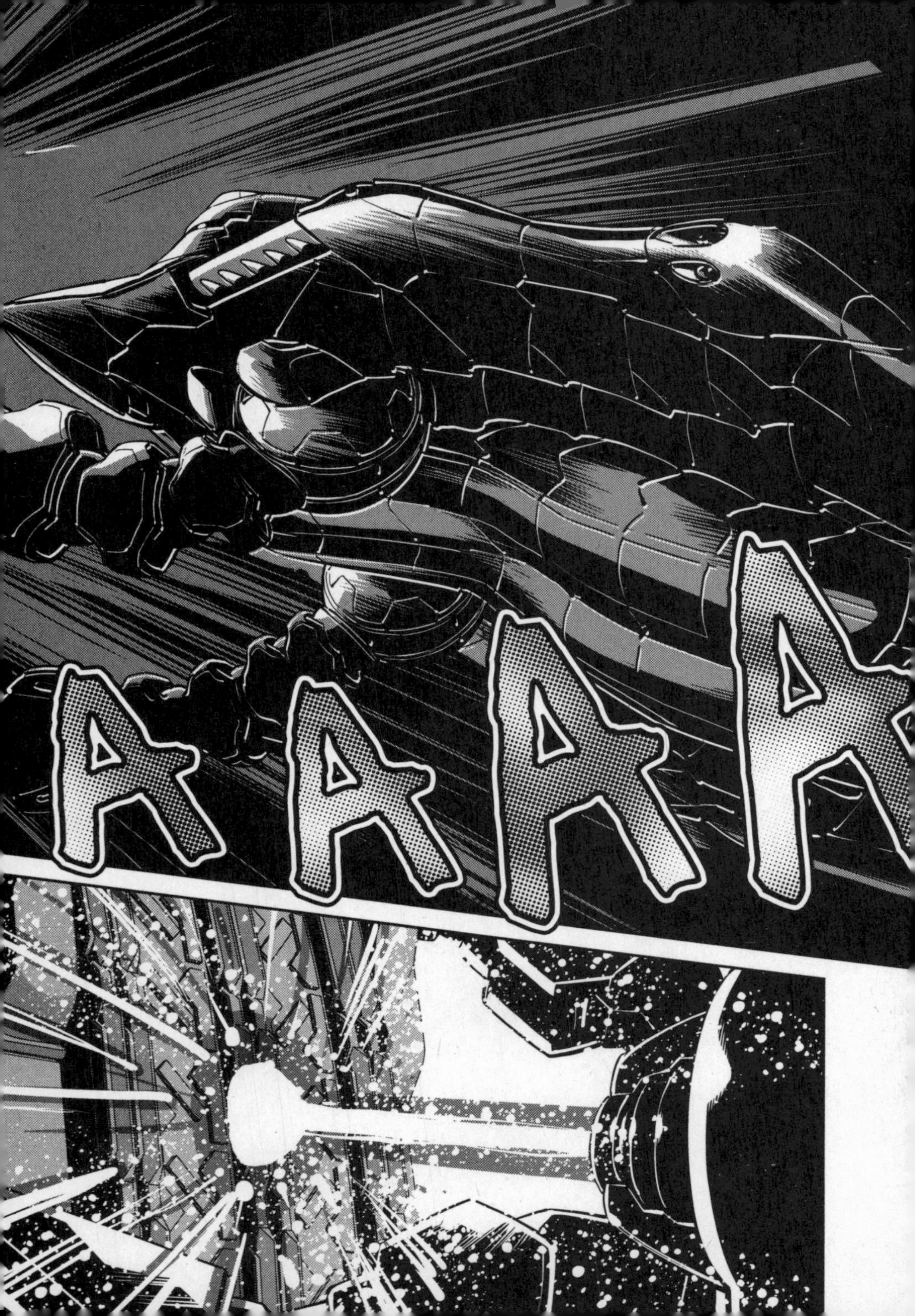
AAAA

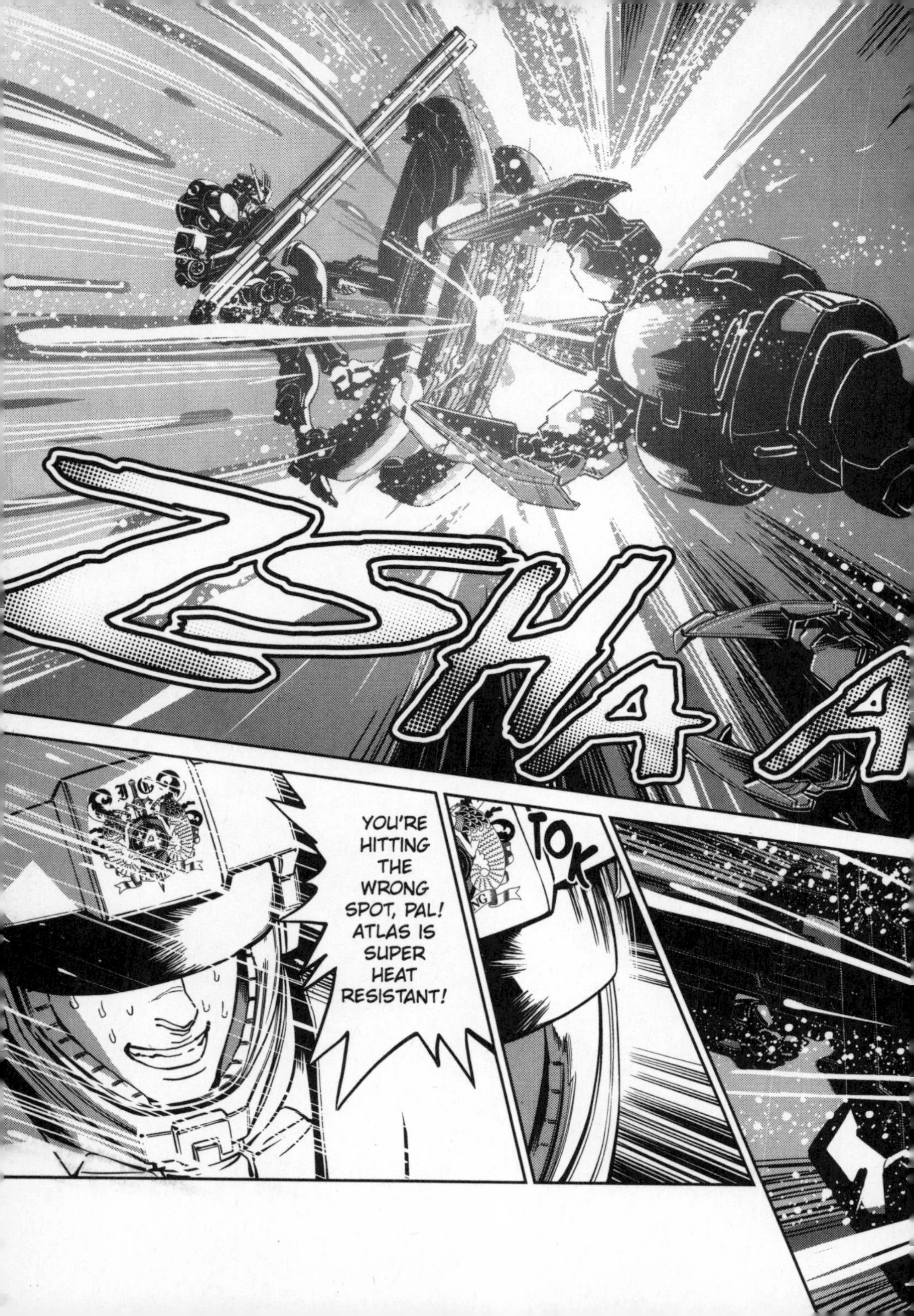
ZSHAA
TOK
YOU'RE HITTING THE WRONG SPOT, PAL! ATLAS IS SUPER HEAT RESISTANT!

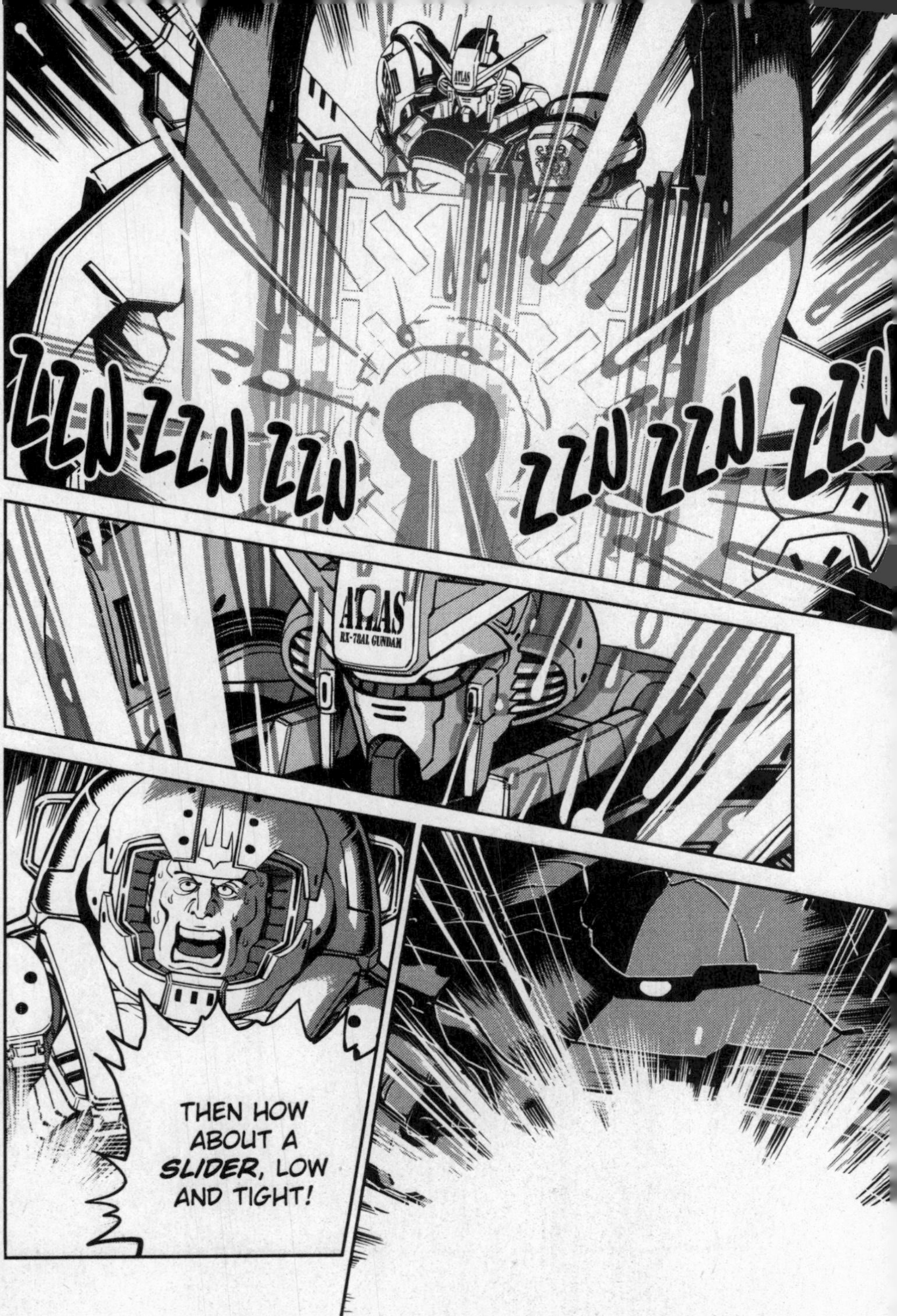
ZZN ZZN ZZN
ZZN ZZN ZZN
ATLAS
ATLAS
RX-78AL GUNDAM
THEN HOW ABOUT A *SLIDER*, LOW AND TIGHT!

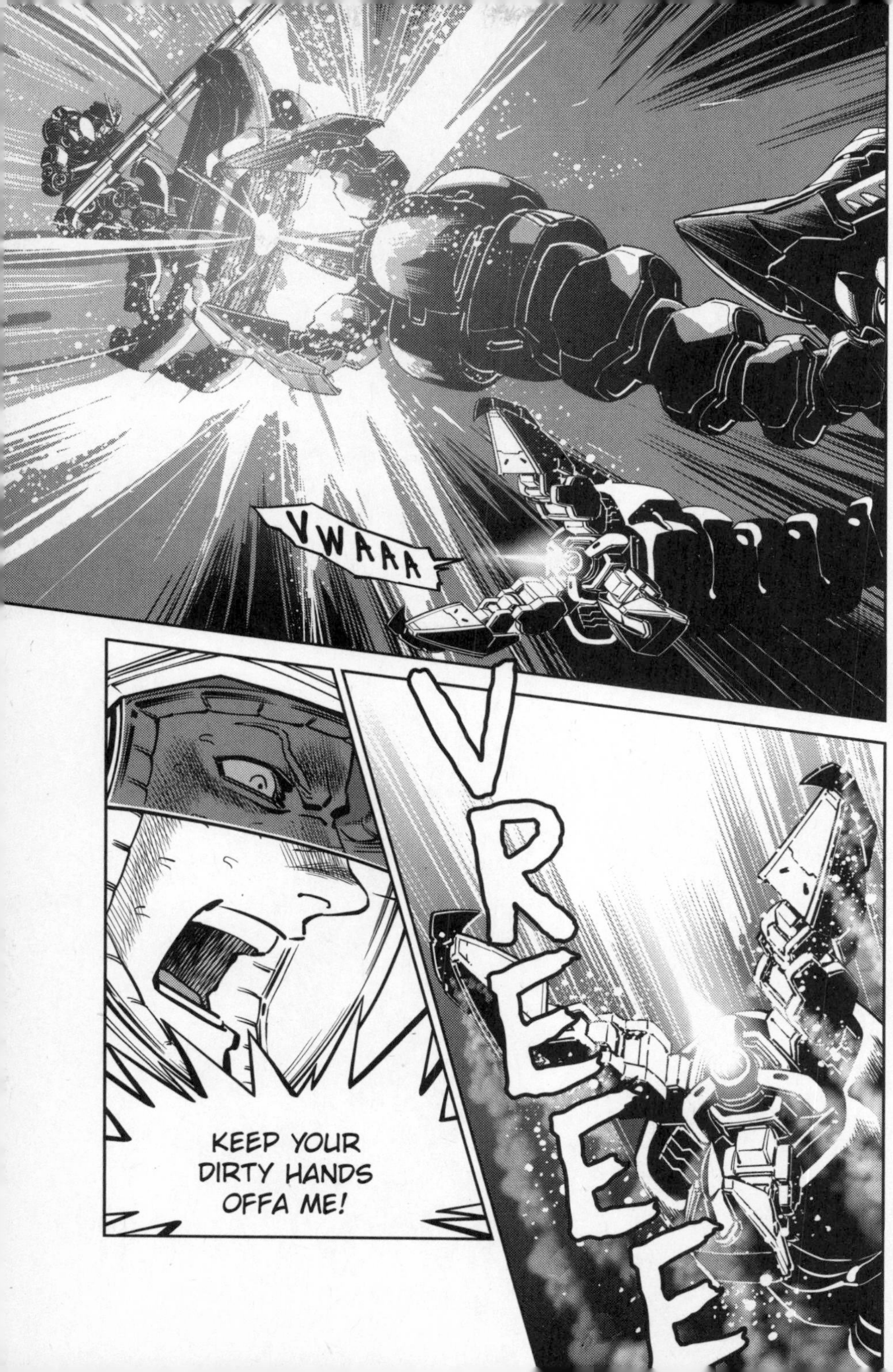
VWAAA
VREEE
KEEP YOUR DIRTY HANDS OFFA ME!

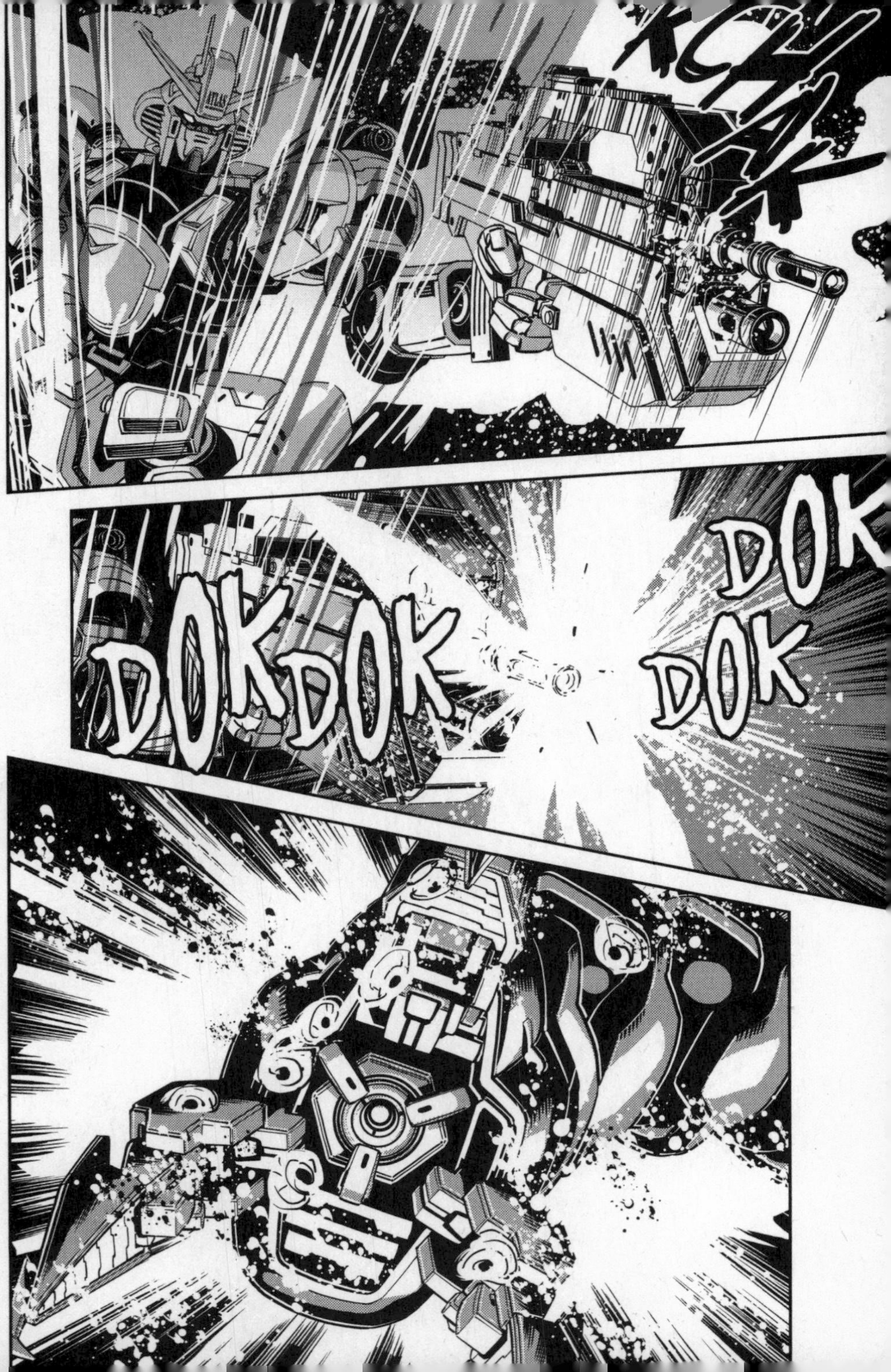
KCHAK
DOK
DOK
DOKDOK

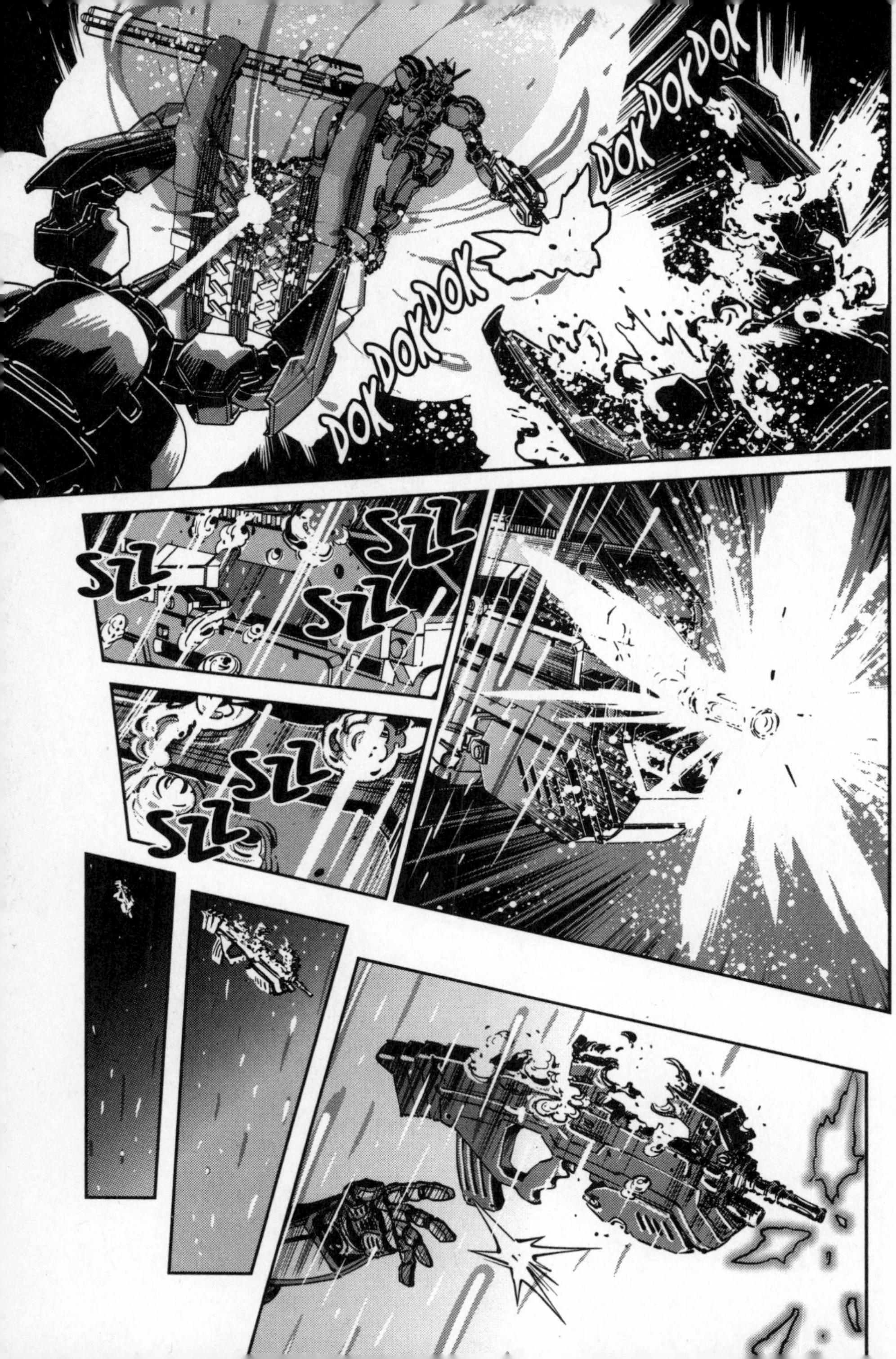
DOKDOKDOK
DOKDOKDOK
SZZ
SZZ
SZZ
SZZ
SZZ

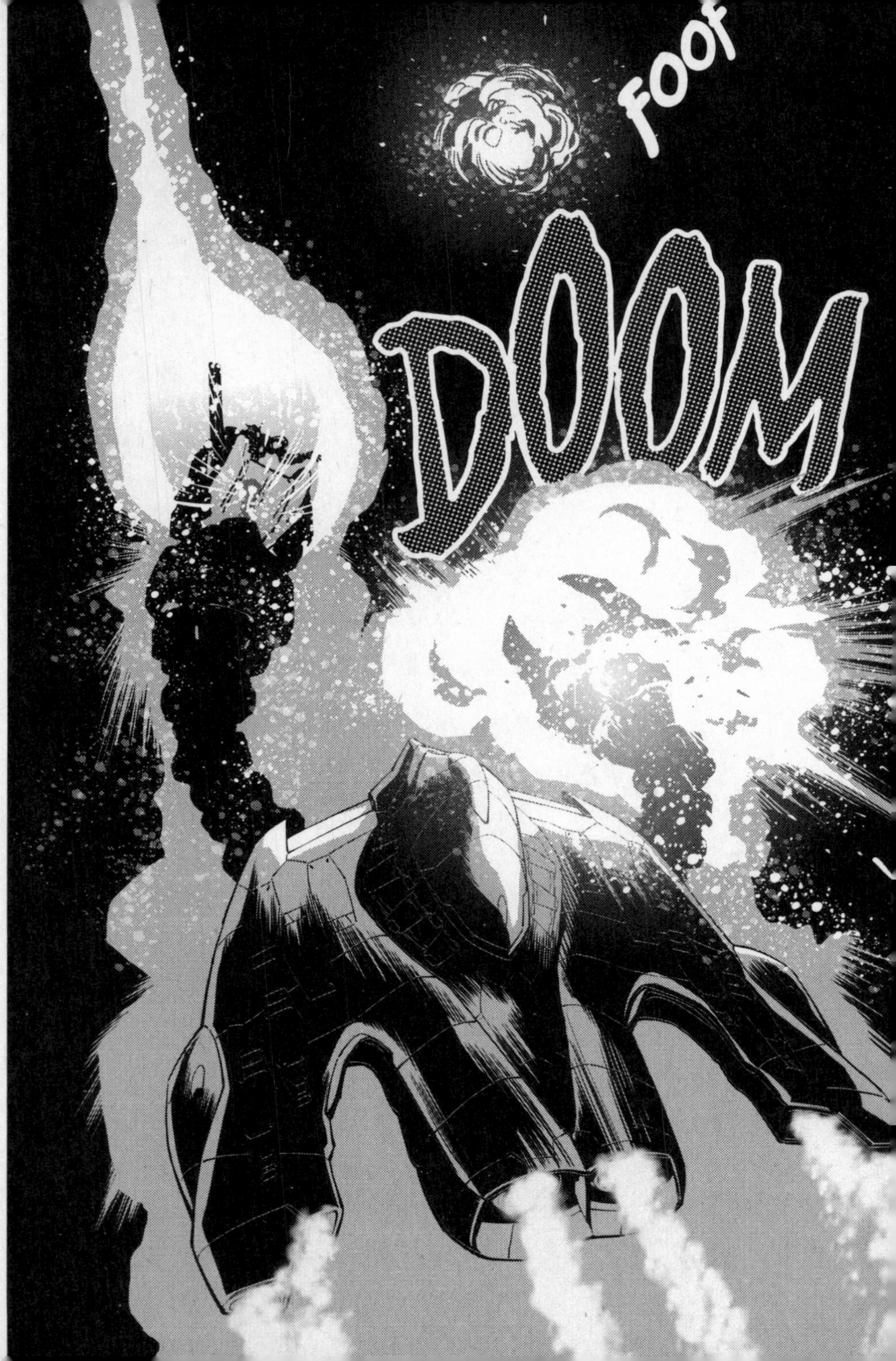
FOOF
DOOM

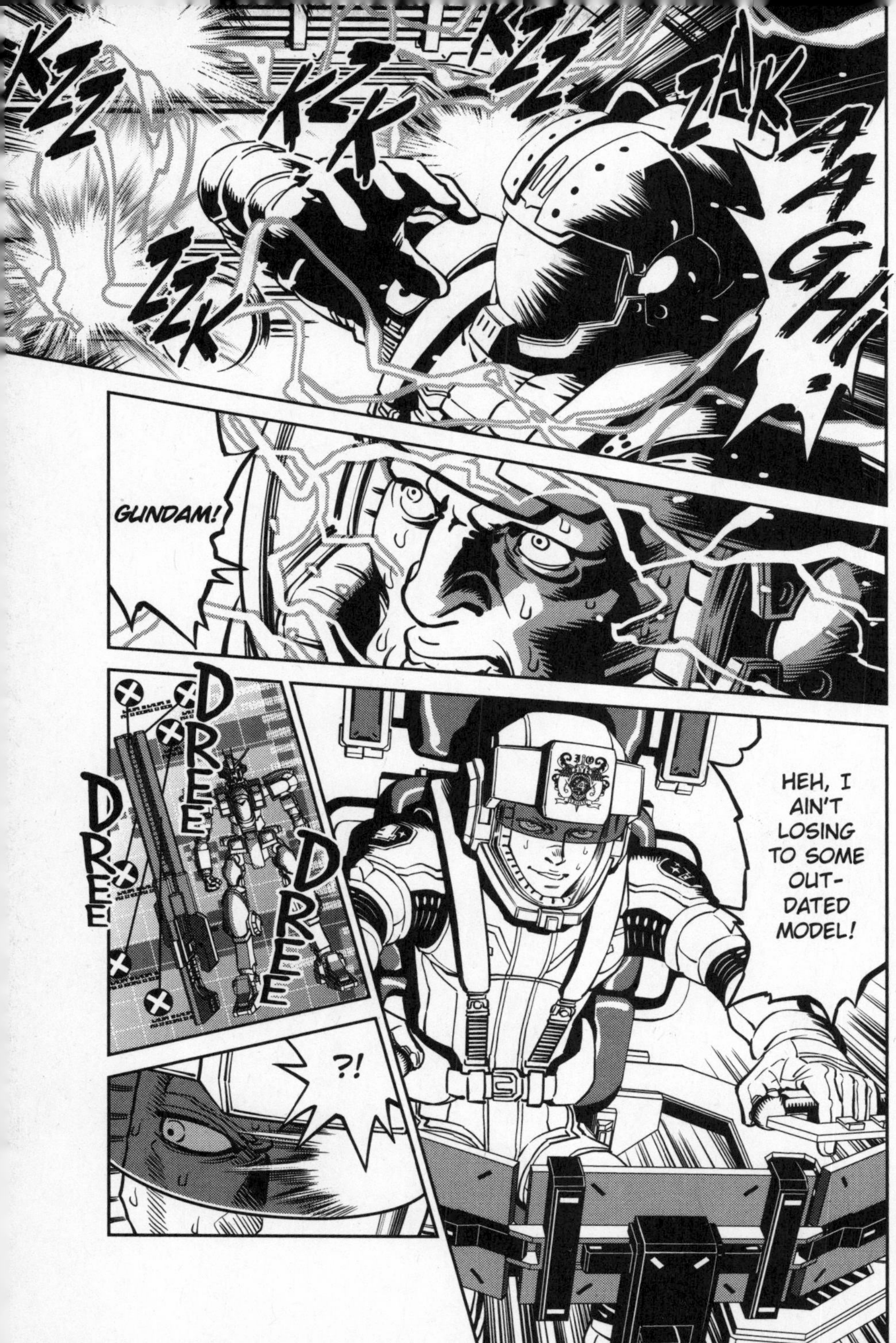
AAGH!
ZAK
KZZ
KZZ
KZK
KZZ
ZZK
GUNDAM!
HEH, I AIN'T LOSING TO SOME OUT-DATED MODEL!
DREE DREE
DREE DREE
?!

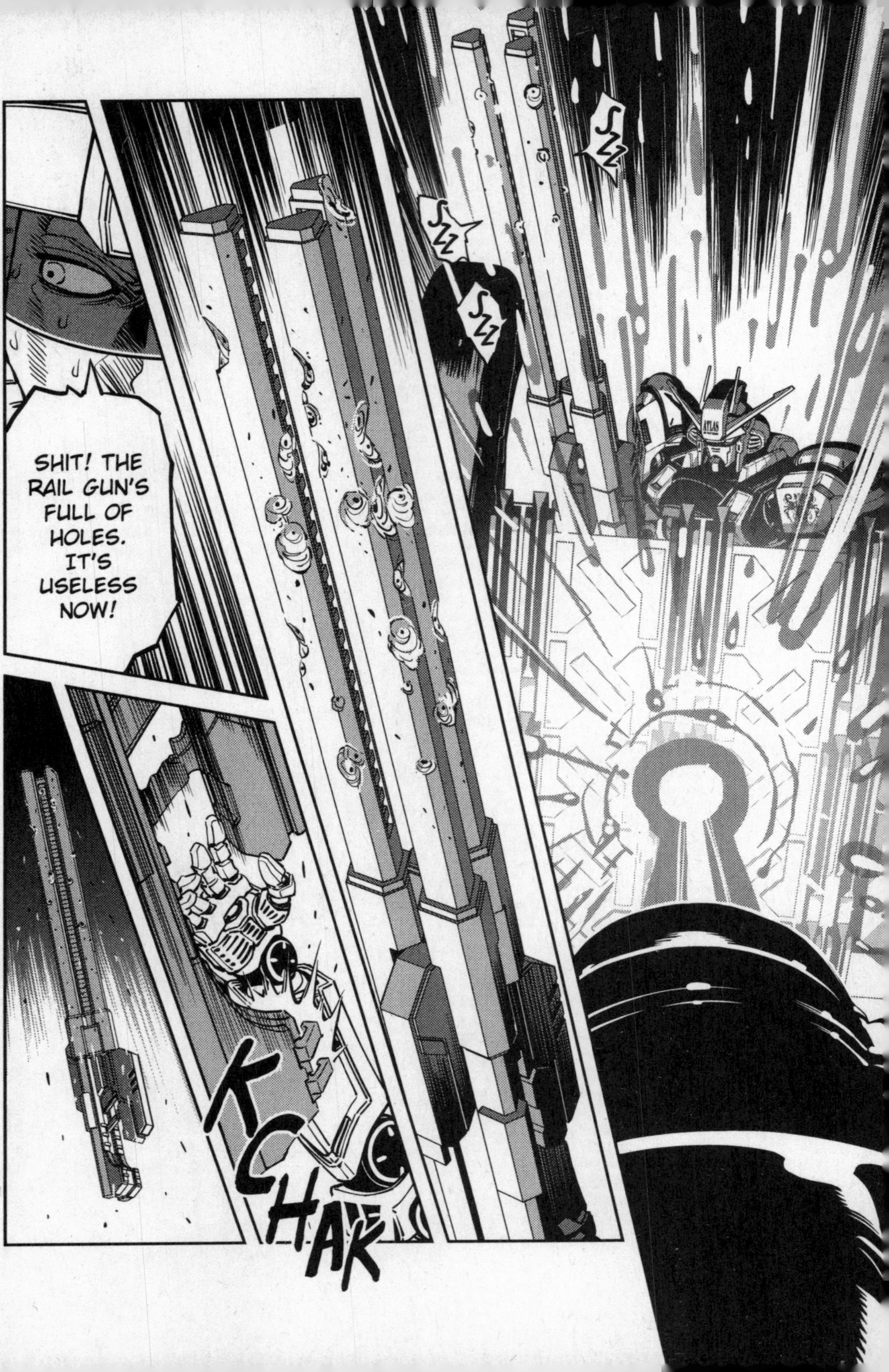
SZZ
SZZ
SZZ
SHIT! THE RAIL GUN'S FULL OF HOLES. IT'S USELESS NOW!
KCHAK

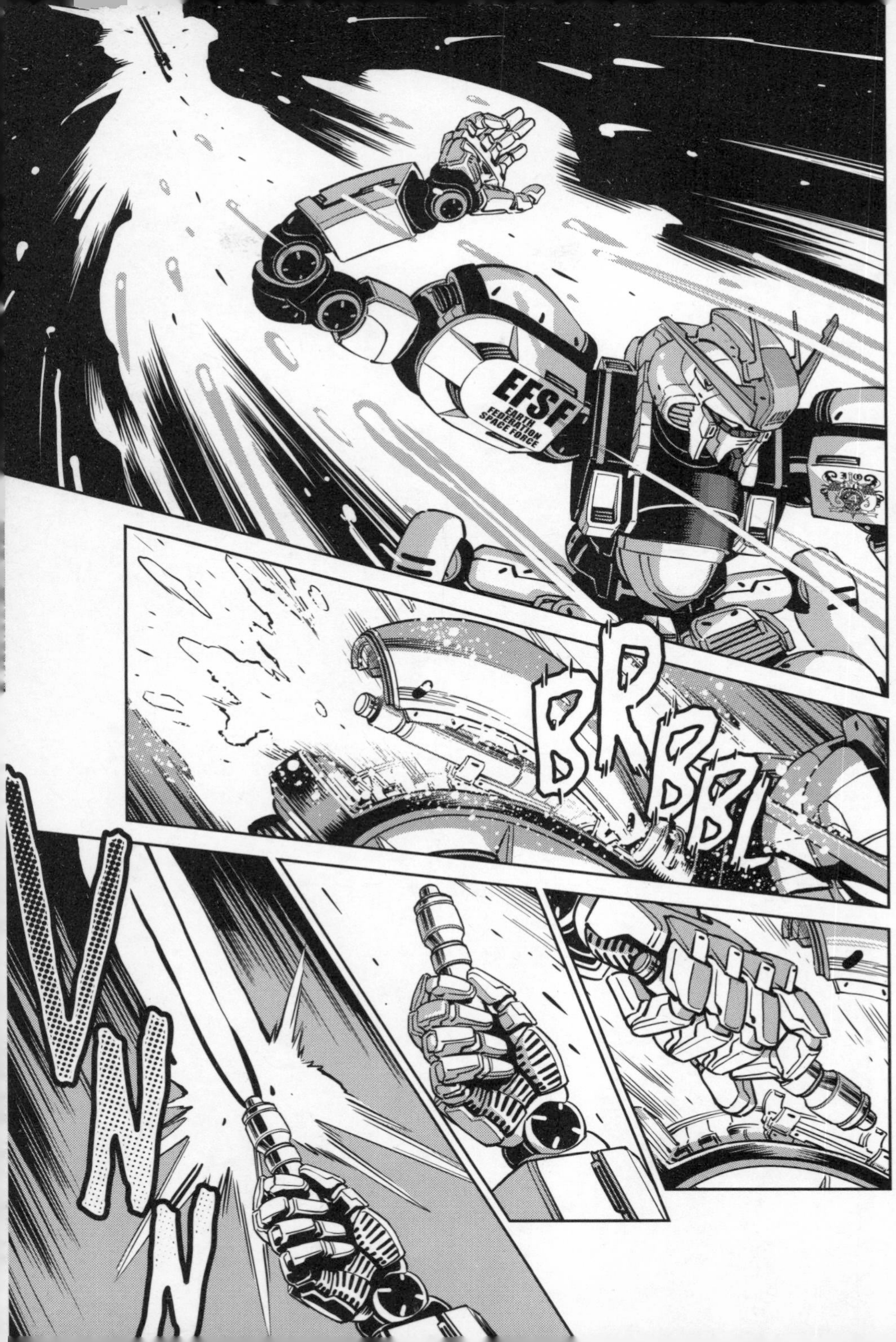
EFSF
EARTH FEDERATION SPACE FORCE
BRBBL
VWN

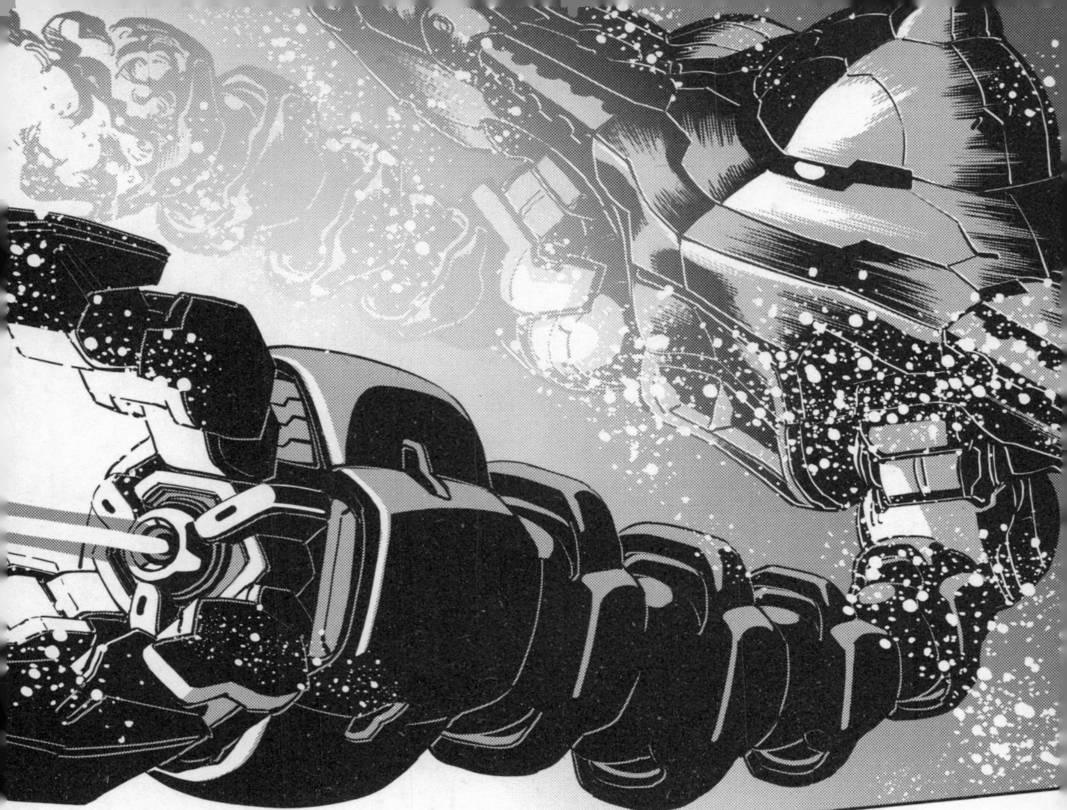

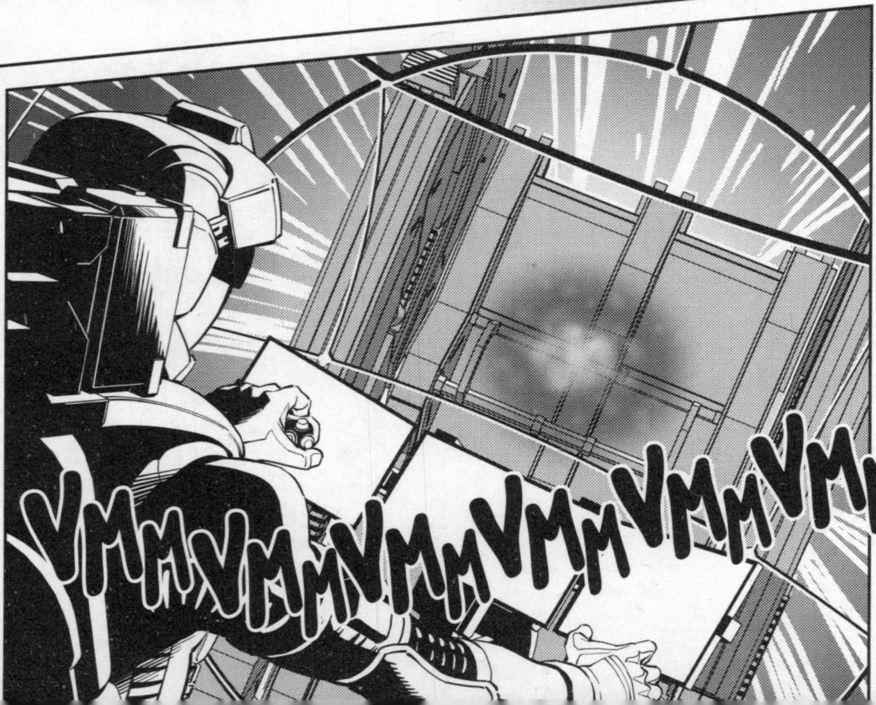
VMMVMMVMMVMMVMMVMM

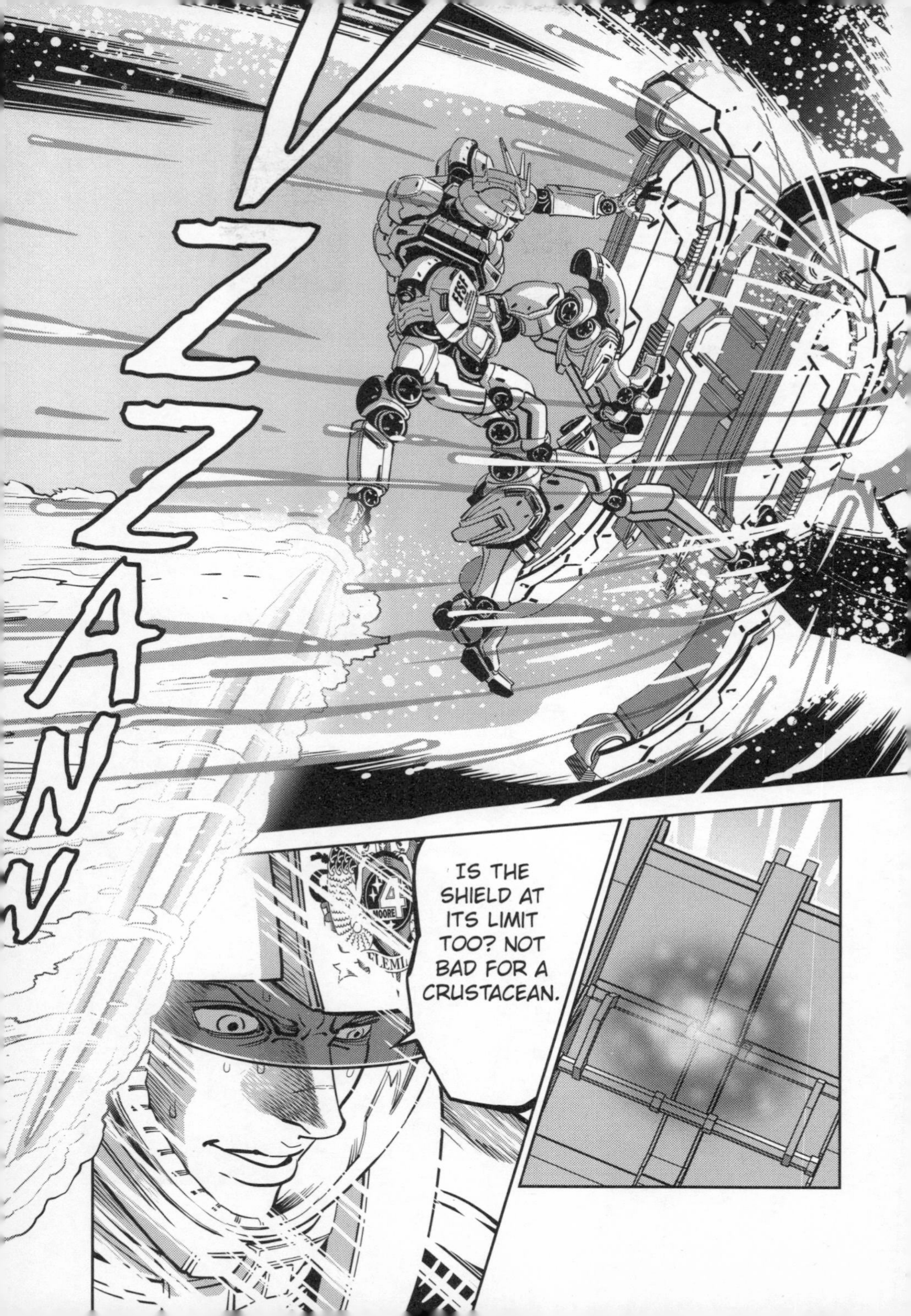
VZZZANN
IS THE SHIELD AT ITS LIMIT TOO? NOT BAD FOR A CRUSTACEAN.

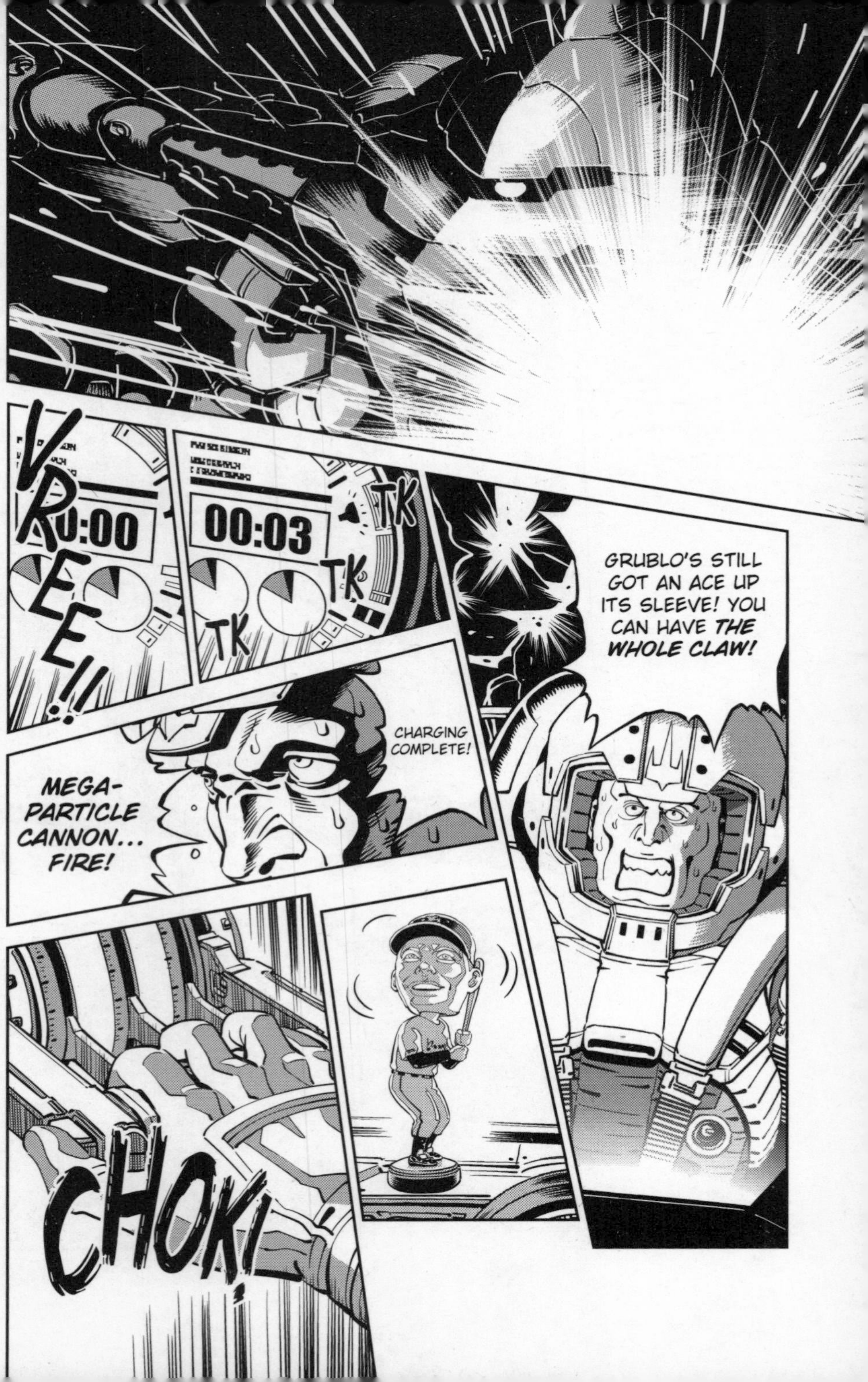
GRUBLO'S STILL GOT AN ACE UP ITS SLEEVE! YOU CAN HAVE *THE WHOLE CLAW!*
00:03
TK
TK
TK
VREEE!!
CHARGING COMPLETE!
MEGA-PARTICLE CANNON... FIRE!
CHOK!

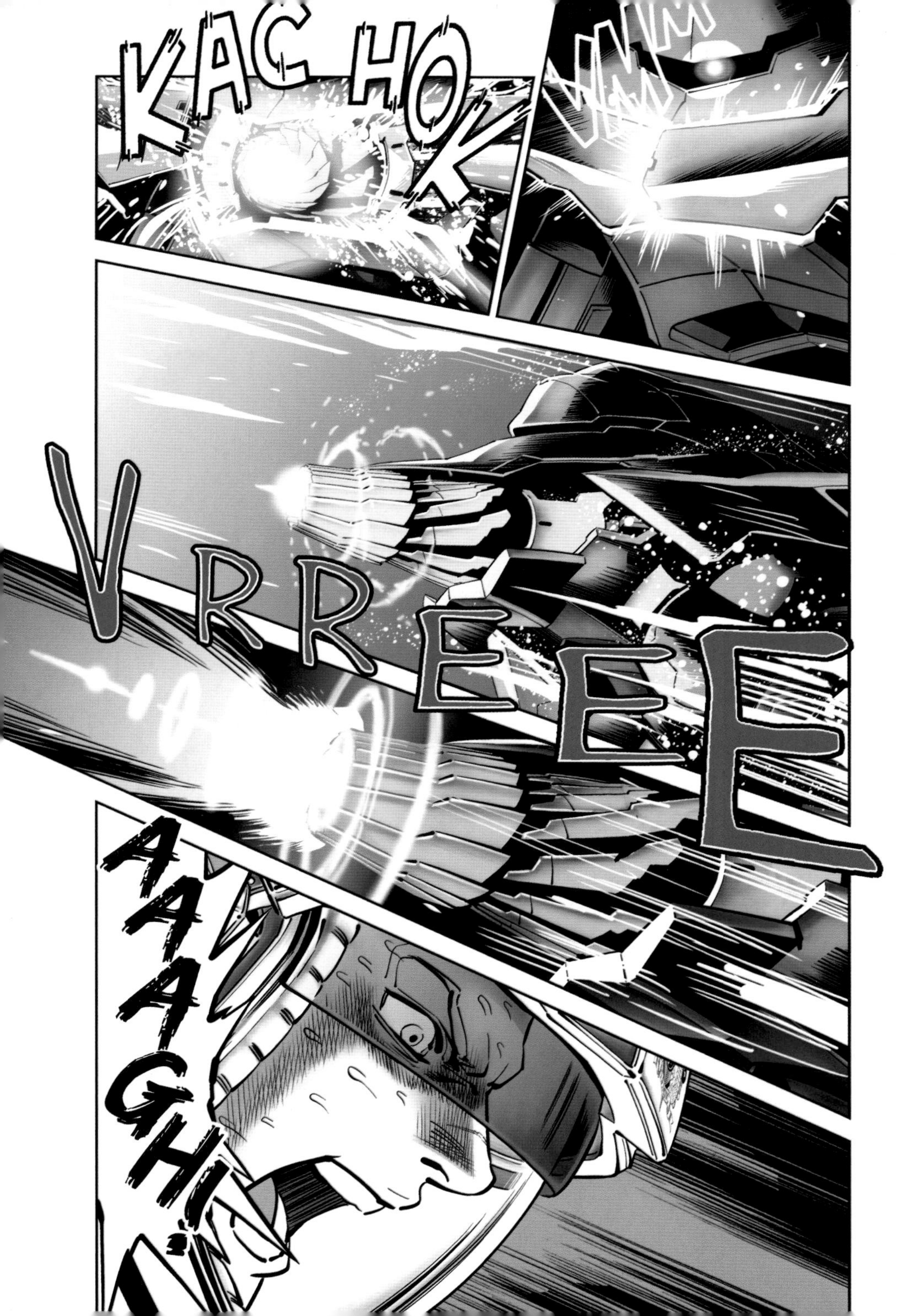
KACHOK
VRREEEE
AAAAGH!

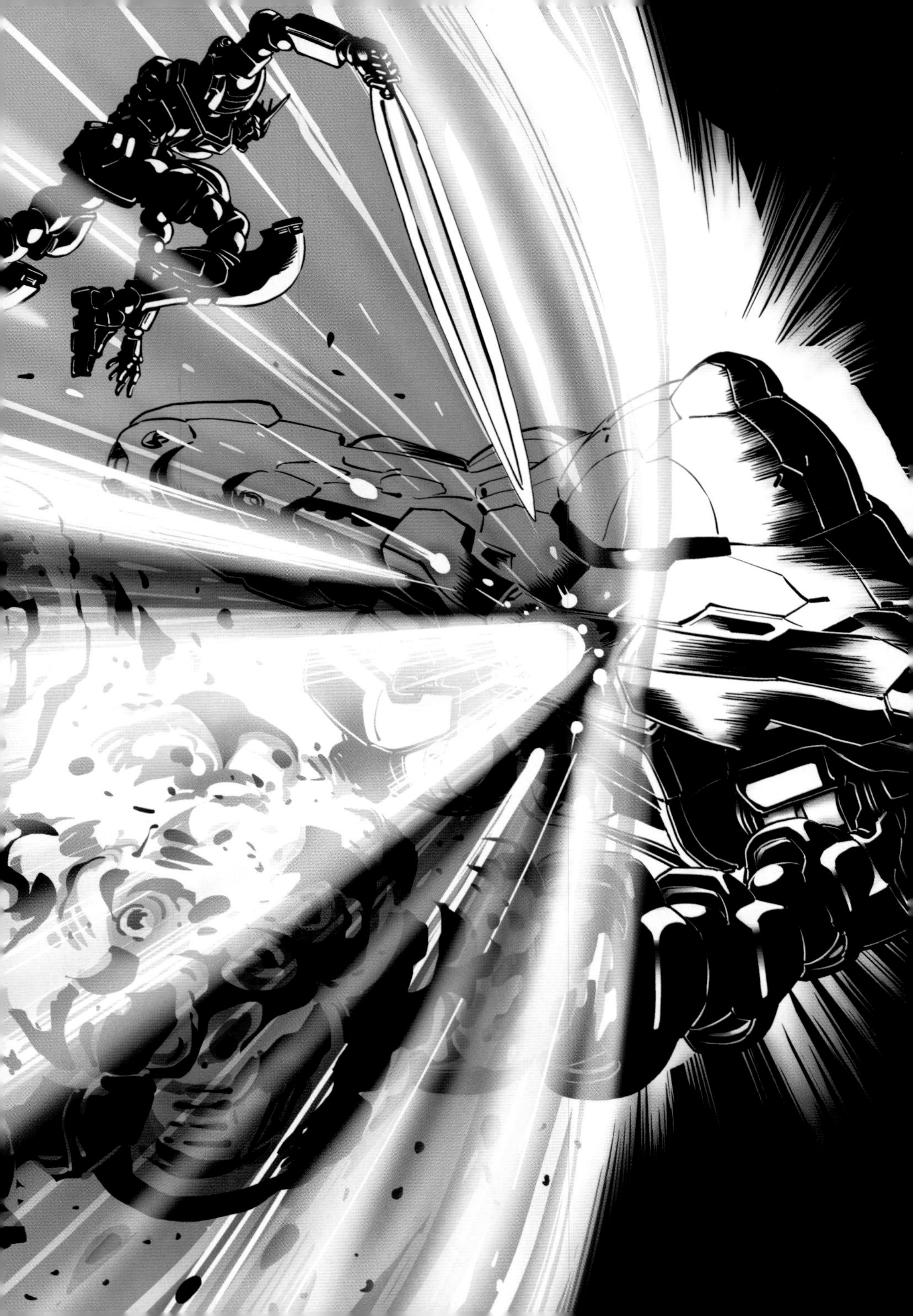

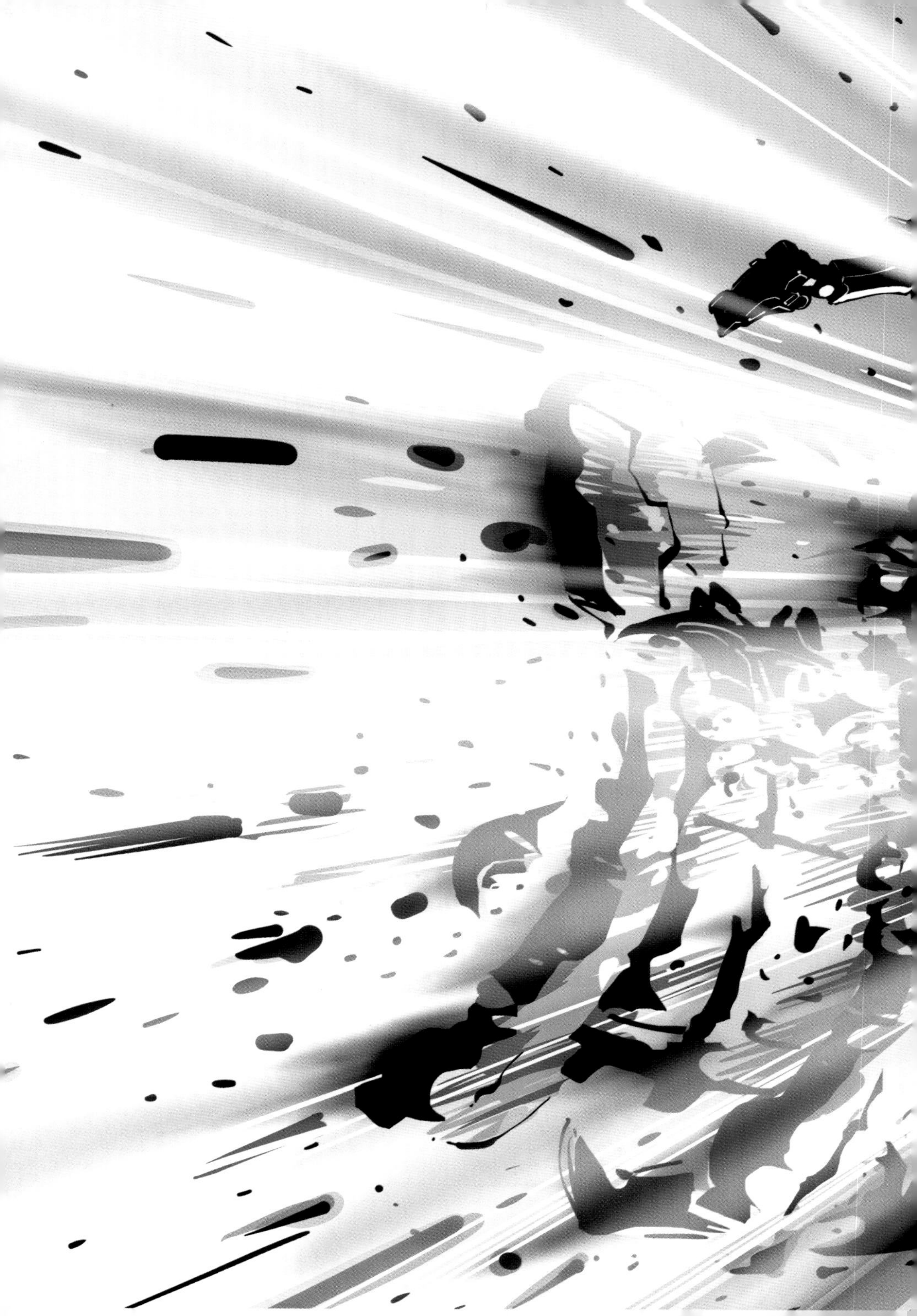

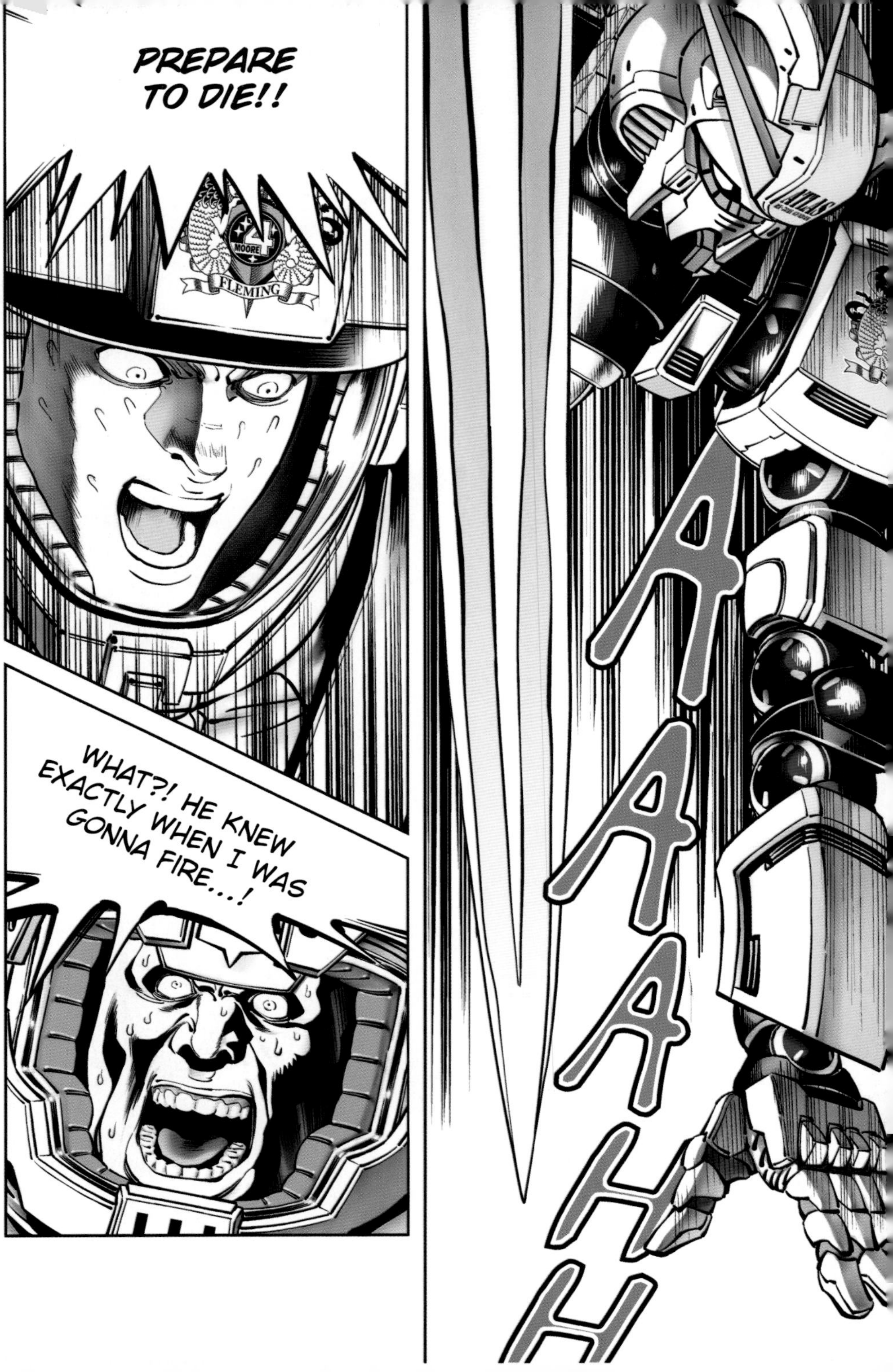
AAAHH
PREPARE TO DIE!!
WHAT?! HE KNEW EXACTLY WHEN I WAS GONNA FIRE...!

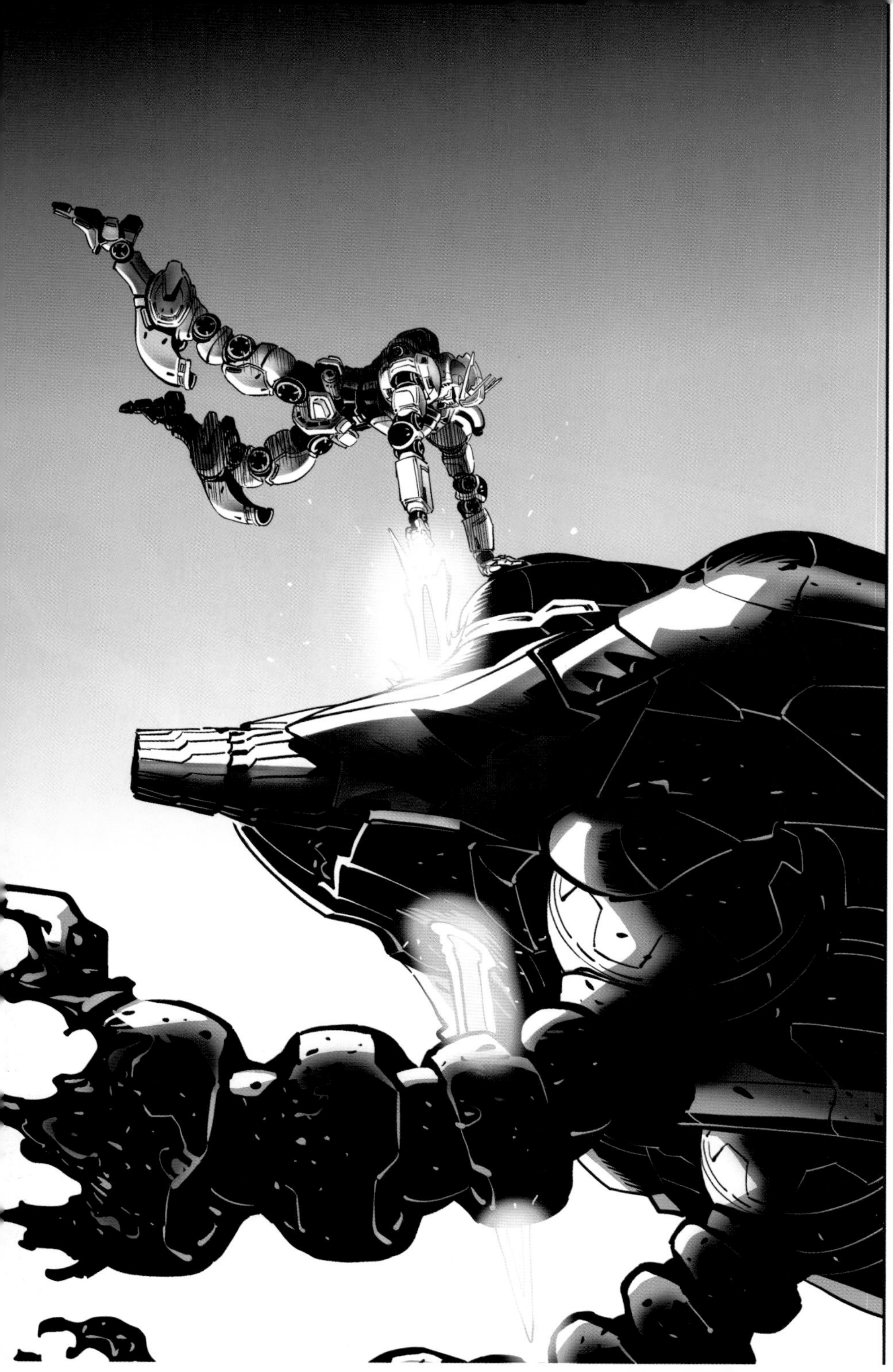

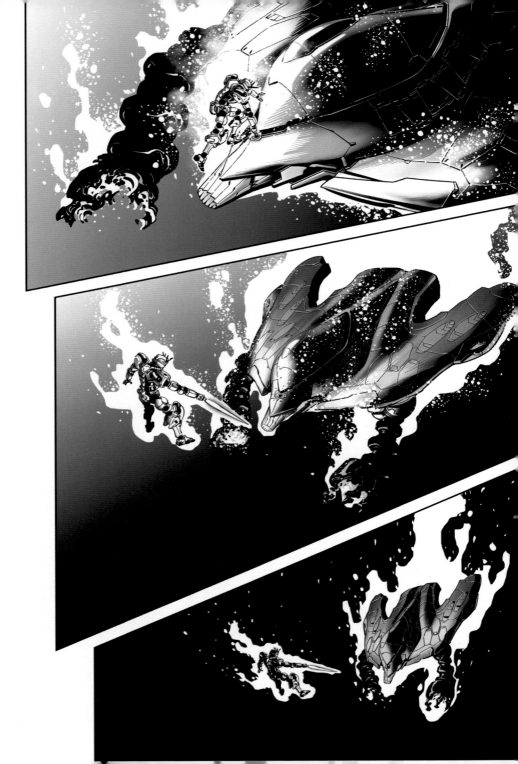

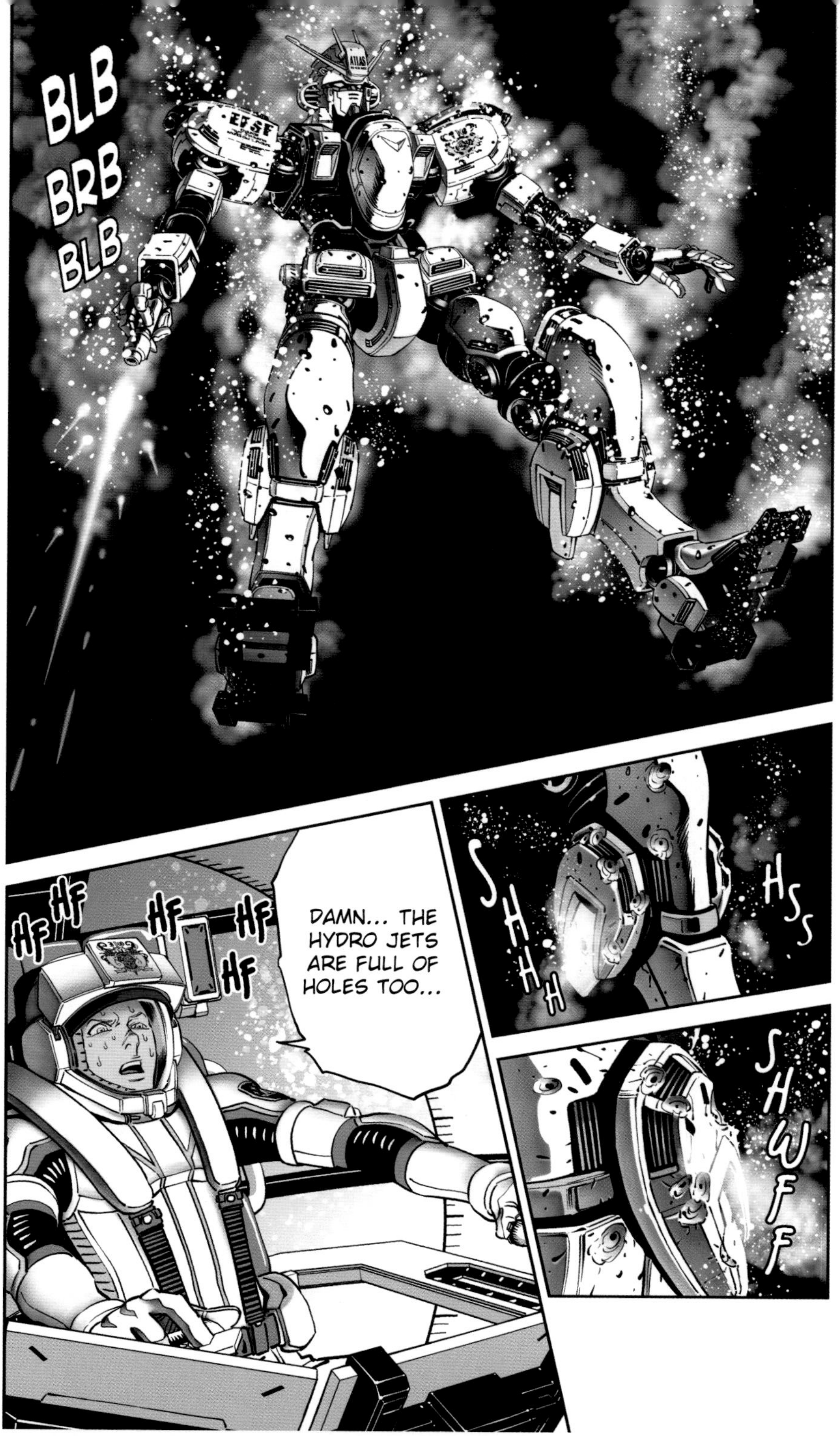

BLB
BRB
BLB
SHHHHH
HSS
SHWFF
HF HF
HF
HF
HF
DAMN... THE HYDRO JETS ARE FULL OF HOLES TOO...

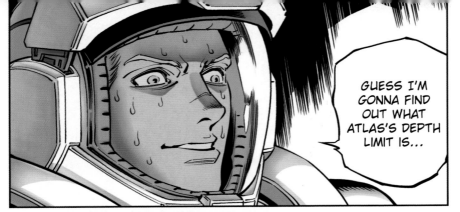

GUESS I'M GONNA FIND OUT WHAT ATLAS'S DEPTH LIMIT IS...

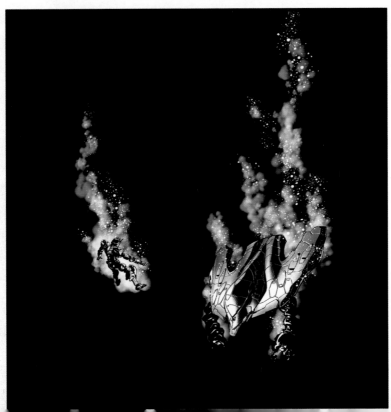

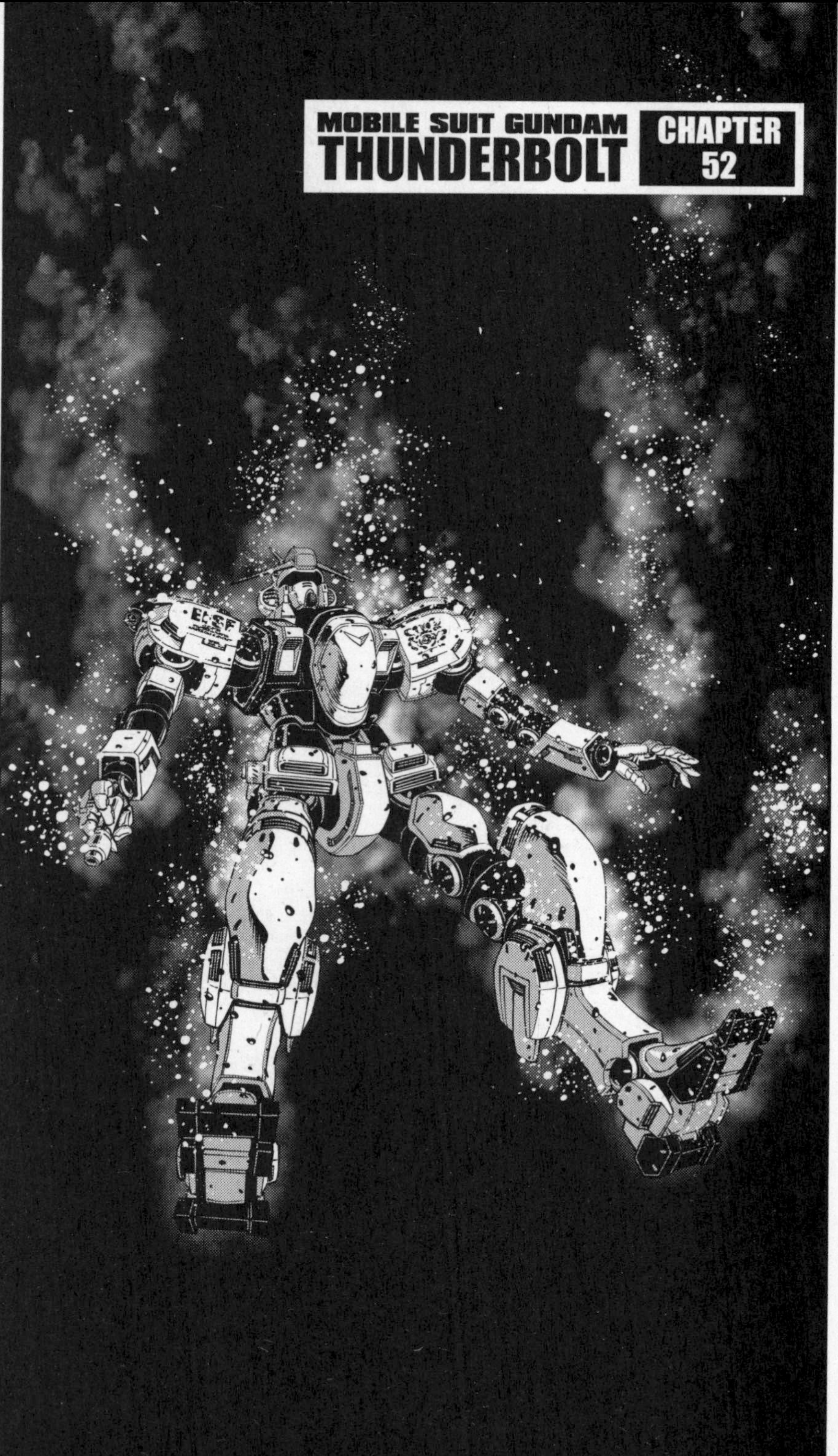
MOBILE SUIT GUNDAM
THUNDERBOLT
CHAPTER
52

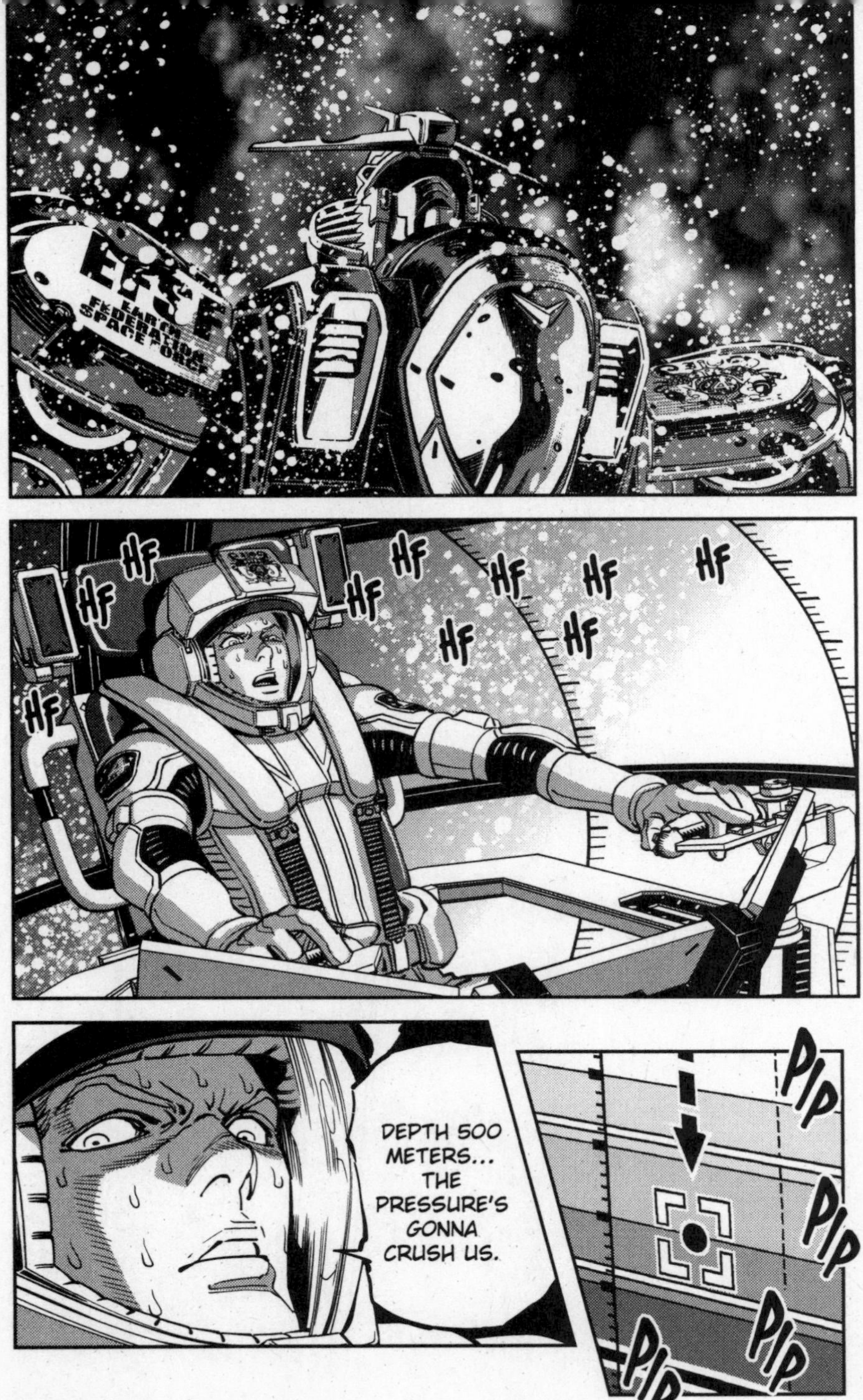
EARTH FEDERATION SPACE FORCE
HF HF HF HF HF HF HF HF HF
PIP PIP PIP PIP PIP
DEPTH 500 METERS... THE PRESSURE'S GONNA CRUSH US.

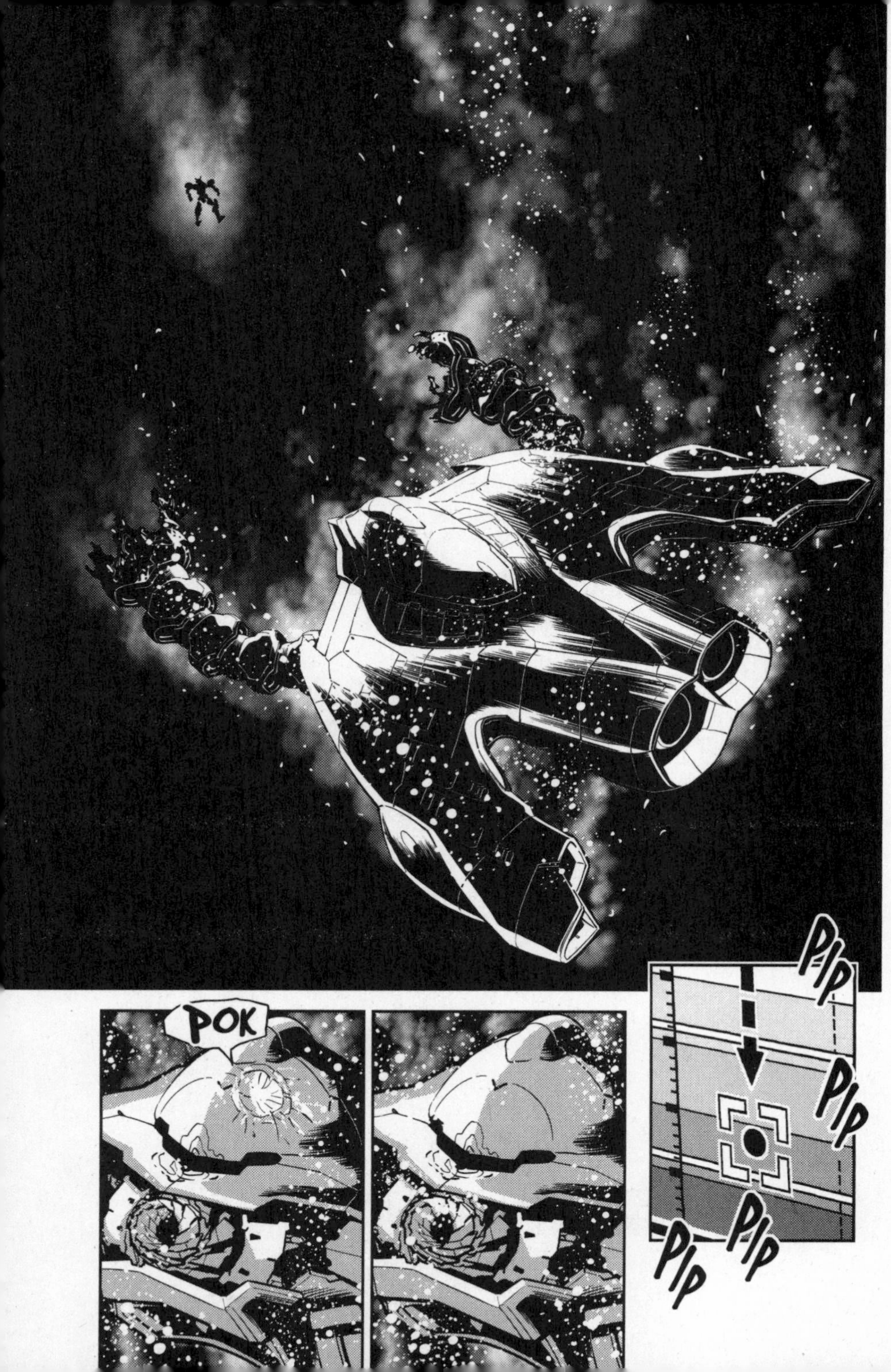
PIP
PIP
PIP
PIP
PIP
POK

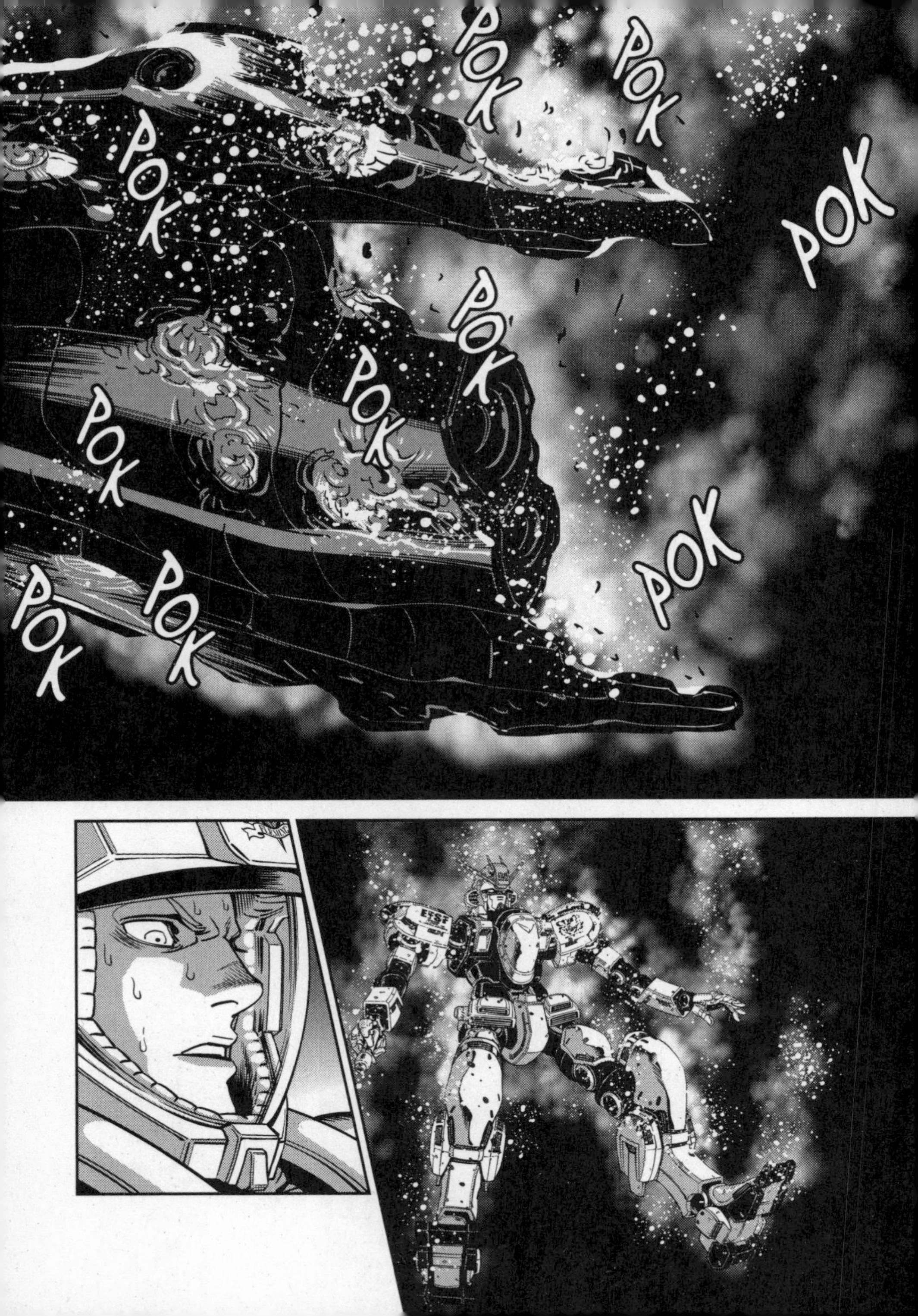
POK
POK
POK
POK
POK
POK
POK
POK
POK
POK

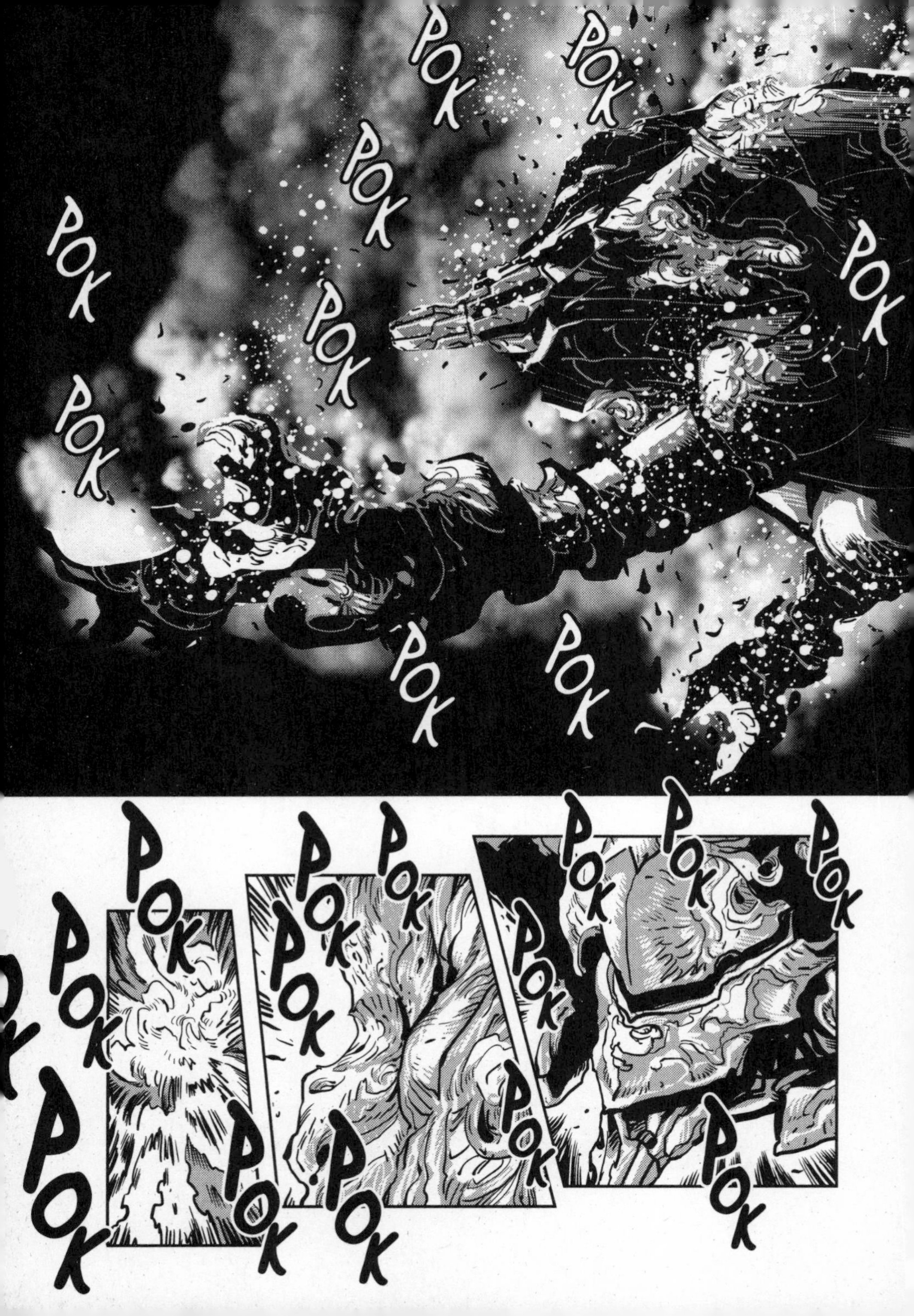

POK
POK
POK
POK
POK
POK
POK
POK
POK
POK
POK
POK
POK
POK
POK
POK
POK
POK
POK
POK
POK
POK
POK

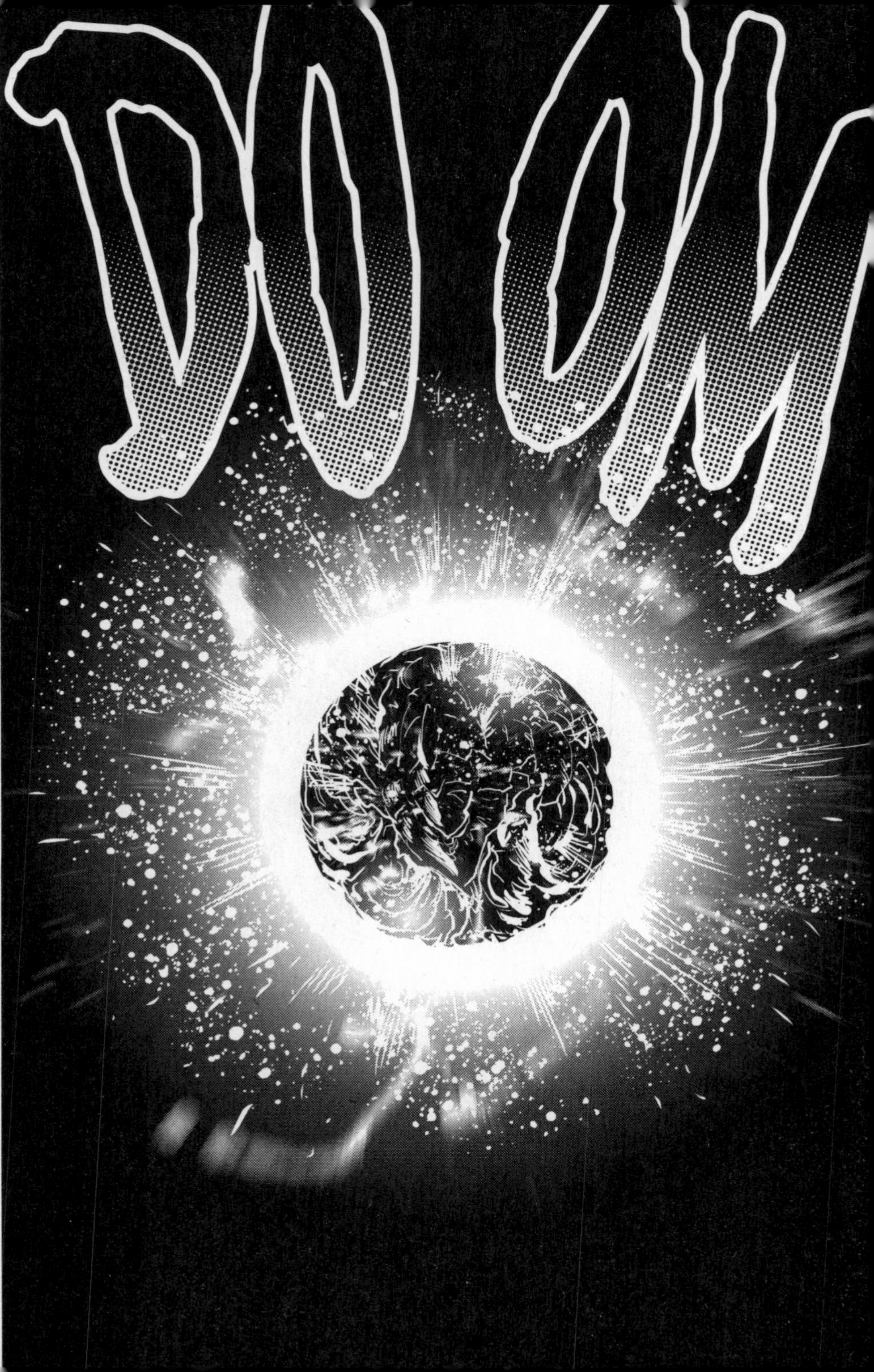
DOOM

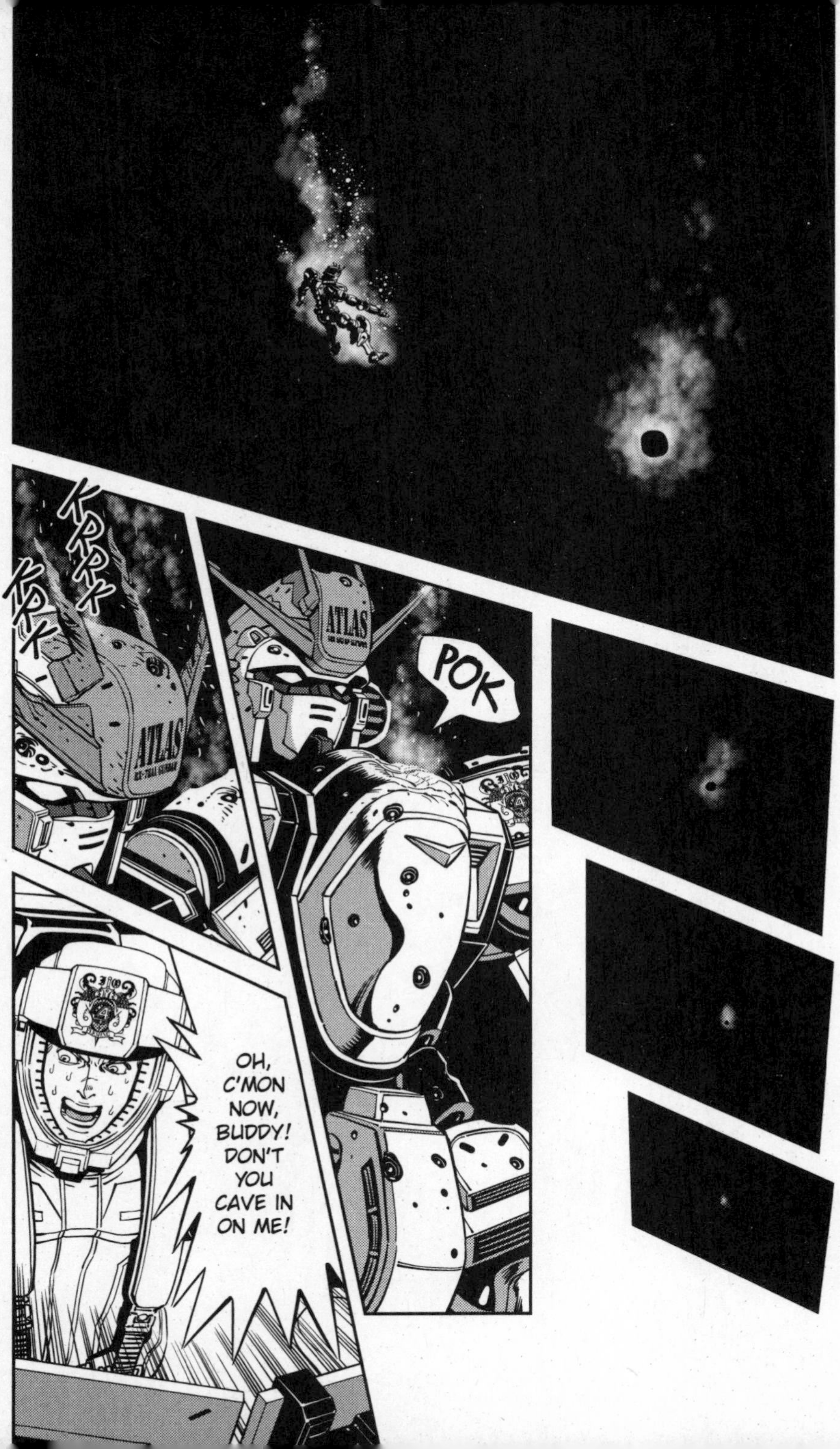
POK
KRRRK
KRK
ATLAS
ATLAS
OH, C'MON NOW, BUDDY! DON'T YOU CAVE IN ON ME!

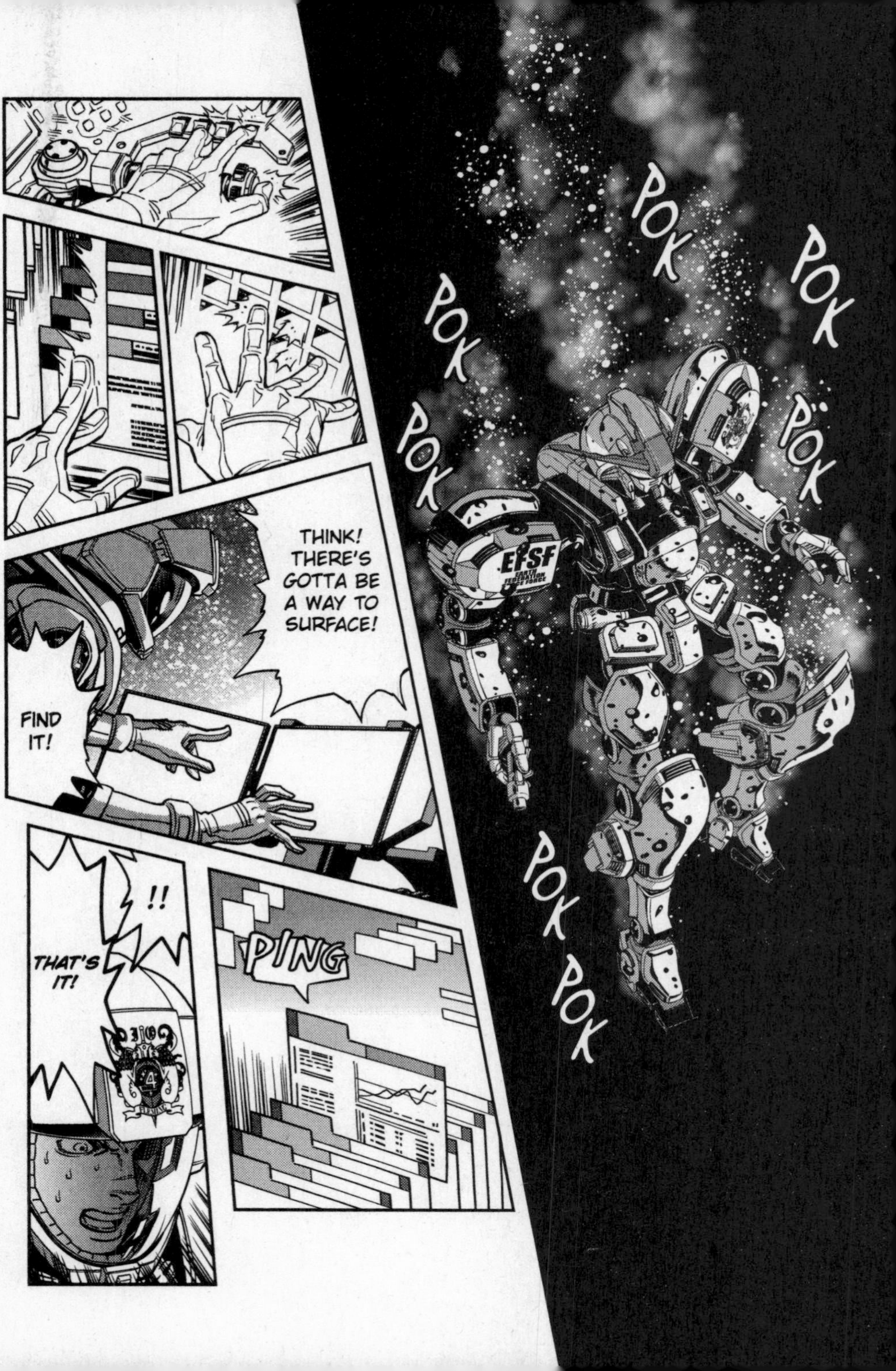
POK POK
POK POK
POK POK
POK POK
THINK! THERE'S GOTTA BE A WAY TO SURFACE!
FIND IT!
PING
!!
THAT'S IT!

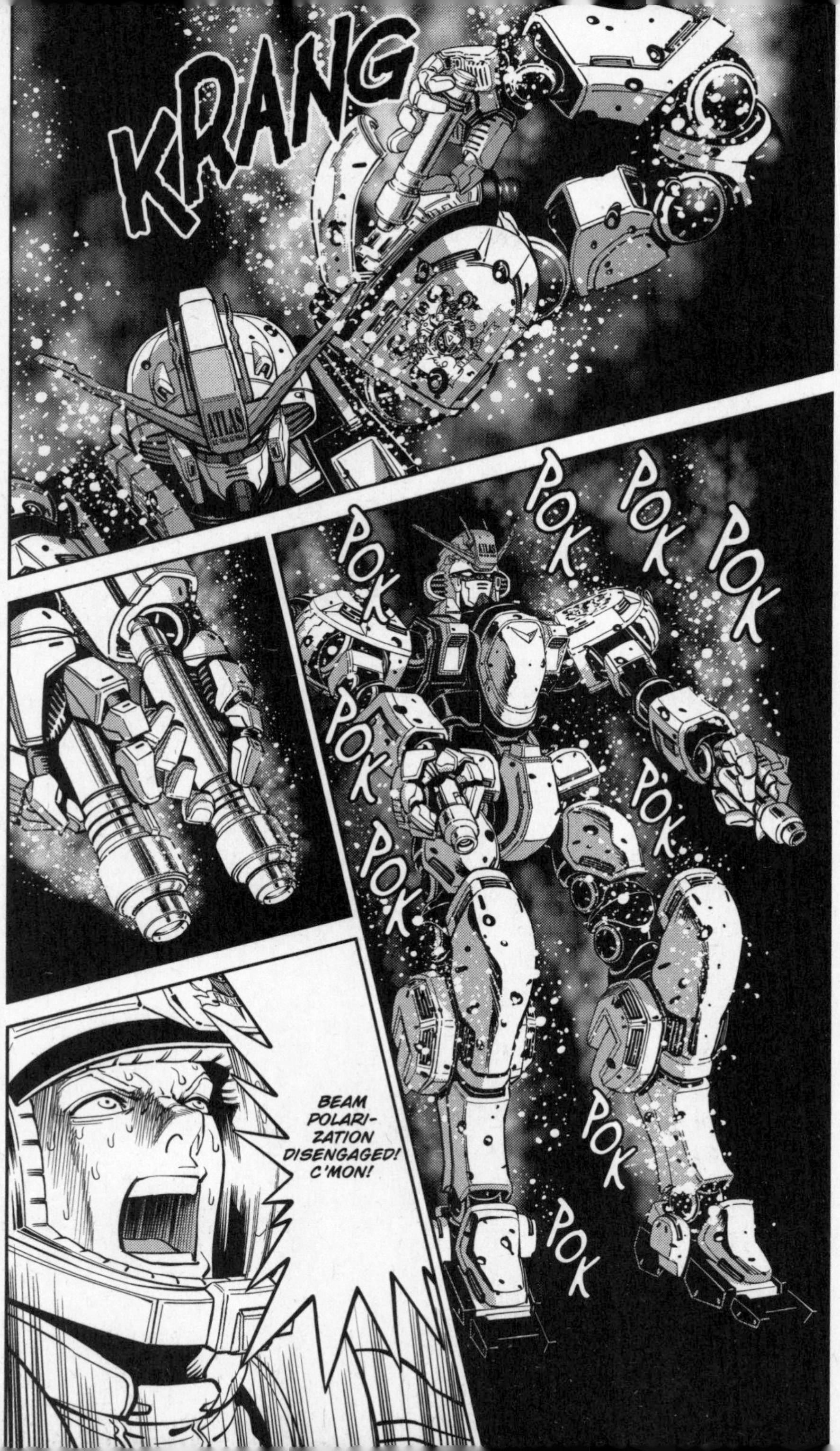
KRANG
POK POK POK POK
POK POK
POK
POK POK
BEAM POLARIZATION DISENGAGED! C'MON!

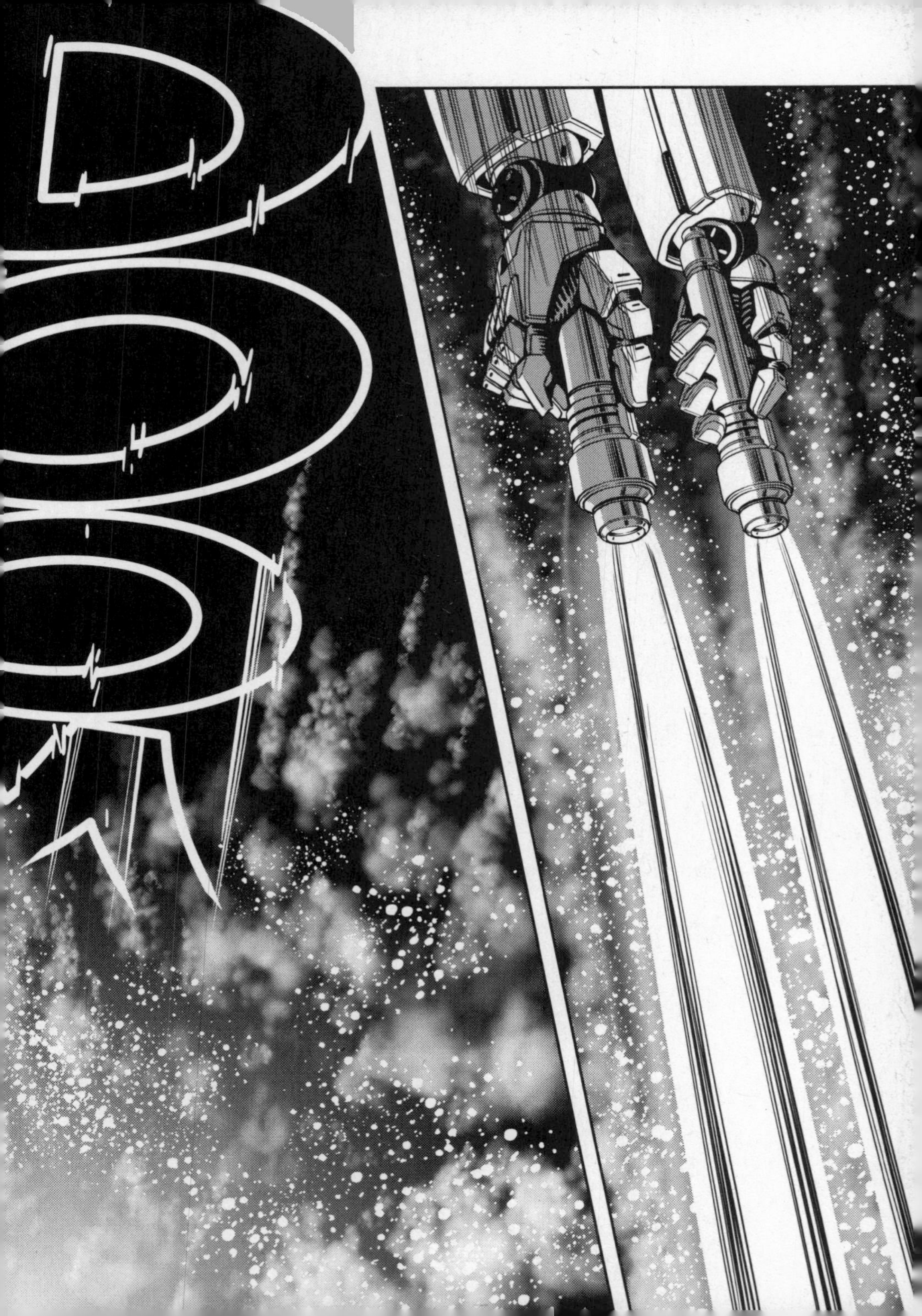
DOOM

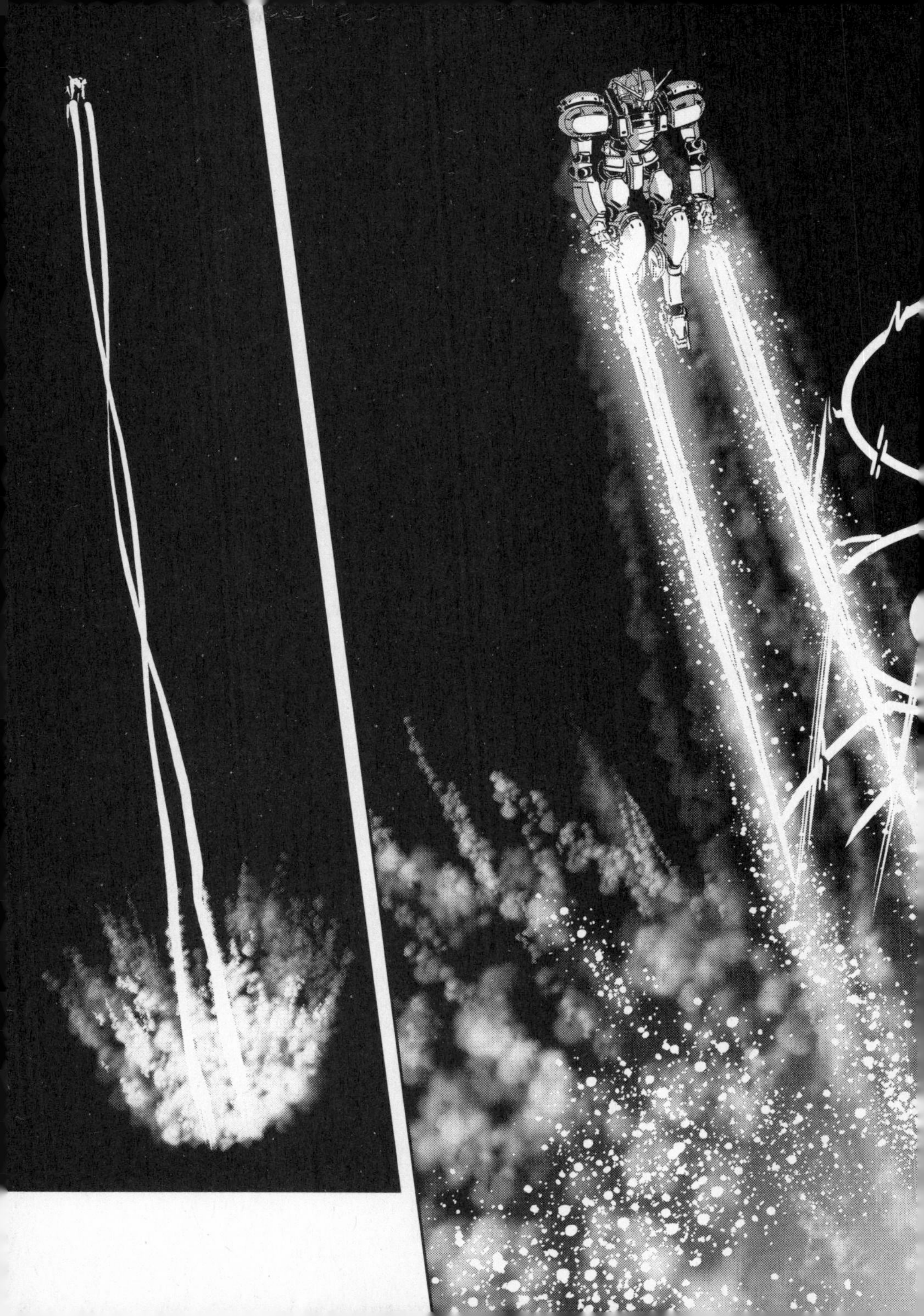

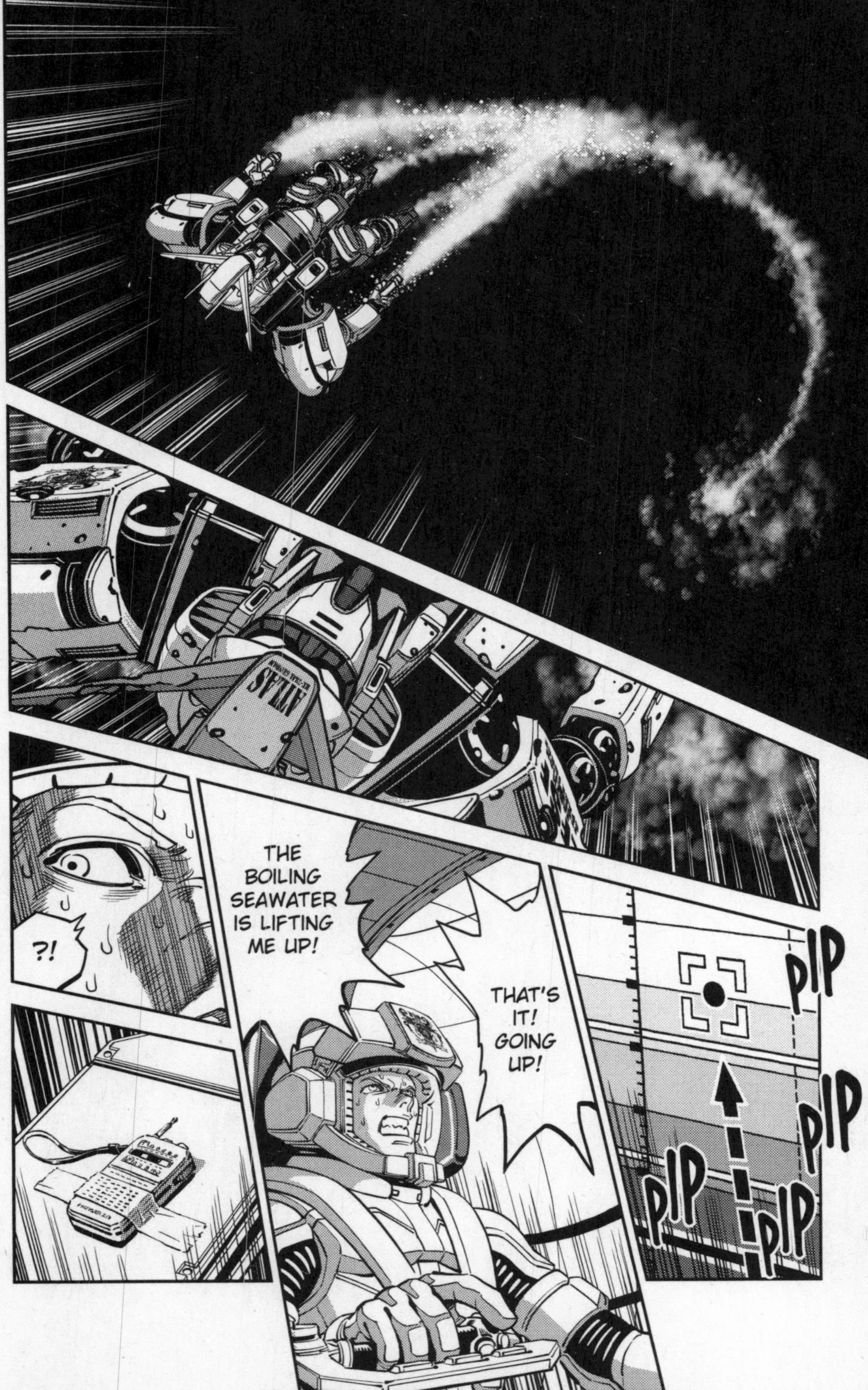

PIP
PIP
PIP
PIP
PIP
THE BOILING SEAWATER IS LIFTING ME UP!
THAT'S IT! GOING UP!
?!

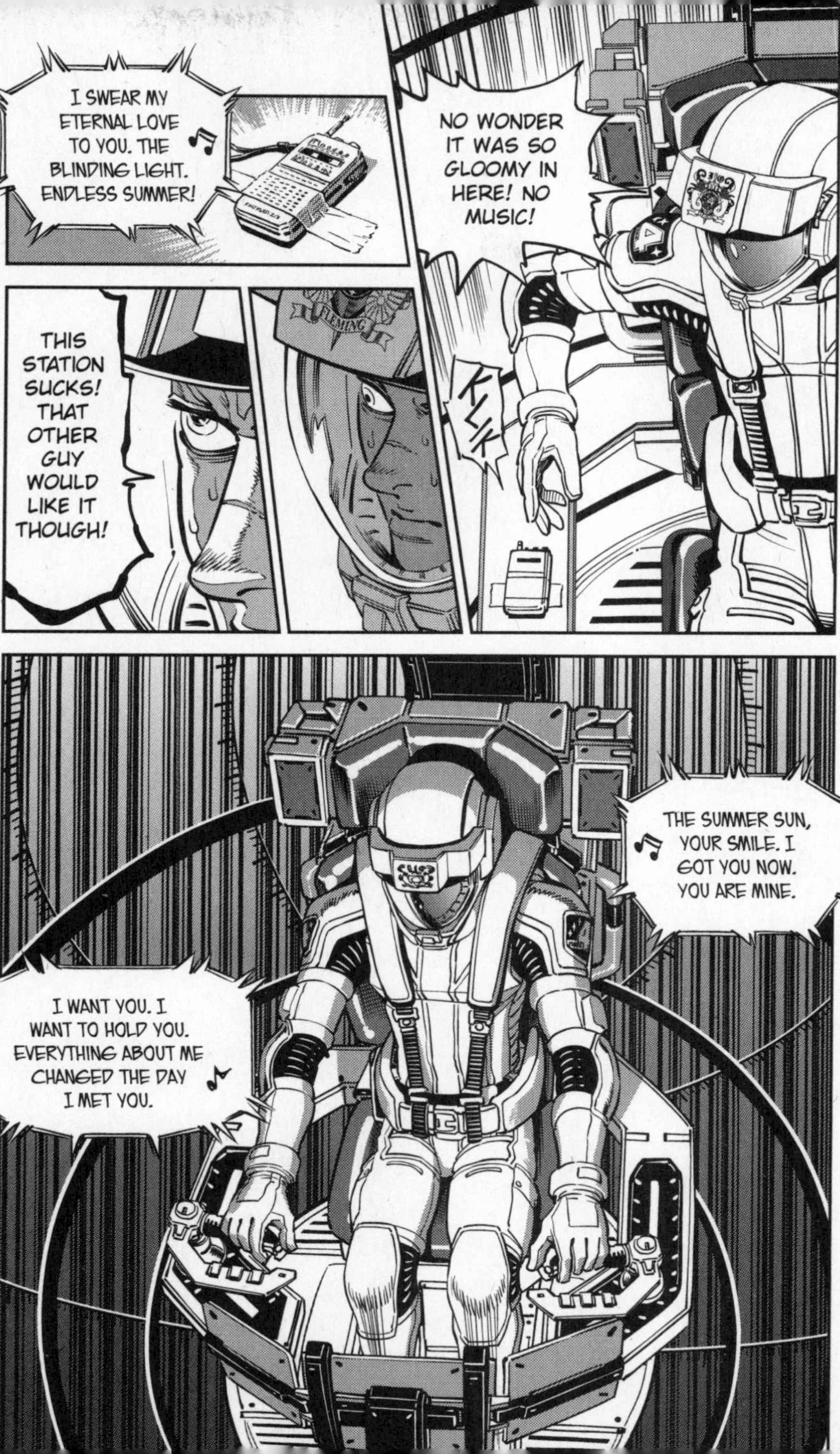
NO WONDER IT WAS SO GLOOMY IN HERE! NO MUSIC!
KLIK
I SWEAR MY ETERNAL LOVE TO YOU. THE BLINDING LIGHT. ENDLESS SUMMER!
THIS STATION SUCKS! THAT OTHER GUY WOULD LIKE IT THOUGH!
THE SUMMER SUN, YOUR SMILE. I GOT YOU NOW. YOU ARE MINE.
I WANT YOU. I WANT TO HOLD YOU. EVERYTHING ABOUT ME CHANGED THE DAY I MET YOU.

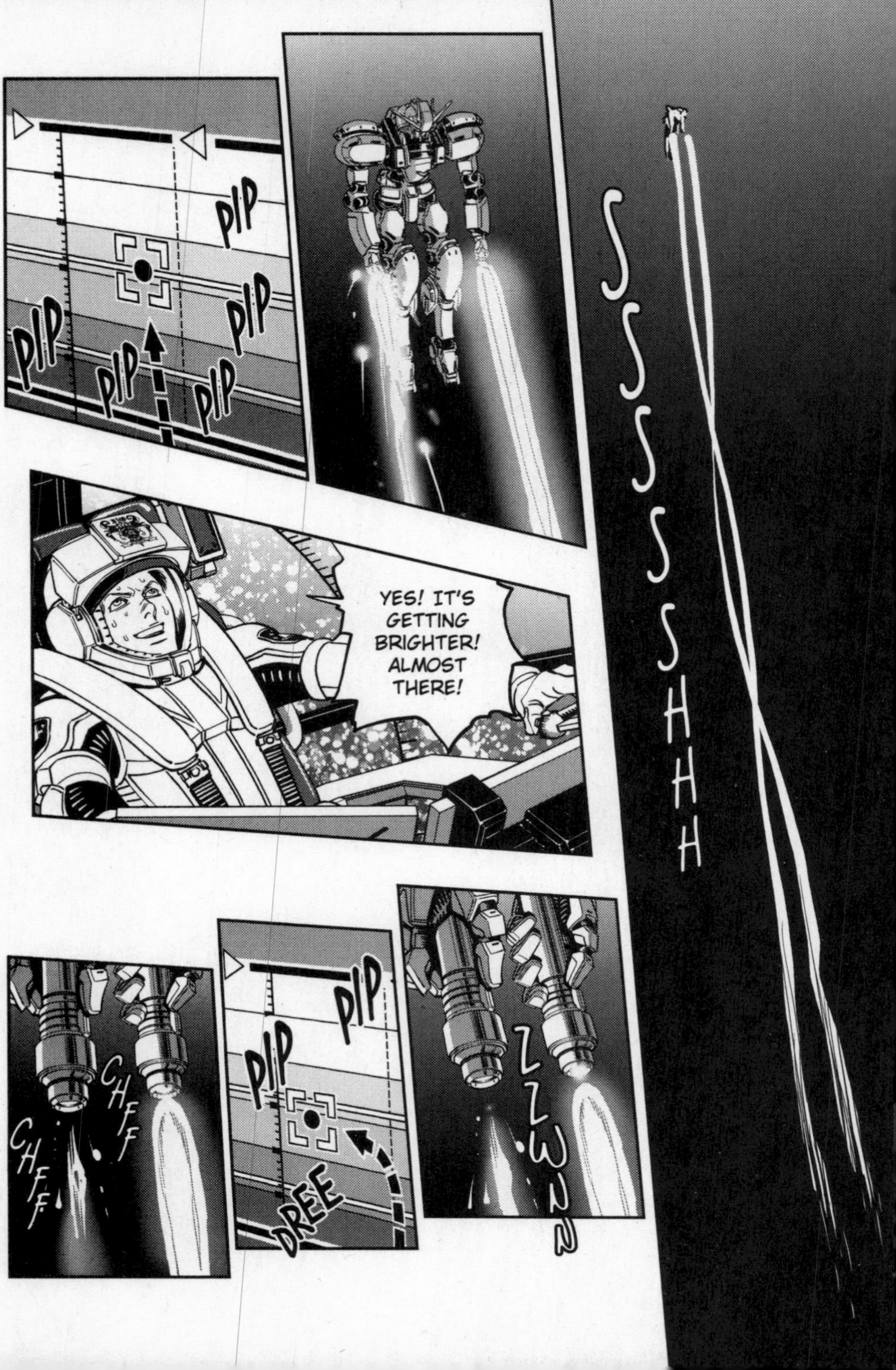
SSSSSHHH
PIP
PIP
PIP
PIP
PIP
PIP
YES! IT'S GETTING BRIGHTER! ALMOST THERE!
ZZWNNN
PIP
PIP
DREE
CHFF
CHFF

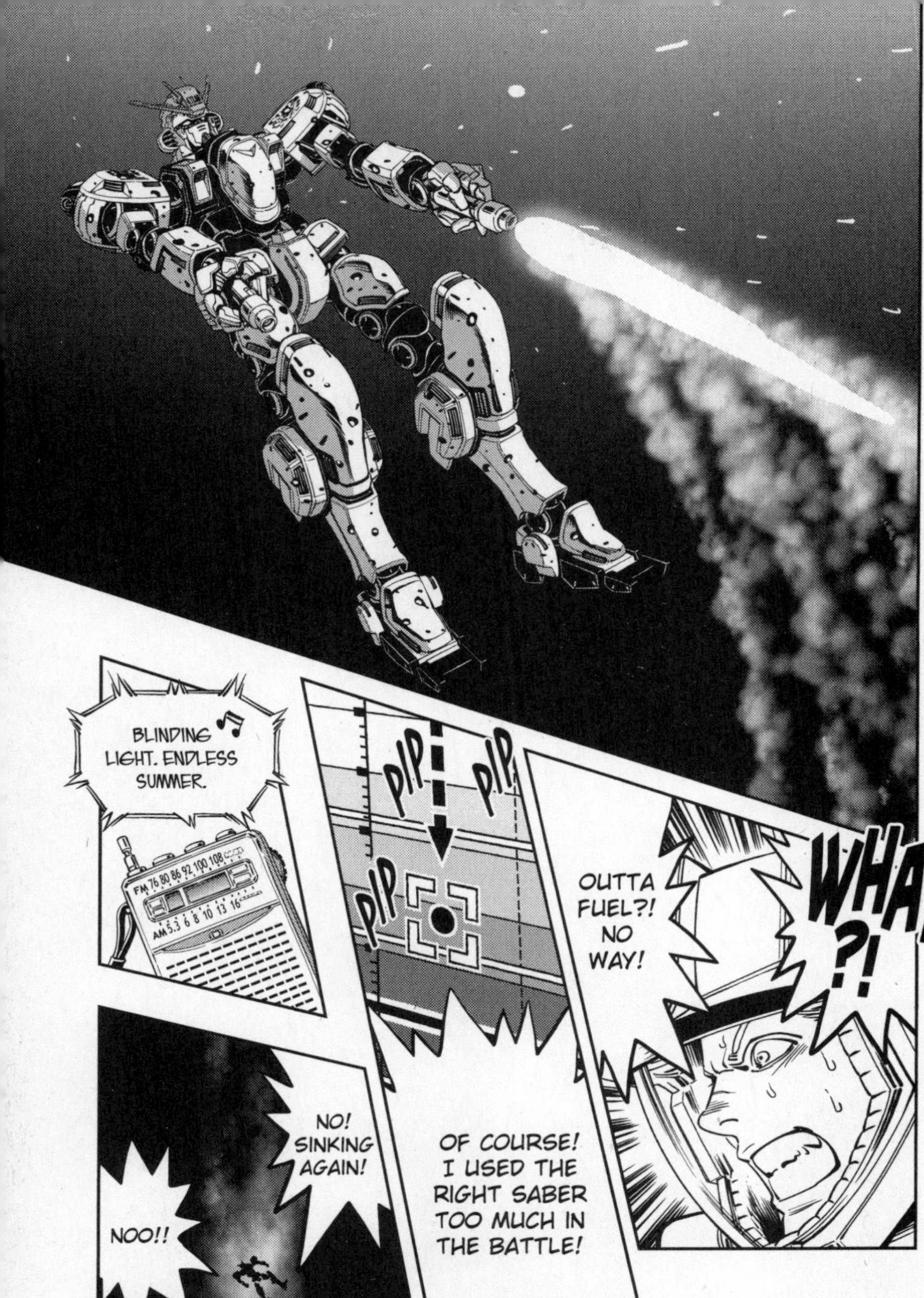
WHAT?!
OUTTA FUEL?! NO WAY!
PIP PIP PIP
OF COURSE! I USED THE RIGHT SABER TOO MUCH IN THE BATTLE!
BLINDING LIGHT. ENDLESS SUMMER.
FM 76 80 86 92 100 108
AM 5.3 6 8 10 13 16
NO! SINKING AGAIN!
NOO!!

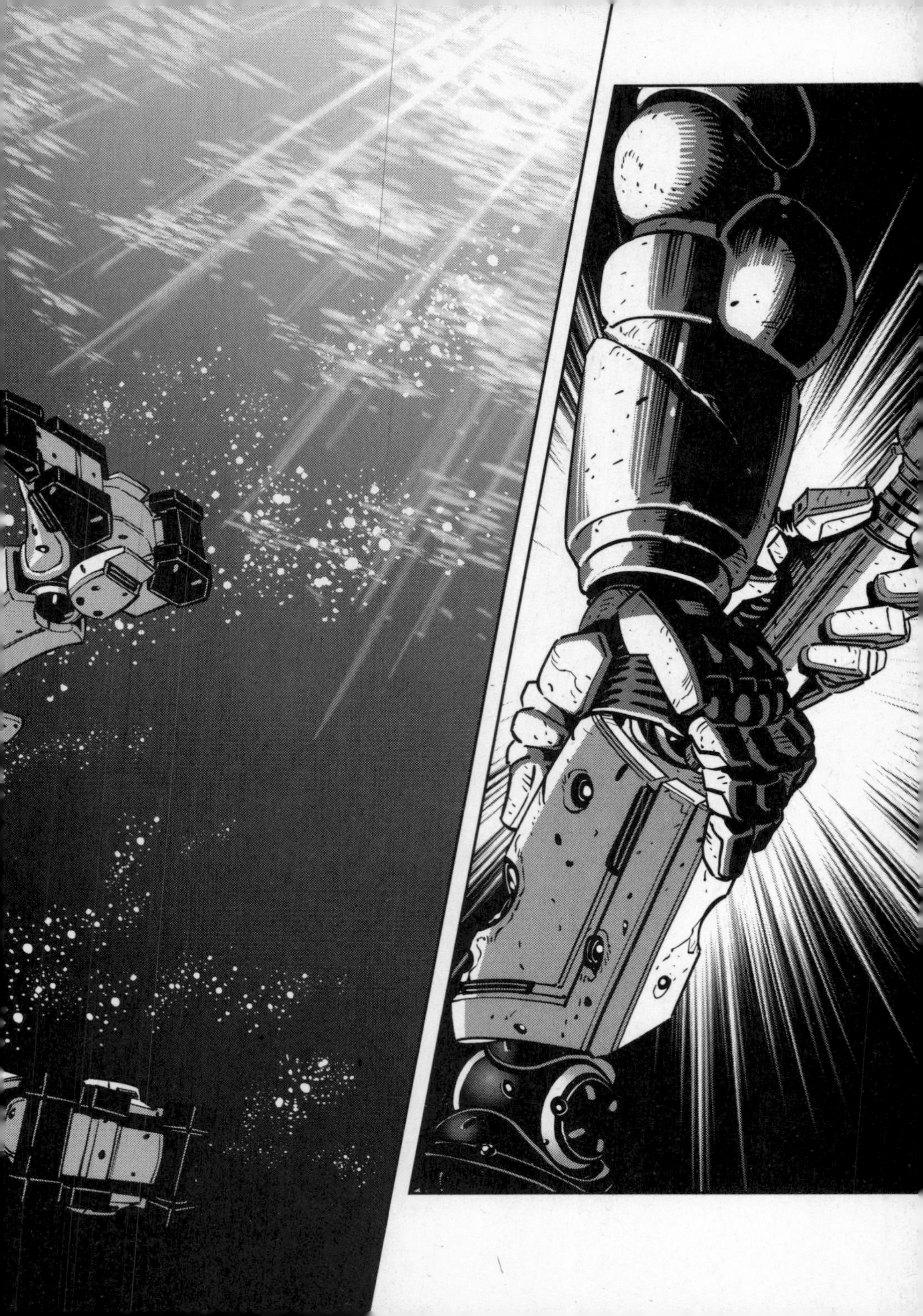

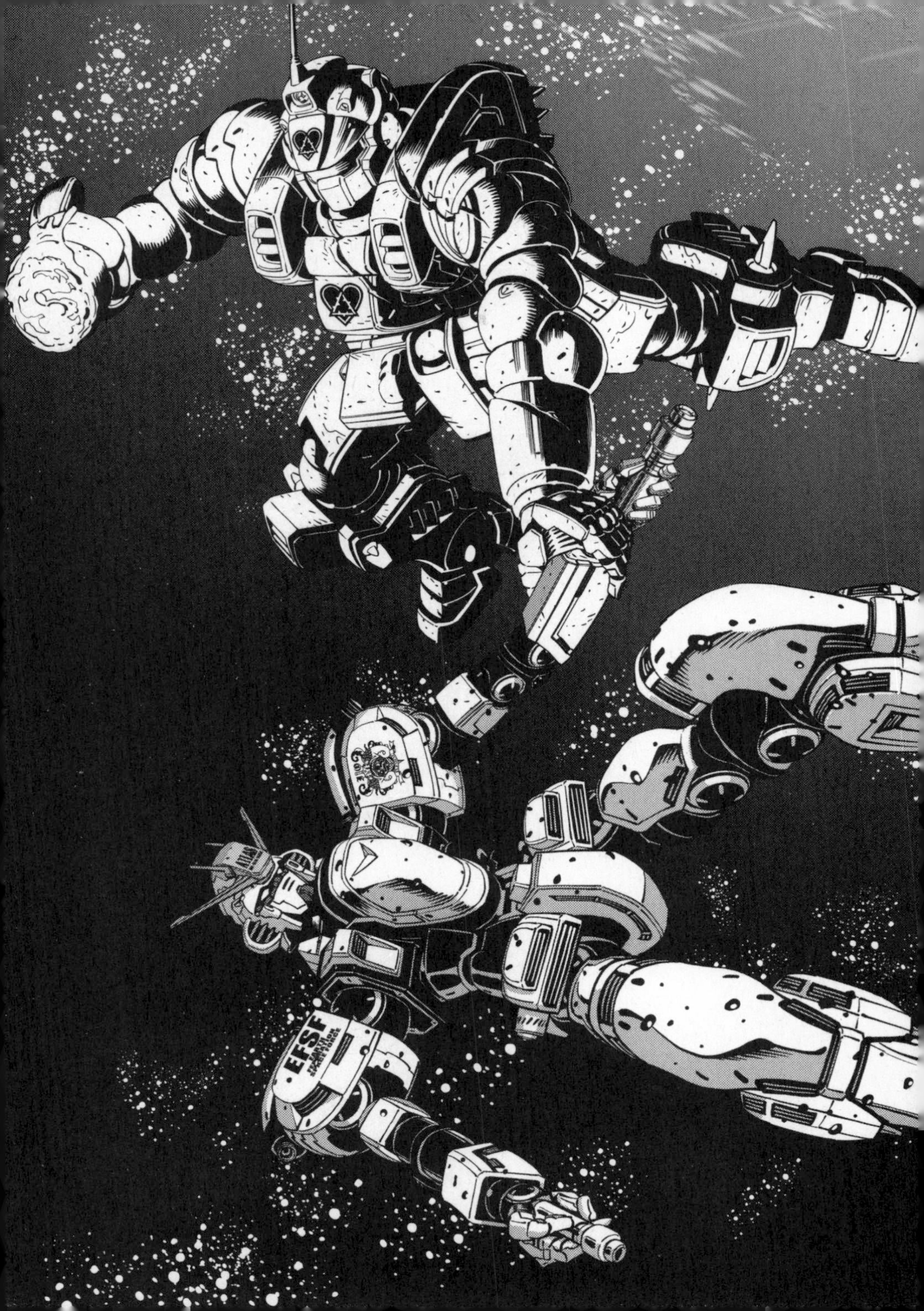
EFSF

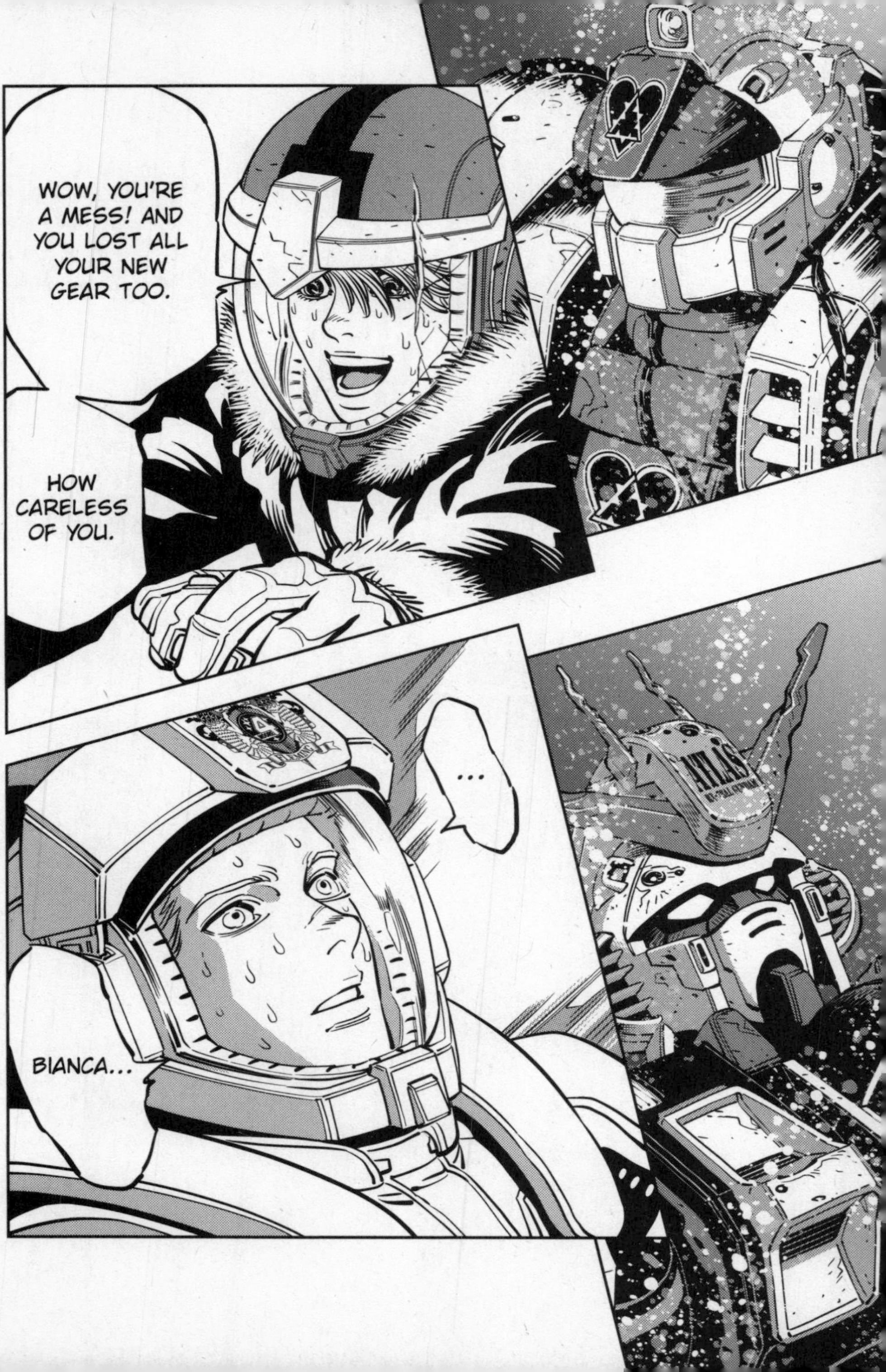
WOW, YOU'RE A MESS! AND YOU LOST ALL YOUR NEW GEAR TOO.
HOW CARELESS OF YOU.
...
BIANCA...
ATLAS

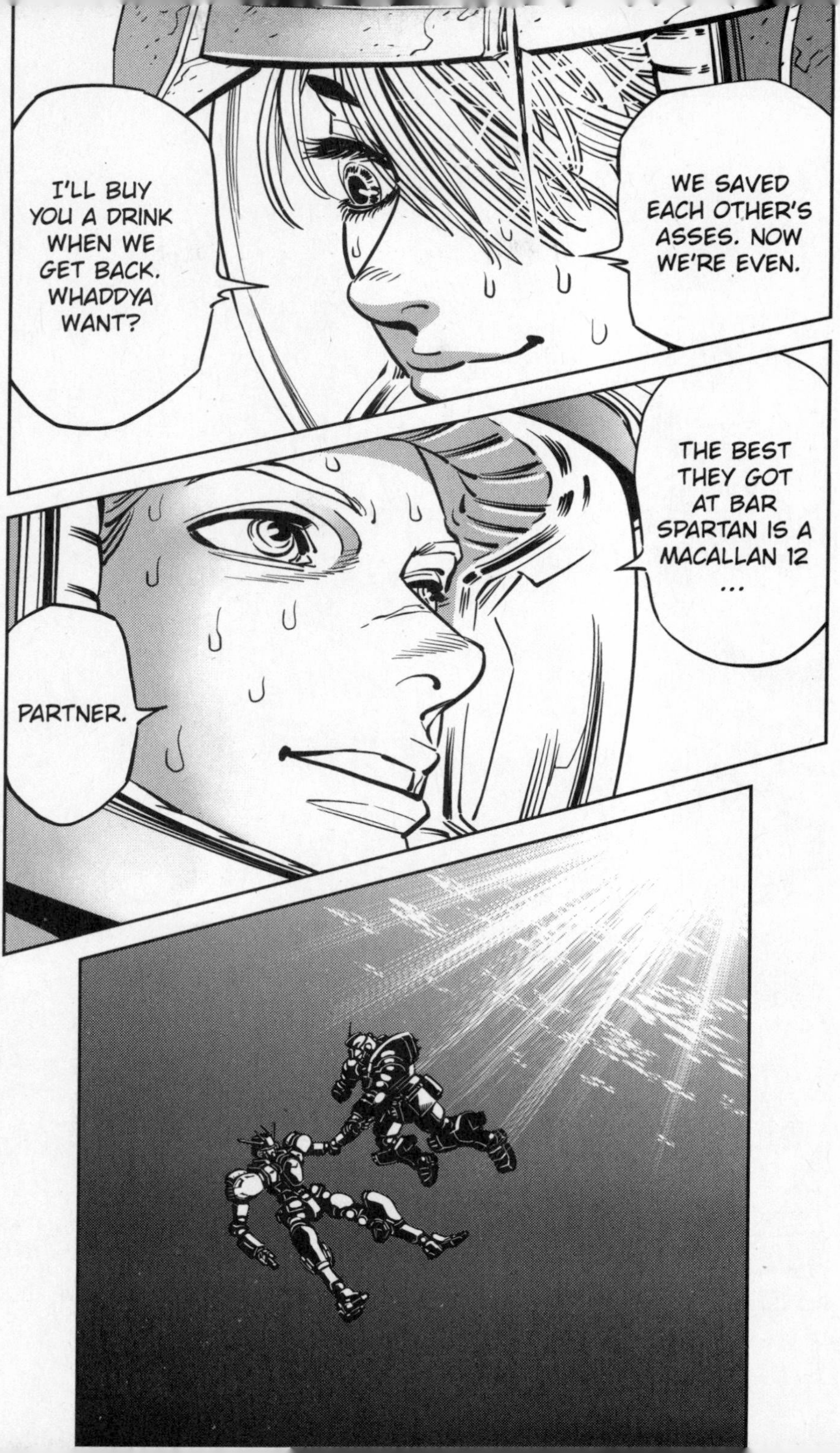

WE SAVED EACH OTHER'S ASSES. NOW WE'RE EVEN.
I'LL BUY YOU A DRINK WHEN WE GET BACK. WHADDYA WANT?
THE BEST THEY GOT AT BAR SPARTAN IS A MACALLAN 12 ...
PARTNER.

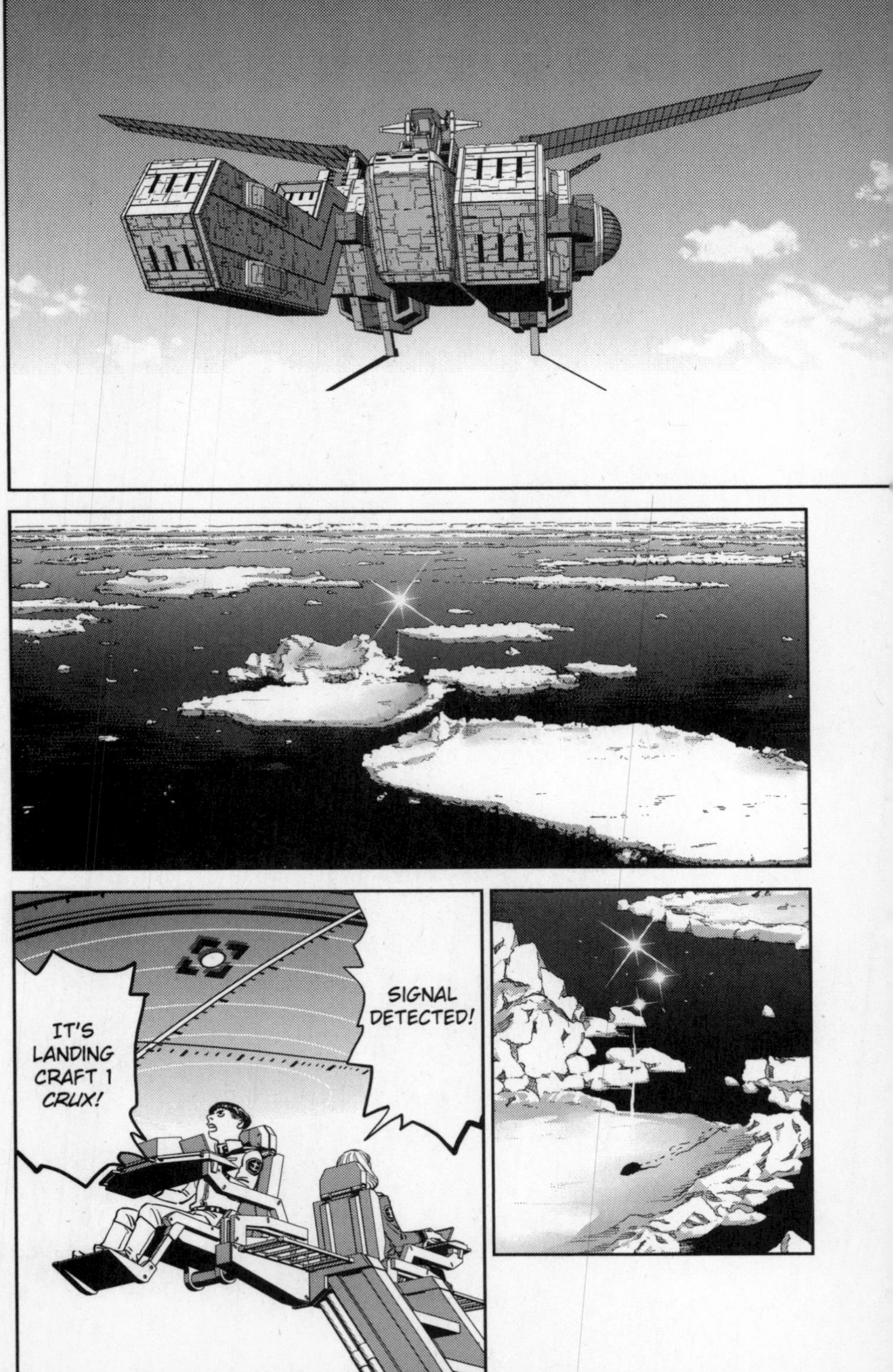
SIGNAL DETECTED!
IT'S LANDING CRAFT 1 CRUX!

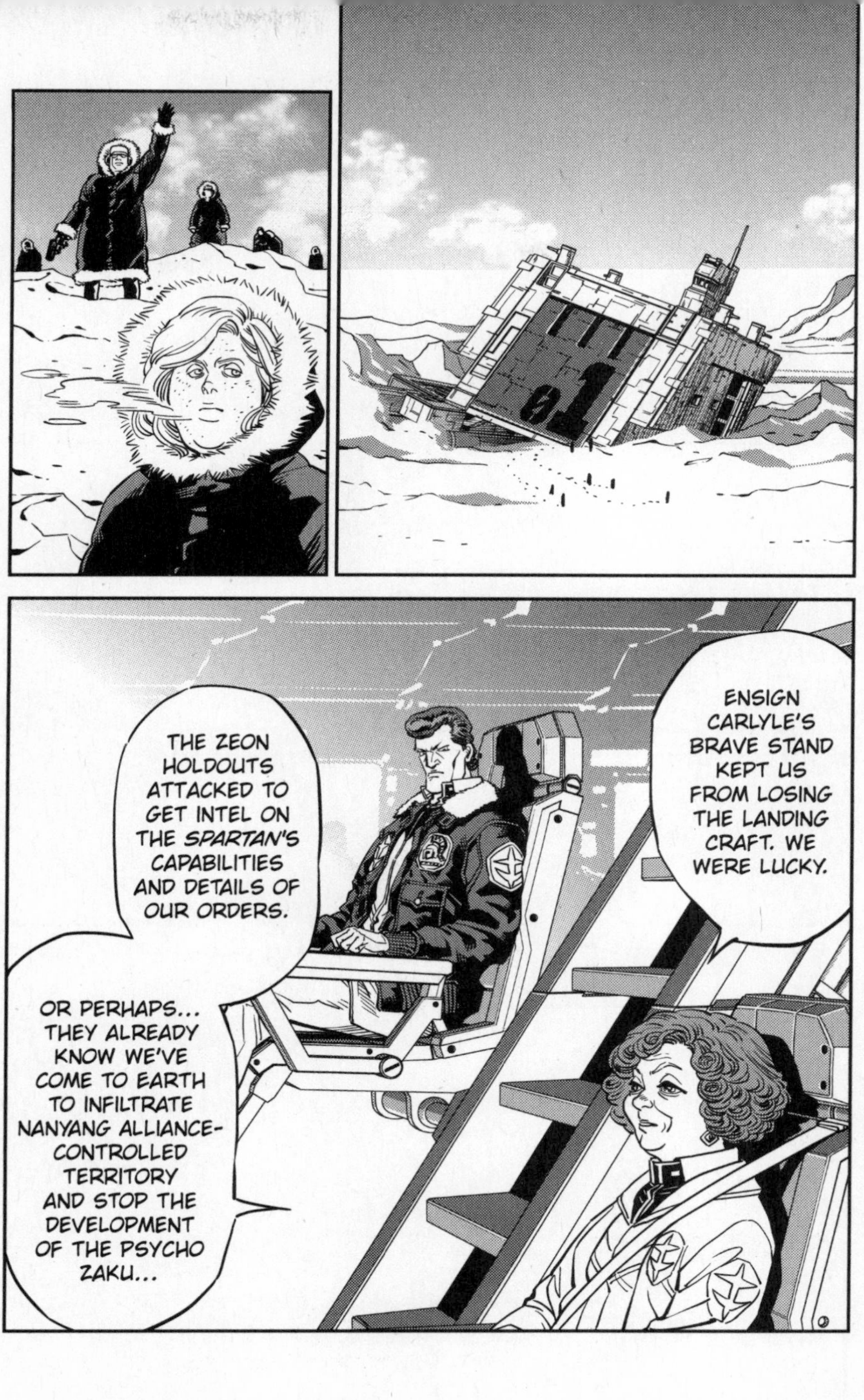
ENSIGN CARLYLE'S BRAVE STAND KEPT US FROM LOSING THE LANDING CRAFT. WE WERE LUCKY.
THE ZEON HOLDOUTS ATTACKED TO GET INTEL ON THE *SPARTAN*'S CAPABILITIES AND DETAILS OF OUR ORDERS.
OR PERHAPS... THEY ALREADY KNOW WE'VE COME TO EARTH TO INFILTRATE NANYANG ALLIANCE-CONTROLLED TERRITORY AND STOP THE DEVELOPMENT OF THE PSYCHO ZAKU...

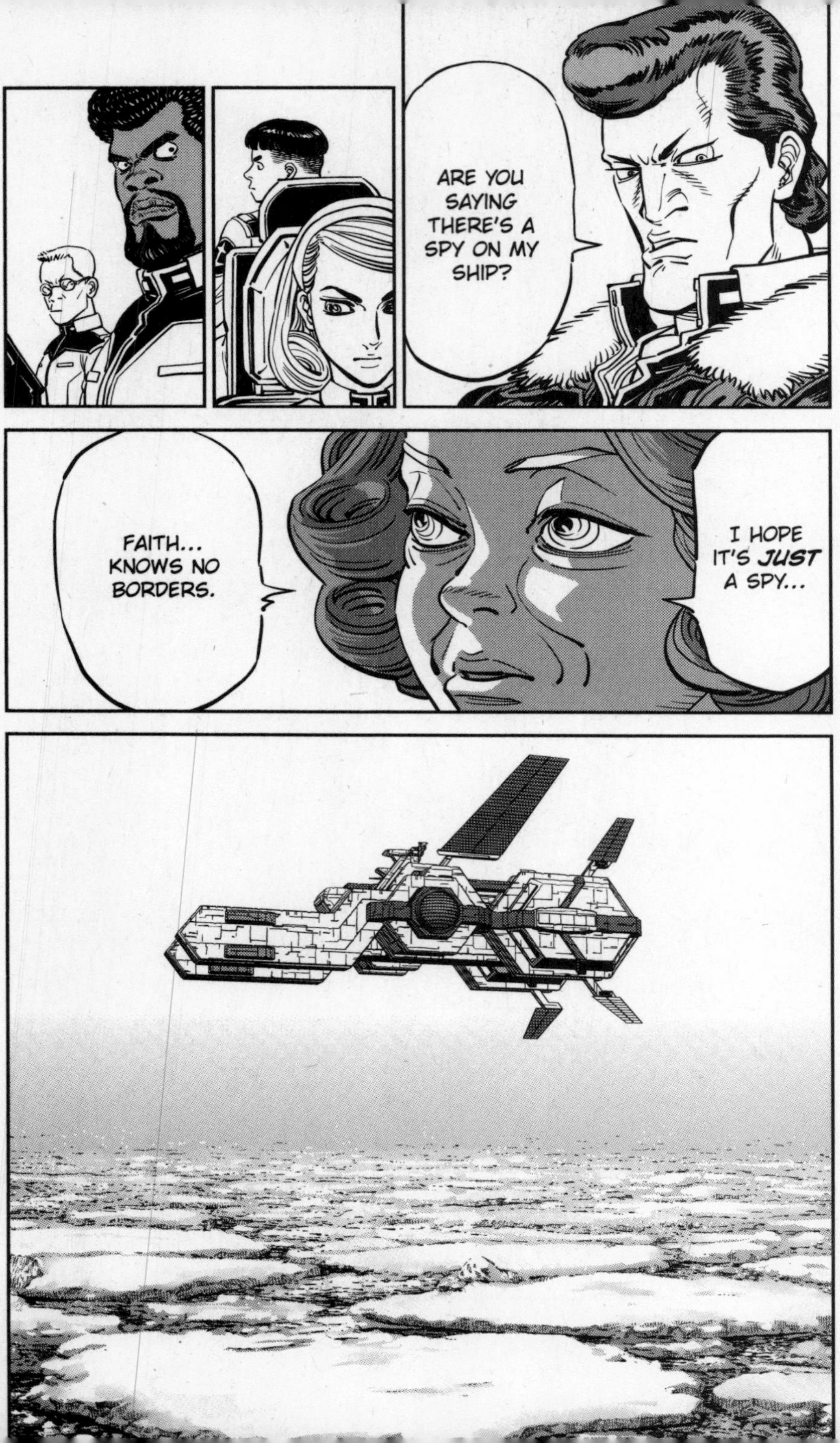
ARE YOU SAYING THERE'S A SPY ON MY SHIP?
I HOPE IT'S *JUST* A SPY...
FAITH... KNOWS NO BORDERS.

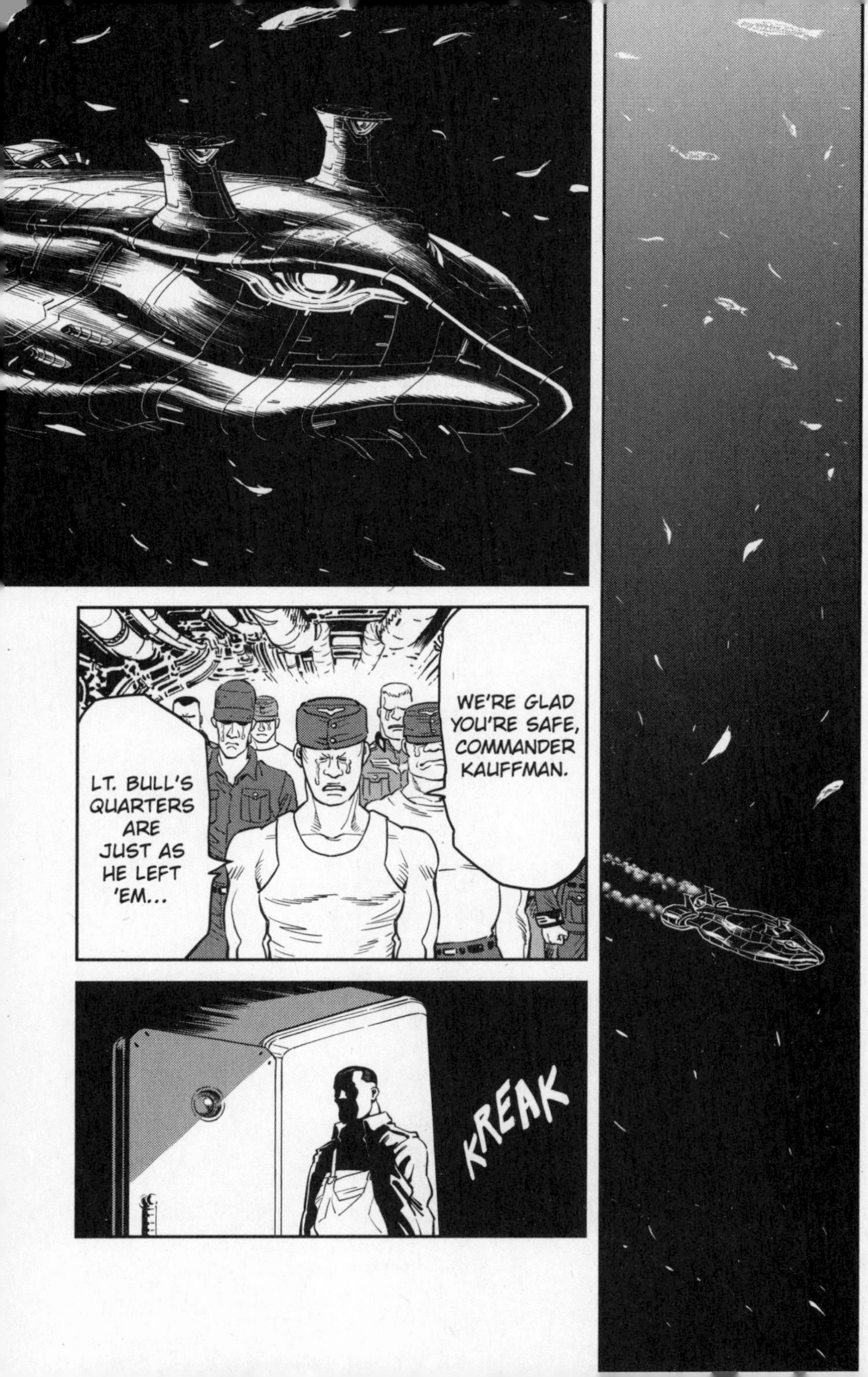
WE'RE GLAD YOU'RE SAFE, COMMANDER KAUFFMAN.
LT. BULL'S QUARTERS ARE JUST AS HE LEFT 'EM...
KREAK

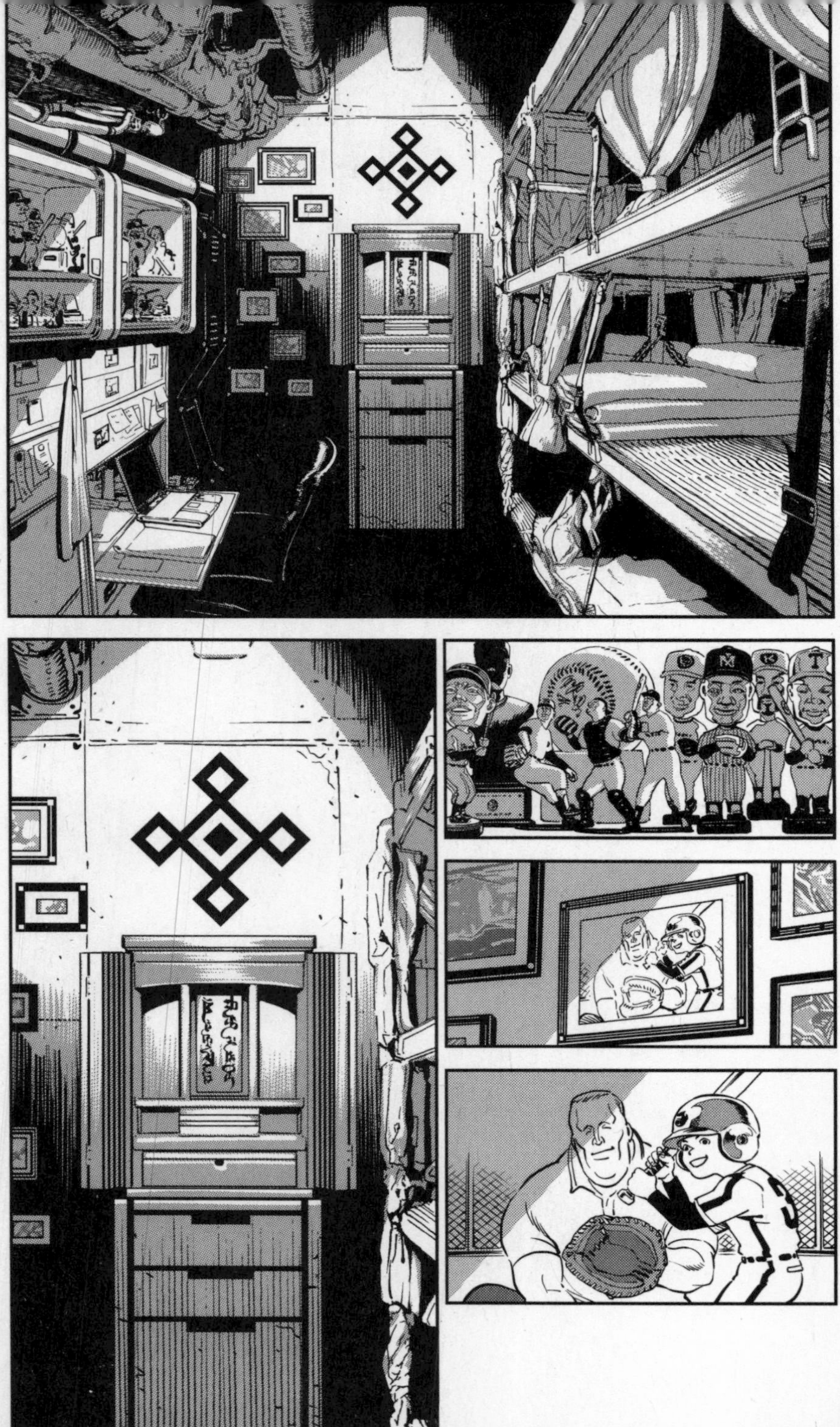

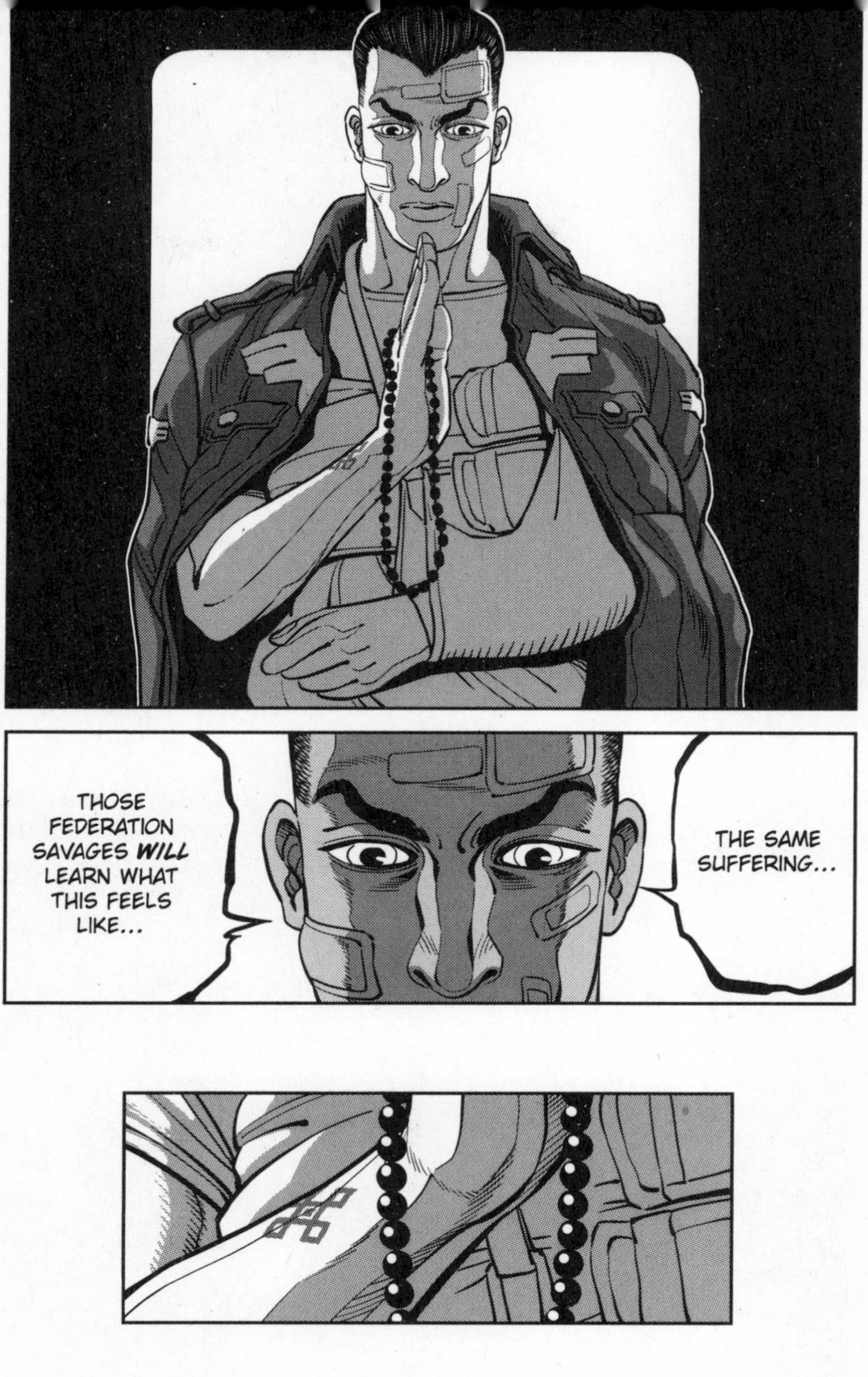
THE SAME SUFFERING...
THOSE FEDERATION SAVAGES **WILL** LEARN WHAT THIS FEELS LIKE...

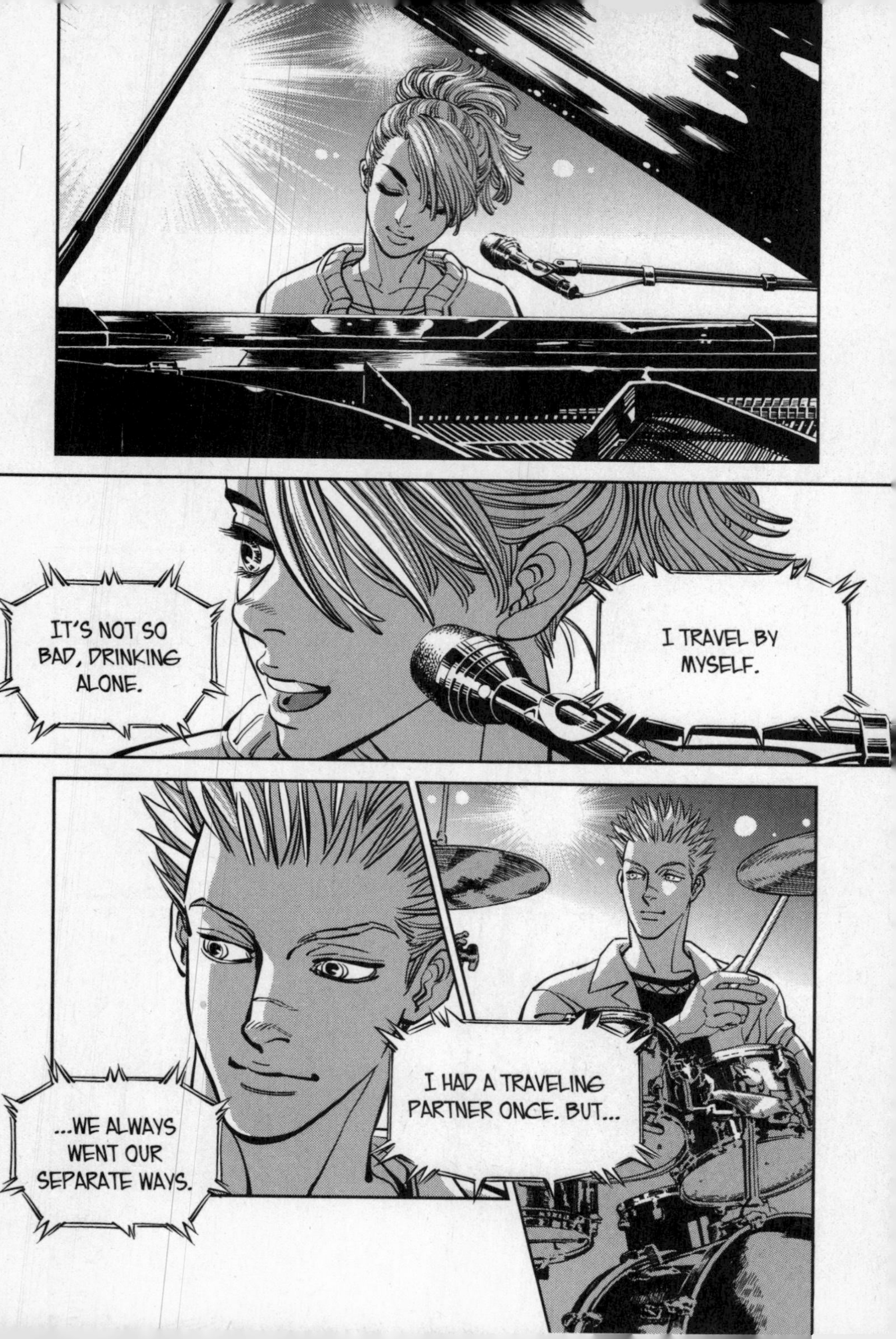
I TRAVEL BY MYSELF.
IT'S NOT SO BAD, DRINKING ALONE.
I HAD A TRAVELING PARTNER ONCE. BUT...
...WE ALWAYS WENT OUR SEPARATE WAYS.

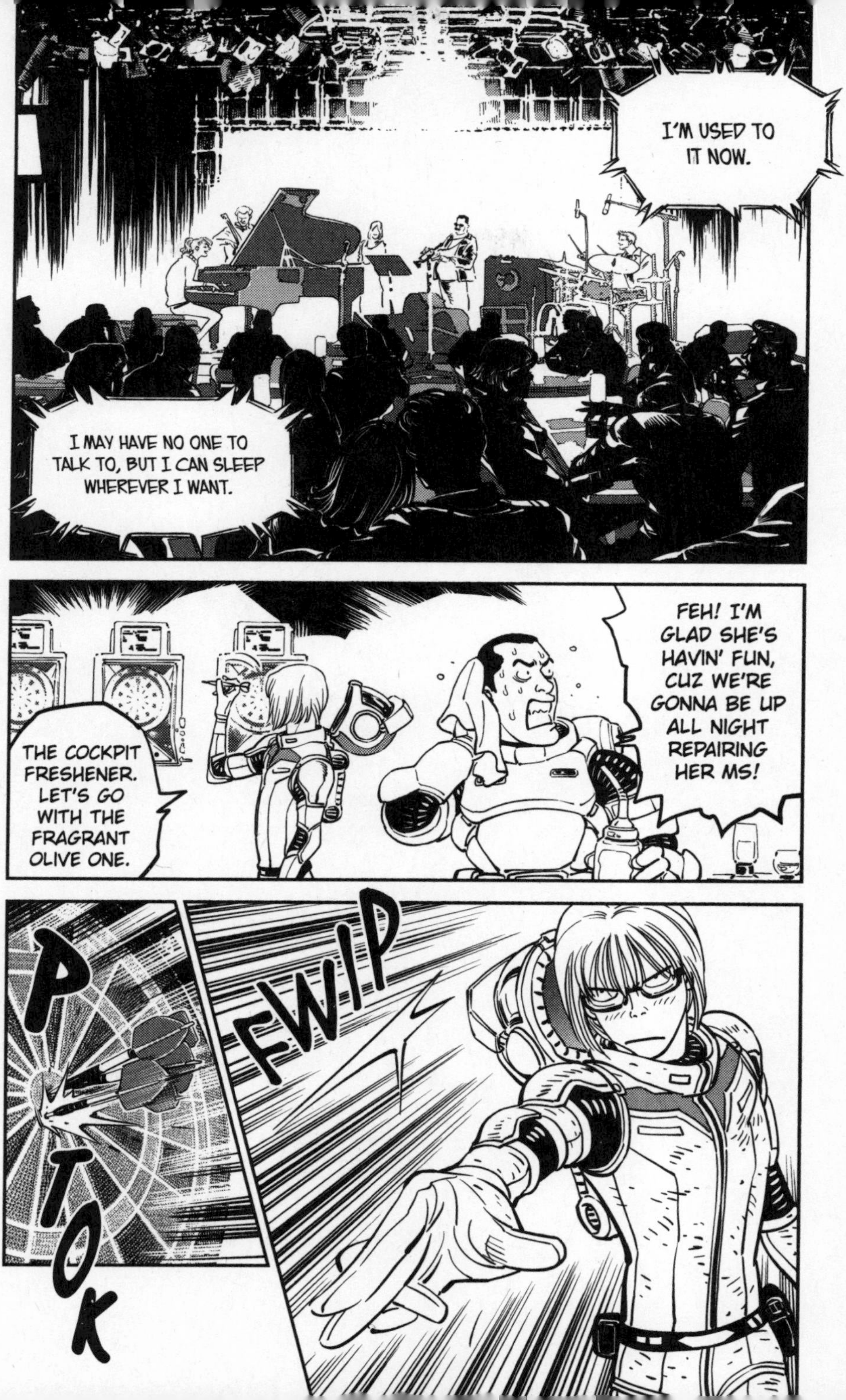
I'M USED TO IT NOW.
I MAY HAVE NO ONE TO TALK TO, BUT I CAN SLEEP WHEREVER I WANT.
FEH! I'M GLAD SHE'S HAVIN' FUN, CUZ WE'RE GONNA BE UP ALL NIGHT REPAIRING HER MS!
THE COCKPIT FRESHENER. LET'S GO WITH THE FRAGRANT OLIVE ONE.
FWIP
PTOK

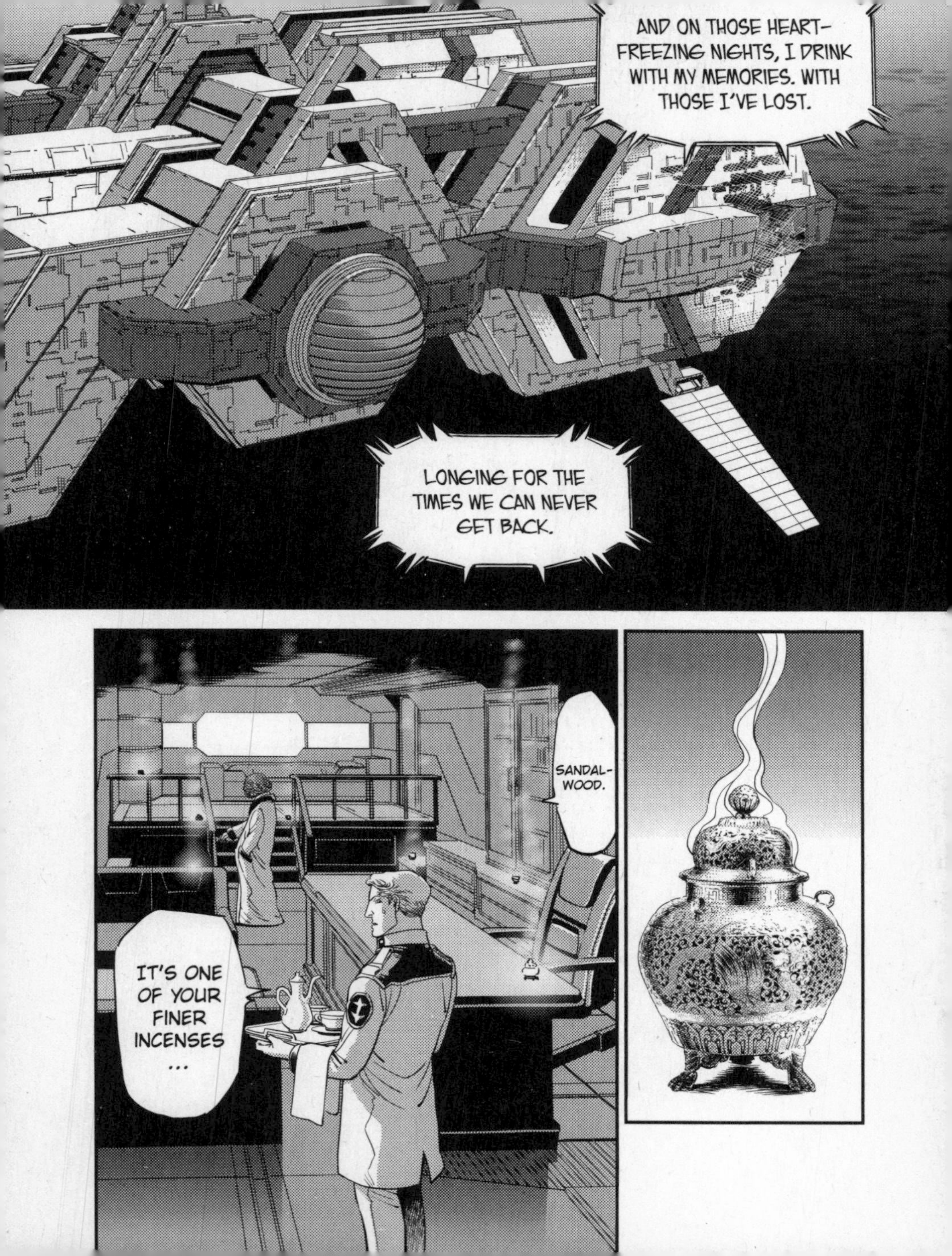
AND ON THOSE HEART-FREEZING NIGHTS, I DRINK WITH MY MEMORIES. WITH THOSE I'VE LOST.
LONGING FOR THE TIMES WE CAN NEVER GET BACK.
SANDAL-WOOD.
IT'S ONE OF YOUR FINER INCENSES ...

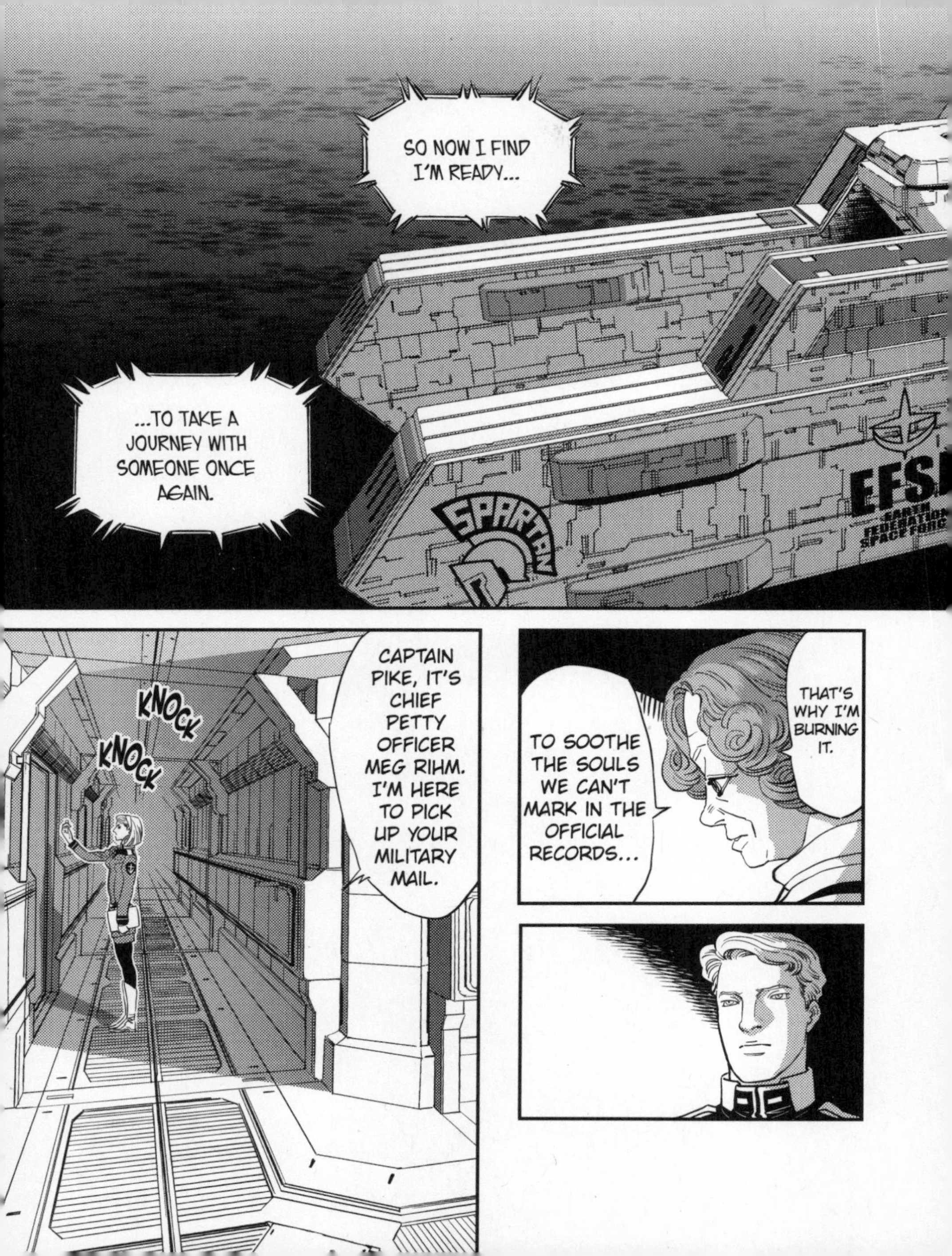
SO NOW I FIND I'M READY...
...TO TAKE A JOURNEY WITH SOMEONE ONCE AGAIN.
SPARTAN
THAT'S WHY I'M BURNING IT.
TO SOOTHE THE SOULS WE CAN'T MARK IN THE OFFICIAL RECORDS...
CAPTAIN PIKE, IT'S CHIEF PETTY OFFICER MEG RIHM. I'M HERE TO PICK UP YOUR MILITARY MAIL.
KNOCK
KNOCK

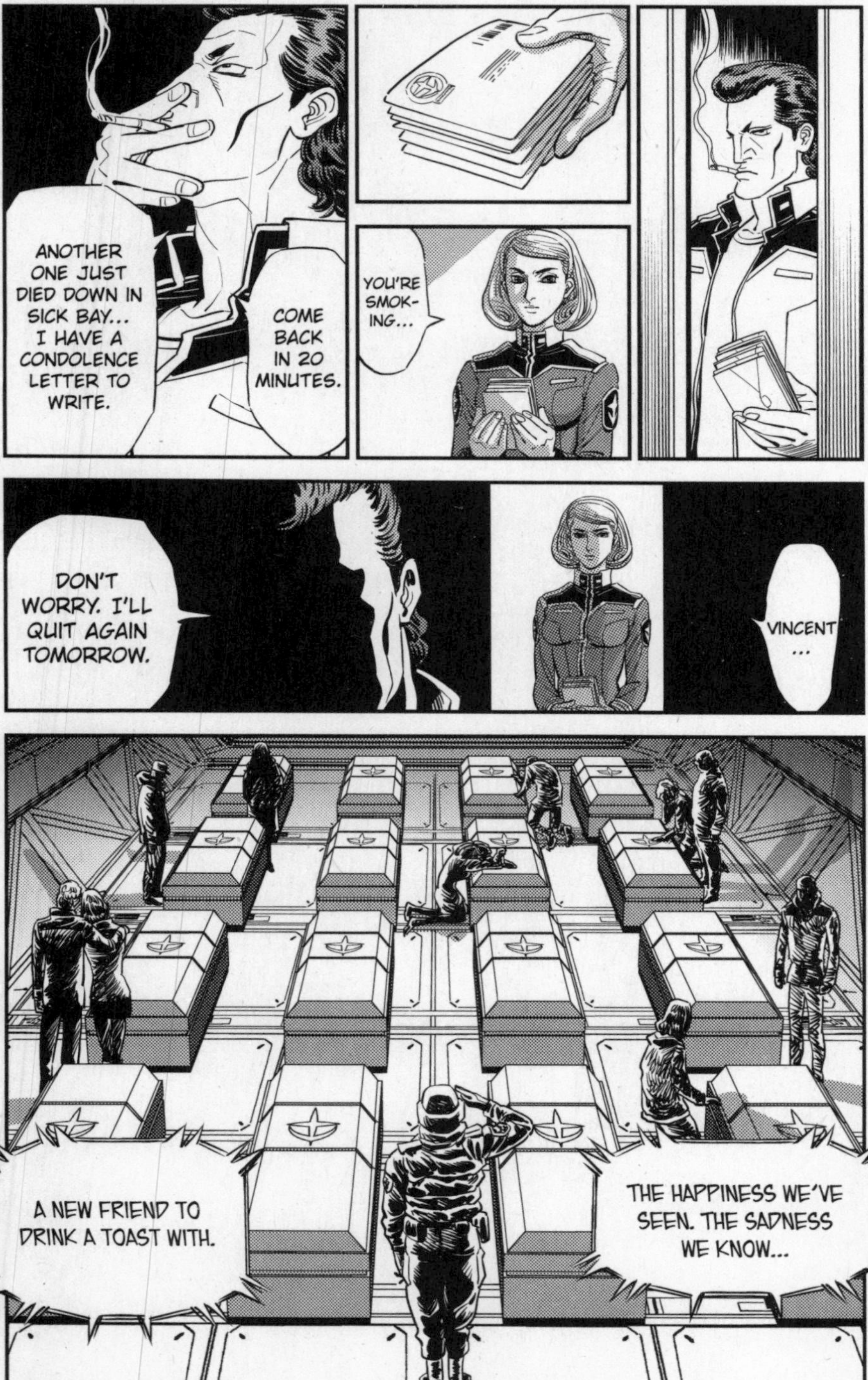
YOU'RE SMOKING...
ANOTHER ONE JUST DIED DOWN IN SICK BAY... I HAVE A CONDOLENCE LETTER TO WRITE.
COME BACK IN 20 MINUTES.
VINCENT...
DON'T WORRY. I'LL QUIT AGAIN TOMORROW.
THE HAPPINESS WE'VE SEEN. THE SADNESS WE KNOW...
A NEW FRIEND TO DRINK A TOAST WITH.

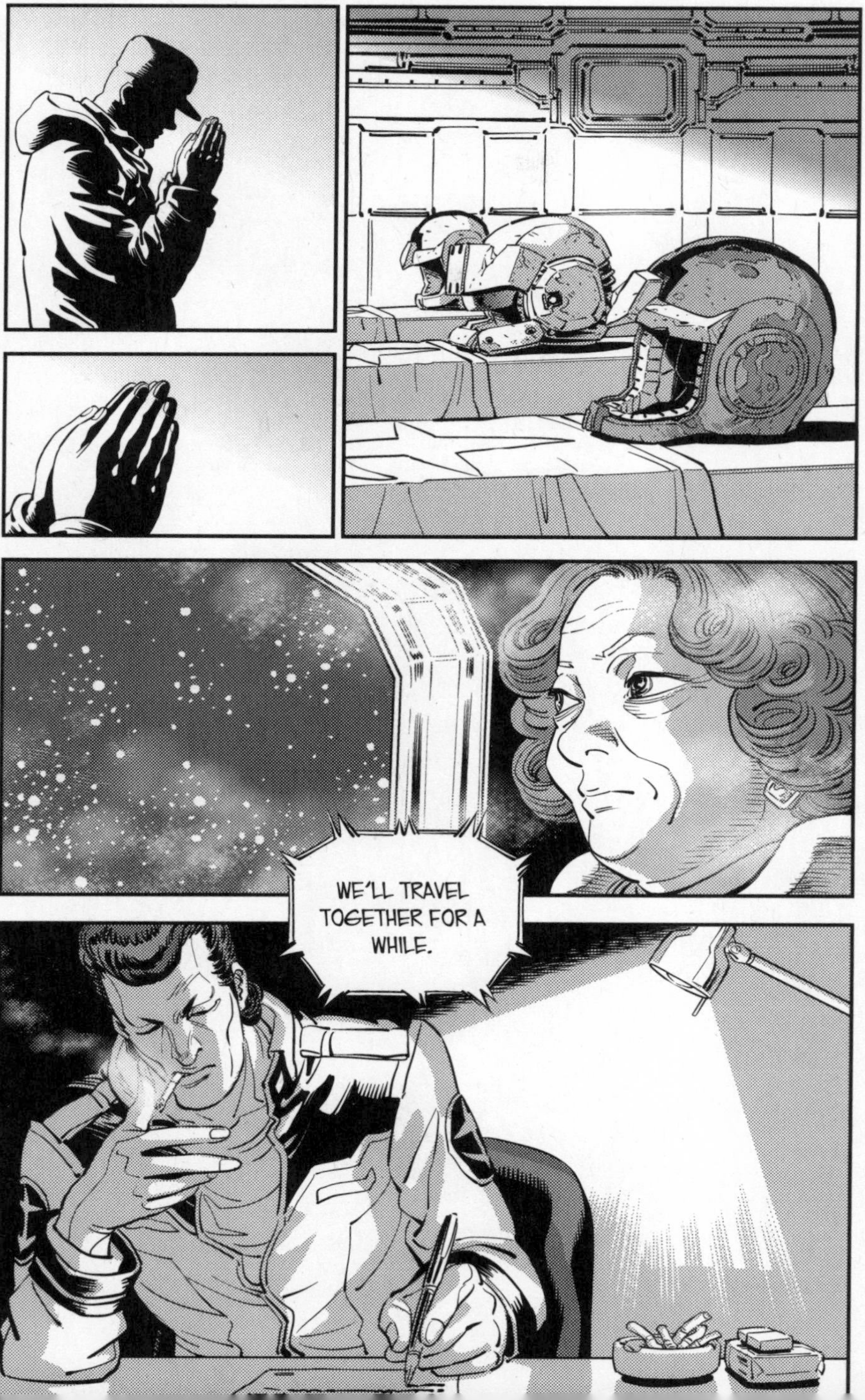
WE'LL TRAVEL TOGETHER FOR A WHILE.

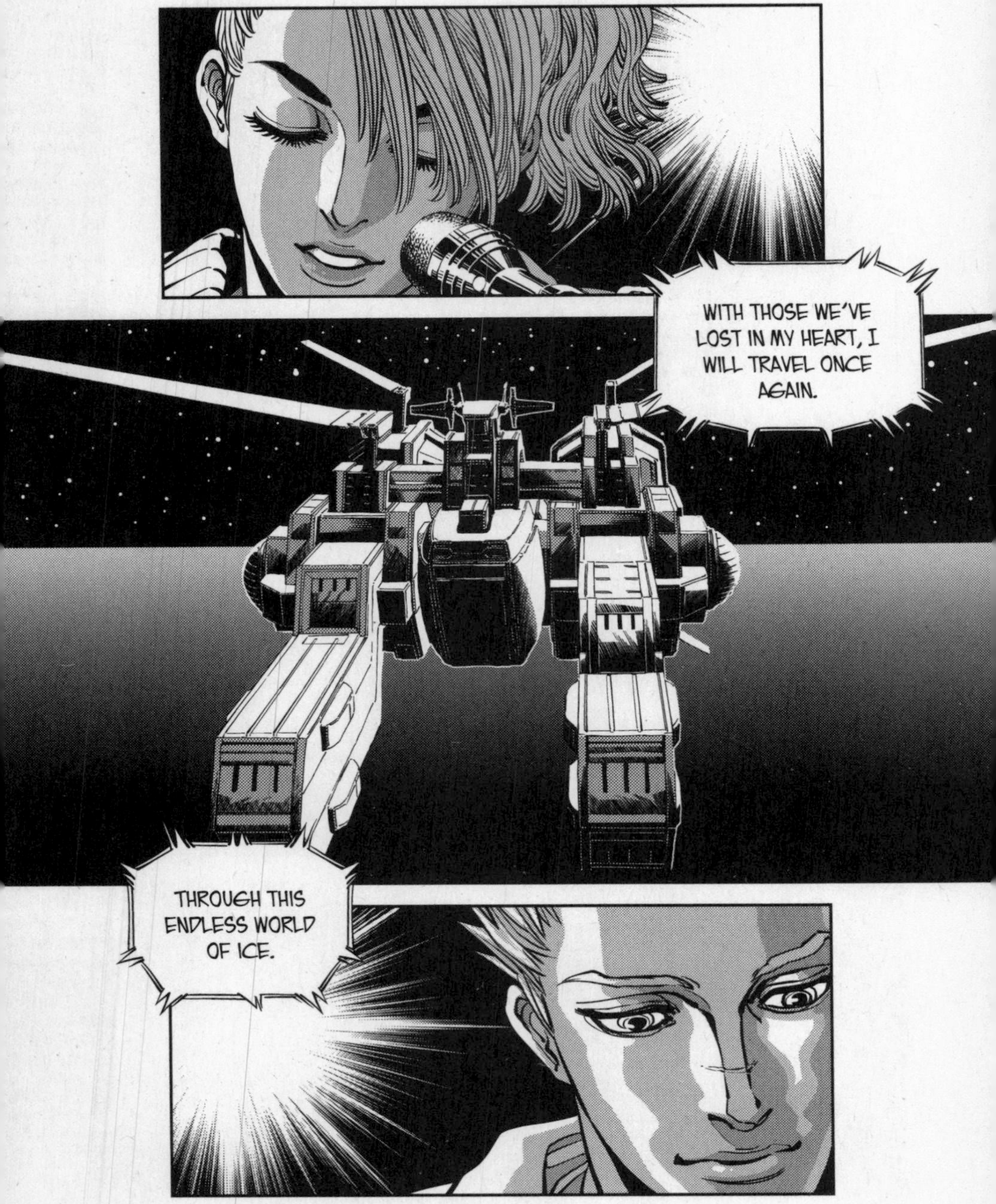
WITH THOSE WE'VE LOST IN MY HEART, I WILL TRAVEL ONCE AGAIN.
THROUGH THIS ENDLESS WORLD OF ICE.

MOBILE SUIT GUNDAM - THUNDERBOLT - VOL. 6 - END

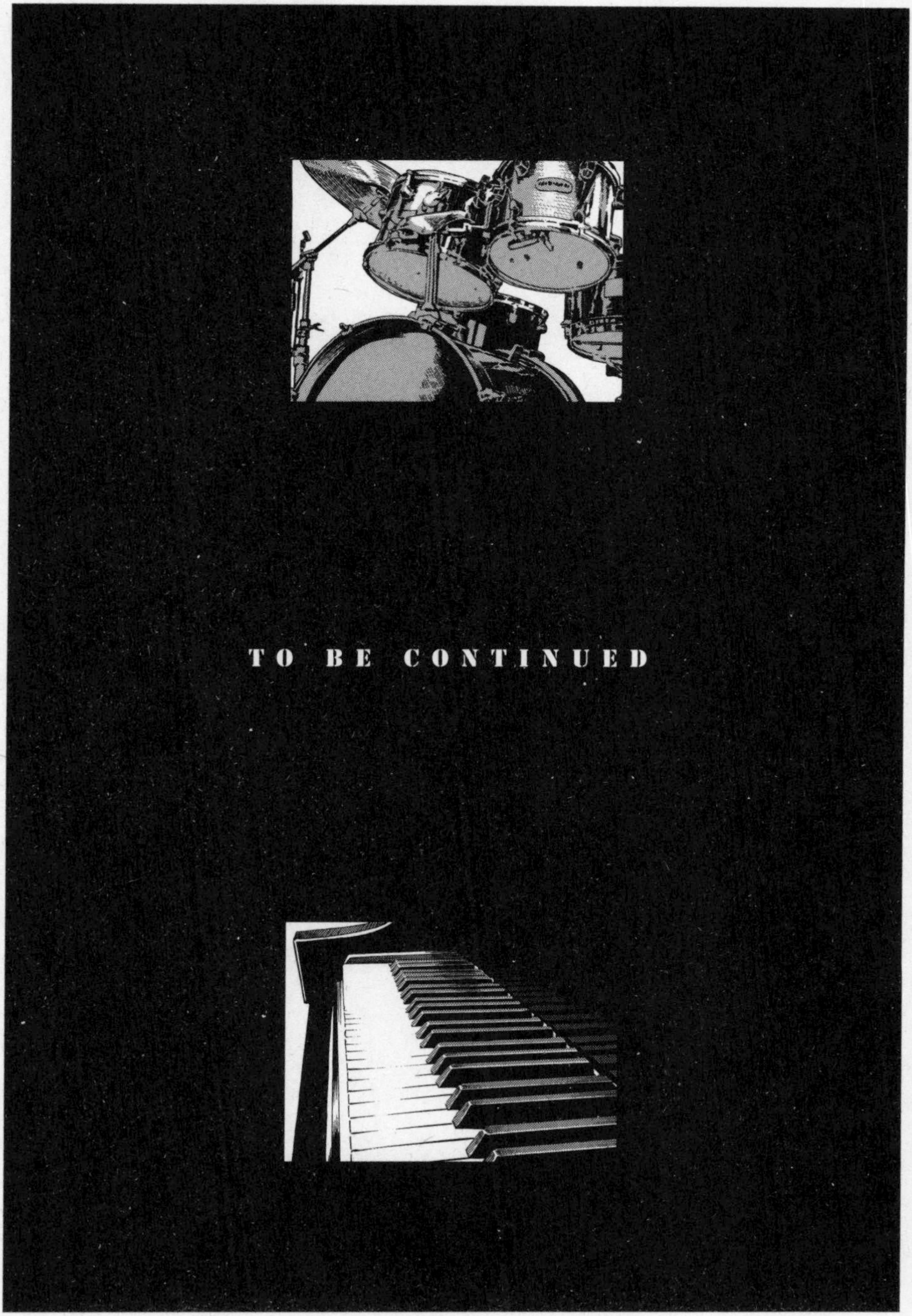
TO BE CONTINUED

STUDIO TOA S.P.A

Executive Director	**Yasuo Ohtagaki**
Chief	**Sayaka Ohtagaki**
Managing Director	**Hideki Yamamoto**
Mecha Design	**Ryosuke Sugiyama** **Yasunori Takahashi** **Shota Sugawa**
Background Art	**Sayuri Nakamura**
3D Modelling	**Suehiro Saruwatari**
Guest Mecha Design	**Takuya Io** **Juu Ishiguchi**
Special Thanks	**Digital Noise**